Pandita Ramabai's American Encounter

Frontis: Pandita Ramabai with her daughter Manorama in England, 1886.

Pandita Ramabai's American Encounter

The Peoples of the United States (1889)

BY **PANDITA RAMABAI**

Translated and edited by Meera Kosambi

INDIANA
University Press

Bloomington & Indianapolis

This book is a publication of

Indiana University Press
601 North Morton Street
Bloomington, IN 47404-3797 USA

http://iupress.indiana.edu

Telephone orders   800-842-6796
Fax orders   812-855-7931
Orders by e-mail   iuporder@indiana.edu

© 2003 by Meera Kosambi

The paper used in this publication meets the minimum
requirements of American National Standard for
Information Sciences—Permanence of Paper for Printed
Library Materials, ANSI Z39.48-1984.

Manufactured in the United States of America

Library of Congress Cataloging-in-Publication Data

Ramabai Sarasvati, Pandita, 1858–1922
   Pandita Ramabai's American encounter : the peoples of the United States
(1889) / by Pandita Ramabai ; translated and edited by Meera Kosambi.
      p.   cm.
Includes bibliographical references and index.
   ISBN 0-253-34190-6 (cloth : alk. paper) — ISBN 0-253-21571-4 (pbk. : alk. paper)
   1. Women social reformers—India—Maharashtra. 2. Ramabai Sarasvati, Pandita,
1858–1922—Journeys—United States. 3. United States—Description and travel.
I. Kosambi, Meera. II. Title.
   HQ1744.M33 R34 2003
   303.48'4'092—dc21

                                                                    2002006851

1 2 3 4 5   08 07 06 05 04 03

To the memory of

my grandfather, Professor Dharmanand Kosambi

my father, Professor D.D. Kosambi

who were involved in the academic life of the USA,

mainly through Harvard University,

during a major part of the twentieth century

Contents

∞ Introduction

∞ *The Peoples of the United States*   PANDITA RAMABAI

Preface and Acknowledgments

It was a hundred and fifteen years ago that Pandita Ramabai first stepped on American soil. She was so struck by "the marvelous things" she saw there that she immediately embarked on her Marathi book *The Peoples of the United States* in order to share with her compatriots her newly acquired knowledge of "the true worth of the United States, the activities of its people, its social conditions and political system, and other such things." The avowed patriotic objective of her book was to inspire in her readers a greater "desire to serve our Mother India." Today the descendants of Ramabai's contemporaries in Maharashtra and other parts of India are quite likely to have a firsthand knowledge of the USA and its "marvels." To them this translation offers a comparative historical perspective and a glimpse of a courageous woman who traced a similar though lonely path a century ago.

This book is intended primarily for American readers—the descendants of Ramabai's American contemporaries, who were impressed enough by her charismatic personality to generously support her efforts for Indian women's emancipation but who were unaware of Ramabai's account of their country. And the book's objective has been inspired by another concern: the need to recognize the achievements of an Indian woman traveler of the late nineteenth century who not only traversed a world that was plotted on a Western, imperialist, and patriarchal meridian, but who also strove to establish the USA for her compatriots as a more progressive country than imperial Britain and as a more suitable model for a colonized India to follow in its pursuit of freedom and advancement. The book is aimed also at a worldwide English-speaking readership that shares the general interest in old travelogues and in unearthing women's forgotten achievements. It is presented as my tribute to an extraordinary Indian woman who cherished a vision of a free, egalitarian, and prosperous India as an integral and proud part of the global community of nations.

That a research-based book about Pandita Ramabai should have a peripatetic and international history is in the fitness of things. The final version of this translation has benefited greatly from the careful reading and suggestions made by Anne Feldhaus and Margaret Allen. Also, constructive critiques of the introduction offered by Anne, Antoinette Burton, and Sumit Guha have been of great value. Much of the first draft of the translation was prepared in bits and pieces during my month-long conference-lecture tour in the USA in January–February

1998. Great help on this tour, in the form of research-related facilities coupled with warm hospitality, came from Barbara Ramusack in Cincinnati and Lynn Zastoupil in Memphis. Antoinette entered into the idea of the book with her usual enthusiasm, and helped it along not only with encouragement but also by sending me some much-needed published materials that were difficult to obtain in India. Relative leisure for translation work was made available, along with good food and good company, by my cousins Hemi and Bonnie Sathe in San Jose and my friends Polly and Harry Fischler in Cherry Hill, New Jersey, during my short stays with them in 1998. Some of the materials for my long-term research on Pandita Ramabai and her contemporaries were collected at the New York Public Library during my earlier visit to the USA in 1995–96, while I was a guest of Mahadev and Judit Apte, and at the Philadelphia Free Library while I enjoyed the hospitality of the Fischlers. My former student Abby McGowan contributed greatly by finding useful source materials in Boston.

The book was originally planned during my six-week stay in 1997 as a visiting scholar at the University of Adelaide, when I started translating the chapter on women in my spare time. Margaret Allen, a constant source of help, support, and encouragement, and a willing listener and discussant, introduced me to the university's Barr Smith Library and the State Archives of South Australia. The idea of translating the rest of the book as well was suggested by Kay Shaeffer and Robert Iseman, who assured me that it would interest American readers. Encouragement was also forthcoming from other colleagues who were fascinated by Ramabai—especially Susan Magarey, Sue Sheridan, Chilla Bulbeck, Jane Haggis, and Susanne Schech. Betty Gray, former superintendent of the Pandita Ramabai Mukti Mission at Kedgaon, made materials available from the archives of the Australian Council of the Pandita Ramabai Mukti Mission, Melbourne. Work at the University of Sydney was made possible by a generous conference invitation by Jim Masselos in January 1999, and the warm hospitality extended by Vivienne and Alex Kondos.

During my visit to England in late 1999, archival materials were made available by Janet Johnstone and Kath Boothman at the Cheltenham Ladies' College, and by Sister Joan Elizabeth of the Community of St. Mary the Virgin at Wantage, where I was hospitably received for a short stay. In June 2000, my reference work in London was helped along by Naina Shah, who introduced me to the Newspaper Library of the British Library, and by Keith and Ruth White, who extended their generous hospitality for the second time.

The actual preparation of the manuscript was done in India. Over the years my research on Pandita Ramabai has been greatly helped by the Pandita Ramabai Mukti Mission at Kedgaon. Mukti's former superintendent Heather Johnstone, current superintendent Venu Ingle, and the Board of Governors have kindly allowed me access to the Mukti archives, which contain valuable published materials, including Ramabai's personal collection. They have also made available the photographs published in this book. Bobby John, always a supportive friend, has been involved in my research at both Kedgaon and Pune (formerly Poona) as a matter of personal commitment to Pandita Ramabai's work. He has provided help at various levels, ranging from discussions about Ramabai to locating research materials in the Mukti archives.

The work of translating *The Peoples of the United States* proved to be more massive than originally anticipated, although I discovered what was involved when I prepared two chapters—on women and on religion—for publication in my earlier book *Pandita Ramabai through Her Own Words* (Delhi: Oxford University Press, 2000). Help with the translation, especially regarding the right choice of English words (with a nineteenth century flavor), was willingly given by my friends Pareen Lalkaka, Aban Mukherji, and the late Ramesh Sirkar in Mumbai (formerly Bombay) and Zia Karim in Pune. Also in Pune I have drawn freely, for the translation and references, on S. R. Chunekar's vast knowledge of Marathi literature and S. S. Bahulkar's equally vast knowledge of Sanskrit literature. Over the last many years the staff of several libraries and archives have helped my research work—in Mumbai the American Information Resource Center, the Asiatic Society's Library, and the Fort Library of the University of Mumbai; and in Pune the Bhandarkar Oriental Research Institute's Library, the British Library, Gadgil Library of the Gokhale Institute of Politics and Economics, Jayakar Library of the University of Pune, archives of the Kesari-Mahratta Trust, and the libraries of the United Theological Seminary and the Union Biblical Seminary.

Work on the introduction was considerably facilitated by innumerable discussions with my enthusiastic friends—Aban, Zia, Naina, Bobby, and others—all of whom have allowed themselves to be subjected to a crash course in American history and Pandita Ramabai's views on America. The final touches to the manuscript were added in the inspiring milieu of Meenakshi and Shama Pawar's lovely and hospitable home in Hanumanahalli, Karnataka (coincidentally the state where Ramabai was born), overlooking across a low river the grand ruins of the historic Vijayanagar empire.

The process of preparing the manuscript for publication was efficiently managed at the Indiana University Press by Rebecca Tolen, Jane Lyle, and Susanna Sturgis, who have been very supportive throughout.

I am deeply indebted to all these people for their assistance. I am also very grateful to all my friends for their warm encouragement and unfailing moral and practical support. But, as we say in Marathi, there is joy and honor in carrying this debt of gratitude.

Meera Kosambi
Pune, India

Abbreviations

Chambers	*Chambers Biographical Dictionary*
CSMV	Community of St. Mary the Virgin (Wantage and Poona)
DAB	*Dictionary of American Biography*
Letters	*The Letters and Correspondence of Pandita Ramabai*
NAW	*Notable American Women*
OCUSH	*The Oxford Companion to United States History*
RICW	*Report of the International Council of Women*
USLP	*United Stateschi Lokasthiti ani Pravasavritta*
WCTU	Woman's Christian Temperance Union
WMCP	Woman's Medical College of Pennsylvania

Introduction

Returning the American Gaze

Situating Pandita Ramabai's American Encounter

BY MEERA KOSAMBI

The annual commencement of the Woman's Medical College of Pennsylvania,[1] celebrated with customary splendor in March 1886, had a wider resonance than usual. It was to serve as a crucible in which international women's history was made. By pioneering women's medical education in the world the college had done Philadelphia proud; and the city's educated elite now responded by thronging to the event. They "stood against the wall . . . , filled every aisle and doorway and sat on the steps," while the students filled the front rows, the faculty the stage, "and a mass of flowers in baskets, bouquets and different designs covered the footlights three deep" (*Philadelphia Press*, 12 March 1886). The college's wide outreach had attracted students from all over North America and even from across the seas.[2] This discursive intersection of feminism and internationalism was most visibly—and exotically—symbolized by Anandibai Joshee, who had sought in the USA the medical education still denied to women in India, vowing to qualify herself to meet "the growing need for Hindu lady doctors in India" (Dall 1888: 84). Stepping on the stage for her degree, "little Mrs. Joshee, the Indian lady, who graduated with high honors in her class, received quite an ovation. Her native costume, a graceful robe of white linen bordered with gold, was in pronounced contrast against the background of sombre-robed ladies and black-garmented men on the stage" (*Philadelphia Press*, 12 March 1886). That Anandibai became India's first woman doctor further reinforced the college's existing Indian connection and its pioneer credentials: the earliest Western women physicians to expand India's medical field were Americans, led by a WMCP graduate.[3]

Building on these international linkages the college dean, Dr. Rachel Bodley, had invited Pandita Ramabai—a reputed champion of Indian women's education and distantly related to Anandibai—to be a guest on the occasion. Ramabai, a Brahmin widow and Sanskrit scholar, was then a teacher-pupil at the Cheltenham Ladies' College in England, and had recently converted to Christianity. Her fame had preceded her arrival in Philadelphia thanks to Dr. Bodley's judicious advance publicity (*New York Times*, 7 March 1886), and her visibility was further heightened by her public lecture the day after the commencement. Under the rubric "A Hindoo Widow Talks to American Women—A Unique and Striking Scene," the *Philadelphia Evening Bulletin* gave a glowing account of this "Hindoo [i.e., Indian] woman of high caste, her slight figure wrapped in the white robe of Indian widowhood, out of which looked a face of most picturesque beauty and expression"; and of the unwritten address she delivered in fluent, idiomatic English:

> Standing in an easy attitude, with her hands clasped upon the desk before her, and speaking with a voice of the most musical sweetness and distinctness, and with the unembarrassed manner of a genuine simplicity, she told the story of Hindoo womanhood to her American audience in a fashion that won all hearts and rivetted all attention. . . . [She proved] herself a woman who would be remarkable under any nativity. . . . And when the earnest little lady suddenly closed her address by asking an American company of educated and refined men and women to join with her in a moment's silent prayer "to the Great Father of all the nations of the earth" in [*sic*] behalf of the millions of her Hindoo sisters to whose cause she has given her life, there was something almost startling in the strangeness of the unique situation. (*Philadelphia Evening Bulletin,* 13 March 1886)

In its coverage the paper succinctly captured the warm and richly complex American response to Pandita Ramabai, whose potentially alienating "Indianness" and "Hinduness" had been significantly mediated by her multicultural persona and Christian faith. The English-educated and Christian Ramabai was similar enough to be "one of us," while her Sanskrit learning and her Brahmin mystique, dress, and diet made her an exotic "other." She was perceived to have transcended the fate of the highly troped "oppressed Hindu widow," and to have arrogated to herself championship of other widows; to be enlightened enough to have acquired a secular English education in England, and capable enough to impress America's educated elite; to have traversed the globe, straddled cultures and religions, and to now have come to envelop Americans in Christian fellowship.

Ramabai, who had already made a dispassionate and critical study of her own society and that of England, now subjected the American continent and culture to an Indian—albeit internationalized and eclectic—gaze. The product was her Marathi travelogue-journal *United Stateschi Lokasthiti ani Pravasavritta,* or *The Peoples of the United States* (henceforth *USLP*), which was published in Bombay in December 1889, some months after her return.[4] This unique historical document—a critical ethnography of American society, spanning a wide range of subjects from polity to economy, and from religion to domestic life—was to confirm Ramabai's credentials as a courageous and independent social thinker despite being a colonial subject in a world plotted on the meridian of imperialism and Orientalism.

USLP is located precisely in the interstices between British imperialism and American Orientalism, which is why it confirms many current notions about travelogue-journals while challenging others. Recent theorizing about travel narratives as a Western genre bears the imprint of Edward Said's landmark analysis of the Western discourse of the Orient—"almost a European invention"—as its civilizational Other. Of direct relevance here is the spearheading role of travelogues, among the whole spectrum of literary productions, in the process of "Orientalizing the Orient" (Said 1991: 1, 49). Further situating Western travel narratives in her influential work *Imperial Eyes,* Mary Louise Pratt (1995: 4–5) has introduced the notion of the "contact zone"—the social space "where disparate cultures meet, clash and grapple with each other, often in highly asymmetrical relations of domination and subordination," like colonialism. The result is the Euroimperialist "production" of "the rest of the world" for a European readership. In Indira Ghose's summing up, "the 'other' constructed in travel writing has not only played a role in the consolidation of colonialism but has also simultaneously served to stabilize the Western constitution of 'self,'" so that "travel writing about the other really serves as a mirror held up to the self" (Ghose 2000: 2–3).

Western women's entry into this Western and male preserve partly subverted the genre while partly reinforcing the categories of race and culture, and the incursion of a non-Western woman like Ramabai introduces further complexity. Women travelers to colonial India could not transcend colonialism and did not attempt to build feminist bridges; Ramabai, traveling in the opposite direction to the USA, was able to make feminist connections across the racial-cultural divide, partly through the shared bond of Christianity. This was in marked contrast to her contestation of Western hegemony and Orientalism, which was reserved solely for colonial Britain. As Antoinette Burton (1998: 1, 3) has discussed, Ramabai challenged British imperial power "at the heart of the empire," and penned through her letters a critical ethnography of British society. Inderpal Grewal (1996: 5–6) has identified Ramabai's writings about both England and America as an inversion of the Eurocentric, imperialistic travel narratives based on a permanent Othering of the "Natives." Grewal situates her study in the broader conceptual framework of "Home"—the domestic space of the Western traveler, the space of return and of consolidation of the Self enabled by the encounter with the Other—and "Harem," the space of seclusion and incarceration of "Eastern" women, which the colonial power hopes to access and liberate. Both Burton and Grewal expand Pratt's notion of the contact zone, and demonstrate that it could be shifted to the colonial metropolis or other spaces in the hegemonic West which were accessed by the relatively rare non-Western traveler in the nineteenth century. In her nuanced documentation Ramabai further identifies the binary fissures effected by imperialism within the hegemonic West. For a colonial subject like herself who had visited both countries, America as a "contact zone" could not be ideologically as conflictual as England was.

Despite its primary focus on American society, *USLP* conceptually weaves together three narratives—about the USA, England, and India—written with multiple objectives. The principal theme is a multilayered account of the USA imbued with Ramabai's appreciation of the country's anti-colonial ideology, and her admiration for its system of government and civil society, as well as its liberal and feminist thinking. Through its historical location the text preserves a slice of American history and provides primary historical source materials, such as personal accounts of landmark events and famous people. At the same time Britain is a very real presence in the book through Ramabai's repeatedly voiced critique of the country's system of government, its rigid class-based hierarchy of privilege, its religious intolerance, and the oppressiveness both of the colonial relationship itself and of British officialdom in India. In addition, *USLP* preserves a slice of Indian history from Ramabai's own vantage point. The India and Indians she critically inscribes into the narrative often diverge from the Indian self-image projected in her compatriots' writings, although her overt nationalism softens the edge of these scattered critiques. The emphatically nationalistic book provides glimpses of the new India of her aspirations, suggesting the major ideological role of America in its construction.

At first glance *USLP* appears to be an idealized account of the USA that shares Ramabai's new experiences with her compatriots. It is a celebration of a land of progress, equality, and opportunity, of collective action and citizens' rights. But underneath all this, it serves as Ramabai's nationalistic and anti-British attempt, significantly mediated by Christianity, to install the USA as an acceptable Western model for India's independence and many-sided progress. This attempt to inspire and consolidate anti-colonial protest projects England as an oppressive imperial power, with the USA as an ideal liberating force and indirectly as a precedent for India to follow in its pursuit of political freedom and social reform. Ostensibly a description of America and its people, *USLP* is in reality a vehicle for a strong, nationalistic, and anti-colonial theme whose explicit articulation would certainly have incurred the charge of sedition from the British government. Ramabai's message is thus encoded within the general framework, which extols liberty and freedom, and makes repeated references to the American success in overthrowing the British.

Ideologically *USLP* is almost as loaded as the Western Orientalist travel narratives, though with a partial endorsement and a partial reversal of the prevalent power equation. Instead of a superior Self looking down at an inferior Other, it presents a Self that is politically colonized and self-critical (colonized, therefore self-critical) looking up to a superior Other which uniquely embodies the strength of the colonizer combined with an anti-colonial value system. But it also presents a Self which resists mental and cultural colonization, and is confident in the possession of the "gaze." There is no indication that Ramabai's explicit admiration for America has diluted her pride in her Indian identity, or deflected her from her nationalist goal of working toward building a modern India. But her vantage point and perspective remain distinct from those of other Indian nationalists and reformers. Ramabai's project of establishing a valorized American model might have succeeded if the Self she presented had corresponded with that of her average Marathi reader. The project floundered, I would argue, primarily because her unique international, liberal, feminist, and introspectively critical Self confronted a parochial patriarchal and male reader (given the low level of female literacy) who was acutely vulnerable to Western assaults on his status. The mismatch was magnified by the predictable Hindu reaction to one who had defected to the Christian fold. Additionally Ramabai's (perhaps imperfectly understood) promotion of a Western country—racially and culturally both alien and hegemonic—as a model for emulation was resisted by the prevalent state of Indian nationalism. Today Ramabai's anti-colonial but pro-Western stance, implicit in her anti-British and pro-American rhetoric, provides a fascinating theme for a postcolonial exploration of a (relatively tension-free) diasporic consciousness, of "the fissured identities and hybridities generated by colonial dislocations" (Loomba 1998: 180). For her compatriots it might have smacked of cultural distancing or condescension.

Ramabai's divergent perceptions of India and the West paralleled the different personae conferred upon her, as evinced by the publicity surrounding her maiden speech in Philadelphia. While it established her in the Western world as an icon of "progressive Indian womanhood," the response was far different on the other side of the globe. Reproducing the *Philadelphia Evening Bulletin*'s report of the speech, *The Mahratta*, western India's socially conservative English-language weekly, sought to negate Ramabai's achievements through a patriarchal strategy. It installed Anandibai Joshee as an alternative role model and the real icon of Indian womanhood—a conventional wife, submissive to her husband despite her high professional education, and more importantly, still firmly within the Hindu fold, even after spending some years in the USA (*Mahratta*, 2 July 1886). It is within this complex international scenario that Pandita Ramabai and *USLP* need to be situated.

In presenting *USLP* to a wider, English-speaking readership, this book has an agenda which combines several historical strands and scholarly traditions. Translating the text is primarily an exercise in retrieving and reinstating a significant component of Ramabai's prolific but now obscured literary legacy.[5] It serves the wider feminist agenda of reclaiming women's writings[6] and the postcolonial interest in old travelogues which challenged the established paradigms. This introduction seeks to situate *USLP* by sketching the Indo-American historical backdrop; tracing the contours of Ramabai's life; and discussing the book's commonalities with other products of the genre to highlight its distinctiveness, including the multiple authorial positions which inhabit it.

The Indo-American Backdrop

While spatial and cultural distance inhibited easy communication between the USA and India until the twentieth century, historical parallels had created a tenuous bond since the serendipitous discovery of America. Almost simultaneously the voyages of discovery inspired by the European desire for direct oceanic access to India's fabled riches led Columbus to identify the Americas as the "Indies" in 1492, and conveyed Vasco da Gama successfully to India in 1498. A stronger Indo-American connection was finally to be forged some centuries later on the British imperial anvil. The volume of direct trade between the USA and western India remained small (*Gazetteer of Bombay City and Island* [1909] 1977: 420). But the operation of the global economy under imperialism was most dramatically and somewhat unexpectedly manifested during the American Civil War. The wartime disruption of cotton supply to British textile mills created an alternative demand for the raw cotton of western India. This in turn expedited railroad construction to link the cotton-producing areas of the interior to the port city of Bombay, propelling the city to unprecedented growth and prosperity during the short-lived boom.

At the time of Ramabai's visit in the mid-1880s, the Civil War was still within living memory, and Reconstruction still recent history.[7] While solving old problems, the Civil War had raised new questions about the agency and modalities for reconstructing the South and reinducting it into the Union. The contentious issue of the social and political status of freed slaves revealed pervasive racism even in the North. The enfranchisement of the blacks was effectively undercut by imposing a poll tax and literacy tests, which also eroded the support base acquired by the Republican Party through its liberal policies, and allowed the Democrats to ensure white rule. Social assimilation of blacks remained a dream; they were either excluded altogether or segregated in "Jim Crow" sections of public facilities (Nieman 1991: 78–113). The country's apparently successful pluralism embodied in the "melting pot" ethos welded native and immigrant communities into one nation, united by a common language and ethos, bridging the divides of nationality, ethnicity, and race. But fissures were apparent just beneath the surface. Federal policies regarding American Indian tribes—subdued through warfare or peaceful means—had oscillated between forced expulsion and forced assimilation. The increasing pressure on their lands for white settlements and farms, combined with the gold rush in California, had led to Indian tribes being gathered in a few reservations; and warfare and genocide had decimated their population from the original five million to 125,000 in 1880 (O'Brien 1989: 14, 77). Prejudices also grew against the Irish and the Germans (who had together constituted 70 percent of the 4.3 million immigrants to the United

States between 1840 and 1860); and Chinese immigration was barred on purely racial grounds (Dublin 1993: 8–10).

But the economy was rapidly growing stronger. Industrialization had introduced prosperity in the manufacturing sector and created a wide railroad network to carry raw materials to the factories and finished goods to the retail outlets. Mechanized agriculture led to flourishing villages. Urbanization, aided by improved transportation, burgeoned; and by 1870 a quarter of the population already lived in towns and sprawling cities. New York City had crossed the one million population mark in 1880; Chicago was to join it in 1890, with Philadelphia just behind. The industrial sector, increasingly dominated by gigantic corporations, raised the country's output to the combined levels of Britain, France, and Germany. But the exploitative labor relations compelled the workers (both men and women) to organize themselves through the Knights of Labor, and the American Federation of Labor, an association of autonomous unions, both of which were active in the 1880s. Rapid industrialization also threatened the farmers of the cotton-growing South and the wheat-growing West, who were to mobilize themselves politically in the 1890s for the electoral success of the short-lived People's Party, or the Populists.

What impressed Ramabai most was women's entry into the public sphere through various occupations, and through their newly founded organizations aimed primarily at "self-improvement" and increasingly also at social reform. The landmark convention at Seneca Falls, New York, in 1848 had launched the women's rights movement under the leadership of Lucy Stone and Elizabeth Cady Stanton. Temperance reform and "home protection" had gathered momentum through the founding of the Woman's Christian Temperance Union in Ohio in 1874. It broadened its scope to most walks of life with its "Do Everything" policy under Frances Willard's leadership, and expanded into an international network. The National Woman Suffrage Association, led by Susan B. Anthony and others, struggled for women's political rights—a contentious issue foregrounded by the (at least nominal) enfranchisement of the freed male slaves —which was to claim women activists' energies for a few more decades until they won the vote in 1920 (Evans 1989: 119–43).

In capturing this social landscape Ramabai offers not a sociological analysis but a model of a relatively homogeneous American society (resting implicitly on a white Anglo-Saxon Protestant base). The Philadelphia-Boston axis of her activities slants her account toward New England–based reform campaigns for ethnic assimilation, educational innovation, and humane causes. And her absorption in American feminism turns sections of the book into a veritable who's who of women achievers. Significantly she is silent about her own visibility in the reform circles, and also about her treatment as an Indian, or about the

American perspective on India. The Indian diaspora was yet to contribute in any substantial measure to the American pluralism, and India itself remained largely peripheral to America's culture and economy. But it had registered on the American consciousness through the European Orientalist discourse, and through its emblematic "oppressed Indian woman"—the cruelly treated widow, and the pitiable "heathen mother" who wantonly threw her babies into the river "with her own maternal hands" (Forbes 1986: WS 2)—whose liberation was a Christian responsibility.

It was no accident that America's direct and most abiding encounter with India was channeled through evangelizing efforts. In 1812 some young missionaries from Massachusetts had arrived in Calcutta, and then Bombay, only to be turned away by the English East India Company's ban on missionary activity within its territories (a history which Ramabai alludes to in chapter 2 of *USLP*). The Charter Act of 1813 introduced curbs on the company's monopoly of India trade and allowed missionaries to function; and the American Marathi Mission was immediately set up in Bombay. It proselytized, produced a new Marathi translation of the Gospel, and opened the first public schools in Bombay City—a boys' school in 1815 and a girls' school in 1824, which preceded similar initiatives by other American and European missions, and by the government. In 1842 the mission started an Anglo-Marathi journal *Dnyanodaya* (Rise of Knowledge), which today remains the region's oldest continuously published periodical (Hewat 1953: 22–70; David 2001: 109–11). The journal acknowledged that "[t]he work of the American Mission falls into two departments, the directly Evangelistic, and the Educational, a difference which is more in name than in reality for the end is but one. The young have to be elevated through Christian education, and *all* through the direct preaching of the Gospel of Christ" (*Dnyanodaya*, 8 April 1886; emphasis in the original). The mission overtly supported the British government, whose protection was essential for its functioning, in an article entitled "The Destiny of the White Race" (*Dnyanodaya*, 6 August 1885): "It is fortunate for India that it is England that rules over her. No other of the white races is so fitted to fulfil her high mission over so great an empire. Better than all, it is the mission of the white race to be the instrument through which is carried to the world a pure religion, a true idea of God, a knowledge of a real Saviour."

The civilizing mission of the white race was a crucial part of the high imperialism of the 1880s, and western India's response had evolved through various phases since the beginning of English colonial rule in the early nineteenth century. The Bombay Presidency incorporated the politically and economically dominant western part of the Marathi-speaking region known as Maharashtra (which was administratively fragmented but enjoyed a cohesive cultural identity), along with some neighboring regions. The Maharashtra region was largely rural and agrarian, although its capital, Bombay, then the largest city in India, was approaching the one million population mark. While British Bombay inducted the region into the orbit of international maritime commerce and industrialization, its cultural heartland remained Poona, the inland precolonial capital. The region's population was chiefly Hindu, with a Muslim minority and small Christian and other religious communities. The contrast between the affluent pockets of British presence and the vast and increasingly impoverished host country was considerable, as was the urban-rural divide in terms of incomes, education, and levels of living—which explains Ramabai's fascination with the prosperity and general advancement of rural USA. Additionally, a consciously deployed British policy highlighted religious tensions, while the mainstream Hindu community was inherently divided by a hierarchical caste structure. This societal fragmentation effectively precluded collective action, which Ramabai found to be an impressive hallmark of American society: it forms yet another pervasive theme of *USLP.*

The traditional Hindu caste hierarchy, based on a broad but fairly rigid division of labor, was dominated by Brahmins. In Maharashtra their ritual supremacy was reinforced by the political-military and economic power they had enjoyed in pre-British days. This multiple hegemony of Brahmins survived their loss of political power and was articulated in their undisputed leadership of the reform movement. By the mid nineteenth century, the region's public life was influenced by the first generation of educated Maharashtrians, who in turn were impacted by the advanced British technology, secular education (accessible to all social strata and both sexes, at least in theory), and a more efficient and formalized system of administration and justice. Prodded by the social critique inherent in the English system of education and Christian missionary propaganda, they strove to introduce social change through public associations, aided by a spectrum of socioreligious movements for revival (like the Arya Samaj), and for reform (like the Prarthana Samaj, partly modeled on the Brahmo Samaj of Bengal).

The social reform initiatives were loosely aligned along the twin axes of caste inequalities and gender injustice, with a considerable degree of initial overlap. Given the existing structural inequalities and the region's unique social history of Brahmin dominance, caste-related reform attracted the lower castes, while gender-related reform preoccupied the upper castes known for their rigid patriarchal control of women. The campaign against "Brahminocracy," or Brahmin oppression of the lower castes (known as Shudras or Sudras), was led by Jotirao Phule (the only low-caste leader of the reform movement) through his caste- and gender-egalitarian Satyashodhak Samaj, or "Truth-seekers' Society." Inherent in Phule's work was an interesting statement of crosscultural and international ideological solidarity with other oppressed groups. His most militant anti-Brahmin booklet, *Slavery*, published in 1869, was dedicated in both Marathi and English to "The Good People of the United States, as a token of admiration for their Sublime Disinterested and Self-sacrificing Devotion in the cause of Negro Slavery; and with an earnest desire, that my countrymen may take their noble example as their guide in the emancipation of their Sudra Brothers from the trammels of Brahmin thraldom" (Keer and Malshe 1969: 66–67).[8] Phule's multi-pronged social reform initiatives led him also to open the first private (nongovernmental and nonmissionary) girls' school in India in 1848, in which his wife Savitribai, whom he had educated at home, worked as a teacher in the face of stiff public opposition and harassment. By the mid-1850s he had added more schools for low-caste girls and boys, and also opened a private shelter for victimized upper-caste widows, which was another radical innovation (Keer 1974: 20–45, 86–87).

But gender-related social reform remained primarily an upper-caste concern, its site the well-regulated family unit, which was hierarchically organized along the sex-age grid, sanctioning the dominance of men over women, and of older members over younger ones.[9] In urban and relatively affluent families—which enjoyed greater visibility on the reform scene, and which formed Ramabai's reference group—the extended family collected under one roof all its adult males with their wives and children (and their married sons' families as well). This small community, to which women were confined by the curbs placed on their mobility, inspired the metaphors of "prison-house" and "parrot's cage." Its sex-segregated social landscape matched the spatial division of the house, with the front portion—the buffer zone between the public and domestic spheres—serving as the male domain, and the rear portion as the female realm. Men and women spent their daytime in these separate realms—except at mealtimes, when women served the men and children first, and ate later by themselves in the dining area located in or near the kitchen, which was the women's domain. The contrast between the Indian extended family and the American nuclear family prompted Ramabai to comment, in *The High-Caste Hindu Woman*, that in India "there is no such thing as the family having pleasant times together" (Kosambi 2000d: 149) and for her to savor such moments enjoyed by the average American family, through detailed descriptions in chapters 4 and 5 of *USLP*.

The rigidly patriarchal upper-caste definition of woman primarily as a wife-mother had led to the community's customs of prepubertal marriage for girls, immediate postpubertal consummation of marriage, and early and perpetual motherhood. The trope of the tragically oppressed widow captured her superfluity in this social scheme, which led to her acute marginalization within the family, and her relegation to a life of mandatory religious austerities.[10] Remarriage remained forbidden for widows, though allowed—and even encouraged—

for widowers. Traditional education, religious in content, was reserved solely for Brahmin men. Although the newly introduced secular Western education was available to women, few women were allowed schooling, tied as they were to domesticity. A glimmer of change came from the young men who were inspired by the new ideas of companionate marriage to teach their wives basic literacy at home. But education geared to self-actualization and independent thinking (potentially subversive of the family's established authority structure) remained beyond their reach. The opposition to women's higher and professional education included a startling echo of the earlier Western discourse on women's education.

The core issues of social reform—the abolition of child marriage, improved treatment (and possible remarriage) of widows, and introduction of women's education—were promoted increasingly in tension with "political reform," or the nationalistic demand for political autonomy. The first generation of social reformers was pioneered by G. H. Deshmukh along with Jotirao Phule. Both sought to remodel traditional society by reconciling their admiration for the progressive aspects of British rule with their patriotism. A liberal ideology, a consensual approach to social change, and interventions through the British legal system characterized the second generation of social reformers, led by the Sanskritist R. G. Bhandarkar and Justice M. G. Ranade (both members of the Prarthana Samaj), as well as Justice K. T. Telang. Ramabai's social activism of the early 1880s coincided with the advent of the third generation, dominated by B. G. Tilak and G. G. Agarkar, whose initial friendship changed into bitter enmity as the former pursued political goals and the latter stressed social issues. The priority of political over social reform, first articulated by Telang, was effectively transmuted by Tilak into the privileging of political rights as the only legitimate goal for all Indians. The construction of nationalism as a prioritized and male project thus succeeded in both sidelining social reform (potentially beneficial to women) and excluding women themselves from the political arena (Kosambi 2000c).

In this scenario of overlapping reform generations and factions, Ramabai's greatest support came from social reformers like Deshmukh, Ranade, Bhandarkar, and Telang, all of whom were on the advisory board of the Sharada Sadan, the residential school she opened in 1889. Agarkar championed her cause through his journalistic writings, and Phule was the only social reformer to endorse her conversion to Christianity. In true feminist fashion Ramabai also mobilized some prominent women for her reform effort—notably Ramabai Ranade (Justice Ranade's wife) who later entered the reform arena herself; Kashibai Kanitkar, the first major Marathi woman novelist; and Rakhmabai Thakur, who was to work as Maharashtra's first Hindu woman doctor. Unfortunately Ramabai incurred Tilak's implacable hostility mainly because of his patriarchal dislike of women's agency and visibility in public life (Kelkar 1923: 331). Tilak's ascendance on the pan-Indian scene at the end of the nineteenth century fixed Maharashtra's reform priorities in favor of political rights, chiefly through extremist nationalism, in competition with the moderate nationalism of G. K. Gokhale.

Maharashtra's parallels with other regions of India further clarify the picture. Bengal is particularly rich in studies of the tension between the struggle for women's liberation and men's nationalistic aspirations in the late nineteenth century. In Partha Chatterjee's reading of the situation, the "woman question" was satisfactorily resolved by male nationalists by formulating the dichotomy between "home" and "outside," which coincided with the private and public spheres of activity, the Indian and colonial areas of influence, and the contrast between the "spiritual East" and the "materialistic West" (Chatterjee 1999). Having constructed women as symbols of the domestic sphere and bearers of the Indian culture and tradition, reformers then allowed them full freedom to actualize their potential, according to Chatterjee. We see the Maharashtra situation to be quite divergent, and to parallel more closely what Sumit Sarkar identifies (also for Bengal) as a selection process at work in dictating the "limited and controlled emancipation" of women to suit the needs of their husbands (Sarkar 1994: 101–104). Both these scenarios reveal the absence of women's agency in creating opportunities and shaping their own lives. The most succinct and famous statement of women's marginalization in the social reform discourse that purported to focus on their well-being comes from Lata Mani, in the context of the discourse on widow immolation in early nineteenth century Bengal: "women are neither subjects nor objects, but rather the ground of the discourse" (Mani 1997: 117). Since women's discursive marginalization marked western India as well, Ramabai's appropriation of social leadership became a predictable and perpetual source of friction.

It was during this turbulent period of social reform that the USA was first placed on Maharashtra's cognitive map, albeit peripherally, through a massive compilation of knowledge in Marathi. During this "translation era," the government and the missions sponsored translations of books on history and biography, including the lives of George Washington, Benjamin Franklin, and Columbus (Jog 1999: 541–49; Date 1944: 917). It was England that the educated classes had learned to live with as a remote but real frame of reference, one that possessed a high degree of intrinsic interest. But the recognition of India's affinity with the American people was indicated by isolated references which cropped up in a variety of predictable and even unpredictable contexts.[11]

Personal experience of the USA remained a rarity, and in the narrative fragments of the few travel accounts written between 1880 and 1920, the dominant themes are not America's prosperity and independence, as in Ramabai's text, but

Orientalism, Christian proselytism, education, social engagement, and, briefly, domestic conditions. Western India's predictably limited personal acquaintance with the USA was initiated by Anandibai Joshee's sojourn there for medical studies (Dall 1888; Kosambi 1996). Encouraged and educated by her husband, Gopalrao, eighteen-year-old Anandibai sailed alone for the USA in April 1883 under the escort of American missionary wives. After graduating from WMCP she started working as an intern in Boston at the New England Hospital for Women and Children. But she was unfortunately compelled by incurable consumption to return to India, along with her husband who had arrived earlier. She died in early 1887, without being able to practice medicine.

Anandibai's American experience reached a wide readership through excerpts from her letters, which were published in a local newspaper by her husband (*Kesari*, 6 November 1883). They described American technological advances and also Anandibai's own activities, like an Indian banquet for her new American friends, through which Maharashtra had made cultural forays into that Western land. Anandibai was liberal in religious matters but a quintessential Hindu, and sensitive to critiques of Hinduism. Her response to America was refracted through intense nationalism, coupled with an unwillingness to probe the depths of India's social problems (and especially to discuss them with outsiders). Bristling at the Christian missionary censure of Indian women's multiple oppression—oppression which Ramabai openly condemned in *The High-Caste Hindu Woman*—Anandibai wrote to her husband: "This is the wisdom and reform of the Westerners we praise so highly! It would not be really surprising if they conclude that we [Indians] are the missing link between ape and man. . . . I had no idea that India is such a cruel and barbaric country! And until I met these people I had no idea either that it is such a heathen country!" (Kanitkar 1912: 207; my translation). A Marathi readership cast in this ideological mold was unlikely to share Ramabai's enthusiasm for America's Christian and missionary reformist ideas.

Gopalrao Joshee had educated his wife, Anandibai, partly to fulfill his reformist ambition vicariously (Kanitkar 1912; Kosambi 1996). A year after her departure to the USA Joshee set out to join her, traveling by the Pacific route via Ceylon and Burma, from which he sent travel accounts to a Poona newspaper. He followed this with indiscreetly candid discussions and interviews on social and religious matters that left a trail of newspaper reports from California to Philadelphia, which he reached in the summer of 1885. Joshee's critical assessment was that "America is a great country—great in splendor and grandeur. The Americans are a mighty people who have mastered all elements of nature . . . [and delivered] a death blow to the institutions of Royalty and aristocracy, kings and queens." But he faulted the Americans for their vanity, for pampering false flatterers, and for the color discrimination he had suffered (Joshee 1886: 3, 15). He also questioned their egalitarianism: "America boasts of having abolished slavery, and yet when Americans get rich, they like to have slaves to serve them, and therefore go to England" (*Index*, 18 November 1886). But Joshee's primary targets were missionary evangelical methods and American social critique of India. Creating exaggerated social dichotomies, he defended the Indian custom of "early and permanent" child marriage as conducive to a stable, peaceful, and harmonious relationship, and thus preferable to the "late or choice [*sic*] marriages . . . made and unmade according to the demands of lust" and leading to a high divorce rate (*Index*, 1 April 1886). At the annual meeting of the Free Religious Association in Boston in 1886 Joshee mounted a severe attack on what he considered questionable missionary proselytizing strategies, prompting the association president's remark that evangelical Christians would perhaps "now begin to understand how a pagan may feel when he hears his religion characterized by an Orthodox Christian" (*Index*, 10 June 1886). The fulcrum of Joshee's argument, the popular binary of the spiritual East and materialistic West, was to be later introduced forcefully into the American cultural discourse by Swami Vivekananda of Bengal at the Parliament of Religions in Chicago in 1893.

Two other eminent Maharashtrians who visited the USA during Ramabai's lifetime displayed widely divergent reactions. Pioneer Buddhist scholar Dharmanand Kosambi, while working as a lecturer at Calcutta University, was invited by a Harvard professor of Sanskrit to join his colleagues in compiling Buddhist texts. During his four trips to the United States (totaling about eight years, between 1910 and 1931), he was deeply impacted by the general advances in the social sciences and the philosophy of socialism. His resultant awareness of the elitist bias of Indian social reform showed him the need to redress the poverty and ignorance of the masses (Sukhtankar 1976). This consciousness of class disparities complemented Ramabai's own consiousness of gender disparities. His contemporary, Parvatibai Athavale, followed partially in Ramabai's footsteps when she went to the USA with the objective of learning English and raising funds for the Widows' Home established by her brother-in-law, the social reformer D. K. Karve, in Poona in 1896 on the model of Ramabai's own Sharada Sadan. Unfortunately Parvatibai was compelled to eke out a living by doing domestic work, and achieved her ambition only during the last few months of her two-year stay (1918–1920). Her response to American homes strengthened her views about woman's primary role as a wife-mother-homemaker, and the need to instill an Indian version of the "feminine mystique" (Athavale 1928, 1930). Three decades after Ramabai's first visit, a fellow Maharashtrian woman—nurtured by an institution inspired by Ramabai but promoting liberal patriarchal reform—was to subvert her feminist message by transmuting her own American experience into its polar opposite.

This spectrum of Maharashtrian responses to American society acquires additional interest because all five travelers shared a Brahmin background and in-depth exposure to contemporary (and largely upper-caste) sociopolitical reform discourse. Anandibai and Parvatibai reveal the tensions inherent in fashioning new emancipatory spaces for women; Joshee asserts the moral and spiritual superiority of the East over the material prosperity of the West; Kosambi and Ramabai in their larger societal visions locate reform respectively in the realms of economic and political restructuring.

Pandita Ramabai across Continents and Cultures

It was almost in the interstices of the extreme social pressures circumscribing the lives of her upper-caste contemporaries that Ramabai's own life unfolded.[12] She was born in the sylvan setting of a "forest home" in April 1858 to Dongre, an orthodox Brahmin scholar, and his young second wife. Dongre's ancestors had emigrated from Maharashtra to neighboring Karnataka; but he had lived as a young Sanskrit student in precolonial Poona and imbibed the radical but rarely practiced idea of teaching women Sanskrit, the "sacred language" expressly forbidden by tradition to women and the lower castes. After defending in an assembly of his Brahmin peers his decision to teach his wife Sanskrit, he withdrew to a secluded forest site to run a residential school for Brahmin boys.

When Ramabai was a baby, the youngest of the three surviving Dongre children, the family started on a continual pilgrimage, traversing the entire subcontinent over the next sixteen years. Never exposed to life in an extended family, or even in a settled community, Ramabai was also saved from an early marriage by the unhappy experience of her elder sister. The Dongres, including the three Sanskrit-educated children, eked out a meager living by reciting stories from the sacred Hindu texts known as the Puranas, which provided Ramabai an early training in public speaking (and also the background for her comments on women and religion in India in chapter 7 of *USLP*). The family's ritual austerities, coupled with constant travels, claimed the lives of Ramabai's parents and sister during the famine of the 1870s. With her elder brother she continued the familiar Brahmanic lifestyle despite terrible hardships, which reinforced her unique individualism, migratory consciousness, and objective social critique—which were conspicuously absent in her conventionally nurtured contemporaries.

This peripatetic existence lasted until the siblings arrived in Calcutta in 1878. Twenty-year-old Ramabai was instantly lionized by the city's reformers, and publicly examined by a panel of Sanskrit experts, who awarded her the titles of "Pandita" (learned woman) and "Saraswati" (Goddess of Learning). The reformist Brahmo Samaj inducted her into its efforts to popularize women's education through public lectures—an activity she was to pursue later under the auspices of the Prarthana Samaj of Bombay. But the two intervening years had been eventful in personal terms. In rapid succession had come her brother's death; her happy but brief marriage to Medhavi, a Bengali non-Brahmin lawyer; the couple's ostracism by his family because of the scandalous intercaste and interregional marriage; and Medhavi's death shortly after the birth of their daughter Manorama.

At the age of twenty-four Ramabai was left alone in the world—an impecunious widow with a baby daughter, lacking a family or other social support. On the invitation of the Bombay Presidency's social reformers, she came to the home of her ancestors in 1882, making Poona a permanent base for her activities. She wrote a Marathi book, *Stri Dharma Niti* or "Morals for Women" (Ramabai [1882] 1967; Kosambi 2000d: 35–101), to sculpt the "New Woman" envisioned by Indian reformers, as described by Geraldine Forbes (1999: 28–30). Circumscribed by the parameters of "benign patriarchy," Ramabai's New Woman was an educated, companionable, but submissive wife, an efficient housewife, and an enlightened mother who would nurture sons capable of restoring India to its former glory. The book was supported by the education department officials and welcomed by the reformers because "the task of championing the women's cause and of speaking or writing on their behalf, which hitherto fell to the lot of men, has now been undertaken by one belonging to the female sex herself" (*Kesari*, 1 August 1882; my translation).

But her more radical intervention was a women's club called the Arya Mahila Samaj, with branches throughout the Presidency, which pioneered women's agency as subjects rather than objects of reform, against the grain of the contemporary "associations for women founded by men" (Forbes 1999: 65–70). It met with the predictable male hostility and even the warning that women should not interfere in the "men's task of eradicating the evil social customs," and that "women would have to submit to male control for a long time to come" (*Kesari*, 8 August 1882; my translation). After testifying on women's general and medical education before the Hunter Commission on Education in 1882 (as she mentions in chapter 1 of *USLP*), Ramabai decided to study medicine herself in England.

Support for Ramabai's plan came from the Anglican Community of St. Mary the Virgin (CSMV) at Poona, which arranged for her to stay at their headquarters at Wantage, England. In return for accommodation, living expenses, and education, Ramabai agreed to teach Indian languages to the Wantage Sisters selected for work in India. In her Marathi booklet *Voyage to England*[13] Ramabai claims to have clarified to the CSMV that she would not convert to Christianity. In April 1883 Ramabai sailed with her baby daughter Manorama for England, and gave a cheerful account of her new surroundings, only to shortly suffer severe shocks. Her female friend and companion on the voyage suddenly committed suicide, and she herself was refused admission into medical college because of defective hearing.

In September 1883, Ramabai was baptized into the Anglican Church as Mary Rama, along with Manorama (Manorama Mary), rather unexpectedly and in contravention of her earlier assurance that such a step was not contemplated (Ramabai [1883] 1988: 3, 7–8). The actual circumstances of her conversion and baptism still remain unclear, but the news was greeted in India with a wide spectrum of interpretations and responses. At one extreme was the insistence of the Anglican Father Luke Rivington of Bombay that this was inevitable because Ramabai had earlier been engaged in a serious study of Christianity, and now felt the need to convert after realizing that "Christianity logically follows from Theism" as preached by the Brahmo Samaj and the Prarthana Samaj (*Times of India,* 12 November 1883). *The Times of India* (14 November 1883) termed Rivington's general rhetoric "indiscreet exultation" and took sensitive note of the fact that "the sudden news of Ramabai's conversion . . . has fallen like a thunderbolt upon her followers and admirers," and "created a profound sensation among the native communities of Western India." The conservative Hindu skepticism was voiced in *The Mahratta*'s (4 November 1883) cynical assertion that "the learned lady has deceived and disappointed alike her friends and foes" and "enrolled herself into the charitable clan of Christ" for monetary reasons. In her subsequent writings Ramabai herself explained her conversion as a natural outcome of her spiritual quest and intellectual conviction (Ramabai [1907] 1992: 26; Kosambi 1992). In any case, if Ramabai's conversion resolved her spiritual tensions, it also created fresh problems. Her theological doubts and contestation of colonialism led to considerable friction with the Anglicans. She spent the subsequent two years at the Cheltenham Ladies' College (where the CSMV had enrolled her) studying English and natural sciences, and training to be a teacher, with only occasional visits to Wantage.

Ramabai's conversion experience remains an intriguing research focus. Gauri Viswanathan provides easily the most sophisticated analysis, mainly on the basis of *The Letters and Correspondence of Pandita Ramabai,* of Ramabai's "anguished search for a personal God" and her "protracted effort to define a conception of divinity that satisfied her craving for interpretive freedom," and at the same time stresses Ramabai's ability "to see the divide between two possible meanings of religion as the source of cultural and national identity on one hand and, on the other, as universal moral value" (Viswanathan 1998: 121). I have examined the problematic against a somewhat different canvas while locating Ramabai as "the site for a series of overlapping encounters—primarily that between Hinduism and Christianity, rationalism and dogma, individualism and Church hierarchy," surrounded by "the larger confrontation between Indianness and Western culture, nationalism and colonial rule, feminism and patriarchy in its multiple guises" (Kosambi 1992: 61). Both these works rely on Ramabai's own written word, her own explication of her religious and spiritual search. A new dimension is added by Susanne Glover, who concludes on the strength of other source materials that pressure was exerted upon Ramabai to convert to Christianity, though not necessarily amounting to coercion, while at the same time "Ramabai actively sought her own conversion," which gave her "affirmation and status within an internationally powerful religious system, as well as opportunities to further her own education and to realize her ambitions" and, most importantly, "salvation as a woman" (Glover 1995: 77, 75).

Despite being a colonial subject on her first visit to the empire's metropolitan core, Ramabai was astute enough to immediately decipher the contrasts inherent in Britain's rigid class hierarchy: "The people of the numerous good families here are highly cultured and polished. At the same time, the people of the lower classes are uncouth beyond limit" (Ramabai [1883] 1988: 27; my translation). She also reacted to the divide between the arrogant British officialdom in India and the hospitable Britons at home: "whatever may be said of the English in India, I have almost in all cases found them very polite and kind to strangers at home" (*Letters*: 175–76). Her acquaintance with the entire class spectrum can be surmised from the discriminatory treatment expected of the man in the street, and from her documented interaction with officials like Sir Bartle Frere (former governor of the Bombay Presidency) and the prime minister, Mr. Gladstone. Her steady support came from Max Mueller, professor of Sanskrit language and literature at Oxford, who praised her "excellent Sanskrit" and "equally excellent English," endorsed her scheme to open a widows' home, and later wrote admiringly about her in his memoirs (*Times*, 22 August 1887; Mueller 1899: 121–29).

Long after leaving England Ramabai mentioned that "[s]he had been everywhere received most kindly, and she had found the English women at home quite different from what she had expected from seeing their sisters in India" (*Hong Kong Daily Press*, 16 January 1889). There is no direct evidence of the feminist support she received from British women, only indications such as Miss Manning's help with the private distribution of *The High-Caste Hindu Woman*, published in the USA in 1887 (*Letters*: 222), and the famous English feminist Frances Power Cobbe's review of the book (Kosambi 2000d: 28). The noted Quaker Matilda Sturge marveled that "one of the Hindu race" had set aside "traditions that have been held sacred for many generations," seeing this as an indication of "a spirit that rises above the tyrannies of custom, and longs to break a galling yoke" (Sturge 1889: 217). A deep imprint was left on Ramabai by the ideas and personality of Miss Dorothea Beale, the pioneering champion of women's education in England, and the "Lady Principal" of the Cheltenham Ladies' College who had nurtured the fledgling institution to maturity (Raikes 1908; Clarke 1979: 33–86).

She was also a close friend with whom Ramabai discussed a range of topics, from intricate points of Christian theology to British rule in India.

The only detailed knowledge we have of Ramabai's stay in England revolves solely around her interaction with her spiritual mentor Sister Geraldine and the Anglican establishment, which subjected her to the full force of the asymmetrical power relations of the empire through its racism, Orientalism, religious insularity, authoritarianism, and patriarchal beliefs. The Anglicans viewed Ramabai as an essentialized "Hindoo Native" who shared her "deceitfulness" and "want of candour and sincerity" with "the generality of the Hindoos" (*Letters*: 114–15). But some remained hopeful about the British contribution to her future: "I think that Mary Ramabai's knowledge of Indian ways, etc. will give her a power of influence which no English woman can have. All that she needs is an English development of her Indian brains" (*Letters*: 45). Ramabai's potential value as a Brahmin-Anglican wedge into Hindu society made the Anglican Church try to control Ramabai rather possessively, and guard her from all non-Anglican (or "heterodox") Christian influences. Sister Geraldine, whose refusal to countenance Ramabai's theological doubts caused most of the friction, identified as the nationalistic crux of the problem the title "The Church of England": "Had it been The Church of Christ in England, the results with Ramabai might have been different. But the last society such a woman (with her great inspiration to work for the benefit of her people) would ally herself with would be—not Catholic Christianity, but the Christianity which bore the impress of their conquerors" (*Letters*: 404–6). The friction resulted in Ramabai's ultimate choice of nondenominational Christianity and her deep appreciation of the religious freedom enjoyed by Americans (which she discusses in chapter 7).

The attempted bonding between British and Indian women was doomed to failure given the asymmetrical structure of imperialism. In India the attempt was spearheaded by women missionaries who were, as Geraldine Forbes has shown, "like all missionaries, clearly implicated in the colonial policy of the British. . . . They were not only the helpmates of the imperialists, they were themselves cultural imperialists" (Forbes 1986: 8). Barbara Ramusack has explored "how the categories of race and gender influence efforts to promote social reforms within an imperial relationship," and concluded that some British women intervened in India's social reform discourse as "cultural" and not "religious" missionaries, functioning also as "maternal imperialists" (Ramusack 1992: 119). In "The White Woman's Burden" Antoinette Burton examines the imperial lens through which British feminists of the late nineteenth and early twentieth centuries viewed Indian women, "not as equals but as unfortunates in need of saving by their British feminist 'sisters' . . . [and] as helpless colonial subjects" (Burton 1992: 137). Elsewhere Burton shows that Ramabai's "travels to the metropole reveal . . . some of the limitations placed on women's international solidarity by the constraints of imperial power relationships on the one hand, and by some Western women's collaboration in the ideological work of empire, on the other" (Burton 1995: 30). Here Burton reads Ramabai's relationship with the authoritarian Sister Geraldine, and even with the sympathetic Miss Beale, as "less a question of sisterhood than a struggle for authority—authority over which version of reform for women would prevail in India," so that sisterhood itself became "a contest for authority because of its imperial context" (Burton 1995: 42). In a different context I have myself identified in Sister Geraldine's case a "conflation of spiritual and racial/cultural authority with maternal authority," whose successful exercise in Ramabai's case was prevented by the latter's contestation of colonial power (Kosambi 2000a: 64).

Ramabai did not write an account of her three-year sojourn and travels in Britain, which included visits to London, Oxford, Bristol, and Devon, in addition to long periods spent at Wantage and Cheltenham. Nor was she able to fulfill her earlier promise to write about "the domestic arrangements in this country . . . [which] are worth emulating by our countrywomen" (Ramabai [1883] 1988: 27; my translation). When she wrote in detail about the domestic, social, and other conditions of the USA, the references to England did not suggest anything worthy of emulation.

In February 1886 Ramabai left England and sailed with her daughter for Philadelphia to attend WMCP's annual commencement. Her intended stay of three months was to stretch to almost three years. In a case of instantaneous mutual admiration, Ramabai caught the American imagination, and was in turn fascinated by the country and its people. After sending little Manorama to England and then on to India under care of the CSMV, Ramabai traveled throughout the USA from coast to coast, lectured on the need to educate Indian women, especially widows; and also published her internationally acclaimed book, *The High-Caste Hindu Woman,* in June 1887 (Ramabai [1887] 1981; Kosambi 2000d: 129–80). The book offers an incisive feminist analysis of the upper-caste woman's seamless oppression through all stages of her life, a deconstruction of sacred Hindu books and their misogynist bias, and a constructive agenda for women's education. As an unofficial Indian feminist manifesto (in a tone which sounds militant even to modern Indian ears), *The High-Caste Hindu Woman* reveals the ideological distance Ramabai had traversed since her *Morals for Women.* The book was privately published and promoted by Dr. Bodley and by Frances Willard, president of the Woman's Christian Temperance Union (WCTU); and sold about ten thousand copies worldwide within a year.[14] The highlight of Ramabai's American sojourn was the establishment of the Ramabai Association in Boston in December 1887, under the presidency of the Rev. Dr. E. E. Hale, the well-known Unitarian minister, with Frances Willard as one of the vice presidents. It pledged financial support for her proposed secular school for high-caste widows in India for ten years (after which Ramabai assumed that the school would be self-supporting). The "Ramabai phenomenon" seemed to sweep right across the country. By October 1888 the association also had a subsidiary at San Francisco; sixty-three "circles" across the country, including some in schools; an annual pledge of $5,000 for her school; and $11,000 collected for the school building (*Letters*: 182). Two years later the circles had increased to seventy-five; and in some cases the annual membership pledge had been reduced from one dollar to twenty-five cents, "to suit the purses of Sunday-school children and others of small means" (Ramabai Association 1890: 6), demonstrating the pervasive appeal of Ramabai's cause to a wide spectrum of age groups and regions.

Ramabai's appeal for help worked on several levels. She was the very first Indian to turn for leadership and guidance to the USA as a nonimperialist Western power—which elicited generous support, contrasting sharply with the treatment she had received in England. The USA and Britain thus found themselves locked in competition for "enlightened" social leadership of India, and Ramabai's much-publicized case strengthened the international perception of America stepping in to compensate for Britain's failure. An article in the British paper *Echo* admitted that "it had been reserved for American women fully to appreciate and generously to aid this modern apostle of culture to her fellow women of India. . . . [I]t was not until her foot touched American soil that enthusiasm, practical and permanent, was enkindled for herself and her cause. . . . We look upon the Hindu . . . woman as one of a conquered race, a dweller in our Indian dependency. The American regards her as an equal and a comrade" (*Dnyano-daya*, 24 November 1892). Even years later Sister Geraldine thought it necessary to exonerate Britain: "we may say, perhaps, that the body of [Ramabai's] work was given by America, the soul by her sojourn in the Wantage Community" (*Letters*: 415).

Most of the close friends and acquaintances Ramabai made during her American visit retained a lifelong contact. She did not make a personal comment about any of them, other than to praise their warmth and generosity. But their descriptions of her, though affectionate, provide clues to the complexity of their perception. The most immediate reaction to Ramabai was prompted by her appearance and personality. The *Philadelphia Bulletin*'s glowing account of her beauty, expressive face, and petite frame also hinted that her light skin and hazel eyes established an instant racial affinity. The valence of this appeal comes across vividly in the writings of Caroline Healy Dall, the feminist reformer and writer who was also a personal friend, and whose biography of Anandibai Joshee—"A Kinswoman of the Pundita Ramabai"—expressed the hope that a "rapid sale" of the book would "aid the projects of her friend and cousin, the Pundita Ramabai Sarasvati" (Dall 1888: iv). Dall's first reaction to Ramabai's appearance, as noted in her journal, was couched in overtly racial terms: "Ramabai is strikingly beautiful. Her face is a clean-cut oval; her eyes dark and large, glow with feeling. She is a brunette, but her cheeks are full of color. Her white widow's saree is drawn closely over her head and fastened under her chin. There is nothing else about her to suggest the Hindu" (Dall 1888: 130–31). That this was a statement of racial acceptability rather than merely one of aesthetic appreciation is confirmed by her description of Anandibai's appearance, "like a stout dumpy mulatto girl not especially interesting until her yellow face lights up" (Dall 1888: 115). The adjective "little" repeatedly applied to both women had a patronizing ring that went beyond a reference to their short stature—itself believed to be a sign of racial inferiority.

As significant as racial acceptability was religious affinity. The Christian underpinnings of the American women's movement have been well documented. Morantz-Sanchez, for example, has noted that among many nineteenth century women reformers, "the religious impulse was transformed into a social commitment and the pursuit of a profession" (Morantz-Sanchez 1985: 104). Barbara Welter has similarly noted the feminization of American religion in interaction with the reform movement of the same period (Welter 1974). Ramabai herself melded a Hindu Brahmin mystique with faith in Christianity, an Oriental aura with a Western education, an insider's knowledge of the "oppressed Hindu womanhood" with an outsider's constructive critique, and an authentic "Hinduness" with the missionary discursive practice. Orientalist overtones dovetailed neatly into admiration and respect in Rachel Bodley's description of Ramabai, "the high-caste Brahman woman, the courageous daughter of the forest, educated, refined, rejoicing in the liberty of the Gospel, and yet by preference retaining a Hindu's care as regards a vegetable diet, and the peculiarities of the dress of Hindu widowhood" (Bodley [1887] 1981: xvii).

Arguably, the greatest impact on Ramabai was made by Frances Willard, president of the WCTU, with whom she formed a personal friendship and who served as a vice president of the Ramabai Association.[15] Willard also speaks admiringly of Ramabai's "perception, conscience, benevolence, and indomitable purpose"; of her being "a woman-lover, not as an antithesis of a man-hater, for she is too great-natured not to love all humanity with equal mother-heartedness, but because women need special help" (Willard 1889: 558). But her tone toward "this gentle Hindu woman" is patronizing: "She is delightful to have about; content if she has books, pen and ink, and peace. She seems a sort of human-like gazelle; incarnate gentleness, combined with such celerity of apprehension, such swiftness of mental pace, adroitness of logic, and equipoise of intention as make her a delightful mental problem" (Willard 1889: 557). At the same time Willard admitted to viewing Ramabai as a Christian wedge into Hindu society: "I cannot help cherishing the earnest hope that, under Pundita Ramabai's Christian sway, women never yet reached by the usual missionary appliances of the church may be loosed from the prison house of ignorance, lifted out of the habitations of cruelty, and led from their darkness into the marvelous light of that gospel that elevates women, and with her lifts the world toward heaven" (Willard 1889: 561). It was to Frances Willard that Ramabai owed her intensive exposure to feminist circles—partly through an invitation to the meeting of the International Council of Women held in March–April 1888 in Washington, D.C., and attended by notable women (some of whom Ramabai mentions in chapter 8 of *USLP*), including Susan B. Anthony, Mary A. Livermore, Elizabeth Cady Stanton, and Lucy Stone (*RICW* 1888: 12–18).

In the course of her travels Ramabai met a large number of eminent people. Her primary contacts were in the field of education, such as Mr. McAlister, the public school superintendent, and Miss Anna Hallowell, the subprimary school superintendent, who facilitated her visits to Philadelphia's schools and colleges (*Letters*: 194; Bodley [1887] 1981: xvi). She was also to personally meet pioneering women educators (some of whom are mentioned in chapter 6), such as Elizabeth Peabody, and also Mrs. Quincy Shaw, who was later closely associated with her school in India.[16] This school served as a conduit for the entry of America, specifically American women, into western India's social reform movement, for the first time under nonmissionary (albeit Christian) auspices. On her return journey to India Ramabai was accompanied by Emma Ryder, an American medical doctor; and awaited in Bombay by Miss Demmon, a schoolteacher who would help with the teaching work (*Letters*: 230–34; Ramabai Association 1890: 17, 21). The Ramabai Association soon sent Sarah Hamlin of San Francisco for organizational assistance in 1889–90, and Judith Andrews of Boston to inquire into the problems in Ramabai's school in 1893–94 (Ramabai Association 1890: 22–23; 1894: 12–26). They were followed by a stream of American women missionaries who worked with Ramabai over the years, the most prominent being Minnie Abrams (see fig. 2).

The American involvement in Ramabai's plans exposed two sites of tension. One was the question of American women's exercise of agency on behalf of their disprivileged, ignorant, passive, and "heathen" sisters. In her introduction to *The High-Caste Hindu Woman* Bodley refers to the "zenana" or women's secluded quarters in conventional Indian homes. She assumes that Ramabai "has written in the belief that if the depths of thralldom in which the dwellers in Indian zenanas are held by cruel superstition and social customs were only fathomed, the light and love in American homes, which have so comforted her burdened heart, might flow forth in an overwhelming tide to bless all Indian women" (Bodley [1887] 1981: vi). Ramabai would have agreed with Bodley's identification of American women as a source of inspiration and aid to herself, but not as agents of Indian women's liberation; the linchpin of Ramabai's efforts was her faith in self-help as the only deliverance. In the same introduction, Bodley conveys Ramabai's request to tell the American readers "to help me educate the high-caste child-widows; for I solemnly believe that this hated and despised class of women, educated and enlighted, are, by God's grace, to redeem India!" (Bodley [1887] 1981: xix). This difference in perceptions of agency was crucial.

The second source of tension was the identification of Indian women's needs and their implicit or explicit construction as passive recipients of aid. Kumari Jayawardena shows, in her novel analysis of Indo-American women's (and men's) interaction, that Ramabai's project provided "an early example of the dilemmas of 'global sisterhood' and the predicaments caused by policy diasagreements between Western fund-raisers and Eastern recipients" (Jayawardena 2000: 197). A mutually acceptable mix of feminism, nationalism, and Christianity remained elusive.

Ramabai's range of interests was extraordinarily wide, and her circle of acquaintances extended beyond white America. She met Harriet Tubman, the African American activist who had "led many slaves out of slavery into the free land, like Moses of old," as she wrote to her little daughter. During her two visits to Tubman's home in Auburn, New York, Ramabai "saw some orphan children and old people unable to work for themselves" whom Harriet and her husband supported (*Letters*: 208). However, there is no mention of this meeting in *USLP*, nor any indication of Ramabai's firsthand experience of African American homes, lifestyles, and problems. Her sympathy for their plight seems to have stemmed from the prevailing liberal rhetoric rather than personal knowledge. This is true also of American Indians and the ethnic minorities whose living conditions and discriminatory treatment she describes in chapter 5 from her own assumed niche within white America.

A more personal engagement with humane concerns brought Ramabai into contact with Mr. G. T. Angell, president of the Massachusetts Society for the Prevention of Cruelty to Animals (SPCA), to whom she addressed a succinct letter in February 1888:

> As I travel about this country I see thousands of young ladies and old women, as well as little children, wearing whole and half bodies of birds on their bonnets. It shocks and grieves me. There is cruelty enough in my own country, but our gentlewomen do not at present think of beautifying themselves with dead birds. Please send me some leaflets on this subject, and I will distribute them on trains and street-cars, as well as give them to my friends. God bless you and your humane work. (Pundita Ramabai Humane Pamphlet 1888)

The letter was used by Mr. Angell for a pamphlet sold by the SPCA in Boston.

The beauty of Nature was another major interest which pervades *USLP.* Ramabai's travels took her all across the North American continent, "this wonderful land, so grand and inspiring to the lover of nature, with all its mountains and lovely lakes and rivers" (*Letters*: 183). Part of her impressive itinerary following her arrival in March 1886 can be reconstructed from her *Letters* and *USLP.* In September 1886 she visited, with Anandibai Joshee, Niagara Falls, "one of the most beautiful and grandest sights of the world; no words are sufficiently expressive to describe its beauty and grandeur. . . . I do not wonder that the ancients were moved to worship the Almighty Being manifested in such objects. I stood there stupefied with wonder. Death, Life, Eternity seemed to stand before me" (*Letters*: 174). The party returned via Carlisle, Pennsylvania. In May 1887 Ramabai was in upstate New York and in Jamaica Plain, Massachusetts; in summer 1887 in Chicago and Saratoga, and probably also in Iowa and Nebraska. In November 1887 she visited Lekoy and Auburn, New York; and then attended the annual meeting of the WCTU in Nashville, Tennessee, traveling via Louisville, Kentucky. In December that year she was in Boston, overseeing the setting up of the Ramabai Association.

In January 1888 Ramabai went from Philadelphia to Indianapolis by the scenic route through the Allegheny Mountains; the next month she was in and around Hartford, Connecticut; in March she traveled from Philadelphia to New York in thick winter snow; and then to Washington, D.C., to attend the International Council of Women meetings. In April 1888 she was in Baltimore, Philadelphia, and Boston. In May Ramabai visited Toronto, and gave a "most interesting lecture, so clever and amusing," in the words of a former Cheltenham student who found her to be "very hard on the male sex" and to hold "very extreme views on the subject of women's rights" (*Letters*: 209, 181). In July 1888 she unexpectedly traveled by train west from Philadelphia to Denver, where she stopped a few days to visit friends. From there she went through the impressive Royal Gorge, where "solid walls of granite . . . [rise] on both sides as if to meet the sky. The rays of the sun never reach the depths of this Grand Canyon, the river [Arkansas] flows merrily between the two walls so cool and fresh. The blue sky makes a lovely canopy of the great temple of the grand beauty of mountains," and the "more beautiful and grander" Black Canyon of the Gunnison, where "the rocks are cut as if by heavy iron instruments by flowing water and its winding course seems to have formed a grand castle for the dwelling of wild beauty of the mountains" (*Letters*: 216). Ramabai's final destination was San Francisco, the "largest city in California," renowned for "fruits and flowers," with its "vast bay girded on three sides by high hills and [forming] a splendid harbour," to attend the annual meeting of the National Education Association, where she was given "a splendid reception" by friends (*Letters*: 214–15, 217). From there she made an excursion in

September to the Washington Territory and to Portland, Oregon, and had an opportunity to admire their "snow-clad mountains" and their "immense forests of pine and fir trees" (*Letters*: 223). On November 28, Ramabai sailed for India from San Francisco.

Ramabai's return voyage to India in late 1888 via Japan and Hong Kong was also publicized by the newspapers of those countries (among them the *Japan Weekly Mail* and the *Hong Kong Daily Press*). Her residential school for high-caste widows, the Sharada Sadan ("Home of Learning"), was opened in Bombay in March 1889 as the first such initiative for women—offering an education and vocational training in a respectable residential setting principally to widows who were marginalized within the family and who could be spared from domestic duties. The city's social reformers extended full support for this landmark venture, having overcome their earlier disappointment at her religious conversion in their admiration for her enterprising spirit, and success in single-handedly collecting substantial funds. In late 1889 Ramabai published *USLP,* within whose multifaceted description was embedded Ramabai's image of the "New American Woman," worthy of emulation by Indians. But this was to be Ramabai's last feminist text—in fact, her last literary intervention in the social arena before her writings veered markedly toward a religious and Christian goal.

Soon after the school moved to Poona in 1890, allegations erupted about Ramabai's violation of religious neutrality. The irreconcilable tension at the core of the Ramabai Association's policy now surfaced: its insistence on secularism was coupled with the expectation of the pupils' voluntary acceptance of Christianity because, as the Rev. Mr. Hazen of Vermont phrased it, "Superstition will disappear before the light of Christianity, just as false ideas of astronomy have disappeared before the light of science" (Ramabai Association 1890: 10). In the same vein Bodley had endorsed, in her introduction to *The High-Caste Hindu Woman,* Ramabai's plan to keep the sacred books of Hinduism and Christianity side by side on the school's library shelves, "and for the rest, earnestly pray that God will guide them to His saving truth" (Bodley [1887] 1981: xviii). This attempt at tightrope walking exacted a heavy price. Ramabai's practice of allowing interested students to attend her private prayers, and then sending them to a mission for further lessons in Christianity, caused a scandal and rift with the city's Hindu social reformers, who resigned from the school's advisory board. The association instituted an inquiry and exonerated Ramabai, but a social boycott inevitably resulted, and many girls were withdrawn by their guardians. Despite the damage, the school continued to function. In 1894 it had two buildings, ran a kindergarten and primary school, and boasted a library called "The Dean

Bodley Memorial Room," as well as orderly dormitories for the fifty-one pupils (including thirty-four widows) who had stayed on, with an efficient kitchen and dining room (Ramabai Association 1894: 12–26). Equally importantly, the school had also provided an impulse for similar ventures within mainstream society,[17] although Ramabai's own cherished dream of helping Hindu widows was thwarted by the split.

In 1898 the school completed its first ten years without achieving Ramabai's dream of self-sufficiency. The Ramabai Association, having "accomplished all of its original purposes," was dissolved, and then reconstituted as the American Ramabai Association. The previous ten years had shown substantial achievements. In the USA seventy-seven circles (with 4,358 members) had kept their pledge and contributed a sum of about $90,000 for annual expenses and other purposes such as the school buildings (Ramabai Association 1898: 4, 6). The school had helped nearly five hundred Indian girls, including the seventy-five who were then in residence; there were seventy children in the kindergarten; fifty of the past students had been trained to earn their own livelihood; and forty-eight of the girls had converted to Christianity over the years (Ramabai Association 1898: 31, 35).

In the late 1890s Ramabai rescued more than three hundred women and girls from the terrible famine which struck parts of western and central India, and housed them in temporary huts at Kedgaon, a village about forty miles southeast of Poona, where she had bought a hundred-acre farm. This establishment was called the Mukti ("Salvation") Mission, and functioned as an overtly Christian, though nondenominational, institution. It was for the support of the Mukti Mission as well as the Sharada Sadan that the American Ramabai Association was formed in 1898, when Ramabai herself was present in Boston. Meanwhile, in 1896 Ramabai had sent her fifteen-year-old daughter Manorama to England, where she attended a succession of boarding schools; in 1898 Manorama was enrolled in the Chesborough Seminary in North Chili, New York. She graduated in 1900, planning to enter Mount Holyoke College to prepare for medical studies; but was called back to India by her ailing mother.

Ramabai spent the last two decades of her life at Kedgaon, where the Sharada Sadan had to be shifted during the plague epidemic of the late 1890s, and where hundreds of famine victims were already housed in the Mukti Mission. At the turn of the century, the mission housed some two thousand women and girls, in various sections modeled on women's institutions in Britain and America; and introduced a radical innovation in the Indian context. They included the old Sharada Sadan for Hindu widows, and separate sections for famine victims, sexually victimized women, old women, and blind women. In the late nineteenth and early twentieth centuries, Ramabai not only introduced but also put into practice the ideology of self-reliance for women in India, by providing them with an education, shelter, and income-earning skills, which feminist activists still advocate a hundred years later as a crucial measure for empowering women. Visitors to the Mukti Mission were greatly impressed by the sight of girls and women performing not only "women's chores," such as cooking, cleaning, teaching, and nursing, but also tasks which were thought to be a male preserve, such as carpentry, basketry, weaving saris and carpets, running an oil press, and managing a printing press. One admirer described the Mukti Mission as "a female kingdom, from top to bottom" (*Dnyanodaya*, 28 November 1907).

Ramabai's writings during her later years had a distinctly Christian slant. She contributed short articles to the mission's quarterly bulletin, *Mukti Prayer Bell* (which had a picture of the Liberty Bell on the cover), and wrote several tracts and pamphlets, but more importantly also her Christian confessions, *A Testimony of Our Inexhaustible Treasure,* published in 1907, which contained the last sparks of her feminist reading of the Hindu doctrine (Ramabai [1907] 1992). About 1905 Ramabai launched her massive lifework, a Marathi translation of the Bible based on the King James Version, the American Standard Version, and the original Greek and Hebrew versions; in the process she also wrote Greek and Hebrew grammars in Marathi. After years of work, the first proofs of the Marathi Bible were ready just before her death; the complete book was published posthumously in 1924.

Also during these last years, Ramabai created an Indian Christian network, overcoming her earlier alienation from the Indian Christian community, which had objected to the secular policy of her school. Her daughter Manorama, educated abroad, was made vice principal of the Sharada Sadan in 1900. She assisted Ramabai in all her activities, managed the *Mukti Prayer Bell,* and opened a Christian girls' school in the princely state of Hyderabad in the south of India. Manorama's delicate health and overexertion claimed her life at the young age of forty in June 1921. Having faced this last personal tragedy of her life with apparently stoic courage, Ramabai herself passed away the following year at the age of sixty-four, alone in the midst of a very large "family" of women and girls at Mukti Mission.

Reconciliation with and acceptance by mainstream Hindu society in western India was not to occur during Pandita Ramabai's lifetime—or after her death. The overtly Christian Mukti Mission had exacerbated Ramabai's alienation, and a patriarchal resentment of her feminist initiatives had sealed her marginalization. In today's Maharashtra she is still viewed with suspicion tinged with admiration, and charged with having betrayed the national and social cause by her proselytism. Ramabai's nationalism, feminism, and vision of a caste- and gender-egalitarian society still remain to be fully retrieved and appreciated.[18]

The scholarly preoccupation with the fascinating parameters of Ramabai's internationalism has frequently obscured her nationalism. Cast in a pan-Indian Brahmanic mold in early childhood, Ramabai often articulated her love for India through love for its languages, primarily Sanskrit, which symbolized the country's cultural unity and heritage. She seriously shifted her attention to modern Indian languages when the linguistic unity of the ethnically diverse USA inspired her idea of developing the cohesive potential of Hindi—spoken by a plurality of Indians—as the national language, and ousting English as an unwelcome foreign usurper (as she spells out in chapter 6). This was among the earliest suggestions in this regard, if not the first; it anticipated independent India's linguistic policy by more than half a century.

Chafing against colonial subjugation, Ramabai repeatedly voiced her anti-British sentiment and her cultural and political nationalism. Initially the opening of her school was welcomed even by her earlier adversaries, who absolved her of the charge of being "denationalized": "[I]t is to her credit that she did not discard her patriotism along with her religion" (*Kesari*, 28 May 1889; my translation). In December 1889 Ramabai had participated as one of only eight women delegates in the annual meeting of the newly established political association, the Indian National Congress, and the meeting of the social reform body, the National Social Conference, held in tandem in Bombay. Subsequently, during the plague epidemic of the late 1890s, Ramabai had a brief but effective alliance with moderate nationalists. She was most vocal in protesting against the stringent government measures, high-handedly implemented by British soldiers, and her courage was celebrated in a Marathi ballad (Kelkar 1923: 331; Nanda 1998: 106). The gradual elision of Ramabai's nationalism in India's reform narrative can be traced mainly to two causes: her major interventions coincided with the ideological cusp when social reform priorities gave way to political objectives; and her feminist efforts were coupled with a Christianizing agenda which drew down upon her the antagonism of those nationalists who were also social conservatives.

The dilemma of private and public domains of social criticism was a sensitive matter that was resolved in various ways by Ramabai's contemporaries. Most common was a bifurcation of private critique from public justification (especially in confrontation with the West) as a nationalistic gesture. Anandibai Joshee, for example, privately agreed that "early marriage is no doubt a bane" and should be dealt a "deadly blow" through government intervention, but she publicly defended the custom at a meeting of American missionary women in the USA (Kosambi 1996: 3193). Women's public protest against oppression was doubly condemned because the reform arena was constructed as a male domain, and verbal as well as active participation in it as men's responsibility and right. Ramabai's analysis of the situation—in her introduction to *The Wrongs of Indian Womanhood,* by the American missionary Lucia Bierce Fuller—was that most Indian reformers did not realize the extent of women's oppression and "even those who have suffered the greatest wrongs are reluctant to tell the truth to the world, even if they have the opportunity, for fear they may lower themselves and their nation in the eyes of other nations" (Ramabai [1900] 1984). Her own solution, that any action for "the salvation of woman in India" needs to be predicated upon naming the problem, informed her repeated critique of Indian society in all her writings, including *USLP.*

This "naming" raises the interesting question about how Ramabai's voicing of these problems differed from the Western Orientalist perceptions (for example, Fuller [1900] 1984), and what discourses it fed into. Ramabai's representation of Indian women, often imbricating the missionary discourse of "the oppressed Hindu womanhood," focused not on women's seclusion but on the related concealment of their problems, ranging from marital harassment to institutionalized oppression of widows, from the plight of deserted women to the ever-present danger of sexual victimization. Only a blurred line separates these almost monolithic representations of "the oppressed Indian woman" (which started in the 1880s and continued for the next twenty-five years) from the Orientalist and missionary emancipatory rhetoric. Another complex question which needs to be posed is whether Ramabai was justified in her claim to act as the voice of the disprivileged and silenced women of India—the "subalterns" or low-status masses as opposed to the articulate and influential elites. Gayatri Spivak has forcefully center-staged the issue in her "Can the Subaltern Speak?" (Spivak 1994). The variously victimized women depicted by Ramabai were obviously female subalterns, but how far Ramabai could legitimately represent them as an insider (a ritually low-status widow despite being an internationally famous elite Brahmin) is debatable.

On the issue of Ramabai's nationalism, some scholars (e.g., Grewal 1996) have read her alienation from the social scene of western India as a result of her conflict with the "nationalists." This locates the conflict within the arena of nationalist politics (whereas it properly belongs to the arena of social reform), and inadvertently brings Ramabai's own nationalism into question. The "nationalists" referred to are obviously extremist nationalists like Tilak who were also social conservatives, and opposed to Ramabai's feminist initiatives for that reason. Jayawardena makes explicit both this identification and the context of Ramabai's support of the British government, dating it from about 1905. In fact, this was the time when Ramabai's Christianizing agenda claimed center stage and she embarked on her massive Bible translation project. Jayawardena contrasts Ramabai's initiatives for women's education with those of Annie Besant (an adherent of Theosophy, which drew heavily on Hinduism) and Sister Nivedita (née Margaret Noble, a "Hindu" nun and a follower of Swami Vivekananda of Bengal), and concludes that "in seeing British rule as the protector of Christianity, Ramabai lost the opportunity to emerge as a truly national woman leader who could also challenge colonialism" (Jayawardena 2000: 203). I would argue that Jayawardena has herself shown the inevitability of this outcome. Both Besant and Nivedita were of Irish ancestry and thus opposed to English domination; as white and British women they were valuable assets in the anticolonial struggle. Both operated within the patriarchal paradigm (Besant opposed widow remarriage and Nivedita glorified the Indian woman chiefly as the mother of sons who would fight for India's freedom); as non-Indians both were beyond the purview of Indian male control. At the same time Ramabai's promotion of feminism and interrogation of Indian patriarchy further undermined her chances of playing a key role in the nationalistic project, which had already been decisively constructed as an exclusively male preserve. The shift in Ramabai's anti-colonial stance and her gradual accommodation of the British government resulted from the ideological antagonism of the political reformers. This dialectic provides a key to the understanding of Ramabai's various ideological evolutions (Kosambi 2000d: 1–32) and brings us back to *USLP* as her most nationalistic text.

USLP: **Text and Context**

Travelogues as a Marathi literary genre had a mixed ancestry. They derived in part from the authentic historical and geographical fragments embedded within the fictitious contents of the sacred Hindu Puranas, and of the semisacred glorifications of pilgrimage sites and rivers.[19] But travelogues in a recognizably Western form were slow to appear.[20] Despite oft-quoted Sanskrit verses eulogizing travel as part of a man's learning process, India did not have the equivalent of the European "Grand Tour" that was so essential for the contemporary upper-class Englishman. Long-distance travel usually occurred within the paradigm of pilgrimage to holy places and was not basically oriented to the secular experience of excursion and education (although exceptions did exist); travel outside India remained a rarity. In fact, credit for scripting the first foreign travelogue in Marathi belongs to Ramabai herself for her *Voyage to England,*[21] which prefaces the account of the actual voyage with a general background and ends with a few first impressions of England. Another related genre was the descriptive accounts of cities, specifically Bombay (Madgavkar [1863] 1961) and Poona (Joshi [1868] 1971), which introduced local history in the 1860s. Possibly influenced by these, *USLP* had the distinction of being the first—and for a long time the only—travel narrative of the USA written in Marathi; its successor was to appear thirty-five years later.[22] But in the interim, fragments of personal experiences of the United States had appeared in Marathi writings, as described earlier.

The other tradition in which *USLP* was located was the foreign—mainly European—visitors' accounts of the USA which had appeared in large numbers by the late nineteenth century. Pride of place in this voluminous literature was claimed by Alexis de Tocqueville's *Democracy in America* in 1835 (Tocqueville [1835] 1966), described by Max Lerner as "not only the greatest book ever written on America, but probably the greatest on any national polity and culture" (Tocqueville [1835] 1966: xxv). Among woman-authored texts, feminist Harriet Martineau's now classic *Society in America* published in 1837 (Martineau [1837] 1887) has an obvious affinity with *USLP*. Like Tocqueville, Ramabai was fascinated by the democratic political institutions and egalitarianism of American society. Their fascination stemmed from the direct relevance of the American developments to the political scene in their home countries: in Tocqueville's case the democratic present shared by France and the USA; in Ramabai's case India's present shared with America's British colonial past. Again, viewing American women through their respective British and Indian societal lenses Martineau and Ramabai reached almost diametrically opposite conclusions about American women, partly as a result of the intervening, eventful half-century. Whether Ramabai was familiar with Tocqueville's book is not certain. But she does cite Martineau (in chapter 8, "The Condition of Women"). Martineau obviously wrote for a dual audience, at home and in the USA, as did Tocqueville, whose book was published in an English translation almost immediately; both had points of departure in a shared Western culture from which they Othered the specificities of the American experience. Ramabai belonged to a culture and society Othered by the entire West. Yet she displays an unusual ability to bridge the cultural divide; her critique comes from a position almost of a surrogate American and becomes a form of introspection. Ramabai seems not to have anticipated an English translation of *USLP*. How well an Indian woman's critique of American society would have resonated with her contemporary American reformers, and what validity it would have been accorded, makes for interesting speculation.

Other Eastern responses to America pivoted on the country's generally admired technological advancement and generally criticized cultural norms. Successive Chinese travelers, venturing out of the ancient land which ensconced them, reacted most sharply to the rootlessness and restlessness of Americans (Arkush and Lee 1993).[23] Visitors from colonized India responded variously to their American encounters, but generally preferred to assert their cultural superiority (as discussed earlier). Ramabai remained a lone crusader for modernizing Indian social institutions along American lines.

Permeated with the educational ethos characteristic of all nineteenth century literature, *USLP* (started in 1887 in the USA and completed in India by late 1889) aims to share with the Marathi readership (as stated in the Preface) Ramabai's "happiness [at] seeing the marvelous things in the United States." The first chapter recounts Ramabai's voyage from Liverpool to Philadelphia, interspersed with lyrically sketched seascapes; and sets the tone for the informative narrative punctuated by social critique and personal comment, and specifically the theme of American solidarity with the women of India across the geographical-cultural divide, contrasted with the British failure to honor their imperial obligation. The second chapter presents a brief history of Columbus's discovery of America (or the "Nethermost World," where the sacred Hindu cosmology might locate it), dwelling on the exploitation of the mistakenly identified "Indians" (or "our Red brethren"); it condemns the ruthlessness of the Spanish and Portuguese conquistadors, and also that of the early English settlers who are, however, then transformed into good American fighters for independence from Britain. The roots of the system of self-governance as the key to the country's greatness—particularly the merits of a republic over a monarchy, and the concept of equal rights for citizens—are described in the third chapter, "System of Government."

Chapter 4, "Social Conditions," stresses the seeming classlessness of American society (which Ramabai unconsciously contradicts on occasion later in the text), its egalitarian ethos, and ability as the sole criterion of success; and describes civic amenities in cities, the prosperity of villagers, and the cozy nuclear family. The most interesting (and the least focused) chapter is "Domestic Conditions." It starts appropriately by describing the typical American house, the housewife's daily routine, family interaction, and social etiquette. It then digresses to women's fashions, and finally branches out in diverse unconnected directions: racial and ethnic discrimination, characteristic American traits, the seasons, and American national holidays involving meat eating and cruelty to animals. The importance of universal education, the benefits of the kindergarten system, and the production of books and newspapers are described in chapter 6. The next chapter, on religion, is essentially an endorsement of American secularism as guaranteed through a separation of church and state (as opposed to their integration in England), appreciation of its religious freedom, and a description of various charitable initiatives. The longest chapter (spanning almost a quarter of the text), "The Condition of Women," is the core of Ramabai's agenda; it is also the most cogently developed, through a treatment of women's education, employment, struggle for legal rights, organizations and clubs, and lastly the origin and growth of the WCTU. Here Ramabai's militant feminism comes across through a coalesence of facts and critique, and passionate personal engagement. The last chapter, "Commerce and Industry," does not jell well with the rest of the text, being mainly a statistical description of government departments, growth of cities and the communication network, agriculture, industries and mining, and lastly philanthropy. But it does highlight Ramabai's faith in the progressive potential of industrialization.

These nine exhaustive chapters did not cover the whole book as originally planned, and were published as Part I, with the expectation that additional material would be published separately as Part II.[24] The original text had several etchings—of George Washington, of the Star-Spangled Banner and the eagle as the U.S. emblem, and two of American Indians (captioned "Our Red Brothers"). It also had a photograph of Dr. Bodley and one of Frances Willard.

Conceptually the text falls into two parts—Ramabai's original narrative and the factual descriptions derived from secondary sources. (Derivation seems to form an integral part of travel narratives: most nineteenth century British travelogues of India borrowed heavily from older ones, although written in the same language and intended for the same readership.) The derivative part draws chiefly on Andrew Carnegie's *Triumphant Democracy, or Fifty Years' March of the Republic*[25] for the informative and statistical material on government, education, religion, and commerce and industry—material which rarely interested a woman of the time. Although the debt is heavy, the process of selection, condensation, and comment itself provides an authentic personal touch. Carnegie's reiterated stress on the superiority of the American republic over the British monarchy dovetails neatly with Ramabai's own, independently documented anti-colonial stance, and also with her distaste for hierarchy as reflected in the rigid class structure of Britain (and in the even more rigid caste system in India), and her admiration for the egalitarian American ethos. Her valorization of liberty (most emphatically and ornately articulated at the end of chapter 3, in a heavily Sanskritized and involved sentence running to twelve lines) as a colonial subject constantly chafing at this subjection adds a strong enough personal slant to transform the borrowed material. Also Ramabai's interests are wider than Carnegie's: the discussion of the country's social and domestic conditions is an enriching addition, as is her discussion of the status of women, for which she has relied on the International Council of Women held in 1888 (which she attended) and its report.[26] Other books which have left an imprint on *USLP*, and which formed part of Ramabai's personal library, are Frances Willard's *Woman and Temperance* and *Woman in the Pulpit*, and possibly also *Berard's History of the United States* and John Stuart Mill's *On Liberty* and *The Subjection of Women*.

Ramabai's original narrative comprises mainly her description of American domestic conditions, her eyewitness accounts of events such as the annual convention of the WCTU in November 1887, reports of meetings with eminent personalities (e.g., the educator Elizabeth Peabody), and her frequent ideological interventions and social critique. Predictably this is a more readable narrative, with its impassioned prose (as in the protest against animal slaughter), vivid and lyrical passages about landscapes and seasons, and occasional self-deprecating humor as well as sarcasm. It is ideologically underpinned by nationalism (associated with anti-colonialism, and valorization of political freedom and self-government); a constructive critique of Indian society (coupled with a belief in social progress through self-reliance, in social equality, and in the abolition of caste/class distinctions); feminism and occasional anti-male rhetoric; and contestation of all forms of elitism, authoritarianism, and religious bigotry. Ramabai's empathy with oppressed peoples—those as obviously alien to her as African Americans and American Indians ("our Red brethren," despite the use of the prevalent label of "savages," which is descriptive rather than derogatory)—is endearing, considering her contemporary upper-caste Indians' general insularity and assumption of superiority. It stands out against the backdrop of the later Indian diaspora which made Indians complicit as white America's "solution" to the Afro-American "problem" (Prashad 2000). Ramabai also displays a pronounced tendency to moralize especially from natural phenomena—either a seastorm suggestive of life's adversities, or a devastating snowstorm illustrating the combined strength of individually fragile snowflakes. The pervasive Sanskrit idiom and profuse Sanskrit quotations show how firmly the narrative is embedded in the Indian tradition—only a Sanskritized worldview could spontaneously perceive American universities as "temples of the goddess Saraswati." Interestingly, as a Christian Ramabai distances herself from the doctrine but not the culture of Hinduism. The opening sentences of the chapter on women are a masterly evocation of a Sanskritic Brahmin childhood contrasted with a wiser Christian adulthood, and an invocation of a Hindu goddess to validate the agency and achievements of American women to an Indian audience.

Complex issues arise from an analysis of the multiple authorial identities which inhabit the book, without overt fragmentation. The occasional tensions arise mainly from Ramabai's differential perceptions of Britain and the USA, and the occasional inconsistencies from her overwhelming desire to highlight the positive elements in American society, while having to reluctantly concede the negative (such as the obstacles to the assimilation of Afro-Americans or to the egalitarian treatment of women). One is tempted to argue that such relatively cohesive multiplicity of subject positions was more easily possible in an age which predated the Indian diaspora and the ambivalences of multiculturalism and hybridity as described by Homi Bhabha, with their inherent disorientation, dislocation, borderline existence, and also the general "unhomely" condition of the modern world (Bhabha 1997). One might add that Ramabai's migratory consciousness, developed early in life in India, enabled her to better withstand the stresses of modernity and encounters with the West. An ability to draw eclectically upon diverse cultural, religious, and ideological influences seems to have saved her from a fractured identity. Antoinette Burton (1998: 73) sees Ramabai as an early subject of the Indian diasporic movement, whose temporary exile in Britain nurtured resistance to colonialism. I would argue that in *USLP* Ramabai juxtaposed a staunch anti-British stance with an equally strong pro-American one, as a consciously deployed strategy of resistance.

Ramabai's gaze is bifurcated (not fragmented), with a consistent set of double standards: everything British is automatically interrogated and rejected, everything American is lauded, with reluctant exceptions. Although Ramabai makes a reference to the distorted British and American accounts of Indian society (in the opening paragraphs of the chapter "Social Conditions"), she does not engage this Orientalist gaze which embodied and reproduced "historically inscribed inequalities and patterns of discrimination," in Reina Lewis's words (Lewis 1996: 1). The contours of Ramabai's East-West encounter are unique. Arguably her psyche had remained uncolonized when she shifted the "contact zone" to England, as shown by her interrogation of the term "native" to mean a British colonial subject, and of its deployment to "embrace under one term 'native' inhabitants of India, America, Africa, Australia, and all the islands of the Pacific" (Kosambi 2000d: 119). Significantly, in *USLP* she herself uses the term "native" in its correct original sense, to describe the inhabitants of America.

But *USLP* provides room for misinterpretation of her stance as an assertion of personal superiority over fellow Indians (which probably weighed heavily with her readers) by its constant critique of India, which amounts to Othering. Additionally, her constant valorization of America and the Americans becomes a reverse Othering—emulatory and empathetic rather than distancing and condemnatory—and almost reinforces the effect of Orientalism. She misses no opportunity to critique Britain and assert America's comparative superiority—sometimes unfairly or absurdly so, as, for example, when she acknowledges the USA's but not Britain's adoption of the progressive kindergarten method; and when she valorizes the USA not merely for its more impressive industrial progress, but also for having a richer mineral base than Britain. Having protested against Britain's political colonization Ramabai seems to have succumbed to America' cultural hegemony; having faulted Americans for being prone to boasting (at the end of chapter 4), she proceeds to boast on their behalf. But the nagging dilemma remains: for all her nationalism, Ramabai sees liberation only through a Western model for India's progress.

The nineteenth century hegemonic Western travel accounts of non-Western countries projected the newly developed "gaze" (Burton 1998; Grewal 1996). The complexity of Ramabai's own gaze stems from its basic duality: her ideological location is such that she partly shares the American gaze directed at India while partly contesting it. Her "shared gaze" is represented by her strictures on the Indian inertia and pauperism (chapter 7), the absence of cooperative effort in the Indian social tradition (chapters 4 and 5), and the treatment of the highly troped "oppressed Indian woman" (chapters 1, 5, and especially 8). These observations parallel the American (and Western in general) perception of India to such an extent that they were probably construed by her Maharashtrian (male) contemporaries as a form of the "transculturation" and "autoethnography" described by Pratt, that is, forms of self-representation by colonized groups through the mediation of the colonizers' cultural and conceptual apparatus (Pratt 1995: 6). That this was not the case, and that Ramabai's self-critical responses were derived from her earlier experiences in India (which long predated her Western travel), is shown by her earliest books such as *Morals for Women*. Interestingly it is precisely Ramabai's preconversion Brahmanic cultural mindset (vegetarianism, kindness to animals, ritual purity) which provides the strongest critique of America.

Ramabai's various speaking positions shift and imbricate throughout the text, reinforcing her status as a simultaneous insider-outsider who straddled several cultures. Her consciously chosen authorial position is that of an upper-caste, Sanskrit- and English-educated Maharashtrian social reformer with a Sanskritized Hindu cultural worldview. The unique combination of Christian religion with Hindu culture which has shaped only this one of all Ramabai's books contrasts with the conspicuous proselytism of nineteenth century Indian Christian literature, including fiction. Baba Padmanji's novel *Yamuna-Paryatan* (The Wanderings of Yamunabai), which ushered in the genre in Marathi in 1857, holds out religious conversion as the only release to the variously oppressed Hindu widows (Padmanji [1857] 1994). Krupabai Satthianadhan's autobiographical English novel *Saguna,* serially published in India in 1887–88, is a beautifully crafted vehicle for the emancipatory message of Christianity (Satthianadhan [1887–88] 1999). Ramabai's own objective analysis in *The High-Caste Hindu Woman* of the Hindu woman's oppression which continues seamlessly through all stages of her life reflects her Othering of Hindu society from a Western vantage point—if it lacks an ostensible Christian motif, it is also devoid of the Hindu idiom. This strong correlation of Ramabai's English prose with a Western, Christian culture, and her Marathi prose with a Hindu culture—both transcending the simple need for rapport with the readers—presents a fascinating avenue for further exploration.

Whether Ramabai succeeded in establishing rapport with the Marathi readers of *USLP* is doubtful. The intended inclusiveness of "we Maharashtrians" must have been undermined by the obvious exclusiveness of the like-minded community she really addressed, for which not many could have qualified: the Sanskrit- and English-educated, upper-caste, progressive, feminist Mahrashtrians whose perspective was shaped by Christianity and who were interested in the details of government and industry in the remote USA. This unintended elitism was aggravated by the constant Othering of Indians, no matter how well-intentioned it was. But even her Indian elitism surrenders itself to American superiority so that while Othering Indians she imperceptibly Others herself. This parallels what Mary John calls (in the very different situation of late twentieth century anthropological research) the "split subject of Indian feminism"—a "subject composed of the investigating subject and the subject of inquiry, at once populated by 'selves' and 'others'" (John 1996: 126). It can be argued that in *USLP* we glimpse Ramabai's split Self—the Self which has experienced the American encounter (as an empathetic, internationalized Christian feminist) being distinct from the Self which invites the readers to share her narrated experiences (as a Maharashtrian Brahmin nationalist).

Other speaking positions blend with this principal authorial stance. As a Christian—an internationally oriented nondenominational Christian—Ramabai addresses issues related to the separation of church and state, the occasional double standards of the Church, the various Christian denominations and their interrelationships. With an unusual ability to share ideologies and solidarities across cultural divides, she assumes a New England liberalism which included sympathy for the plight of the African Americans and the American Indians, and adopts a Northern American feminist ideological stance from which to view the Southern American women's lack of progress. Ramabai's unexpected advocacy of the temperance cause, explained chiefly by the influence of Frances Willard and the WCTU, also flows spontaneously from a puritanical mindset.

The book's strength is precisely its breadth of scope, largeness of vision, and plurality of vantage points. Ramabai's "insider" position makes her a Hindu critic of Hinduism and a Christian critic of Christianity;[27] she critiques India as an Indian and America mainly as a surrogate American.

USLP met with a varied response at home. The sharpest reactions were drawn by Ramabai's feminism. In its pointedly brief review, *Kesari* gave a neutral assessment of the contents and narrative style ("elegant and appealing style" and "vivid descriptions"); obliquely suggested that the author's stated policy of seeking the good and ignoring the bad in the American society should be more generally applied (to India, for example); and bared its patriarchal hostility: "It is not surprising that Panditabai has lashed out at the male sex; that is a bad habit she has formed. Who knows how she intends to fulfil her object without the help of men!" (*Kesari*, 7 January 1890; my translation). The fellow Maharashtrian so boldly and knowledgeably returning the Anglo-American gaze was a woman—a sight disturbing to the male psyche, further aggravated by her enviable international acclaim and foreign travels—both of which had eluded most of her male compatriots. Resentment at her criticism of Hindu doctrine and practice, and of male dominance in India, coupled with a supposedly blind admiration for all things American, ensured for the book at best a lukewarm reception from the mainstream newspapers.

If in the male perception the book's subtext of feminism obscured that of nationalism (conceived as a solely male project), its few educated female readers were strongly impacted by its feminist agenda. In her book review Kashibai Kanitkar, a writer of repute, starkly contrasted the constricting, illiterate existence forced upon Maharashtrian women with the envious lot of the emancipated American women:

> Incarcerating us, women, in the prison of social system, locking up the doors and keeping a strict watch is a task which our menfolk perform loyally and with great pride. . . . Even the American women suffered not a little at the hands of the short-sighted men there; but they were at least able to read and write. They were not obliged to ask for permission to visit a temple on a holy day, or to beg obsequiously for a few pennies to buy coriander leaves to garnish the vegetable. They were therefore able to show their courage. It would be hardly surprising if every one of our countrywomen who reads this book mutters dejectedly that such a golden day will never dawn for us. However, we will have to swallow these words hastily before they reach anyone's ears for fear of committing "treason against men," just as our men are afraid of committing treason against the [British] Government. (Vaidya 1991: 236; my translation)

The words, perhaps inspired by Ramabai's account of the American women's dual struggle against the slavery of Africans and women's subjection, also anticipated by a century the currently popular trope of women as a colony. Ramabai's explicit "naming" of the existence of "colonies within colonies, oppressions within oppressions" described by Julia Watson and Sidonie Smith (Smith and Watson 1992: xvi) could not expect to win popularity with the male readership of *USLP*.

Ramabai's *USLP* might have succeeded in temporarily feeding the incipient and fragmentary feminism in western India, but it did not appeal to the Maharashtrian nationalistic sentiment as she had intended. Given the contemporary reform climate which prioritized and privileged nationalism as a male project over social issues, which were considered women-oriented and therefore subsidiary, Ramabai's feminist advocacy proved counterproductive to her effective functioning as a social leader. Arguably Ramabai's feminism as much as her Christian proselytization was responsible for her marginalization through a patriarchal backlash, and it was possibly the same reason why this remarkable book failed to make a long-standing impact; except for occasional and partial airings, it was relegated to dusty obscurity, from which it has only recently been retrieved.[28]

A Note on the Translation of *USLP*

Stylistically there is an amazing contrast between Ramabai's easy-flowing English and her more contrived Marathi, although the latter was her mother tongue and she picked up English only at the age of twenty-five, after reaching England in May 1883. (Her self-deprecatingly humorous account of a one-sided conversation with an Englishman on board the steamer to England describes her attempts to communicate with him through a few words and a great deal of gesticulation. See Ramabai [1883] 1988: 16.) Ramabai's Marathi style veers from ornate ponderousness to impassioned fluency to colloquial ease, often pervaded by a polemical didacticism. A conscious attempt has been made in this translation to preserve the tone and texture of the original Marathi text, to retain its nineteenth century flavor, and to avoid anachronisms. The nineteenth century English words (e.g., "Mohammedan" instead of "Muslim") and spelling of place names (e.g., "Bombay" instead of the current "Mumbai," "Poona" for "Pune," "Calcutta" for "Kolkata") which were used by Ramabai herself in her English writings have been retained in the translation—and the old place names also in this introduction—so as to avoid confusion. The translator's classic dilemma of fidelity versus readability has been settled in favor of fidelity, and by consciously avoiding the use of compact, modern English words and phrases which would negate Ramabai's skill in describing alien cultural concepts and artifacts to her Marathi readers. A reference must be made here to Ramabai's efforts to enlarge and enrich the Marathi vocabulary by coining new words (none of which, unfortunately, were to be absorbed into standard Marathi) for citizenship, collective effort, (women's) clubs, and the like, in order to capture their exact nuances.

The book's (Sanskritized) Marathi conceptual structure poses a predictable problem in the task of translation. A classic case is the frequently used Sanskrit word *jati*, also common in Marathi, which can denote caste, community, race, nationality, or tribe. This problem is resolved by using the appropriate English equivalent in the translation. Another example is that of figures such as a *lakh* (100,000) and a *crore* (10,000,000); these are given in numerals as far as possible. Amounts originally given only in Indian rupees have been presented here in U.S. dollars (at the exchange rate of three rupees to a dollar mentioned by Ramabai—unbelievable though it seems today, when a dollar fetches about forty-eight rupees!). Amounts originally given in both currencies are retained unchanged.

Many of the Marathi words and expressions used by Ramabai are now archaic, or have undergone a radical change of meaning. As a corrective against a misreading of her text, I have relied on *Molesworth's Marathi-English Dictionary* (a 1994 reprint of the second edition of 1857) for her contemporary Marathi usage. No liberties have been taken with the text, except to divide very long paragraphs and sentences into shorter ones; and care has been taken to achieve a translation as faithful as possible to the letter and spirit of the original.

Notes

1. The college was started in 1850 as the Female Medical College of Pennsylvania; it became the Woman's Medical College of Pennsylvania (henceforth WMCP) in 1867, and the coeducational Medical College of Pennsylvania in 1970 (MacMartin 1995: 4, note 5).

2. The thirty-three graduating students included sixteen from Pennsylvania, fourteen from twelve other states, one from Russia and two from India (one "Indian" woman being in fact British) (*Philadelphia Record,* 12 March 1886). Also, during the nineteenth century thirteen African American women graduated from WMCP, including Rebecca Cole, the second Afro-American woman doctor (MacMartin 1995: 4).

3. Clara Swain, a WMCP graduate, arrived in North India in early 1870 and was followed by Clara Seward in 1871 and Sarah Norris in 1873. They were attached to different U.S. foreign missions, and they preceded British women physicians into India (Balfour and Young 1929: 16–18).

4. *United Stateschi Lokasthiti ani Pravasavritta,* Mumbai: Nirnayasagar Press, 1889; reprint Mumbai: Maharashtra State Board for Literature and Culture, 1996. The book, written in Marathi (the language of Maharashtra in western India) is referred to by Ramabai's biographers by its English title *The Peoples of the United States.* This was presumably the title under which the book was copyrighted, to meet the requirement of registering vernacular books under an English title. (The two extant copies of the original publication which I have located do not contain the customary English title page.) The title translates literally as "The Social Conditions and Travel Account of the United States." This is the first time that *USLP* has been translated into English; existing analyses of the text are usually based on its brief summary by Sengupta (1970: 195–201).

5. This interest had inspired Adhav's selection of Ramabai's writings (Adhav 1979). My own edited compilations, including translations (Kosambi 2000d, Kosambi forthcoming) span, together with the present book, all Ramabai's non-religious writings; and constitute the "Pandita Ramabai canon."

6. A retrieval of women's words as a step toward reconstructing women's history has been the primary impulse for the present book. The emergent feminist field of women's history strives to explore the structures of patriarchy and their

impact on society, and to recover women's voices and experiences (Ramusack 1990: 139). The most overarching compilation of Indian women's history utilizing existing research is Barbara Ramusack's own "Women in South Asia" (Ramusack 1999). Also easily the most intricate and impressive exploration of the historical reconstitution of patriarchy in colonial India is *Recasting Women*, Kumkum Sangari and Sudesh Vaid's collection of essays (1997).

A number of writings by and about Indian women have recently been reprinted and republished. Krupabai Satthianadhan's *Saguna*, the first (and superbly crafted) woman-authored autobiographical novel in English, has been edited equally beautifully by Chandani Lokugé (Satthianadhan [1887–88] 1999). Also edited by Lokugé is Cornelia Sorabji's *India Calling* (1934), an autobiographical narrative of India's first woman barrister (Sorabji [1934] 2001). The most "famous and infamous" foreign text about Indian women is the American author Katherine Mayo's controversial *Mother India*, republished with Mrinalini Sinha's scholarly and nuanced introduction (Mayo [1927] 1998).

The most panoramic representation of Indian women's literary endeavors in the major Indian languages is the anthology of translated extracts by Susie Tharu and K. Lalita, spanning several centuries (Tharu and Lalita 1993). Significant among women's serious Marathi writings is Tarabai Shinde's *A Comparison of Women and Men* (Shinde 1975), recently translated into English by Rosalind O'Hanlon (1994). Haimabati Sen's unpublished Bengali memoirs, written from about 1923 to 1933, translated and edited by Geraldine Forbes and Tapan Raychaudhuri, present the personal narrative of a medical woman's struggle in a male-dominated world (Forbes and Raychaudhuri 2000). Another retrieved personal account is Rashsundari Debi's autobiography "Amar Jiban" (1868) in Tanika Sarkar's sensitive and scholarly translation and exploration (Sarkar 1999).

7. The general background for this brief overview of the late nineteenth century USA comes from *OCUSH*.

8. Structural similarities in the status of low-caste Indians and African Americans continue to be drawn in India.

9. This description of the upper-caste family life and the reform discourse is based on Kosambi (1988, 1998b, 2000b, and 2000c).

10. Upper-caste widows in Maharashtra were compelled to shave their heads and wear dull maroon saris; in Bengal widows had close-cropped hair and wore plain white saris. Ramabai dressed like a Bengali widow, for reasons explained in the next section.

11. For example, an informative and apparently innocuous book on "Vegetable Substances" concluded with general thoughts on farming, referring among other things to the hard work and innovative methods of the English-speaking European settlers in North America (so unlike the luxury-loving Spaniards of

South America), which led to great prosperity and (in a veiled nationalistic message) eventual political independence (Malshe and Chunekar 1970: 216–17).

12. This life sketch is based on Adhav 1979; Chappell, n.d.; Macnicol 1926; Sengupta 1970; and Shah 1977. See also Kosambi 2000d.

13. *Voyage to England* (Ramabai [1883] 1988) is a long letter by Ramabai describing the background, the actual voyage, and her first impressions of England. It was written and first published in 1883. For a translation, see Kosambi (forthcoming).

14. The edition of the book published in 1888 mentions on the title page that it was the "tenth thousand." A draft of Dr. Bodley's handwritten letter to the present and past students of WMCP appealing to them to buy the book for themselves and to give as a present is preserved in the archives of the Medical College of Pennsylvania. *The High-Caste Hindu Woman* was reviewed by a spectrum of newspapers across the American continent, judging by the old clippings preserved in the archives of thc Pandita Ramabai Mukti Mission.

15. Willard herself was impacted deeply enough by Ramabai to keep her photograph on her desk (Willard 1889: 423). Ramabai remained in touch with the vast international WCTU network (which she describes in chapter 8). It was also to serve as a support structure for her daughter Manorama in Australia in 1902–1903 (*Our Federation,* 15 October 1902, 15 April 1903).

16. Mrs. Quincy Shaw was a trustee of the Sharada Sadan from 1889 to 1898, and one of its vice presidents from 1894 to 1898 (Ramabai Association 1890–1898). See also chapter 8, note 31.

17. Ramabai's most prominent ideological follower was the social reformer Professor D. K. Karve, who established a residential school for destitute widows in 1896. A college was added and in 1916 also the first women's university in India, which is still flourishing as the SNDT Women's University, the oldest and largest women's university in India. In the early twentieth century Ramabai Ranade managed the Poona branch of the Seva Sadan, which provided shelter and vocational training for destitute women. Both these institutions operated within a liberal patriarchal paradigm.

18. The erasure of Ramabai's contribution from the collective memory of Maharashtra and the rest of India—including feminist activists—has lasted up to the present. It unfortunately belies the assumptions by excellent scholars like Viswanathan (1998: 118) and Jayawardena (2000: 203) about Ramabai's inspiring influence over "succeeding generations of Indian women," although one willingly endorses the sentiment.

19. I am indebted to Dr. S. S. Bahulkar for this information and insight. For a description and analysis of the glorification of rivers, see Feldhaus (1995).

20. Dean Mahomed, a hesitant herald of the Indian diaspora, wrote an En-

glish account of his fifteen-year career as a soldier in the East India Company's army, and published his *Travels* after immigrating to Britain in 1794—which made him, according to Michael Fisher, the only Indian to have "appropriated the English genre of the eighteenth century travel narrative" (Fisher 2000: 7). But few followed his example, in either English or the vernaculars.

21. Ramabai's *Voyage* was said by a reviewer to be the second such description available in Marathi. The first to be written originally in Marathi, it was preceded by *Englandatil Pravas* [Travels in England], an 1867 translation of a Gujarati book; and succeeded by an account of travel to England in two parts, published in 1889 and 1892 (Date 1944: 844).

22. A travel guide to the USA (translated from the Hindi) and a travelogue-journal were published by the same author in, respectively, 1925 and 1926 (Date 1944: 881).

23. The title of Arkush and Lee (1993), *Land Without Ghosts,* derives from a Chinese visitor's observation (which was generally shared by his compatriots) that American children grow up reading Superman comics infused with a forward-looking dynamism; they do not hear ghost stories which symbolize reverence for the past.

24. A notice to this effect appears in one of the extant copies of the original *USLP.* Part I was published in haste in time for the annual meeting of the Indian National Congress held in Bombay in late December 1889.

25. The archives of the Pandita Ramabai Mukti Mission contain Ramabai's personal, heavily marked copy of Carnegie (1886).

26. Ramabai's personal library also contains a copy of this report (*RICW* 1888).

27. The idea has been suggested by the phrase "Christian critics of Christianity" used by Tyrrel (1991: 83).

28. The book is hailed as a classic in all histories of Marathi literature. Macnicol (1926: 69) mentions that a generation after its publication "the students of the University of Bombay were studying it as a model for the charm and beauty of its language." My senior colleagues read an extract (from the "Seasons" section in chapter 5) in their Marathi school textbook in the late 1940s. I first discovered an original copy of *USLP* in a neglected corner of an old library, and referred to it in Kosambi 1988. The book's chances of being "rediscovered" have increased since it was reprinted by the Maharashtra state government in 1996.

Figure 1. Pandita Ramabai in the United States.
Photo courtesy archives of Pandita Ramabai Mukti Mission.

Figure 2. Pandita Ramabai (*seated, center*) with Manorama (*standing behind her*) and American missionary Minnie Abrams, with children at Mukti Mission.

Photo courtesy archives of Pandita Ramabai Mukti Mission.

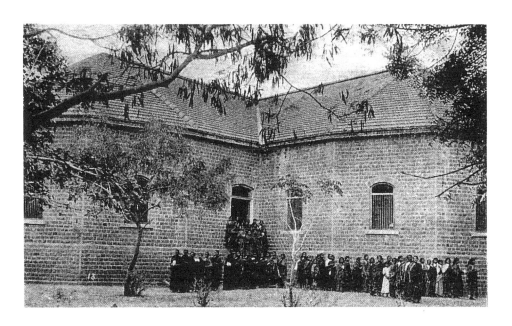

Figure 3. Women coming out of the church at Mukti Mission.

Photo courtesy archives of Pandita Ramabai Mukti Mission.

युनाइटेड् स्टेट्सची लोकस्थिति

आणि

प्रवासवृत्त.

❖

हा ग्रंथ,

पंडिता रमाबाई

यांणीं केला.

सुंबई,
निर्णयसागर छापखान्यात छापला.

सन् १८८९ इसवी.

Figure 4. Title page of *United Stateschi Lokasthiti ani Pravasavritta*, 1889.

The Peoples of
the United
States

PANDITA RAMABAI

Preface

The "United States of America" is a name that would be familiar to many; and many must have seen the map of the country while studying geography. But very few in our country can have any knowledge of the true worth of the United States, the activities of its people, its social conditions and political system, and other such things. When I went from England to the United States at the beginning of 1886, I knew nothing at all about the country other than its name. But within a few days of my arrival, I began to grasp, little by little, the greatness of that nation. As a result, I developed a desire to stay there a little longer and acquire a better knowledge of these matters. Accordingly, I stayed there from March 1886 to the end of November 1888, traveled about 30,000 miles in the country, and obtained information about several things. The happiness I derived from seeing the marvelous things in the United States will remain incomplete unless I share it, at least in some measure, with my dear countrymen and -women; that is why I am publishing this small volume. Most of it was already written in the United States, the rest has been written since my return [to India].

A few days ago I delivered altogether eight or nine lectures in Bombay and Poona on the topic "The Peoples of the United States." Some of those who heard them might have thought that I was exaggerating.[1] But I assure them that there was no exaggeration in what I said. Anybody who doubts the veracity of the vast figures cited in connection with trade and commerce, education, etc., should consult the U.S. census returns for the year 1880.[2] There are numerous American men and women in this city of Bombay who are learned and also proficient in Marathi. I request them to correct my mistakes, should there be any inaccuracy in what I have written.

There are also those who belong to a particular [ideological] faction, who have faulted me for having described only the good things about the United States and having totally omitted any reference to the bad. To them I can only say that they will find, at several places in the book, a mention of the very bad things which are obvious to all. But I do concede that I have not found fault with the people of the United States to the extent that many have desired. A pious countryman of ours,[3] who visited the country before I did, has made a note of the faults of American society. (I think he found nothing but faults in America; although it is true that he received sufficient funds to cover his travels throughout the country, and also back to India!) While traveling in the State of New York, I was asked by a man, "What is the most deplorable thing you have noticed in our country?" I said, "Friend, I have not come to your country to detect your faults, I want only your good qualities. They are what I am looking for, and they are what I find!" It was very rarely that I noticed any faults among the American people, like stumbling unexpectedly upon a stone or a thorn while walking along a very broad and spacious street; and I could not but mention them. There are good and bad people everywhere, and everyone has good and bad qualities. Needless to say, we will find good qualities if that is what we are looking for, and the result will be contrary, if our objective is the opposite.

The proofs of this book have been read with great care; nevertheless some errors have unavoidably remained.

I shall regard this meager effort of mine to have been fruitful if a perusal of this book increases in some measure the diligence and desire to serve our Mother India, which currently prevail in the hearts of my dear countrymen and -women.

Ramabai

Sharada Sadan, Bombay
December 1889

1   Voyage from Liverpool to Philadelphia

In January 1885, Doctor Rachel Bodley, Dean of the Woman's Medical College of Pennsylvania, wrote me a letter, earnestly inviting me to attend the graduation ceremony in Philadelphia in March 1886, at which Mrs. Anandibai Joshee would receive her medical degree.[1] At the time I was studying and teaching at the Ladies' College at Cheltenham in England. At first I did not accept her invitation for reasons of my own;[2] but she entreated me to come to America by writing again herself and by getting Mrs. Anandibai Joshee and Mr. Gopalrao Joshee to write to me, so that I could not bring myself to decline the invitation, despite my several problems. For one thing, Miss Bodley has put us under a great obligation by showing such concern for Hindu[3] women, although she herself belongs to another race[4] and religion. Secondly, Anandibai Joshee's is the very first example of a Hindu woman having studied a difficult subject like medicine and earned a degree. So I had a great desire to witness the happy occasion when she would receive her degree. That is why, despite the many obstacles to my coming here, I entrusted myself to God Almighty, and sailed with my daughter for America on February 17, 1886, from the port of Liverpool in England, on the ship[5] *The British Princess.*

My English friends did not at all wish me to come to this country; so they disapproved of my voyage, needless to say. Many of my women friends even prophesied that we would be shipwrecked and would drown in the ocean, because February is not a propitious month for sea voyages. Moreover, there were a great number of storms during the month that year, and several ships were wrecked off the coast of America. Severe cold had frozen the ocean around New York City and within a radius of twenty-five to thirty miles; and the continent of [North] America was ringed with ice. Be that as it may, there was no sign of a storm for three days after our ship left the port of Liverpool; but on the fourth day our ship approached an area in the Atlantic Ocean, midway between England and America, which is known as the "Devil's Pot." That is when a terrible storm broke, and we began to witness the dreadful aspect of the ocean.

There were not many passengers on our ship as the time was not favorable for voyages. The First Class had four men and three women, and the Third Class had altogether 190 passengers, including men, women, and children. These 190 people had come from different countries of Europe in order to settle in America. (See the brief account of the condition of immigrants, which appears later in the book.[6])

On Sunday some pious persons among these 190 gathered together on the middle deck, held a service, and sang hymns. That night there was a dreadful storm. I heard such a strange tale from a woman at the time that I cannot resist recounting it here. This woman had the First Class cabin next to ours, so I became particularly friendly with her in the course of the voyage. She was of the Roman Catholic persuasion. She told me that there was a man on the steamer who could not tolerate the above-mentioned passengers singing hymns; and he complained about their behavior, prophesying that there would definitely be a storm that night. He said that the people were provoking the Devil by praying to God, and that the Devil would certainly retaliate with a storm. By a coincidence, a storm did break that night, and his prediction came true. A few days later the same people started singing hymns one night, which enraged the man even more. He predicted another storm like the one before; and this prediction also came true. The following Sunday was calm and pleasant, so some children went to the upper deck and started singing "Hallelujah, hallelujah" (a Hebrew word meaning "Praise the Lord"). Our leader[7] could not control his rage then; he immediately rushed out and shut the mouths of the thoughtless children. But one could say that the Devil really persecuted our leader that day, because our ship was about to be submerged in the ocean. If this anecdote be true, one can say that many of the educated and progressive people in England still harbor a staunch belief in the powers of ghosts, spirits, and demons! Be that as it may.

The storm caused us a great deal of hardship. Huge ocean waves would dash against our portholes every moment, and make us wonder whether the ship would sink in that very instant or a little later. For three to four days we could not even lift up our heads, let alone get up and walk about. In the end the air in our cabin became too stale to breathe. So I resolved to go up on the deck, come what may, and left the cabin, gathering up all my courage. But how was I to move forward and climb up? The rocking of the ship made it difficult for my feet to stay on the floor. Finally I somehow managed to go up and sit on a chair. Within a quarter of an hour, it was as if the fresh ocean air infused a new life force into my body. Half an hour[8] earlier, when the ocean waves dashed against the porthole, I was unable to even look at them because of a strange fear, and had suffered palpitations. But see what a miracle occurred in half an hour! Now I felt not an iota of fear while standing on the deck when the ship seemed about to drown, and while observing the vast and dreadful aspect of the ocean. On the contrary, my heart surged with energy, joy, and peace. I shall never forget the lesson I learned from this natural phenomenon on this occasion. Man dreads adversity and enemies as long as he refrains from confronting them bravely. The more a timid person tries to bury his head in a corner of his house or in his bed in a cowardly manner, the more his fear increases and the more does despair darken his surroundings. But, friend, just make a resolve that "I shall either accomplish my task or give up my life,"[9] and confront your foes and your adversities, such as despair. Then the word "fear" will vanish from your memory, you will become fearless like a liberated soul,[10] and you will accomplish your tasks on the strength of Truth and Courage, even though the whole world be against you! How many storms are our scattered boats required to face in this endless Ocean of Life? If we fight the dreadful ocean waves courageously at such times, we shall certainly gain victory as well as peace of mind. But our condition will be pitiable indeed if we are overcome by the specter of false fear and start to tremble while climbing up or down the mast in order to furl or unfurl the sail.

Our ship danced about in the "Devil's Pot" for five to six days. It developed some trouble with the steam engine after entering the "Pot." Had the ship picked up speed without repairing the engine, it would have been offered up to the ocean without further delay; but the engine could not be repaired because it was impossible to hold the ship steady in one place against the onslaught of the waves. The poor captain was in a sad plight indeed; but finally the engine was repaired gradually and the ship began to sail as before. Even after leaving the "Devil's Pot," there was no dearth of storms in the ocean. When the force of the mountain-high ocean waves tossed our ship first into heaven and then into the netherworld, one would naturally wonder whether it would drown that very moment or the next. Above that infinite, boundless ocean was the canopy of the sky—sometimes clear and at other times cloudy—and below were waves the size of the small hills in the Himalayan range, against which our ship dashed continually, looking like a small leaping fish floating on water, when compared to the scene around us. It is not possible to describe the kind of thoughts which ripple into the minds of the spectators at the sight of such a gripping, dreadful, and strange scene. At the time of a storm, seabirds called "gulls" are seen floating on the ocean everywhere. They are truly the heralds of storms. They begin to fly about at great speed when a storm is about to break; and during the storm they ride the waves joyously and playfully. The happy birds remain unaffected even when tall waves surge up from all sides and clash together, a fierce wind blows, a thick fog is spread over the surface of the ocean, and the waves and thunder roar deafeningly. They just enjoy themselves. The birds almost race each other, riding tall waves, just as an Arab rides his youthful and splendid steed swiftly like the wind. At times Lord Sun would break through the cover of clouds and shine forth in the sky like a victorious warrior; the sight of the full rainbow across the heavens would then be truly entrancing and well worth describing. At times, one and a half or two rainbows would be visible. Occasionally when the ocean waves clashed against the ship or against each other, and strong winds carried a spray of water drops into the distance, sunlight would transform it into a rainbow. Oh, how can one describe the beauty of the ocean and the sky at such a time! It was so attractive and pleasing to the eye that one wished to watch it unblinkingly. When the storm abated somewhat and our ship came within three days' distance of the coast of America, we saw numerous leaping fish jumping up from the ocean.

On March 3, at about half past four in the afternoon, we sighted the coast of the American continent in the Western Hemisphere—the same continent at the sight of which Christopher Columbus had concluded in 1492 that he had sailed around the entire globe and reached India. I cannot describe the joy I felt at that moment. I thought to myself, "My Indian friends, just now the soles of our feet are turned toward the soles of yours. It is high noon here, and your part of the world is cloaked by night. Here we are strolling on the ship and chatting, and there you are snoring in bed. What a marvel!"

Extreme cold had frozen the water near the shore, and the coast of America was surrounded by ice, as mentioned above. It reflected the rays of the sun, and dazzled the eyes. When our ship reached the mouth of the Delaware River in the evening, a pilot familiar with the area and with the river came on board, and our captain entrusted to him the charge of navigating the ship.

No matter how adept a person may be in his work, he is likely to make a mistake some time or other; so it is not surprising that the pilot made a mistake at this juncture. Perhaps in a sleepy or a drowsy spell, he speeded our ship up the Delaware River so fast that it ran aground in the mud about sixty miles from Philadelphia, and did not even budge for the next couple of days. For the previous seventeen days or so, we had not sighted land; it had taken us seventeen days to cover the distance of twelve. At long last we had sighted land, but were prevented from reaching it by this fresh obstacle, even though our destination was so near. Our plan was to conclude our voyage that night and to disembark in Philadelphia at dawn; this unexpected disruption of our plan disappointed us very sadly indeed. But we did offer profuse thanks to God for having rescued us from the danger of dreadful storms and from engine trouble which might have set us adrift, and for having brought us safely to this hemisphere.

When we got up the next morning, we found our ship surrounded by ice. Four or five small steamboats arrived that day and the next, went around our ship breaking up the thick slabs of ice into smaller pieces with their sharp prows, and freed our passage. Even so, our ship would not budge. Then, at high tide, three or four boats together tried to pull the ship out of the mud with thick ropes tied to it. This attempt also failed, and the ship did not budge. Then, on March 6, the passengers in our class were put into another boat and sent on to Philadelphia. The boat could not accommodate passengers from the other class, and so they watched us with disappointed faces as we left. We felt very sorry about this, but what could we do? There was no choice. So we left them on the ship and came away. The next day, arrangements were made to take the rest of the passengers to Philadelphia. We reached Philadelphia at eight o'clock on the evening of the sixth. Both Mr. Gopalrao and Mrs. Anandibai Joshee received us at the wharf on the river, welcomed us warmly, and took us home. We headed straight for bed, utterly exhausted as we were.

On March 11, 1886, at eleven in the morning, we went to the assembly hall known as the Academy of Science in Philadelphia. About 3,000 to 3,500 people, both men and women, had assembled there to witness the ceremony of awarding degrees to the women students who had graduated from the city's Medical College. On the same day, our countrywoman Mrs. Anandibai Joshee received her medical degree. The occasion presented a very attractive scene. It was a particularly happy day for us, because Anandibai is the first Hindu woman to have studied medicine and earned a degree; I feel additionally very proud of her because she is my kinswoman.[11]

Until about four years ago, there was no facility for women in India to study medicine anywhere except in Madras. And even in Madras, the education imparted was not of a very advanced level. Popular opinion did not favor even general education for women; needless to say, it was violently opposed to giving women medical education. In the year 1883,[12] I was invited by the Education Commission at Poona to give my opinion on the changes and improvements necessary in the prevailing system of female education, and suggested that it was essential to give medical education to women. Dr. Hunter, president of the commission, told me later that the commission would not be able to make a suggestion to the Government in this regard, because medicine was not a subject included in general education; but that he would privately bring it to the notice of the higher authorities.[13]

Subsequently, through the efforts of several good people, a large fund was collected for bringing women doctors from England to India.[14] The Government also made a provision for women to study the subject, and opened classes for them in men's medical colleges. But, true to convention, they first sought the opinion of very learned men on this matter. Needless to say, the Government received a variety of responses from the variety of people who were consulted. The only surprising thing is that even some of the people who call themselves reformers and supporters of the upliftment of women opined that women should not be taught medicine. In Bengal, Keshub Chunder Sen, the leader of the Brahmo Samaj of India,[15] gave his opinion that women should not even be allowed to sit for university examinations and that medical education would deprive women of their womanliness, also that they are not capable of studying such a difficult subject, and so on. Even so, a number of learned men were convinced that women could study medicine, that their physique and smaller brains would not obstruct their studies, and also that they would not lose their womanliness by studying the subject. The Government opened the doors of medical colleges to women in accordance with the favorable opinion of these gentlemen, but hardly any Hindu women have come forward so far to study medicine. Two girls were studying medicine in Madras and one woman in Bengal; but, so far, I have not received news of their having graduated. There is an acute need for women doctors in India. Our bashful Hindu women feel very embarrassed to convey their condition to men regarding many gynecological complaints, and especially at the time of childbirth. Many a time they would rather die than reveal their condition to a male doctor. Under these circumstances, the need for women doctors would be obvious to anybody. But no country is free from prejudice. Some oppose women's medical education through ignorance, some through selfishness.

Just as Mrs. Anandibai is the very first Hindu woman to qualify as a medical doctor, the college where she studied is the very first medical college in the whole world to be established specially for women. It was consecrated[16] in 1850. Initially it met with opposition from popular opinion; and the founders and teachers of the college had to suffer a number of hardships, such as poverty, public censure, and the like. But the college is flourishing now, by the grace of God. It receives financial and other aid from a number of people. The dean of the college, Rachel L. Bodley, exerts herself day and night with utter dedication, in order to make it prosper in every way. It is during her tenure that the college has reached such large proportions. We pray to God to reward her with ever greater success in her endeavor. "Friends," or people of the Quaker sect, provide substantial assistance in this work. People of this sect are usually very liberal-minded, and not prejudiced, as I have mentioned elsewhere.[17]

When the women doctors of this country, especially those trained at the college in Philadelphia, started to practice medicine like male doctors, an association of male doctors, known as the Philadelphia County Medical Society, declared that it disapproved of women teaching, and made a rule that their members should not consult women doctors or encourage women in any way to study medicine.[i] But this rule of theirs did not at all hinder the passage of time or the progress of women. Time changed as it was bound to, and women progressed as they were bound to.

Note in the Original Text

i. However, in June 1888, the very same County Medical Society requested and begged the learned Dean Bodley of this women's medical college to join them, and made her a member.[18] A couple of days later, news came that she had suddenly passed away. Dean Bodley was a very dear friend of mine. She sincerely loved Dr. Anandibai and me. I am deeply grateful to her for the concern she felt for our countrywomen and for the help she extended to both of us in our efforts.

Dean Bodley left her mortal body and departed from this world; and we find this separation very difficult to endure. However, we content ourselves with the knowledge that she will live on eternally on this earth through her fame for meritorious deeds. We pray to the All Merciful God to send good and virtuous women like her to earth, in order to emancipate our lowly and wretched female sex.

2   The "Nethermost World," or Continent of America

Before describing what I saw on my arrival in the United States of America, and what its social conditions are like, it would be necessary to give a brief history of this country. My educated countrymen and -women would probably be acquainted with that extraordinary history. But there may be those who have not read about the discovery of America and the subsequent settlement of Western people there. If such people happen to read this book, they would not grasp how the foundation of the American political system and social conditions, described here, was laid. A brief account is therefore given of the discovery of America, its original inhabitants, and the creation of the nation of the United States.

Centuries ago, when people lacked adequate knowledge of the shape of the earth, they indulged in all sorts of speculations in this regard. The ancestors of the Hindu and other communities[1] believed the earth to be flat; as a result, they imagined the universe to be multi-storied, like the large multi-storied city houses, with the earth occupying the middle story. According to the Hindu Puranas, the universe is a fourteen-storied mansion, of which six stories or "worlds" are situated above the earth, and seven below; the lowest of these stories has been named the Nethermost World.[2] Now that all these ideas have been disproved by new discoveries, everyone has understood that the universe is not like a fourteen-storied mansion, and that the earth is not flat.

In the year 1435, a boy named Christopher Columbus was born in the city of Genoa in Italy, in the continent of Europe. No one realized his worth when he was young. His father was poor, and worked as a wool carder. But when Christopher was old enough to understand things, he expressed a desire to become a sailor and sail the seas. He made a thorough study of geography, mathematics, and navigation so as to be a good sailor, and embarked on his first voyage at the age of fourteen.

About seven or eight centuries ago, the Christians of Europe fought wars, known as "Crusades," with Turks and other Mohammedans. These wars brought Europeans into contact with the Mohammedans, from whom they gathered a great deal of knowledge. From the Mohammedans they heard descriptions of our country, that is, India. The people of the olden times, especially the Mohammedans, had a habit of exaggerating a hundredfold the good and bad qualities of whatever they described. It was not surprising, then, that in the accounts of India which they gave the Europeans, the Turks made a mountain out of a molehill and a bird out of a feather. They described India in a nutshell as "a golden goose," implying that the country was filled with gold and was fabulously wealthy. From the end of the tenth century A.D., Mohammedans had started raiding India and looting the gold, silver, and jewelry of its people. The Mohammedan tales of these sumptuous loots made the European mouths water with greed for the riches of India; and the Europeans started searching for an easy route to India. The overland route from the north through Afghanistan was riddled with obstacles, so they looked for an independent sea route. Some had already thought of a sea route to India by sailing around the continent of Africa. But Christopher, having become well versed in mathematics, geography, and navigation by the time he grew up, declared that, because the earth was round, he would sail westward and circumnavigate the globe to reach India directly.

Having vowed to prove his theory, Christopher sought help from the Kings of Italy, Portugal, England, and France; but they thought he was insane and refused. He did not abandon his efforts even after such setbacks, but obtained an audience with the King of Spain and requested his help by promising to chart an easy route to the wealthy land of India. The King did not heed him, but the Queen, Isabella, took pity on him. She summoned him and promised to provide money for his expedition by selling her own jewelry. Thus Christopher Columbus started his voyage with three ships, a promising crew, and enough victuals to last a number of days, and sailed westward to capture the "golden goose" of India.

After many days' voyage, Columbus' ships reached the Canary Islands to the northwest of Africa. After leaving the islands, the crew saw only the endless stretch of ocean all around, without even a hint of land anywhere; and they were terror-stricken. But Columbus urged them not to be anxious or afraid, but to sail on. During the third month after leaving home, that is to say, on October 12, 1492, Columbus sighted an island. It was overgrown with jungle in which a number of savages were wandering about. When day broke, Columbus himself was the first to set foot on the island, Spanish flag in hand. With a naked sword in one hand and the Spanish flag in the other, Columbus claimed sovereignty over the island in the name of the King of Spain. In the belief that the island was somewhere close to India, he set the custom of calling its inhabitants "Indians." On sailing further, he sighted the island of Haiti. Columbus made four voyages to this new land; he sailed even further and discovered South America. In the strong belief that the land he had discovered was India, he started calling it the "Indies," that is, India. Subsequent discoveries revealed that the country was not India, so the Europeans gave it the name "America," because Amerigo Vespucci, Columbus' friend, sailed to this newly discovered land after Columbus' death.

On his return voyage he described this new land in a number of letters; a German geographer who published these letters expressed a desire that the new land be known for Amerigo. Henceforth the continent of America came to be known for Amerigo (also pronounced Americo). In truth, the land discovered by Columbus should be known as "Columbia," but such is the way of the world that one man sows and another reaps the harvest. That is how the land discovered through the labors of Columbus became famous in the name of Amerigo. There are some islands to the east of Mexico and Central America which are still known as the "West Indies" or Western Indian Islands. The practice of calling the original inhabitants of America "Indians" has still not changed. In order to emphasize the distinction between them and our own countrymen, their name has the label "Red." Thus these "Red" brethren of ours and their land, the Nethermost World, were discovered in the fifteenth century A.D.

Charity at the Expense of Others

The reader might feel a little surprised at this heading. There are some bluffs, cheats, and misers who practice charity and philanthropy only by words or by robbing others, without spending a single penny of their own; in our country it is customary to describe the acts of such people as "charity at the expense of others." An important and unparalleled example of such charity occurred in the course of European history, and must be narrated here because of its close connection with our Red brethren of the Nethermost World. It happened in the following manner:

Rome, the capital of Italy in the continent of Europe, rose to great fame during the rise of the Romans. Even during their decline, the city rose in stature because of the Popes. These days even the Popes are on the decline and hardly retain any of their former greatness. Even so, many scholars and admirers of antiquity still visit Rome because it is an ancient city. The above-mentioned Popes are the chief religious teachers of the Roman Catholic denomination among Christians. Just as in our country the disciples of Shri Shankaracharya[3] have bestowed on him the title "Teacher of the World," similarly the Catholic Christians have given their principal teacher the title of "Pope," which means "Father." For about a thousand years, from the fifth to the fifteenth century A.D., the influence of the Popes increased enormously throughout Europe. Initially the Popes were the chief abbots of the monasteries of poor, devout Catholic monks, and had no connection with money or politics. From the time that the Roman Emperor Constantine embraced Christianity in the fourth century A.D., the "honorable" abbots gained entry into political intrigues in a small way. Later the Pope*jis*[4] became so powerful that they would snatch one person's kingdom and give it to another without a thought. The Pope*jis* then started to believe that they were the real Teachers of the World—nay, even Masters of the World, next only to God; that God had given them the power to turn anyone into a prince or pauper; that they could never sin or do wrong; and that if they said the West was the East, so it was! Countless gullible people took their word to be the absolute truth, and started to worship and obey them. The Pope*jis* excommunicated any obstinate person who refused to obey them. The Pope possessed the power to excommunicate such a person during his lifetime; he was believed to also possess the power to prevent such a person from going to heaven after death, which made all credulous people terribly afraid of the Pope. Even mighty and powerful kings and learned men would tremble in fear of the Pope, let alone the poor common people. However, not all the kings who honored the Pope did so out of piety; some hypocrites among them flattered the Pope to win favors for themselves.

When knowledgeable and resolute men like Columbus started to traverse the globe by sea routes and discover new, rich lands, one Pope*ji* of Rome practiced "charity at the expense of others"! In the fifteenth century, the Kings of Spain and Portugal were the favorite disciples of the Pope. In 1493 a Pope*ji* named Alexander VI was highly pleased with these two dear disciples of his, and rewarded them with two great endowments. The Pope published an order, known as a "bull," declaring that all the new countries or islands which had been discovered with the help of the states of Spain and Portugal should be regarded as possessions of their respective rulers. He prevented any possible dissension between the two by drawing an imaginary north-south line in the middle of the Atlantic Ocean, and stipulating that all new islands and continents, such as America, which had already been discovered or which would be discovered in the future in the Western Hemisphere should belong to the King of Spain; and everything east of the line, such as Africa, India, and the islands around them, should pass to the King of Portugal.

Did Africa, America, India, and the islands in their vicinity form the Pope's patrimony? How did he get the right to bequeath them to the Kings of Spain and Portugal? But there is no saying what the hypocrites and the heterodox would do at any given time. That is why I think that this act of the Pope qualifies for the epithet "charity at the expense of others."

Gold! Bring Home the Gold!

In 1492 Columbus returned from his westward voyage to America (or to India, as he believed) with help from the Queen of Spain. Later, in 1497, Vasco da Gama sailed to India around Africa, with the help of the Government of Portugal.[5] The only reason why the people of Spain and Portugal discovered new lands was gold. The European strategy was to turn like a weathervane to deal with a situation. If the newly discovered countries were in strong hands, an appeal was to be made to them for the freedom to trade. But if the inhabitants were ignorant savages and unable to offer resistance, their country was to be annexed forthwith, and the people were to be made slaves by force or by torture, to be sold like cattle in the market. That this was their strategy is evident from their conduct. When Columbus first came to San Salvador,[i] its original inhabitants were so impressed by him and his companions because of their skin color, build, and strange-looking ships as to think they were gods. So they began to serve these White gods with great devotion. The White gods, without even inquiring whether their Red devotees had a claim to the island, immediately annexed it to their own dominions in the name of King Ferdinand and Queen Isabella of Spain!

They did not stop at that. Later, from the time of Columbus' second voyage, many more Spaniards (people of Spain) began to arrive there. They captured the poor harmless inhabitants of the Nethermost World and took them to Spain to be sold into slavery. And they forced many more into slavery right then and there, and made them work in gold mines. As a result, hundreds of Red people immediately died of overexertion and ill treatment. If a person was obstinate enough to refuse to work as a slave, the Spanish "gods" would beat him severely. If this failed to cure him of his obstinacy, they would torture and kill him in full sight of his own people. So the fear that obstinacy would lead to this dire fate would make the Red devotees of the White devils do the bidding of their masters without a murmur. But, being unused to such incessant labor, they would die quickly. The Red inhabitants of the Nethermost World had been free from birth, and unused to slaving for any one. When the Spaniards and other Europeans began to force them into slavery, they would kill themselves by starving to death or by hanging themselves, preferring death to lifelong torture through slaving for greedy and brutal people like the Spaniards.

Once it so happened that a number of Red people selected a specific day on which they would all hang themselves together, in order to escape their cruel foreign masters. This plot came to the knowledge of a White man who supervised slave labor. He was extremely cruel by nature, and would torture with regular beatings the Red people forced into slavery. When they gathered together at their secret meeting place on the appointed day, carrying ropes to hang themselves with, this cruel man appeared in their midst, rope in hand. It is impossible to describe the fear and shock which the poor people felt at the sight of him. He then said to them: "Slaves, did you think I would not discover your plot? I can even read your minds. You can go ahead and hang yourselves. But do you see this rope I have in my hand? You can begin to hang yourselves. I too shall put this noose around my neck and die along with you, so that I can torture you a hundred times more in the next world!" The poor credulous people believed him and abandoned their plan to hang themselves out of fear that if he really died along with them, he would inflict much more misery on them in the next world; and they continued to slave to death under the White masters as before. This incident demonstrates that the Whites had mastered the art of controlling the foolish, credulous people by cunning and stratagem whenever they failed to do so by force.

Even great men like Columbus did not hesitate to practice deceit. Columbus had incurred a heavy debt from the exorbitant expense of his voyages. In order to repay the debt, he thought of the trick of luring or forcibly capturing about five hundred Red people of the West Indies on different occasions, loading them on board his ships and sending them to Spain to be sold into slavery. He used the money from their sale toward repaying part of his debt! What is well worth remembering in all this is that Columbus and those who followed him believed that they acted in accordance with the will of God. When Columbus wrenched the poor innocent people from their families, homes, motherland, the enjoyment of freedom, and other such invaluable things—things which make life worth living—and ruined their hopes of happiness; when he sold them as slaves in Spain and inflicted on them the indescribable agonies of slavery; he believed that he did them a great service. These people were idol worshippers. He was convinced that he had served God to the best of his ability by sending them to a Christian country like Spain and having them converted to Catholic Christianity! How sad that a great man's conduct should be tarnished by such an extraordinarily demonic deed!

The ability of the human mind to discriminate between good and bad is known as the conscience. A person's mind makes him feel guilty while doing a bad deed, or after he has done it. Therefore, he has to think of some way of making his act appear good, so as to ease this mental agony. Acting in the name of religion is one such measure. When the King of Spain sent Columbus and subsequent voyagers back to the Nethermost World with substantial assistance, he—and other kings who assisted similar expeditions—made three pacts with them. The first and foremost was that they should find gold and bring it back; the second was that they should convert the Red Indians to Christianity; and the third was that they should discover new lands and, if possible, annex them to their dominions. Their chief objective was to go to foreign countries and loot their wealth; but that would not have appeased their conscience, so the second objective, of propagating their religion, was pushed forth. The people who went in search of gold were accompanied by a number of good, benevolent people who went to the Nethermost World to evangelize in earnest, and who sincerely helped the Red people. On numerous occasions they intervened to save those poor people from oppression at the hands of the gold-hungry Europeans. Such good people are to be praised and lauded not only by us, but by people of all countries and races.

Our Red Brethren, and Their Customs and Manners

The inhabitants of the Nethermost World have been labeled "Red," as mentioned above. Now I intend to briefly explain how they acquired this label, and also describe their customs, manners, and conditions in different parts of the country. It helps greatly to understand accounts of a people or an object, if one grasps their nature and their good or bad attributes.

In our own country we see a variety of skin colors every day—some of our countrymen are fair-skinned, some shiny black, some are wheatish, some pale and hazel-eyed, and some present such a mixture as to defy all these categories, as we all know.

When the Spaniards discovered the Nethermost World, as mentioned above, they observed that the people there were of an ochre hue like red earth. At first they unknowingly called these Red people "Indians"; but after discovering their mistake they set the practice of calling these original inhabitants of the Nethermost World the "Red people" or "Red Indians" because of their color. No one knows how and when these people came to North America; many conjecture that they were preceded by another race of people, because the finds in different parts of the country, such as the walls of old ruins, caves dug into mountainsides, large dams, and the pottery, arrowheads, and ornaments found through deep excavations show that they were not made during the era of the Red people.

The "Red Indians" are big-built, tall, strong, agile, and good-looking. The women are somewhat shorter than the men, and many of them are very pretty. By nature these people are no different from the people of other countries. They do not unnecessarily bother anyone who leaves them alone; but they know very well how to retaliate if anyone harms them. And who does not? Some White people say that the Red people are knaves, cheats, untrustworthy, murderous, and cruel; but that is not true. Many good-natured White people have lived among the "Reds" and tested them. They say that the "Red Indians" are very respectable, grateful for services rendered, hospitable to strangers, and affectionate. Now, it is not that all of them are good; but nor are all the Whites good! In sum, whether people are good or bad does not depend on a particular race or country; good and bad people are found in all races and all countries, and so also among the "Red Indians."

In the fifteenth century A.D., almost all the Red people lived like savages. They painted their bodies in different colors, they fashioned tunics and blankets out of the skins of animals they had hunted, and they decorated them with colored feathers. This custom still prevails among them. Nowadays they have started wearing cotton and woolen clothes, and have acquired many other advanced practices, from contact with the Europeans. Earlier they were not familiar with the use of iron, but would make do with arrowheads, lance tips, knives, etc., made of sharpened quartz. They were expert archers and skilled in the use of clubs, but totally ignorant of the use of gunpowder, swords, guns, cannons, and the like. They did not know how to build houses with stones, bricks, and mortar. They did not do much farming, although in some areas maize would grow plentifully without much labor. Their diet consisted of fruit gathered from the forest, the meat of hunted animals, fish, etc. They did not have a script in which to write letters or books. They had many tribes, each with a language that was different from, but in some ways similar to, the others. There is an area known as Mexico at the southern tip of North America, where the people were not complete savages but fairly advanced.

The dwellings of these savages are tiny huts. A dozen long straight sticks would be pegged into the ground in a semicircle, their tips tied together, and the whole covered with animal skins, the bark of trees, or mats to make a small tent. It would have a hole in the center of the roof to let out smoke, and a small door in front, not made of wood but consisting of a small curtain which could be lifted to go in or out. The chief daily activities of the men are hunting, fishing, making boats from tree trunks, making tools from quartz and fish bones, etc. Women have to do almost all the other chores, of which plowing, guarding the fields, sowing, cooking, and such are the chief ones. Their fields produce mainly corn, tobacco, pumpkins, squash, beans, and other crops. These people are very fond of smoking tobacco. Tobacco was quite unknown in the Eastern Hemisphere four centuries ago. This "gem"[6] first came to Europe from the Nethermost World, and the people of almost all the countries of the globe have become addicted to smoking ever since.

Although the Red savages did not give much importance to trade, those in the east sold strings of beads called "wampum," and those in the west sold copper which they mined themselves. "Wampum" consisted of necklaces of white, black, or blue shells threaded with a string, which were used instead of coins, like rupees, *pice*, or *mohurs*;[7] moreover, belts made of such strings would serve as instruments of treaties between kings. In addition, many tribes had the custom of sealing a treaty by exchanging eagle feathers or smoking a pipe.

Their political system was also very simple, and comprised the unanimous selection of a strong man as a king who would be obeyed by the whole tribe. Kingship was hereditary. If occasion arose to fight a war with a neighboring tribe and if the king happened to be weak, he would have a brave and clever man of his tribe unanimously selected as his general. If the king was brave, he himself would serve as the general. They had many tribes which engaged in frequent fights and conflicts.

Their religion, in a nutshell, was the belief in a great, powerful divine spirit as the creator and protector of the world, who ruled over all and who was assisted by many minor gods and spirits—both good ones giving happiness and evil ones causing unhappiness. The evil spirits were to be propitiated through sacrifices. The future could be divined through dreams and omens. After death, good people attained immortality and spent an eternity in the enjoyment of sports like hunting, which, according to them, was the ultimate happiness.

Their custom was that a man captured in war would either be killed as a sacrifice in the temple, or tortured to death. His capacity to endure torture would indicate the extent of his courage. That it was their custom to torture people to death does not mean that they were cruel by nature. Savage and ignorant people have many strange customs. The people of England made human sacrifices when they lived in a savage state. Subsequently Christianity spread all over Europe and civilized the people, but the practice of burning alive or torturing to death a person found guilty of religious offenses or treason still continued.[8] Recently, Burma was annexed and the "rebels" there were horribly tortured, as has become widely known.

The "Red Indians" of many tribes made human sacrifices before a god, and ate their flesh as a sacred offering. It has been observed that, except for aquatic animals, no other creature in Nature eats the flesh of its own kind. But man, being such a superior creature, still eats the flesh of his own kind, which is sad indeed. Usually civilized people do not in reality eat the flesh of fellow human beings; but they have mastered the art of "eating" others of their kind without actually eating their flesh. The history of every country and every race is filled with descriptions of such cannibalism. These days many new varieties of cannibalism are being discovered in Europe, the only difference being that one catches his neighbor and eats him raw, while another roasts, fries, or grinds him into a "chutney" before eating him! Otherwise the practice of cannibalism has not disappeared completely from any country. Take care that you yourselves do not eat one another!

Reasons for the Red People's Loss of Freedom and Annihilation

Thus far I have briefly described the customs and manners of our Red brethren. Now I shall conclude this part with a brief description of the reasons for their loss of independence and their almost total annihilation.

When the Europeans went to the Nethermost World and began to mine gold and bring back captives, the Red people were living in an ignorant and savage state, as mentioned above. They had no knowledge whatever of the existence and use of the weapons of destruction, such as gunpowder, cannons, and guns. Besides, there were no horses in America; and the savages came to believe that these extremely bright, swift, and strong animals which obeyed human beings were not ordinary but divine beings. In our Puranas we hear of miraculous and unconquerable weapons such as missiles of Fire, Wind, and Thunderbolt, but we have no real knowledge of them, their appearance, use, and so on. This being the case, if someone brings such weapons to our country with a view to frightening and conquering us, he can do so with ease. Not even a hundred thousand[9] people, ignorant of such weapons, would last before him; moreover, ignorant people would begin to believe that he is a superior—even a divine—being because of his marvelous knowledge, and would fear him without reason. These poor Red Indians were in the same plight. It is not that they were weaker than the Europeans, or that they did not value freedom and did not resist when the Europeans began to tamper with it. But they were ignorant, gullible, and overly scrupulous. Sometimes they refrained from resisting their foes because of omens or unfounded fears; at other times they were afraid of the enemies' horses and their guns, cannons, and other weapons. What could the poor people do? Even if you are thousands strong and in a state of readiness, you would not be able to withstand just one enemy who single-handedly showers you with fire and hot balls, because you lack the necessary weapons to fight him. In such a situation it is hardly surprising that five or ten thousand Europeans destroyed hundreds of thousands of Indians. Their action can be compared to that of a strong, well-armed man cutting off the heads of hundreds of thousands of unprotected, ignorant, unarmed babes. No one will call this act a truly brave deed. If these same Europeans had discarded their firearms and weapons, and defeated the Red Indians in wrestling or by fighting them with their own weapons, such as bows and arrows, quartz knives, and bone-tipped lances, they would have proven themselves to be truly brave. But sad to say, those who called themselves pious and went forth to enlighten the ignorant, to rescue people from hell and lead them to heaven, ended up by utterly annihilating the poor innocent Indians through deceit, trickery, cruelty, and false speech.

Now, I do not claim that the Red Indians were always totally innocent; but they themselves never provoked the Europeans or employed deceit. On the contrary, when the Europeans first came to their country, the Indians regarded them as the descendants of the Sun and welcomed them most hospitably and respectfully, and tried to please them by offering them gold, fruit, and other gifts, according to their ability. Even so, these White deities were not satisfied; on the contrary, they tried to exploit the Indians as much as they could. Is there anyone on earth who would not offer resistance to such an omnivorous god? I cannot bring myself to blame them for trying to protect their rights in every possible way. Their misfortune was their ignorance. They possessed no means of dispelling that ignorance at the time. A man who does not attempt to overcome his ignorance even though he possesses the means to do so can undoubtedly be faulted. But what is the poor man's fault if he lacks the means? The history of the Indians shows very clearly that one of the chief reasons for their fall was ignorance (under which are subsumed gullibility, excessive scrupulousness, fear of omens, fear of ghosts and spirits, etc.).

A proverb says that when two persons fight, it is a third who profits. Mutual spite is fatal to all families, large and small, and to society and country. In truth, its root cause is ignorance. Spite arises in people's minds out of a mutual prejudice stemming from some slight cause; and once that happens, there are quarrels aplenty. Quarrels turn people into enemies, and each makes every effort to destroy his enemy. Should one enemy be strong, the other finds it necessary to seek help from a stranger; and once a third person enters a quarrel he turns both parties into puppets in his hands, and achieves his own ends. He is the one who gains, while the others lose. It is bad for the people of any family or country to have internal feuds. Our countrymen's feuds allowed foreigners to gain entry into our internal matters, and we lost our independence, as everyone familiar with the history of India knows. Our Red brethren ended up the same way. While they were fighting among themselves, the White people entered the Nethermost World. The weaker among the Red Indians enlisted the aid of the White foreigners to destroy the strong enemies of their own race. They took the Whites to their own countries, and gave them whatever help they needed. As a result, although their enemies were defeated by the Whites, they themselves also incurred a heavy loss instead of gaining anything. The White gods defeated their enemies first, and then kicked their Red Indian allies out of the country—and became the sole sovereigns themselves! Thus, both the weak Indians who helped the Whites to defeat enemies of their own race, and the similarly despicable people in our own country, were guilty of joining the common enemy and helping him to injure their own people.

The Europeans, such as the Spaniards, Portuguese, French, English, and Dutch, made the best of the opportunities described above, and employed different means to wrest away the motherland of the [Red] Indians, made their own colonies there, and established their own kingdoms. Today the Indians are scattered all over America like fragments of a broken glass bowl. Their only aim in life now is to eat and drink whatever is provided by their White enemies and rulers, to be utterly dependent on them, to live out the lives they are born to, and to die like wild animals or birds hunted by the White people.

A Brief History of the United States

After Columbus, a man named Cabot visited America in 1494 during the reign of Henry VII of England.[10] Subsequently, a number of people, such as the French, Spaniards, Portuguese, and Dutch, settled their colonies in America. I shall not dwell on them here, because the subject matter of the present book is unrelated to any but the English colonies. A man named Sir Walter Raleigh went to America in 1585 to settle a colony there. The people who accompanied him on that visit did not live there respectably, plowing and cultivating the land on which they had settled, but, instead, started searching for gold and oppressing the Indians. Therefore their colony in the new land was not a happy event, needless to say. Later on, one John Smith came to settle a colony in the province of Virginia, discovered by Raleigh. The people who accompanied him at the time included a number of women, so that the settlers lived in families. To John Smith goes the credit for having settled the first English colony in America. Afterwards some Puritans went to America and settled colonies known as New England. Thus, one after another, English colonies sprang into existence in North America. These settlers retained their firm resolve even after enduring all kinds of adversities and misfortunes. They cultivated the land in America and built large cities and towns in what used to be jungles. Their arts and crafts flourished everywhere. They possessed the very praiseworthy qualities of adventurousness, valor, strong resolution, and hard work.

At the end of the eighteenth century, there were altogether thirteen English colonies in North America. The English people in England became very envious of the prosperity of their compatriot settlers, and began to feel that they themselves should derive a substantial benefit from the American colonies. Thinking that the English discovery of the new country should serve the prime objective of making England prosperous with its revenues, they employed various measures to extract wealth from the colonies. Chief among these were the barriers to the trade and advancement of the American colonies, erected by acts of Parliament. Parliament had resolved that the settlers in the English colonies should mine gold, silver, copper, iron, and other metals in America, but not use them for manufacture; that all the metal ores from the mines should be sent to England and to no other country; and that the colonies should not trade directly with any country but England. Through these and other similarly oppressive laws, England began to harass the settlers in America. But even such laws failed to satisfy the greed of the English. In order to repay the debt they had incurred during wars with the French and the Red Indians, they resolved to enforce a law known as the "Stamp Act" in the American colonies. This act stipulated that every American was to affix a stamp printed in England on all receipts, contracts, and other legal documents in order to prove them authentic and legal. It became impossible to write a legal document without buying stamp paper printed in England. Therefore the American colonists called it a very oppressive act, and appealed repeatedly to the English officers responsible for enforcing it. Finally the matter was exacerbated to such an extent that the English Government realized that the Stamp Act was destroying the peace of the colonies. The act remained in effect in America for about a year, during which time the English

Government sold stamps worth 16,000 pounds sterling; and as much money was spent on forcing the Americans to buy the stamps. Also, the army maintained there to protect English rule began to cost the English Government five times as much, that is to say, 80,000 pounds sterling per year.

At that time the American people had two political parties: those belonging to the Tory party were favorable to England, but the supporters of the Whig party were opposed to the acts of Parliament. Realizing that the Stamp Act did not bring any profits, the English Government repealed it and levied a tax on many essential commodities, such as tea. Even this was resented by the Americans. The English Parliament had representatives of the English people; but the American colonists did not have a similar right to send their representatives. The Americans began to regard it as a terrible humiliation that they should have to submit quietly to the laws made by the people of England for their own convenience. They declared that they would boycott all goods which were taxed. After the Stamp Act, almost all Americans had resolved not to use those goods manufactured in England which would adversely affect the trade of their own country. This resolution dealt a serious blow to English trade. As a result, the English Government acceded to their request and abolished the tax on all goods except tea. This tax was not very profitable but was merely symbolic of England's domination; even so the Americans could not tolerate it. In order to test its power over the Americans, the English Government sent some East India Company ships laden with tea to America. In 1773 the ships reached the principal ports, like Philadelphia. Their captains, seeing that no one bought their cargo in New York and Philadelphia, headed for New England. In the city of Charleston the tea was unloaded, but not bought by the local people; it was stored in warehouses, where it rotted. When three ships laden with English tea came into Boston harbor, several young men of Boston boarded the ships, broke open three hundred boxes of tea, and dumped their contents into the ocean. This group is humorously known even today in the United States as the "Boston Tea Party," that is to say, the group of people in Boston who went to drink tea.

When the news of this rebellion at Boston reached England, the English Government was furious with the Bostonians, and passed a law known as the "Boston Port Bill" to prohibit any English merchant from trading with that city. This caused a great deal of hardship to the residents, but the people in other parts of the country helped the Bostonians a great deal by supplying them with essential commodities. After this incident, the oppressiveness of the English Government became notorious throughout the American colonies. In 1774 the English army camped in Massachusetts to punish the Bostonians. Later the matter was greatly aggravated. The American colonists began to complain that they had no representation in the English Parliament. They demanded that they should be consulted while laws were being made which would affect them, and they asserted that it would be unjust of the English Government to impose arbitrary taxes on them without consulting them. Not only did the English Government not accept this logical and legitimate argument, but it also arranged to send the army there to control them, at the Americans' expense. On this occasion the American people unanimously attempted to protect their rights. The different colonies sent their elected representatives to Philadelphia, where the Congress of the American people was established. The Americans conducted the work of their national administration and legislation through the principal officeholders of the Congress. Subsequently, many wars were fought between the English and the Americans. At the end of the year 1775, the American Congress appointed George Washington to be the general of its army. Since that time, the Americans gained confidence that they could hold their own against the English. On the 4th of July 1776, the people of America declared to the world that they had severed all connections with the English Government and become totally independent. At that time, the States of America had a total population of 3,000,000 people, including all men, women, and children. They did not possess much wealth, or superior arms such as those possessed by the English Government. But so strong was their desire for independence that it made them regard as mere molehills the mountains of obstacles which repeatedly confronted them. For eight years they fought the English. Finally, in 1781 they won a victory over the English and gained independence for their nation of the United States. Until 1783 the English Government continued to fight intermittent wars with them, but was unable to affect the independent States of America.[11]

The nation was reduced to poverty because of the war; and it faced all the problems which a newly created nation is likely to face. But all these problems were solved through the intelligence and diplomacy of Washington, Franklin, Jefferson, and other learned, farsighted men devoted to the national welfare. In 1787 the United States Congress created and implemented a federal system of government, which facilitated excellent administration and general stability. Let us now briefly consider the federal system of government in the United States, which has led to great happiness among the people of these States and made this nation the wealthiest and most advanced among all the nations on earth.

Note in the Orginal Text

i. This was the island on which Columbus first set foot. It is one of the islands in the West Indies and belongs to the group known as the Bahamas. Its original name was Guanahani; its new name, "San Salvador," given by Columbus, means "The Holy Savior."

3 System of Government

The ancient political philosophy of our country specified seven features of a kingdom; namely, Ruler, Minister, Ally, Treasury, Nation, Forts, and Army. Kingdom meant the country under a king's dominion, and the chief feature of the kingdom was the ruler or king. This has led to the general belief that the nation, the treasury or wealth of the country, the subjects, etc., were created solely for the comfort and happiness of the king. In accordance with the barbaric custom described in the proverb "Might is right," which has prevailed since ancient times, the king was God and controlled the destinies of his subjects. The sayings[1] that the subjects model themselves on the king and that the king shapes the times clearly show how the king's sovereign rule over his subjects and his freedom to do as he wished had earlier made a strong impression upon the minds of the people. It did not even occur to the people of ancient times that a country could do well without a king, that is, without a strong ruler. This is probably why they identified "chaos" or "disorder" as "anarchy," that is, a country without a king, or lacking the authority of a king. Such a belief does not at all exist in the republican nation of the United States. Here there is no king and there are no subjects; even so, the system of government in this nation is the best possible, and there is no "chaos" or "disorder." The chief object of this chapter is to explain the reason why this is so.

The excellent principle on whose firm foundation this marvelous republican nation is built is summarized in the following sentence: "We hold these truths to be self-evident, that all men are created equal,[2] that they are endowed by their Creator with certain unalienable rights, that among these are Life, Liberty and the pursuit of Happiness." The principle which supports all these things assumes equality among the inhabitants of this nation. All its laws, customs and manners, and ideas are based upon this eternal truth. There is no room whatsoever for arguing that a particular right is available to one person but not to another; therefore the distinction between high and low classes and families does not arise. There is only one American community. In our country there was only one caste in the eon known as Kritayuga,[3] which is why all people acted in unison and were happy and equal. Similarly there is only one community in this nation, which is why it enjoys the greatest possible happiness arising from unity. Anyone who boasts about his particular community or lineage is regarded as having insulted the greater American community. Liberty, the patron goddess of the Americans, inscribes the name "American citizen"[i] on the forehead of any person (except the Chinese) who enters the country.[4] The fortunate person whose forehead sparkles with this inscription considers himself to be in possession of greater honor and distinction than the thousands of other people who wear gem-studded crowns. It would not be surprising if kings and princes who wear crowns of gems envy such a person.

The basic principle of American citizens is that theirs is a government "of the people, for the people, and by the people." The vote of Presidents such as Washington, Lincoln, and Grant, or of learned men such as Franklin, Jefferson, and Emerson, does not carry any more weight than the vote of a lowly Negro citizen. Nor is there a single citizen who does not enjoy any of the citizen's rights which were available to those famous people.

The different States within the United States have quite dissimilar systems of administration and different types of laws. When the country came under the rule of the people, the prevalent English laws were retained with a slight change. But, as the people progressed and changed their views, the old laws also underwent a gradual alteration. The new States which have been incorporated into the nation during the last forty years or so are very American and have simple laws. Even the old States are gradually following their new siblings.

Local Government

The Federal Government is only a larger form of the local and state governments. Local government is like a seed, and it is a self-evident truth that the Federal Government, which grows out of it like a tree, will be of the same type as the seed; its quality and productivity will also depend on the quality of the seed. Therefore, before considering this republican, federal government, let us consider its original form.

Iowa is a State of the new American type, and may be regarded as representative. At one time it was covered with forests and jungles. While in Iowa some time ago, I became acquainted with many people who were among the pioneer settlers there. I give below information regarding the manner in which they founded the settlement and its local government.[5]

To begin with, an adventurous and enterprising man goes either alone or along with his wife to the new, forested area in order to seek his fortune. The equipment he carries consists of an axe, some implements, plows, a pair of horses, and some seeds. On reaching a spot of his choice, he fells the trees and builds himself a hut. Then he cuts down the surrounding forest, plows the earth and sows the seeds he has brought along to make a small farm, and plants fruit trees. Some time later a few more people follow suit, build huts or houses nearby on their own plots of land at a short distance from each other, and settle down.

When ten or fifteen such families settle down comfortably in one place, they soon begin to think of two urgent matters. The first is to construct convenient streets and roads from one house or hamlet to others; and the second is to build a school for children. As there is no government to provide these amenities in such a place, the inhabitants of the tiny settlement try to make up for the deficiencies themselves. They soon form a committee of a few people. The members resolve by mutual agreement to pay a certain amount of tax for a certain purpose. Then the need arises to have people to oversee the different tasks, such as assessing the tax to be levied, collecting it, utilizing it appropriately, and keeping accounts, which leads to the appointment of officials, such as the tax collector, accountant, supervisor, and clerk. Subsequently, a constable and the justice of the peace are appointed.

It is by consulting everybody that these works are created and officials appointed for the convenience of the inhabitants of the village. Someone among the assembled inhabitants proposes that a particular person should be appointed for a specific job, and that a certain amount of money should be spent on a certain work. Everyone is then asked for his opinion. (Such an opinion is called the "vote.") Thereafter, in accordance with the favorable vote of the majority, persons are appointed and tasks undertaken. While ascertaining public opinion in this manner, no attempt is made to discover the superiority or inferiority of anyone's family, class, or status. Whatever a man's social background, it is enough if he is an inhabitant of the village, of respectable (lawful) conduct, not a criminal or of an unsound mind, not below twenty-one years of age, and that he is a man (women have not yet acquired legal rights, except in Wyoming and Kansas). It does not matter whether he is poor or rich, learned or ignorant, dark-skinned or fair-skinned; his vote counts for not an iota more or less than the vote of the President of the country.

In this national system of government, the administration of the township, that is, the local government system, is very important. The administration of every township embodies almost all of the basic principles of the federal administration. Each township can be said to be an independent nation in itself. It is very good that the local government of the United States is free from two undesirable elements: too little independence and other shortcomings which weaken the local government system in our own country; and too much independence, which is what led to the loss of freedom in Hellas, that is, Greece. The local government in our country embodies numerous basic principles of self-government. What our people call the *panchayat*[6] may be regarded as one kind of body of people's representatives. But it does not possess the capability of an elected body in a republic, because the council is selected by a few prominent people in the village. It differs greatly from a committee elected by all the people through a well-considered and public vote. The council lacks the support of general public opinion; it has little chance of acquiring the stature and capability enjoyed by something done in a legal and organized manner. Besides, the selection of the councilors is sometimes in the hands of the two parties in the dispute to be settled; it has no representativeness at all. Anything which is not representative cannot possibly be beneficial to all. This is why, although village councils existed in our country, our people were not able to obtain a knowledge of local self-government, its benefits, or the unity resulting from it. (See Appendix A.)[7]

The Hellenese people rated local independence very highly when Hellas had a republican government. A federal republican government as in the United States was never established in that country. The Greeks had not created, and established throughout the country, a general system of government based on strong and farsighted thinking, which would lend permanence to their independence. In Greece, a republic meant each city being independent and sovereign. The proximity of a number of such city-states is bound to lead to conflicts sooner or later, for major or minor reasons. And if one small city goes to war with another, one of them is bound to emerge victorious, which would keep the enmity between them always alive. How would such small city-states, fighting with one another, survive war with a strong nation? Amity and unity were not possible among them because they completely lacked a unanimously accepted, common national ideology which would bind them together. Everyone was independent; everyone did as he wished. The several republics in Hellas collapsed one after another and were demolished by strong foreign attacks because a lack of organization among the independent city-states kept them apart. At one time an attempt was made in the province of Attica in Hellas to forge one nation out of several city-states, but it did not succeed. One reason was that the different city-states failed to voluntarily surrender a sufficient number of their principal rights to the nation in order to strengthen it. Secondly, they did not have sufficient time to think of forging such unity and to work toward its realization. Before the idea of unity emerged and took root in Attica's soil, it was cut down by Attica's two enemies, Macedonia and Rome. Neither the Hellenese nor the Romans even thought of allowing the inhabitants of each city and village to elect their own representatives, invest them with the power to be their leaders and speak and act on their behalf, send them to a general legislative assembly of the state or nation, and implement in their own cities the laws passed by the majority in the assembly. They probably considered it an affront to their independent city-state to implement the laws passed by another city. The Greeks and the Romans had very similar ideas regarding the independence of a city or a province.

The local government in the United States does not have too little or too much independence, as described above; this will become clear when one grasps the system of government in this country. Under this system, the local, state, and federal administration enjoy the amount of independence indispensable for their stability and functioning. Also, it does not at all allow the kind of independence which might create dissension among the towns, counties, and states and thereby lead to disunity, which would be detrimental to the nation.

An area of six square miles is called a township. Government surveyors are made to measure land, and the country is divided into states, counties, etc. When a number of new towns are settled, as described above, a county is formed by combining about a dozen townships.[8]

Counties

All the county officials are appointed to their posts by election, as are township officials, and usually hold office for two years. In several States such officials are elected annually. An official receives a monthly salary according to the regulations at each place, but it is quite modest. The county capital is designated by a common decision of all its people. Officeholders and officials such as sheriff, magistrate, road supervisors, and superintendent of education are elected and appointed periodically; even the lower-level judges are elected by the local people. It is appropriate that judges should be appointed by consulting popular opinion, because the people are closely connected with public matters, such as justice. It is usually officials like judges who control the fates of the families of poor, laboring classes. Needless to say, if these officials are careless, hard-hearted, arrogant, and oppressive, the lives, money, and honor of the poor, powerless people are in danger. Such examples are very common in monarchies, especially in monarchies where the king entrusts all duties to his favorite officers, who are ignorant, and who then spend their own time in idle luxury. It is very harmful if a person or a class holding an imaginary high title possesses powers which closely affect the happiness and well-being of all the people, and if the people do not possess the power to remove them from office. It deprives poor people of proper justice. Usually only the rich, powerful officeholders emerge victorious, and the goddess of justice is constantly sacrificed at the altar of such injustice.

States

As mentioned above, a number of counties together constitute a State. Just as the county government is a larger replica of the local government, so is the state government an enlarged replica of the county government. Each State has a chief official, known as the Governor, who is elected by the approval of all the people in the State. He stands in the same relation to the State as does the President of the United States to all the States taken together. The state government consists of one or two additional features not found in the local and county governments, which are very important. Each State has the power to enact its own laws. The chief city, that is, the capital of the State has a state house which houses the state legislative assembly, the Governor's office, the state high court, and the office of the chief education inspector. The state legislative assembly has two parts: one is called the House of Representatives and the other the Senate. The Representatives and Senators are elected by the people of the State. These two bodies together make all the state laws. The state government has the power to enact only such laws as are compatible with the federal government of the United States. The implementation of the state laws is the task of the Governor. The judges of the state high court are appointed by the President with the approval of the Congress; and they try the cases before them in accordance with the state laws. The state inspector of education supervises all the schools in the State. Each State has its own treasury; and the state government keeps its own accounts. Similarly, each State has its own army; however, the States do not use it for fighting among themselves. Also, no single State in the United States has the power to make war or peace with a foreign country; this power rests with the Federal Government. There is a rule stipulating that the state government is to finance its armed forces, department of education, etc. In sum, the state government possesses the powers and features necessary for an independent kingdom or nation. The state governments have voluntarily vested the Federal Government with important powers, such as entering into treaties with foreign nations, for the convenience of all and for maintaining unity among the States. In all other matters, each State is an autonomous nation.

Territories

The province next in importance to the State is the Territory. The people of a Territory do not have the right to elect their Governor, because a Territory is the common property of the whole nation. A Territory becomes a State when it acquires a sufficiently large population. It acquires all the powers of a State after the Congress resolves, in accordance with the United States system of government, to promote it to the category of State. The local and county governments in a Territory are independent, as in a State. A Territory also has a Governor and a high court; its officials possess the same powers as state officials. These officials are appointed to their posts and sent to the Territories by the President in consultation with the Congress. A Territory does not have the right to send a Representative and a Senator to the Congress; however, each Territory sends a Delegate, that is, a representative, to Washington. Although he cannot join the Congress, he can make important suggestions to the Congressmen in making resolutions and laws regarding the Territory. As a Territory does not have the right to send its Representative, it cannot participate in the election of the President and Vice President.

Nation

The great republican nation of the United States is constituted with thirty-eight States and twelve Territories, as described above. Because no limit has been set for the number of States it can have, any number of new States may be added to it. These States are not merely like small districts; they are independent nations, as explained above. Each State has its own independent features—House of Representatives and Senate, Governor, high court, army, treasury, administration; therefore, all the States are autonomous. If the States secede into separate nations, they would not survive a foreign attack, and the trade and advancement of the country would suffer greatly. Therefore, they unanimously follow certain rules made by mutual agreement. In order to reinforce their unity and strengthen their administration, they have voluntarily surrendered their sovereign rights and created a federal system of government. This Federal Government is controlled by the President; but he is not independent. He has to run it in consultation with the Representatives and Senators of all the citizens of the country.

The seat of the Federal Government is the city of Washington, situated in the District of Columbia. This district is not a separate State, but the common property of all the States in the Union. Departments which are under the common control of all the States, such as the national Treasury, as well as the Supreme Court, Department of Education, scientific societies, and the like, are located in Washington.

Supreme Court

The great and most excellent means of providing stability and strength to the Federal Government is the Supreme Court of the United States.[9] The Supreme Court arbitrates in all disputes regarding national matters, such as the division of powers between the federal and state governments, and the extent to which these powers may be used. Both the federal and state governments are required to abide by the decision of the Supreme Court, until such time as the Federal Government enacts a new law in consultation with all the States. But, should the United States Congress attempt to enact and implement a law in contravention of the Constitution which was ratified by all the States as soon as this republic was established, the Supreme Court deliberates upon its validity and declares it null and void. This, however, does not mean that the Supreme Court possesses unlimited powers. It is true that the President, Congress, and other governmental bodies of the United States obey the orders of the Supreme Court, but it has the power only to settle disputes in accordance with the Constitution, and cannot conduct itself in an arbitrary manner. Nor does it have the power to enact new laws or implement laws already in force. Only when a matter is brought before it according to proper procedure does it give a favorable or unfavorable ruling based on the Constitution. It does not have the right to interfere in the working of the state or local governments, or of the President, unless the matter is placed before it. Also, it is required to make public all its rulings and the reasoning on which the rulings are based. The powers of the Supreme Court have been circumscribed in this manner. Within these limits, when the Supreme Court rules upon any matter, on the strength of the powers vested in it by the nation and in accordance with the Constitution, no one in the country has the power (at least legally) to do other than abide by it.

The legislatures of the States are free to enact the laws they want, but they take good care not to contravene the Constitution while doing so, knowing that the Supreme Court has the power to nullify any law contrary to the Constitution. There is no reason whatsoever to contravene the Constitution, because the citizens of the State would themselves refuse to pass laws contrary to the Constitution of the Federal Government, which all the States have appointed as their administrator for their own protection, by voluntarily surrendering some of their rights. But should such an occasion arise and should a State indulge in an extra-constitutional act, there should be some body with the right to declare it irregular; and it is appropriate that this right is vested in the Supreme Court. Only one such case has come before the Supreme Court since the establishment of the United States. About twenty-five years ago, some Southern States had kept Negroes in slavery and, in order to protect their own profit, claimed that they would secede from the United States, and that they had the right to do so; they also made the attempt to secede. The Supreme Court ruled at the time that secession from the United States is contrary to the Constitution and that a State does not possess this right. The Southern States disobeyed the Supreme Court and rebelled, but were defeated by the combined Northern States, which desired unity.

The disputes regarding limits to the rights of the States are few and far between, and do not come often before the Supreme Court. But it does not have the chance to remain idle, because any disputes between the citizens of the States which involve large sums of money or very important matters can be brought before the Court for arbitration.

The Court has nine judges. They are not changed after a fixed term, like other government officers (such as President, Secretaries, etc.). Once appointed to the Court, a judge continues in his post as long as he is able to perform his duties;

only if he is found incapable of performing his duties, or if the Congress is able to bring a charge against him and prove it, is he removed by the Federal Government. If one of the judges dies, the vacancy is filled by the President by nominating another suitable person to the post; but before appointing him the President is required to obtain the approval of the Senate. The President does not have the right to appoint new members to the Supreme Court without consulting the Senate or against its wishes. The judges of the Supreme Court receive a salary of $10,000 per annum (each); and the Chief Justice is paid five hundred dollars more, that is, $10,500. A judge retires on reaching the age of seventy; he then earns an annual pension equivalent to his salary for the rest of his life.

Many other officers and lawyers in the United States earn perhaps ten times this amount of money. The post of a Supreme Court judge is not very desirable from the monetary point of view. A lawyer or even a teacher earns three or four times this salary. But the status of a judge's position does not derive from money; the greatness of the position itself is responsible for its extraordinary status. All citizens of the nation accord him utmost respect. Governors of States, the President of the country, and great bodies like the Congress extend implicit obedience to their rulings. They are representatives of the Goddess of Justice, and occupy a most excellent position as judges of the Supreme Court. How would the Goddess of Justice preserve her honor if they accepted the position—the position which is probably unparalleled in the whole world—because of the lure of money? It is therefore very good that the desire to occupy this position is not created by the strong temptation of wealth. The Justices of the Supreme Court are usually men of good character, learned, influential, experienced, and possessed of a great deal of practical wisdom. Their style of life and dress are very simple, which raises their status even further.

The Supreme Court is situated in Washington, where it functions at all times. But each of the judges takes turns to visit all the parts of the country every year at a stated time, to help the local judges to settle their cases. In order to facilitate justice, the Federal Government has divided the country into nine circuits and further districts, each of which has its own court and judge. As these courts are federal, their judges are nominated by the President with the approval of the Senate. The appointment of these judges is for life (unless they are proven to be incapable, or guilty of irregular conduct).

Congress

Let us now consider the legislative body which makes the laws according to which judges resolve public disputes and maintain social, economic, and constitutional order in the country.

The federal legislative body, or the Congress, has two branches: the House of

Representatives and the Senate. Both are situated and carry on their work in Washington. They start their sessions on fixed dates in March and December every year. The House of Representatives at present has 325 members. The number of Representatives sent by a State depends upon the number of its inhabitants. The Federal Government takes a population census every ten years, and informs the States about the number of Representatives each State is entitled to send to the Congress on the basis of its population. As the population of the country increases, so does the size of the electorate. In 1870 it was resolved that every 138,000 inhabitants should send one Representative; in 1880 this was changed to every 154,000. This provision gives an equal right to all the States to elect Representatives on the basis of their population, and prevents disputes.

The Representatives serve a term of two years. When the Congress ends its session on the fourth of March, the Representatives' term of office also comes to an end. But if they are capable and popular, they are re-elected and have the right to serve in the Congress for another two years. Thus the members newly elected to this important post are under the supervision of old and experienced officers. Each Representative receives a salary of $5,000 per year and traveling expenses. The salaries of the federal officials are paid from the federal treasury, as per the constitutional provisions.

Senate

Each State elects and sends two Senators to this body. The elected legislative body in each State selects its Senators and sends them to work on its behalf. A Senator's term of office is six years, and he too earns a salary of $5,000 a year and travel expenses. There is a provision that the term of office of all the Senators should not end simultaneously. One-third of the Senate members resign every two years;[10] but, if capable and popular, they are re-elected and hold office for another six years. The Senate members have to support the political party which is in power in their own State; but their political inclinations do not change suddenly in keeping with popular opinion, as is the case with the Representatives. The Senate has very great and important powers, which makes it a powerful organ of the Congress. The drafts of new laws are first approved by the House of Representatives and then placed before the Senate. No law can be passed if the Senate does not approve it. Treaties made with foreign countries cannot be ratified except with the approval of two-thirds of the Senate members.

The ambassadors and agents sent by the United States to other countries have to be approved by the Senate. Although the President is able to appoint a number of officers of his own choice to different posts, he is dependent upon the approval of the Senate; otherwise not even ten Presidents together can appoint their own nominees. For members to be promoted to the Senate after serving in the House of Representatives is regarded as a sign of great honor in American society. This country is very proud of its Senate, and not without reason. Like the Supreme Court, this body is without an equal in terms of status and powers. Even the English Parliament has no equal to this body. The English Parliament has two divisions: the House of Commons, or the body of common people; and the House of Lords, or the body of the nobility. Only in the House of Commons does the general public opinion count to an extent; the House of Lords treats public opinion with contempt and is open only to members of the elite, irrespective of whether or not they are popular among the general public. Lord Salisbury, the present Prime Minister to the Queen of England, says that he is envious of the American Supreme Court and that he has a great desire to have a body like the American Senate in his own country because of its marvelous efficiency and strength. It must be remembered that this marvelous strength and efficiency rest on the strong support of public opinion. The chief strength of a nation is the right of the general public to vote in the functioning of the government on the basis of their own future interests. Why would a Senate, rooted in such vigor and nurtured by public opinion, not develop extraordinary strength and efficacy?

No one in this country has the power to enter into a treaty or to declare war with a foreign country without the approval of the Senate; this and many other such facts have contributed to the greatness of this nation. Thanks to the thoughtful conduct of the Senate, this nation has escaped the terrible effects of thoughtless actions. In a kingdom whose fate is controlled by one person or a handful of persons, these officeholders are likely to develop a strong desire to fulfill their own ambitions and earn public acclaim by doing deeds which appear momentarily attractive and impressive but which lead to the destruction of the nation; and they are also likely to succeed. Such persons do not consider whether the results of an action would lead to the welfare of the nation, but think primarily of the deeds which would dazzle the people and earn praise for themselves at the present time. A republic is not likely to suffer the severe blow which might befall a monarchy where its fate lies in the hands of ministers or army generals. In a republic a shortsighted action is not likely to increase anyone's personal glory, nor is the absence of such action likely to lead to his being ignored. When a matter is not related to any personal interest, it does not bring honor or dishonor upon anyone; nor is there reason for anyone to insist upon it. When the entire Senate deliberates upon a matter and gives its favorable or unfavorable opinion, it is accepted by all. Only an action which leads to the national good should be undertaken and only such an action should be accepted by all. No one here approves of an act which ignores the national good and only preserves an individual's ministership or earns him praise. If an occasion to declare war with a foreign country arises, the Representatives, Senators, and President first deliberate upon the reasons for going to war, whether these reasons are enough to justify the bloodshed involved in war, and the resultant profit and loss. Only after they have won a majority vote in favor of war does the United States government embark on such a horrible course of action as fighting a war. Such deliberations and decisions take a long time. In the meanwhile all the inhabitants of the nation get an opportunity to express their opinion on the matter, and sometimes the very cause for the dispute disappears with the passage of time, making war unnecessary. If a decision is made to go to war, its responsibility is accepted by all the Representatives and Senators, and the President. It never happens that one sahib[11] happens to insult another, who then does what seems right to him and declares war as a form of revenge, and that innocent people suffer the consequences.

A comparison between some of the rules of the British Government and those of this republic would immediately reveal the superiority of the latter. In Britain an undertaking intended for the public good is possible only after the whole Parliament approves it and a law is passed accordingly. But it is possible to fight a war with countries like Egypt, Burma, Afghanistan, etc., and sacrifice hundreds of thousands of human lives, and to suffocate a poor country like India under the burden of a tremendous debt, if only a handful of ministers nod their approval. No one consults the Parliament in such cases. Five or six selfish persons can ruin the entire country, or make a rash treaty with a foreign country and submit their own country and its protectorates to the butcher's knife, in the name of the Queen (and it must be remembered that the Queen or King is not a powerful person but a poor puppet in the hands of these office-holding ministers, dancing to their tune). This is called the advanced political philosophy of an advanced country!

How good it would have been had the British Government followed the example of this republic and been guided by a large number of thoughtful people instead of allowing a handful of persons to interfere in the domestic matters of other countries! The avowed policy of the United States Government is not to interfere in the internal matters of foreign countries and not to allow anyone to interfere in its own domestic matters.

This country has two strong political parties. No matter which of them is in power, they have vowed not to rush into a conflict with another country, even when there are strong reasons for doing so, but to allow neutral mediators to give due consideration to these reasons and attempt to resolve the matter peacefully. Recently a treaty has been signed between the governments of the United States and England, providing that if a dispute should arise between the two, they would not go to war but resolve the dispute through third party mediation. This is indeed a great credit to their civility. The United States Government is prepared to make such a pact with other countries also. But if the other party disregards the suggestion of the United States that a dispute should be resolved by mediation, and if it insists on declaring war, then this government would reluctantly be prepared for war.

President

Thus far we have considered the governing bodies of this nation. Let us now consider its representative who heads these bodies and implements the laws which they have passed as being good and worth introducing in the country.[12] This representative is called the President of the United States. He holds the powers entrusted to him by the nation with the consent of the Congress, and acts on behalf of the nation. His term of office is four years; after his term is over, the people of the United States duly re-elect him if he is very popular, and appoint him to the office of President for four more years. George Washington, Thomas Jefferson, James Madison, James Monroe, Andrew Jackson, and Ulysses Grant each served twice as President of the United States and enjoyed the position for eight years each. No one can be appointed President for more than eight years.[13] In view of the future welfare of the country, George Washington refused the Presidency for a third time in spite of the wish of the people, just as he refused to be King, thereby making his fame immortal. He knew that if the same man remained President for three or more terms, it would deal a severe blow to the independence of the United States. His refusal of a third term was an excellent monument to patriotism and a good example to the future Presidents of the United States.

The President of the United States is not a puppet nominally placed on the throne and manipulated by his ministers. Just as he is the President of the entire nation, he is also the highest magistrate and the supreme commander of the army and the navy. His power is unlimited during his term of office. No change can be introduced and no significant work carried on in the Departments of Justice, Revenue, Defense, etc., without his orders. Everybody is ever ready to implement his orders immediately. The combined standing army in all the States does not amount to more than about twenty-five or twenty-six thousand; but many more than six or seven million strong men would be ready to go to war in defense of their country, as soon as they receive orders from the President. These soldiers do not need to be paid from the national treasury all their lives; it is the duty of the nation to maintain them only for the duration of their service. They fight not as a favor to their country, but for its defense; they do not fight for the glory of one man, but are ever ready to lay down their lives in the defense of their country. The President can remove any army officer from his post for a valid reason.

Nobody wishes to curtail the unlimited powers of the President just because it is the people who have made him their representative. If the President's actions do not find favor with the people, they reserve their judgment until the next election. There is no need for the people to resent the President's use of unlimited powers, because it is not beyond the people to remove from office this highest officer elected by themselves, should he indulge in wrongful activities. During his term of office the President receives a salary of $50,000 per annum, and he is also given possession of a large mansion near the building of the Congress in Washington, and a retreat a few miles outside the city for occasional rest. Every week the President meets with the people for a few hours at the appointed time. Every inhabitant of the country, from a millionaire to a penniless laborer, has an equal right to meet the President; anybody who so wishes can see the President during the time appointed for the purpose. The President must treat everyone with due respect. This and many other similar customs regularly remind the President that the power of the nation is vested not in one person, but in all the citizens in equal measure.

When the people's elected representative assumes the office of President, he appoints his cabinet himself.[ii] As the President is his own prime minister, his ministers, or cabinet officers, do not have a higher or lower rank, but are equal. These ministers are called "Secretaries," as for example, Secretary of War, Secretary of the Treasury, etc. These ministers are not permanent. If proven to be unsuitable, they are replaced without any difficulty. The ministers do not appear in person before the legislature; they send in writing whatever suggestions they wish to make. Earlier, the President would be present at the beginning of each session of the Congress, and make the inaugural speech. But this practice has been discontinued following the realization that it is better for the executive head not to be present when laws are being made. Now the President sends in writing the suggestions he wishes to make to the Congress. He is also free to communicate to the Congress any matter which he thinks will contribute to the nation's welfare.

It has been mentioned that the President's powers are very great. His veto powers are also great. The veto power means the President's right to withhold approval, after showing due cause, for a draft bill which has been passed by the Representatives and Senators, and sent to him for approval. A draft bill which is vetoed by the President cannot become law. If the reasons advanced by the President are not found to be appropriate, and if both the House and the Senate approve it by a two-thirds majority, the draft bill is considered again and passed. Thus, although the President's powers are unlimited, it is within the powers of the Congress to limit them.

The American people rarely make a mistake in electing their President. Most of the Presidents so far have been good. Many of them, like Washington, Adams,

Jefferson, Lincoln, and Garfield, were well suited in every way to be popular Presidents because of their qualities, such as extraordinarily upright conduct and political acumen. Lincoln and Garfield were neither millionaires nor descendants of great sages or kings. They were able to overcome all obstacles, such as their original poverty, difficulty in getting an education, and impecuniousness, thanks to their diligence and uprightness; from being the sons of poor farmers they went on to become learned teachers, lawyers, and Presidents of the United States, and achieved immortality because of their innate civility and other good qualities. This is cause for wonder, indeed. The thought that the common people of the United States can occupy very high positions on merit, without the aid of three powerful factors, namely, social class, family background, and wealth, arouses in our hearts great respect for the country.

Whenever the American people realize that they have made a mistake in electing their President, they possess the means to rectify it. The President's conduct and functioning are under scrutiny by all. It is enough for him to do just one or two things which the people disapprove of, and they are immediately made public in the newspapers throughout the country. They are mentioned in public speeches. Everybody starts to say that the next President to be elected should be more morally upright and more efficient than the present one. This usually restrains a President who is inclined towards immorality. If not, efforts are already under way to replace him when his term is over. If he violates the federal laws of the United States, he can be brought before the Supreme Court like a common man, tried, and removed from office.[14] When his term is over, the President takes up any work of his choice, like an ordinary citizen. Some practice law and some take up farming; some get elected as Representatives from their home States and serve the country in the Congress. A former President does not get a pension. Even as President he is an American citizen, and when his State elects its Governor, he goes back to his home town and casts his vote in the election like other ordinary citizens. His vote as President does not count a whit more than that of James the farmer, or Samuel the coal seller. His visit is not celebrated, except for a special reason, by the town municipality with a big show, by wasting the money collected from the poor; but all are very eager to show him due respect. It is understood that this respect is shown not to the individual, but to the people's power which is vested in him. A past President is not given undue respect. On the contrary, he is thankful to the American citizens for having accorded him the highest honor by electing him President.

It is the people who together elect the President, but not directly. Each State appoints a certain number of "Electors" according to the size of its population. These electors ascertain the popular opinion in their State and go to Washington, to report that such and such a person has won so many votes. The person with the largest number of votes is appointed President. The President is elected once every four years, on November 6. And four months later, that is, on March 4, the old President hands over charge to the new one.[15] On that occasion, the new President takes an oath to implement the laws of the United States and to serve his country faithfully. The presidential election costs $600,000, that is, about Rs. 1,800,000 each time; but the entire expenditure is not incurred because of the President alone. Each State also has to elect the Electors at the time of electing Representatives; this expenditure is merged in the larger one.

In the United States, as in England, two of the political parties are strong at a time. Many such parties have been in existence so far. Their main function is to exert themselves to achieve an important goal. About twenty-five or thirty years ago, the Republican Party came into being; its aim was to free the African slaves. The original aim of the Democratic Party, to protect individual freedom, was very good, but on nearing its sixtieth year, it is beginning to turn senile. The Republican Party is also entering middle age. Three new parties have been formed recently, of which the Prohibition Party, which opposes liquor, is very important. Although it was established not so long ago, it has gathered strength from the upright men and women of the United States. Just as the Democratic Party was on the rise earlier and the Republican Party is victorious now, it is the hope of many that the Prohibition Party's efforts will be successful in the future and that it will deliver the United States from its dreadful foe, namely, Liquor.

As everybody values freedom of thought and expression, nobody harbors enmity against people of opposing parties. The followers of each party justify it openly by providing arguments in its favor; and nobody gets angry if hot words are exchanged during such debates. Even when members of the same family, that is to say brothers, or father and son, belong to opposing parties, they do not lose their love and respect for each other. Elected officials at the federal, state or local level, such as the President, are candidates nominated by one of the parties; they are elected to office by a majority vote, irrespective of the party they belong to.

Revenues of the United States Government

According to the system of government prevailing in the United States, the township pays for its own expenses, the county for its own, and the State for its own.[16] This country has a very small debt compared to its large size. Many States are not in debt at all, but have a revenue which is adequate for managing their affairs. All the city municipalities in the United States have a total debt of $575,000,000. And the national debt amounts to $1,500,000,000 for the whole population, that is, $30 per capita. In 1835 this nation had no debt; moreover, the treasury had a surplus which it did not know how to utilize. The terrible American Civil War from 1861 to 1865 led to a very large debt. In 1866 the nation owed more than $3,000,000,000, on which an interest of $146,000,000 per annum had to be paid. By 1885 more than half this debt was repaid. It appears that in another ten or twelve years the entire debt will be paid off. During the last two years debt amounting to $270,000,000 has been repaid, as a result of which many taxes have been abolished. Also, the soldiers and widows of soldiers who fought for the Government during the Civil War have been granted a 25 percent increase in their pensions. Seeing that the United States Government repays its debt eight times faster than the British Government does, Mr. Gladstone has said that the qualities of wisdom, self-sacrifice, self-control, and farsightedness are found eight times more in the United States Government than in the British Government. It is no mean praise that an eminent politician like the above-mentioned gentleman should express such an opinion about this elected government.

In 1830 the annual revenue of the U.S. Government was $1.25 per capita, and in 1860 it was $1.75, that is, a total of $56,000,000. This revenue accrued mostly from customs on goods imported from foreign countries, and sale of public lands. From 1861 to 1865, a civil war was fought among the Americans over the slave trade; in order to repay the debt of $3,000,000,000 incurred because of the war, several taxes were imposed on the people of the United States for many years. In 1866 the levy of taxes and sale of lands together generated $558,000,000. From 1861 to 1867 the annual levy of taxes alone collected $400,000,000 to $500,000,000. Prior to this period the per capita taxes amounted to $1.75, which had to be increased to $17 due to this debt. Now, with the decrease in the national debt, many of the taxes are being abolished. In 1833 the revenue of the U.S. Government was $400,000,000, of which $50,000,000 was paid as interest on the national debt; $66,000,000 was paid in pensions to the soldiers who fought for the Government in the American Civil War; $64,000,000 was spent on the army and navy (of this amount, $10,000,000 were spent on repairing harbors and improving waterways); and $6,000,000 was spent on maintenance for the American Indian people. (It should not be thought that the U.S. Government pays $6,000,000 per year in charity to the Indians. In return for the vast lands snatched from them by force or coercion, they were paid very small sums of money which were deposited in the U.S. national treasury. They yield an interest in excess of $6,000,000. This is the amount distributed among the several tribes for their maintenance; it is not sufficient for them.) A sum of $68,000,000 is spent on public works (which will be described below). The salaries of the government officials, that is, the President of the United States, the two sections of the Congress (House and Senate), and the Vice President, amount to $2,054,000. These are the main heads of expenditure. There are several miscellaneous expenses.

This is a brief account of the government of the United States. See the picture of the Star-Spangled Banner of the United States reproduced here.[17] George Washington, the first President of this country, had a very beautiful shield, decorated with stars, and red and white stripes. It was very beautiful. The American people felt that their national flag should be like the shield and, out of respect for Washington, copied the same design on their flag. What a beautiful flag it is! It has white stars on a sky-blue cloth, and red and white stripes next to them. No other nation has such a beautiful flag—and where is another such beautifully organized nation of happy citizens to be found? The joyous stars roam freely all over the clear blue skies and provide us, inhabitants of the earth, a sight to delight the eyes. Just so do these free States of America, located midway between the clear blue waters of the Atlantic and Pacific Oceans, delight the hearts of all the people on this earth by their imposing, serene brilliance. The flag of the United States at once gives an idea of its political system. Its fifty States and Territories are autonomous but guided by the Federal Government in Washington—just as the Earth, Mercury, Jupiter, and the other planets move in their independent orbits but are guided by the Sun.

The combined area of all these States is two and a half times as large as our India, and their wealth very great. This vast country has overcome all kinds of obstacles and calamities in such a short time, and become more advanced and prosperous than all other countries on earth, on the strength of a system of government whose greatness is indescribable! The creator of this system of government, the source of all happiness and the real life force of humankind, is Liberty, whose statue stands in New York Harbor—the Delhi Gate[18] of the United States —and captures the minds of the whole world by her serene, pure brilliance. She stands with a torch in one hand to illuminate the whole world with the light of freedom, and a book in the other in order to provide knowledge and dispel the ignorance of the human race. The throne of the Goddess of Liberty, and the home of knowledge and progress, is the United States. It is no wonder that the sight of this land also fills the heart of a proud but enslaved person with joy, allows him to forget his sorry state for a brief while and be immersed in the heavenly happiness of freedom; and makes him earnestly wish that all the people in all the countries of the world would acquire such a system of government, such liberty, equality, and fraternity.

Notes in the Original Text

i. The word *jaanapada* has been used here to translate the word "citizen." The word "citizen" ordinarily means a resident of a city. But in the United States of America this word possesses a far deeper and more significant meaning. A citizen is regarded there as an inhabitant of that nation, one who has a right to participate in its government. There is not a single word in our language which expresses the same meaning. The Sanskrit word *jaanapada* somewhat resembles the American word "citizen." It means a person who inhabits a country or nation. If the word is slightly altered to create a compound which means a person who controls his *janapada,* that is, country, it would be the equivalent of the American word "citizen."[19]

ii. There are a total of seven ministers, ranked as follows: Secretary of State, Secretary of the Treasury, Secretary of War, Attorney General, Postmaster General, Secretary of the Navy, and Secretary of the Interior.

A Vice President is elected at the same time as the President. His term of office coincides with that of the President. His salary is $9,000 a year. In the event that the President dies while in office or is removed from office, the Vice President is made President for the duration of the term. If the Vice President also dies or is removed from office, the presidency passes on to one of the ministers in the council, in the order of precedence given above.

4 Social Conditions

An exercise given to students in an art school is to seat them all around a person or an object placed in the center, and ask them to sketch that person or object. While doing so, some happen to be sitting in front of the object, some behind, and some at an angle; and they sketch it as they see it from their own perspective. This does not mean that if we see the right side of the object in the picture, it has no left side; or that if we see the front portion in the picture, it has no back. It merely indicates that only that side of the object which we see in the picture was visible to the artist, and not the rest. It is impossible for a person to see all the sides of an object while sketching it; the same applies to the description of the social conditions in a country. A single person is not able to see all aspects of a society; therefore one person's opinion of it cannot be assumed to be infallible.

Some English and American people have traveled in India and written descriptions of our customs and manners and social conditions. A perusal of these clearly shows that a foreigner sees the people of the country he visits in a very different light from how the inhabitants see themselves. Therefore, I have refrained from presenting any firm and final conclusions that such-and-such is the nature of American society and that it has only these many types. Instead, I intend to describe how they appeared to me. This is the objective of this chapter and of the book as a whole.

The most distinctive aspect of American society is the public-spiritedness (concern for the good of all) of the people's thinking, government, and everything else of importance. In India, England, or other old nations, all facilities and conveniences are intended for a chosen class, and are not available to the general mass of people. Such a state of affairs is very rare in the United States. The public nature of this system of government is the chief reason for the public-spiritedness in everything else. No one here believes that a king is the lord and master of the subjects, and that the subjects and all other things have been created on earth for his benefit; because here the subjects themselves are the rulers and everyone believes that only what is good for the people should be incorporated into the government. In this nation "of the people, by the people and for the people," all the people are consulted, and whatever is approved by the majority is accepted. The people themselves elect and appoint the chief of the country, state, and town. The people themselves get laws enacted as they want.

This country provides no scope for the willful activities of those who follow the whims of the ruler, impose an arbitrary government upon the subjects, and lead a life of pleasure.

This society does not have upper, middle, and lower classes.[1] Although some class distinction and animosity is to be found everywhere, it is neither rigid nor detrimental to the nation, as is the case in the old monarchies, or like the caste distinctions in our country. A number of measures have been adopted for eliminating the existing class distinctions; chief among them is the free schooling provided to all children. The children of all the inhabitants of the United States receive a free education in schools where they learn to treat everyone in a friendly and civil manner as belonging to the same class and inhabiting the same country. They are taught that all are human beings and should treat one another as such, and not that some are socially superior and others inferior. Every child is convinced that even though he may be poor or destitute now, he can become the President of the country in the future, if he makes the effort. He knows very well that he will achieve a superior or inferior position in society depending on his qualifications. A person's ability, and not his class background, is his principal means for obtaining a high or low position.

In cities and even in villages, the streets, meeting halls, hotels, prices of goods, etc. are designed for the convenience of all the people. The large streets in cities are usually paved with round or square stones or bricks, and fitted with iron rails for the horsecars, in which one can travel conveniently and cheaply. Those who go about in a wealthy style in buggies, at the high charge of five dollars a ride, suffer quite a few jolts on these streets, but not the poor who travel a distance of four to five miles for a fare of a few pennies. This is one example of the measures introduced for the convenience of the general public. Every city in this country has very broad streets, because it is essential to have good, wide streets for people to move about without hindrance. There are paved sidewalks on either side of the street. Underneath the sidewalks or below the center of the street, sewers are built in order to carry the dirty water from the city's drains. The sidewalks make it unnecessary for people to walk in the middle of the street, which is used by carriages. This unhindered movement saves time in going to and from work. Similarly, the absence of open gutters eliminates the foul odor emanating from drains.[i]

It is the great good fortune of the people of the United States that their municipalities are not clever and conscientious like the self-governing, learned municipalities in our country. The learned members of the municipalities in our country spend a fortune on decorating and illuminating the city when a sahib comes on a visit,[2] and on creating a well-endowed, perfect garden at his place of residence, so that they have no money left for keeping the city clean or for providing streetlights where the common people move about. Naturally the ordinary person does not receive the facilities and benefits of cleanliness and hygiene as much as he should. It is simply not possible for such a thing to happen in the United States. Here the residents of a city pay the house-tax for certain amenities. If they do not get these amenities, they do not stop at making a fuss about the negligence of the municipality; they remove from office officials who fail to carry on their duties efficiently even after receiving a notice or two. It is not the practice in the United States to decorate the city with municipal funds, no matter which sahib comes on a visit. Therefore the funds earmarked for street lighting and cleaning the drains are not wasted on erecting arches or raising banners in honor of the sahib.

Attached to the municipality is a sanitary committee which visits different parts of the city and supervises hygiene without being reminded. It pays close attention to testing whether or not the vegetables, fish, milk, butter, and other eatables sold in the market are safe and edible. Similarly, if an epidemic erupts in any part of the city, special precautions are taken to see that the drains there are kept clean, to investigate the causes of the disease and to eliminate them. Public gardens and open grounds are provided throughout the city. These gardens are not laid out in the residential areas of a particular class, but in a place which is easily accessible to all. The rich may spend their own money to have their private gardens and install other amenities; but the municipality would not inconvenience the common people by spending the money of the poor to beautify the surroundings of the houses of the rich. Any kind of information is available without expending much money or effort. Cities and towns have a good police service. The police in our country arrive slowly on the scene of a burglary or street fight, after giving the culprit time to escape, and then start to throw their weight about; the policemen in the United States have not yet learned this art. If a stranger needs information about the city streets, etc., he has only to ask a policeman who returns a courteous answer. At every crossroads, on crowded streets, in alleyways and at street corners, there are policemen posted at a short distance from one another to keep a watch. The drivers of public horsecars, train drivers, ticket collectors, and the like treat passengers with great courtesy. (I have something more to say about the railroad system, which I will mention later in the book.)[3]

Of all the civic amenities in cities, piped water is the most important and excellent. Water for everyday use is stored near the city or a little beyond. Sweet water being abundant here, there is no scarcity. The place where water is stored is called a "water reservoir." Water is carried from there into the city pipes with the help of a steam engine. Tap water is not shut off at any time of the day or night. Public cisterns and taps are provided for animals and for people at various places in the city. Water tanks are built at street corners at short distances from one another; in case a house or warehouse should catch fire, water is available nearby to extinguish it. The methods used for extinguishing fire are excellent and worth remembering. Fire stations, which employ courageous and expert firemen at very high salaries specially for this work, are built at short distances from one another. Just as our Government spends money beyond its means to maintain a vast army in order to sacrifice human lives at the place of execution known as the battlefield, the local government in the United States maintains this army of firefighters to save human lives. Their drill, agility, and orderliness are excellent and astounding.[4] Even their horses are well trained for their work. The horses are needed for carrying the fire-fighting equipment, such as ladders, rubber tanks, hoes, axes, and the steam engine required for pumping water from the tanks. The equipment which is to be carried by the horses is kept in such excellent order in its proper place that it can be mounted on horseback without delay. What is more, the horses are so well trained that on hearing the alarm bell they themselves go and stand near the equipment, and nudge it so that it slides onto their backs. Their intelligence makes one marvel. Throughout the city, at short distances from one another, there are mechanical handles which signal the fire station. They are connected by wires and made to function like a telegraph system with the help of electricity. Every house owner knows where they are located. The handle is to be turned or pressed according to the printed instructions in the niche or box where it is located, so that the connecting wires ring the bell in the nearby fire station. The number of strokes indicates the neighborhood and street where the house is located. The firemen at the nearest station then get ready within five seconds, equip themselves with the weapons and armor necessary for fighting the fire, and speedily proceed to assist the people in distress. No matter how tall the house which is on fire or how terrible the fire itself, they are never too afraid or lazy to climb up and extinguish it.

The people here are never lethargic in helping those in distress. If a carriage is stuck in the street, even very well dressed men step into the mud or the gutter to help extricate it. On such occasions the respectable people in our country would reason that the work is beneath their dignity and walk calmly on.

If the social conditions of a country are to be seen in their true state, one should not sample them in large cities like Bombay or Calcutta, but see the state of the people in villages. Since my arrival here I have had to spend most of my time in cities, but I have also had ample opportunity to get to know the villages. It can surely be said that the States[5] of Pennsylvania, New York, New Jersey, Connecticut, and Massachusetts are examples of the old type and Illinois, Iowa, Nebraska, Colorado, and California examples of the new type of social conditions.

In small towns and villages, almost all the families live in their own houses, and also own the land on which the houses stand.[6] The relationship of landlord and tenant farmer is quite rare in this country, though not entirely absent. A man is not considered great only because he is a big landowner or very wealthy; his status is that of an American like thousands of others. The laws governing the sale and purchase of movable and immovable property are very simple and convenient. Therefore, although a house owner or landowner is the sole possessor of his assets, he is not known as a large estate holder or landholder. In old countries like England and Scotland, there is a separate class of tenant farmers who are continually dependent on the landowners; it is not found anywhere in this country. The owner of even large lands farms them himself, with the help of his sons or hired hands. The owner of a small farm works on his land and in his house, and in his spare time also helps a big farmer in order to earn extra money. This means that the hired help is not considered inferior to the rich farmer; this is the reason why poor and respectable men do not feel embarrassed to earn money in this fashion.

In the house, the wives and daughters of these men do all the work themselves. Domestic help is employed for a month or two during the very busy harvesting season. The women have the freedom to perform any task they are called upon to do at any time, from that of a scavenger, which is considered to be the lowliest in our country, to that of a teacher and preacher, which is considered the highest. There is no work which is considered to be beneath one's dignity, as long as it does not tarnish one's honor.

Thus it is customary for people everywhere to do all kinds of work. Even so, the villagers here do not appear to be boorish like rustics. Rare are the people who are paupers and dressed in tatters like beggars. A person who struts about through the village showing off his rich clothes receives hardly any attention. If a man dressed in somewhat dirty clothes is on his way to work, and if a stranger offers him a little money out of pity for his poverty, it is considered very insulting.

In villages there is hardly any crime, and there are no vices other than drinking and smoking. There is very little fear of theft. Sometimes people go to bed without bolting their doors from the inside, and go out without even locking the house. A village of about a thousand inhabitants usually has a poorhouse or soup kitchen which supports, at the expense of the inhabitants, at the most five or six aged persons or destitutes who are too weak or sickly to work. Just as the villagers are accustomed to all kinds of work, they are also interested in education and learning. A village of a thousand people usually has a public library which stocks not inferior books but scientific, historical, legal, and theological volumes written by very learned men like Huxley; epics (in prose and verse); books on the crafts, art, music, medicine; excellent novels; a few reputable and popular magazines published in Europe and in this country; weekly and daily papers—all of which are available to everyone. Such a village has at least one high school, and five or six elementary schools for small children. An illiterate person is rare indeed. The same man we saw in dirty clothes in the morning on his way to his farm, a plow on his shoulder, or going to fertilize his farm or to chop wood, is seen in the evening in clean clothes, sitting happily by the fire chatting with his wife and children, or reading a book or a magazine like the *Century*, the *Atlantic Monthly*, or the *North American Review*. There is a piano in his parlor, and a couple of newspapers on the table; and volumes by scholars and poets like Milton, Tennyson, Longfellow, Gibbon, Macaulay, and others are kept on the bookshelf not for mere decoration but for serious study by the family. At least five or six paintings are hanging on the walls. The family members are well informed about the events in their own country and in others. In the morning we saw his wife and daughters cooking, washing clothes and dishes, and doing other housework. In the afternoon or in the evening after supper, one of them is seen knitting socks or doing needlework, another playing the piano or painting flowers and other motifs on porcelain cups or on canvas, and a third doing her daily lessons from a book on Latin grammar (with the intention of taking the entrance examination of a college to study there). Every morning and evening the master or mistress of the house reads one or two chapters from the scriptures and says the prayers; and the mother reads to her little ones from religious, historical, or other books to amuse them. Little children hear from their mother historical anecdotes about their brave forefathers who endured sufferings and hardships to create an independent nation and about their great deeds; or stories about one Lincoln who was a poor lad but rose to be President of their country, thanks to his diligence and excellent character. The children then develop patriotism, desire for advancement, and the hope that hard work will win success and excellence for them too, as in the case of Washington, Lincoln, and Garfield.

Nor are the girls without hope. They too hear the lives of great and famous women and hope to be like them some day. When their mother goes to the meeting of an educational, philanthropic, or religious association in her spare time, they accompany her, and see the work that goes on there. This kindles in them an interest in education and a desire for philanthropy. They are not subjected to separation from their mothers and oppression in their husbands' homes, which results from the custom of child marriage prevalent in our country. The budding hope in the heart of an American girl is not scorched by disappointment and unhappiness [as in India] at the thought that she is only a woman and therefore incapable of achieving anything, that she will have to spend her entire life in subjection, that she is not destined for the joy of freedom; that, if her husband dies tomorrow, she will be disgraced as a child widow, tormented, starved, made to slave in the house against her will, cursed, forced to have her head shaven by the barber, or detested as a destitute; that she has no protector in this world or the next! No one humiliates her because she is a wife or a dependent daughter. She is as worthy of her parents' love and affection as her brother is. Like her brother, she also has the facility to study, or learn the arts and crafts. And she has the hope that some day she can be her own mistress, the mistress of her house, and a self-reliant, free American citizen. While describing this happy American family, I clearly see before me several families I have met in this country. It will suffice to describe just one of them by way of illustration.

There is a small town called Gilbertsville in the State of New York, which I visited a year ago.[7] In May 1887 I became acquainted with a number of students at Cornell University, one of whom invited me to visit his town and deliver a speech there. During the vacation he went home and made all the arrangements, and his mother sent me a letter of invitation. When I reached Gilbertsville, George (as the boy was called) brought his carriage to the train and drove me to his house, which was about half a mile from the town. George's mother and sister were standing at the door to receive me. As we reached the house, they came to the carriage, welcomed me most respectfully, and took me inside. In the meanwhile George led the horses to a nearby pasture to feed and let them loose. In the evening his father and brother returned from their farm, in quite dirty clothes. His mother began to cook, and his sister began to set the table with plates, bowls, spoons, etc. When everything was ready, all the family members came to the table, having washed and dressed themselves in clean clothes, and sat down to eat. The people here do not follow the practice of the men eating first and the women afterwards! The master and mistress of the house and the children eat together. A girl, a boy, or someone else gets up to fetch anything that may be needed during the meal, and hands it to the mother. After finishing the meal and the housework, the whole family assembled in the parlor. The mother went to the writing desk to write letters. The father and brother stood behind the girl who was playing the piano and singing sweetly, and began to sing along with her. After a while we spent a happy time together, talking of this and that.

The next morning, the master of the house, George, and his brother went to work on the farm. George's mother and sister were engrossed in housework. Our meeting was scheduled at two o'clock, after the midday meal; and George's mother was to preside over the meeting. She is the president of the evangelical and philanthropic society there. She made a good speech and conducted the meeting extremely well. Anyone who saw her cooking at home would have assumed that she had done nothing but cook all her life. At the meeting she was seen to be well-educated and conversant with social etiquette. Her husband plows the field, feeds the cattle, harnesses carriages, fertilizes the farm, chops wood, cuts grass, and supervises the farm. Seeing him at work on the farm, one would think that he has expertise only in this work, but no knowledge of anything else. But after returning home in the evening, the same farmer expounds philosophy, and discusses things like Greek pronunciation, the close connection between Greek and Latin grammar, the similarity between Arnold's poem *The Light of Asia*[8] and the life of Christ, my opinion of Theosophy and its teachers, the difference between the English and American systems of government, etc. The son is a perfect farmer when at home; but after the vacation he would go back to the university and, on graduating after four years, become a preacher or a trader. Another son has finished his education and has a good job in New York City. The third son stays at home and works on the farm. One daughter has finished her education, married a man of her choice, and is managing her house and family on her own. The mother said, "I hope my younger daughter goes to Cornell University to study with her brother. My Georgie will work for a few days to earn enough for his expenses, and go back to the university to continue his studies. I am very keen that my daughter do the same. She is keen to go and study there with Georgie." How proud the affectionate mother must have been of both her children when she said this! And oh, how happy I felt to hear her wish that her daughter will go to the university like her son! When will the parents in our country begin to say this? When will they give up the awful belief that a daughter is less worthy or capable than a son?

On the third day it was time for George to return to the university. His mother packed a hamper for him with fruit, cakes, etc. His sister accompanied him in the carriage to the train to see him off. On the way the brother and sister started to sing happily. The sight of the innocent, happy pair, singing a happy song on their way to the train through the forest, put me in mind of the children of our ancient sages. How happy and cheerful the two were! Both nurtured the hope of their lives being fulfilled, both possessed equal rights and equal status, and both had free access to the avenues of advancement. One of them is a female, but is not therefore doomed to disappointment born of a lack of freedom. The other is a male, but does not therefore behave arrogantly and humiliate his sister by word or deed. Both are hardworking and aspire to rise high. Because both have equal freedom, they will be able to obtain an education and wealth,[9] albeit with diligence and hard work. It is hardly surprising that a nation where men and women, and all human beings, are equal and where people are the masters of their fate, their wealth, freedom and conscience should advance, and the inhabitants be happy.

Not all American families are like the one described above. The saying "Every village has its Untouchable quarter"[10] is applicable even to America. American villages also have superior, medium, and inferior types of people. Some are absorbed in shallow luxuries and prone to building castles in the air; some are of a serious bent of mind, hardworking and self-controlled; some are leaders of society and some followers; some egotistical and some modest; some are stupid, some clever or scheming—all these types can be found in American society. Even so, American society is free on the whole, and the signs of advancement, which stems from freedom alone, are seen everywhere in this society.

All the qualities of a sea or a river are present in each of its drops. So also, all the qualities which have given rise to a free country like the United States are present in each American town and each association. The excellent system of government which has led to the advancement of this country is the result of the self-government[ii] enjoyed by its towns and its associations. It would appear that an American citizen is fed, along with milk in his infancy, the knowledge of self-government and administrative procedure. The people's unity and organization can be seen both in a small village and in a large city. Whenever anyone wishes to undertake a task, he gathers a few persons of his acquaintance, informs them of his objective, and does what is considered right by the majority. No matter how small the task, it is undertaken by an association; and no matter how small the association, it is managed by at least three officeholders: a president, a secretary, and a treasurer. Even two or three persons together can constitute such an association, and its procedure is laid down in a set of rules. Thus, most of the important tasks are undertaken by associations, the associations are assisted in their proper working by rules, the rules are framed by consulting all the members of the association, and the rules once accepted by a majority are adhered to. These main seeds of self-government are found almost everywhere in this country. It was these seeds from which sprouted the plant of local government; the plant put forth many branches in the form of county governments; it further flowered into state governments; and these flowers have produced the glorious fruit of the Federal Government of the United States. Children are taught this kind of self-government at home and in schools. At home their parents do all the chores according to a plan. In schools they are taught to decide by a majority vote what game is to be played during the sports hour, and to conduct themselves in an orderly manner. It is firmly impressed upon children that, as far as possible, they should themselves do whatever is necessary, and not impose upon others and ask for help in small things.

The system of government in the United States is such that the Federal Government at Washington does not interfere at all in the work which the state governments are capable of doing; the state government does not help with the work which the county government can manage; and the county government does not intervene in the work which can be carried out by the local government. This excellent system has made the American people experts in self-government, and has also made them self-reliant. Every family must contain the seed of such self-reliance; if it does, only then can a nation composed of thousands and millions of families possess this excellent quality. The American family system is like the government. The husband does not push himself to do chores which the wife can do, and the parents do not offer to do the work which their children can manage.

This patriotism and national pride contain a great deal of egotism. The English used to consider themselves the most superior among all peoples. It is natural that the Americans have inherited their egotism from their English ancestors. But this is a new country and everything grows fast in new soil. In keeping with this rule, their native egotism has also grown rapidly in this fertile soil, and these people have outdone their ancestors. While describing anything in their own country, they are in the habit of comparing it with things in other countries, and then pronouncing it the most superior. "Our factory is the biggest, our country is the best, our nation is the most superior, our brains and the arrangement of their cells are the most delicate and exquisite among all." Their habit of saying that they are the best is notorious. If you go to a church to hear a sermon, the preacher says that his own religion, society, or social custom is the best. If you read a book by an army chief like General Grant, he says that the American army is a better fighting force than any other in the world. If you attend a meeting, the speakers are singing praises of the customs in their country and community. They are dazzled by their own brilliance and think nothing of others. The common people display a particular want of modesty. Even so, on the whole, the American people do not hesitate to treat others with respect, because the lessons of self-government learned since childhood have developed in them the excellent quality of self-respect. He who understands the value of his own honor and is able to protect it, is also particular about the honor of others.

Notes in the Original Text

i. In our country, men relieve themselves anywhere they like in the streets; no one does so here. It is very surprising that no one tries to stop this utterly shameless behavior. This improvement is as essential as all other social reforms. It is both dreadful and harmful for respectable women and small children to witness such dirty and shameless things while walking in the streets. If the people of our country insist that the municipalities should build a number of latrines at public places, it can easily be done.

ii. Self-government means well-considered conduct which involves exerting power over oneself without violating the rights of other people.

5   Domestic Conditions

Such, on the whole, are the social conditions in the United States. A few words must now be said about the domestic conditions in cities, towns, and villages. All over the world, the housewife is generally regarded as the central figure in the house; but in American houses the housewife is given special importance. The American housewife is the veritable goddess of the house (although there are exceptions to this rule also). Since a housewife must have a house to live in, it would not be out of place to say a few words about the houses in this country, before describing her.

The internal design of the house is usually the same in cities and villages, though the external construction is different. City houses are usually built of stone and brick walls; the houses in villages and towns are built mostly of wooden planks. Because of the abundance of trees and the general use of coal for fuel everywhere, wood is the principal material utilized for building houses. The foundation of the house is laid with stones or bricks, and the structure above is built of wooden planks, beams, and columns. From the outside the walls look like the panes of a stained-glass window; on the inside they are lined with thick planks or paper, plastered, and then decorated with paper of variegated colors. This wallpaper[1] is very durable and allows no room for bugs, etc. The houses have several windows which let in ample light, and also fresh air which circulates all through. The windows are fitted with large glass panes so that the house does not become dark even when they are closed during the winter.[2] During the summer there is an abundance of flies, mosquitoes, etc.; the windows are therefore fitted with screens of fine wire mesh, so that they reduce the menace of flies without blocking the air. In order to decorate the windows and reduce the glare, they are hung with a variety of curtains made of lacy or plain cloth. There is an excellent provision to pull them to one side when necessary. The entire floor and the stairs, except for the kitchen and the front steps, are covered with a carpet or mats. The floor underneath is made completely even with wooden planks. Once or twice a year the carpet and mats are removed and brushed clean.

Ordinarily a house has a parlor, a dining room, a kitchen, a guest room, and a separate bedroom for each person. There are several conveniences, such as wardrobes to hang clothes, shelves for books, tables, and chairs. Things like fuel, vegetables, and milk are kept in the basement. City houses have a bathroom which contains a large and long vessel like a cistern, lined with enamel, which is called a bathtub. Attached to it are two water pipes, for hot and cold water. The hot-water pipe is connected to a boiler near the stove in the kitchen, which saves the trouble of carrying hot water upstairs or installing a separate stove to heat water. Most village houses do not have bathrooms, which causes a great deal of inconvenience to one used to having a bath every day. Usually the people here do not have a daily bath; they wipe their bodies with a wet towel dipped in a jugful of water poured into a washbasin, and bathe only occasionally. Villagers content themselves for months on end with a mere "towel-bath." In the winter a large brazier is lit in the basement and connected with iron pipes to all the rooms so as to carry the heat throughout the house. The pipes can be opened or closed at will with the help of "registers."

Most of the cities and even small towns have gas lights in houses and streets. This country is rich in combustible mineral gas. In Pittsburgh and many other cities this combustible gas is used also for cooking, running machines, heating houses, lighting houses and streets, etc. Mineral oil is used in the smaller towns which do not have the plants to produce combustible gas. The newly settled cities in the West have mostly electric lighting. Electric lights are occasionally seen also in the old cities in the East.

The domestic arrangements for cooking and dining are like those of the Europeans. The white cloths spread on tables at mealtime; the white napkins for wiping the hands and mouth while eating; the towels for wiping hands, feet, and the body kept in each room for the use of its occupant; bedsheets and pillowcases, etc., are customarily washed at home. The cook or maid, and sometimes even the mistress of the house herself, serves as laundress, and washes and irons these clothes. The cook is usually Negro or Irish. Many poor American women also work as cooks in other people's houses. As is the case with us, there are very few people here who are blessed with good servants. An intelligent and thoughtful mistress learns to do all the housework herself, and also helps the maid in her work. But there are many thoughtless mistresses here. Many cannot cook, which is why cookery schools have been opened here.

It is very expensive to maintain a house in the city; many people therefore take lodgings. A single person can get reasonable lodgings for twenty-five to thirty dollars a month (a dollar being worth about three rupees). The lodger has a separate room to himself and takes his meals with the members of the family. Respectable persons can get lodgings with well-born and good-natured families. Many good women who are reduced to poverty support themselves by taking in lodgers. It is customary also for well-to-do middle-class families to keep lodgers. Hotels and inns are expensive; moreover, they do not provide any domestic comforts.

For almost two years I lived in Philadelphia as a lodger with a woman.[3] She is very good-natured. Not all women are so good-natured and such good cooks and housekeepers; even so, this woman's manner of housekeeping will give a general idea of the daily routine of most housewives. This woman gets up at five-thirty or six in the morning, has her bath (either a proper bath, or wiping the body), finishes her toilette and comes down. (The city houses have three to four stories; the kitchen, dining room, and parlor are on the ground floor.) Then she goes to the kitchen and instructs the cook about what to make for breakfast; and also dusts the dining room and sets the table with knives, forks, spoons, napkins, plates, teacups, glasses, etc. She then puts on her bonnet and shawl, and goes to the market with a basket in hand, to buy fruit and vegetables for the day. At seven o'clock either she herself or the cook sounds the gong. On hearing it, all the people in the house get out of bed, wash their faces and rinse their mouths, have a wash or bath, and get dressed. The gong is sounded again at seven-thirty, and everyone comes down to breakfast on hearing it. By eight breakfast is over, and the cook goes upstairs to dust all the bedrooms and make the beds. The women usually make their own beds and keep their rooms tidy. The men lodgers leave all this work to the maid, either because they have to rush off to work or because they are lazy. In the meanwhile the landlady washes the dirty (porcelain) plates,[4] bowls, cups, glasses, spoons, knives, etc., with soap and hot water, and dries them. After cutting the vegetables for the midday meal, she checks the accounts. Then she reads the newspaper for a while, and finishes other chores promptly. Afterwards she goes shopping if necessary. She also helps the cook, who does the laundry, sweeps and dusts the house, washes the dishes, scrubs the floors and front steps, heats the stoves and heaters, etc. The cook is paid sixteen dollars, that is, forty-eight rupees, as salary and maintenance. From Monday to Tuesday there is continuous washing. A large tub is placed in the backyard and filled with boiling water and soap in which clothes are soaked for a while before they are washed. The clothes are not beaten on a stone here; they are spread on a wooden plank (which has parallel grooves a finger's breadth apart and which is covered with a tin sheet) and rubbed with soap. They are then dipped in indigo water, wrung out, and dried. The clothes are not starched, just ironed and folded. Every house has a laundry of this type.

The midday meal is served at about one o'clock in the afternoon. At this time again a gong is sounded to call the diners. The food is quite good, after their own style. Boiled potatoes, cabbage, turnips, beetroot or whatever other vegetables are in season; meat or fish; eggs; and salad made of chopped leaves called "lettuce," radishes, tomatoes, that is, European eggplant [sic], and sliced cucumbers in season—all these are placed on the dining table. These people do not know how to cook vegetables with seasoning, as we do. Salt, powdered pepper, and chili powder are kept on the table, as is a bottle of vinegar for the salad, which people can help themselves to. Sometimes eggplants or potatoes are fried in cooking fat. In addition, there is a sweet dish called "cake" which, together with many types of puddings, is served at the end of the meal. Fruit is served in season. A person who is averse to fish, meat, or dishes prepared with eggs and animal fat has a very hard time getting enough to eat, and is compelled to manage largely with milk, bread, and fruit.[5]

In the afternoon or after breakfast, the landlady repairs or patches up torn clothes, or stitches new ones. Every house usually has a sewing machine, which is very useful in this cold country. In the morning or afternoon, people pay social visits. After finishing the housework, the landlady reads books and newspapers in her spare time and attends lectures. She also helps many charities. She works as a secretary for an organization which supports a rescue home for fallen women. In addition, she also contributes to many other religious and charitable works with as much money and labor as she can. Sometimes she goes to the hospital to visit and inquire after the patients there.

In families with children, the mothers take excellent care of their children. An American home where the parents and children treat one another well and are eager to do their duty is a place of great happiness. After the evening meal the parents sit with their children in the parlor enjoying the warmth of the heater, and tell them happy, amusing stories and talk to them sweetly. This is a very happy time for them. The children address their parents as "dear Mother" or "dear Father"; the parents address their children sweetly as "my darling" or "baby." Love for their children is expressed in their speech at all times. Husband and wife never fail to address each other as "dear" or "my dear." In respectable families no one ever curses or uses bad language. Swearing, cursing, or rude, impertinent speech is considered a sin and a sign of vulgarity. Generally, if one wishes to ask a favor, one says courteously "Will you please do this?" or "Please do such and such"; similarly when someone has done a favor, conveyed a message, or brought something, or on similar occasions, one politely says "I thank you." One does not pass between two persons who are standing or sitting together, or in front of another person; should one be compelled to do so, one says "Excuse me." If one is called upon to leave the table while others are eating, one asks the master or mistress of the house for permission. If a person has not heard what someone has said, he asks him to repeat himself by saying "Pardon me, what did you say?" Children are taught these manners from an early age, and they stand them in good stead later.

Respectable people treat men and women with due courtesy at home and in society in general. Men show courtesy to women in a variety of ways. While talking to a woman—whoever she may be—they doff their hats and address her as "Madam." At home or at meetings, women are offered seats first. In very crowded trains and streetcars, men give up their seats to women (though not all men show such good manners); and strong young women show the same courtesy to old or weak persons.

Sensible and respectable women do not quarrel with anyone. Quarrels do take place here, because "Every village has its Untouchable quarter," as the saying goes;[6] but they are not full of shouts, curses and bad language, as is the case with us. If a person is angry with someone, it is enough to avoid him. For an ordinary quarrel, it is sufficient to change the tone of voice. Instead of saying "Thank you" in a low, sweet voice, one says it in a somewhat harsh and angry tone. Vulgar and ignorant people make ample use of obscene words; they even come to blows at times.

When people meet, they take each other's right hand and shake it, and ask after each other's well-being with a question which is, literally, "How do you do?" but which means "How are you?" As it is customary to ask this question as soon as one meets someone, the appropriate answer is "I am fine, I am quite well." This answer may not always be truthful, but so strange are the conventions of speech that they leave little time to think of truth and falsehood.

When one person meets another, he has to say something; so the people here start by commenting on the weather. A pleasant day and clear skies bring forth the compliment, "Oh, what a fine day!" But few are the days which thus please everyone; not every day that passes is able to find favor with all. Some dislike rain; some cannot bear the cold and others detest the heat; some are eager for the rains, others are waiting for the snow and for the rivers to freeze so that they can go skating. In sum, the poor weather cannot please anyone. Although these people are accustomed to criticizing the weather, they have a true appreciation of the beauty of Nature. Not that each and every person is sensitive to it, but few are the people here who would fail to praise a thing of beauty.

It is but natural to ask a lot of questions on meeting a foreigner and a stranger. These people ask questions very politely. When these and other Western women come to our country, we ask them many strange questions; similarly, these women also do so without fail.

Fashions

The dress and toilette of the women here contain a great deal of artifice.[7] The women here are usually good-looking, and many are born very beautiful. Their love of natural beauty is easily seen from the arrangement of their houses and homes. The ancient Hellenes had a natural love of beauty which was taken over by the Romans, who imitated them, and imparted to the English and other Europeans. The people of this country have also copied it in everything, as can clearly be seen from the design of their cities, ordinary houses, large buildings, and churches. However, women's dresses, and many other things, show hardly any beauty; also, they change a lot from year to year. When France was a monarchy, the Empress of Paris [*sic*] used to set the standard for dress and toilette for all the women of Europe and America. It was customary to respect and emulate everything done by the Empress of Paris and by other wealthy, fashionable women.

Twenty-five years ago, when my parents were traveling with the family from Kumta to Bombay by boat, they had to stay in Sadashivgad and wait for a couple of days for the next boat.[8] We had put up at a place close to the newly built railroad, on the other side of which was the railroad station. On the day we arrived, three Englishwomen came and sat on a bench at the station in the afternoon. Their skirts were so wide and bulging that each of them would have covered an area of up to two yards in diameter, whether she was standing or sitting. Never before had I set eyes on such a strange kind of dress or on such red-faced[9] women wearing it, and I had already begun to feel afraid as soon as I saw them. Just then a man brought them a small basket filled with things, and one of the women quickly got up, pushed the basket under the bench on which she had been sitting, and sat down again. I was filled with such dread at the sight, and had such a knot in my stomach! Now I laugh at the memory, but at the time I was quite convinced that they were women of some thieving tribe or demonesses who stole other people's children and also other things, and carried them away hidden in their bulging skirts; and that one day they might even pick me up and carry me off in the bag inside their skirts if I happened to be out of sight of my parents!

The bulging skirts which so frightened me in childhood were the creation of the Empress of Paris, and until some years ago all the women of Europe—big and small, rich and poor, educated and ignorant—thought them very beautiful and wore them. The Empress of Paris started to wear bulging skirts when she was pregnant, so that the changes in her figure would not be noticed. All the fashionable women thought it was a new and attractive style, and started to wear it themselves without discovering its origin; what is worse, they even made similar skirts for their little daughters. How the Queen of Paris must have silently laughed at the sight! There was another beauty who was slightly short; she raised the heels of her shoes by a couple of fingers' breadth in order to disguise her lack of height. Other women followed suit and got high heels for their shoes without discovering the reason for this style. This practice of wearing high-heeled shoes is still prevalent.

Those who wear gold and silver jewelry or other types of ornaments, or those who attire themselves in unusual clothes in an effort to enhance their beauty, often manage to spoil their natural good looks. This rule applies not only to our country, but also to England and the United States, which have reached the very pinnacle of progress. The women here profess great sympathy for Chinese women because they have to endure the very painful custom of having their feet bound in order to make them small. Some say that this Chinese custom is a sign of the slavery of women; some see it as proof of the ill effects of Buddhism and Confucianism. They make many strange conjectures while criticizing the evil practices of other peoples. But, like the man with the double packsack in Aesop's fable, they see very clearly the contents of the sack in front, but naturally do not see the contents of the sack at the back. The women here regard a narrow waist as a great sign of beauty, and make their waists small by wearing a "corset," which is a sleeveless bodice made of thin strips of whalebone and steel, shaped so that it is narrow in the middle and quite loose above and below. Ordinarily, a well-built woman of medium height should have a natural waistline of thirty-nine to forty fingers' breadth; the women here tighten their waists and reduce them to between thirty and twenty-four fingers' breadth. A girl is taught the habit of wearing a corset from the age of about twelve. This practice obstructs free breathing and affects the lungs of many women; the pressure of the corset upon the stomach causes the spleen and the abdomen to press upon the uterus. This obstructs digestion and deep breathing, and leads to disorders of the spleen and the lungs; during childbirth it causes far more agony than is normal; and God alone knows what other suffering and trouble it causes![10]

There is another article intended to beautify the figure and the dress; it is called a "bustle." The bustle is made by weaving thick wires together. It comes in two or three shapes. If it is tied to the waist and hung at the back under the skirt, the skirt bulges at the back below the waist. No one but Goddess Satwai[11] knows the beauty of the bustle. Probably she has created it herself because it did not occur to Mother Nature to attach a natural bustle to the backs of European and American women at birth! Two or three thick petticoats are worn over the bustle under the skirt; the combined weight of the petticoats, skirt, and bustle, about six to seven pounds,[12] presses upon the abdomen and, needless to say, causes ill effects.

It is right to protect the feet with shoes in this cold country, but fashionable women wish to have small feet and wear very tight shoes which deform the feet and cause big calluses. Also, as a result of high heels, the weight of the body does not fall equally on the whole foot while walking, but falls mainly on the front part, which damages all the toenails. These fashions are more popular in cities than in small towns. Poor women emulate the styles of rich ones, and both rich and poor women spend lavishly on items of clothing. The leather gloves to be worn on the hands are so tight that they take a long time to put on, and they make women's hands look like fat rolls. These women feel compelled to wear gloves when they go out to dinner, for an outing, or to pay a visit, even during the hot summer, when the whole body is perspiring.

Nowadays "dress reform" has started here.[13] Many sensible women with a knowledge of anatomy have begun to improve the style of their dress. This reformed dress is made scientifically and is comfortable and healthy; moreover, it allows the wearer to do any kind of work and does not obstruct any activity. These dress reformers are engaged in earnest efforts to prevent women in their own and in other countries from wearing harmful fashionable dresses and ruining their natural figure as well as health. The progressive inhabitants of Japan have started to rapidly emulate the bad qualities of Europeans along with the good. The women there have discarded their clumsy clothes and begun to dress like European women. When I called on Miss Frances Willard[14] to bid her farewell, she said to me, "Tell the women wherever you go, especially in Japan, that they must not ruin their health by wearing silly, fashionable clothes. These are my parting words to you. If we wish to do something for the good of the people, all of us must reform our dress."

Most of the women here have forgotten the real use of bonnets, which is to protect the head against the cold and against bright sunshine. Bonnets have now become veritable head ornaments. They are decorated with colored silks, ribbons of silk and velvet, artificial cloth flowers, etc. In addition, it is customary to attach beautiful feathers, or even whole stuffed bodies of dead birds, to bonnets. A few years ago a woman of ill repute in Paris went to the theater wearing a whole bird on her bonnet in order to attract attention; even respectable women imagined this to be a new style, and set the trend of attaching lovely birds to their bonnets, without bothering to discover the origin of this style. Millions of lovely birds are massacred because of this cruel custom; heartless bird hunters make their living on this trade; and respectable women unthinkingly encourage it. As a result, not only do the poor birds lose their lives, but they are also made to suffer terrible agonies. They are skinned while still half-alive, so that their lovely feathers do not fade. Who can adequately describe such cruelty, and the agony of the poor birds? Two years ago, a shop in London sold, in three months, the skins of 404,464 birds from the West Indies and Brazil, and the dead bodies of 356,389 lovely birds from our own India. There are thousands of such shops in Europe and America. Who can estimate how many untold millions of dead birds are bought and sold there? Besides, there is the wanton destruction of innumerable baby birds. The parents are killed by some wicked person when they are out gathering food, and the hungry little ones in the nest pathetically call out to their mother with their beaks wide open. But the mother is not alive to answer them, and they cannot go in search of food and feed themselves because their wings are not yet developed. After screeching for a day or two, they die of hunger. Alas! If there be a stone-hearted person who fails to shed tears at the thought of their plight, he is verily a blot on the human race! If the women wearing bonnets decorated with birds had any knowledge of the suffering of the birds or the harm done to the world because of this practice, they would certainly have given it up. Now in Western countries there are societies known as "Audubon," which have the protection of birds as their objective.[15] We pray to God to crown their efforts with the success they hope for.

It is a part of fashion to wear white powder on the face and to rub pink color on cheeks and nails to beautify them. It is a common practice everywhere to beautify the head by wearing wigs and switches when one's hair begins to fall out in old age, or even in youth due to some disorder. Hair is made to appear curly by wetting it, winding it around bone sticks or paper rollers, and pressing it with hot tongs before going to bed at night. Some use oil and spirits to fix strips of hair on the forehead like inverted Turkish arches.

The custom of wearing false teeth when real teeth start to fall off in middle age is prevalent in some places even in our country. Here, wearing false teeth is like the case of "a man who discards torn clothes and dons new ones."[16] The skilled craftsmen here make dentures which look as good as real teeth. A pretty young woman with crooked teeth goes to the dentist to have them extracted, and beautifies her mouth by wearing nice false teeth. Quite a few people asked me whether my teeth were real. An elderly woman in Philadelphia refused to be convinced that my teeth were real until she opened my mouth and inspected the palate and everything else. Perhaps because these people eat a lot of meat, their teeth lack natural strength, and fall out easily. False teeth are very useful to them; they not only make the mouth prettier, but also help in chewing hard and tough food.

Men are also seen to follow fashions as women do, but they try to appear plain and simple. The fashionable men are usually the very young, or sons of rich families. Boys from poor families also imitate the fashions and clothes of rich and spendthrift men, in great style. Men's fashions involve changing clothes three or four times a day, wearing suits of different cuts, wearing a hat at an angle, stroking the mustache, carrying a slim cane, walking with a dashing gait, and talking smartly. Men's clothes are of a single color (usually black or gray, with a hat to match) and simple, in the European style. Wearing them does not hamper movement while working; they are very convenient for a man who works hard all day at all kinds of things. The clothes of the clergy are different in style; that is, they wear robes reaching down to their knees. Men's formal clothes worn at banquets, etc., are made of high-quality material; some look attractive and some ugly.

Two vices are widespread among the menfolk in the United States: drinking and smoking. The Anglo-Saxons from whom most Americans are descended were accustomed from ancient times to drinking a liquor known as "beer." Later, many more types of liquor began to be manufactured, and at the same time the vice of drinking also increased. From the time that the United States became an independent nation to the present, all peoples of Europe have been coming to settle down here. Hundreds of thousands of people arrive daily to settle down in the United States; preponderant among them are Germans, Italians, and the Irish, all of whom are notorious for drinking. Their large numbers in the United States have led to an increase in the vice of drinking among the original people of America. The vice of smoking has similarly increased greatly. The extent of these two vices can be easily seen from the size of the annual national expenditure given below. The people spend annually as follows:

	US $
Charity	5,500,000
Salaries of the Clergy	12,000,000
Education	96,000,000
Tea and Coffee	145,000,000
Sweets	155,000,000
Shoes, Socks, etc.	197,000,000
Metals, incl. Iron	263,000,000
Meat	303,000,000
Tobacco	490,000,000
Bread	538,000,000
Liquor	900,000,000

The harm caused by drink to public health and to the nation has led hundreds of thousands of American men and women to oppose drinking. All kinds of immorality which are prevalent among the Americans today can undoubtedly be attributed to the two vices mentioned above.

Racial[17] Discrimination and Prejudice

People are the same everywhere.[18] Human beings have the same good and bad qualities wherever and in whatever condition they may be. The United States of America is famous for its wealth, education, and advancement; and with reason. But racial discrimination and prejudice, which are most inimical to all progress and civility, are not altogether absent in this country.

When the ancestors of these people left England and came here, they brought all their outmoded English customs with them. When their country became independent, they had to greatly modify the ancient English class distinctions, in keeping with the motto of their philosophy of freedom, "All men are created equal." However, until 1861 this motto was not applicable to all. Their tradition of buying and selling Negro slaves like cattle led to the belief that the Negro race was inferior to the White race by birth. It was totally forbidden to eat with the

Negroes at the same table or to intermarry with them, while they lived in slavery; this still remains unchanged. The Negro has been freed from slavery, but the hatred for his race harbored by the Whites still persists. I have dined in hundreds of different places so far, but nowhere have I seen a Negro eating at the same table as the Whites. Moreover, I have rarely seen a Negro seated next to a White person at a service in the most holy temple of God. The Negroes have their own churches; their clergy also belong to the same race and are not seen much in White society.

People of the Negro race have been freed from slavery for barely twenty-five years, but the progress they have achieved for their race during this short time through sheer hard work cannot but invite praise for their ceaseless industry and self-reliance. Twenty-five years ago Negroes were forbidden to read and write. They were born and grew up like cattle; like cattle they served the man who bought them, with all their might; and finally they died like cattle. A Negro was not a human being in law, and had no rights as a human being. He did not even have the legal right to enter into holy matrimony, which strengthens social bonds in human society. But praise be to William Lloyd Garrison,[19] Elizabeth Heyrick,[20] Lucretia Mott,[21] Wendell Phillips,[22] and other good people like them! After enduring the agonies of hard work, adversity, and public opposition, they created a public opinion favorable to the emancipation of the Negro race in the United States, and placed all of humanity under an obligation which can never be repaid. Since the end of the American Civil War and abolition of slavery in 1865 to the present, the American Negro has emerged from his animal state and attained the human state with the help of good people and through his own achievements. People of his race have now become teachers, preachers, lawyers, doctors, traders, and even Senators in the United States Congress. Not a single right which is available to the White citizen of the United States is now denied to the Black; and there are favorable signs that the obstacles to social intercourse between the Black and White people which exist today will soon disappear.

Ordinary American people feel a strong hatred also for the Red Indians, the original inhabitants of America. After making treaties with different Indian tribes pertaining to their lands, the United States Government violated the clauses of those treaties and wrested the lands from them; it then turned very respectable and branded the Indians as rogues. Now some good Americans are exerting themselves strongly for the advancement of their Red countrymen. For fear of public censure the United States Government has opened a few industrial schools for Indian children, out of the Indian people's money deposited in its treasury. Of these industrial schools, the Hampton Institute in the State of Virginia, the Carlisle Indian School in Pennsylvania, and the Lincoln Institute in Philadelphia are being run very successfully.

The Indian people have no rights as American citizens; moreover, they do not even have the right to file a suit against anybody in an ordinary court of law in the United States. The United States Government has granted designated lands for the settlement of different Indian tribes, which are called "Indian reservations." Any Indian who ventures outside the bounds of the reservation either loses his life to the bullet of an American hunter, or is sentenced by a judge for having left the reservation without permission. On every reservation lives an agent, called the "Indian agent," appointed by the United States Government to keep an eye on the Indians. This agent is an all-powerful autocrat, ruling over the Indians. The United States Government entrusts to him the responsibility of supplying foodstuffs to the Indians on the reservation. His is the last word on everything. Very few of the Indian agents are honest, and the poor Indians suffer a great deal at their hands.

The Indians are a very long-suffering people, either because of ignorance or by nature. They are careful that no complaint reaches the Government as far as possible; and even if it does, there is little chance of their receiving justice. Whenever the efforts of kind people succeed in creating public opinion in favor of the Indians, the Government is shamed into appointing "commissions" to investigate their true condition. These commissions include good and nonpartisan men and women. They have exerted themselves to bring the oppression of the Indians to the notice of the American citizens; and their efforts have also been successful to an extent. Many kind men and women have established a society for the welfare of the Indians, with branches in many places in the United States. Foremost among the true benefactors of the Indians must be counted a woman named Helen Hunt.[23] Until she presented information to the American citizens about the true condition of the Indians, based on historical evidence and her own experience, no one had a clear idea of the matter. Helen Hunt was appointed to an Indian commission by the United States Government. She spent five or six years in a dense jungle in the company of these savages, and wrote a book entitled *A Century of Dishonor*, describing their true state, which opened the eyes of the people of the United States. She also wrote a novel entitled *Ramona*, describing the sad plight of the Indians. The numerous efforts she made for the welfare of the Indian people are now bearing some fruit. Another woman of similar stature, named Alice Fletcher,[24] is now working ceaselessly for the welfare of the Winnebago and Omaha Indian tribes. Her own efforts, and those of her friends, have borne fruit, and the United States Government has granted these two tribes the right to cultivate the land in their reservations. These people are now farming the land successfully, and have begun to learn other trades as well. A resolution has been passed to the effect that they should be granted all the rights of American citizens in a few years' time, when they are able to read and write, manage common trades, and understand social customs and conventions. There is a tribe called Cherokee Indians in the area known as the Indian

Territory, which has achieved a surprising degree of advancement on the strength of its intelligence and industry. They have established a government in their reservation on the model of the United States Government, and made their little state comparable to one of the United States of America. A man of this Indian tribe even thought of an alphabet for his language and invented a script. These progressive Cherokee Indians have totally abolished slavery in their tribe. They have given up all savage customs and concentrated attention on spreading education among their own people. If other Indian tribes make the effort to uplift themselves like the Cherokees, their condition will improve very soon.

The Americans do not mind if the Japanese people come and settle down in their country and become American citizens, but they have a great dislike for the Chinese.[25] The Americans hate the Chinese for petty reasons, for example that the Chinese in America do not discard their native dress as the Japanese do and dress in the American style, that they do not cut off their queues, discard their wooden clogs in favor of American leather shoes, etc. This is a stigma on this so-called respectable, freedom-loving people. The Chinese are very hardworking by nature and travel to far-off countries for work. They are very moderate in their conduct and spending habits. They are not accustomed to lavish spending like the Europeans, and do not charge exorbitant rates for their labor. That is why the narrow-minded Westerners dislike them. They claim that the Chinese lower the price of labor; that they are of inferior character, dirty, immoral, and likely to ruin the morals of the Americans. Many Westerners feel that the Chinese people have no good qualities but are the repositories of faults, and that their very touch or their company would ruin their own morals. Therefore many wicked people feel an intense hatred for the Chinese. They harass them as much as possible; some loot their houses, some massacre them, some are busy spreading prejudices about them among the people of the country. Two years ago many shortsighted people reduced the Chinese inhabitants of the Northern States to dire straits, and even killed many of them. Even so, this does not mean that there are no sensible people here. They champion the weak, harmless Chinese and secure their good as much as possible. Many writers experienced in conducting research have written books and essays to prove that the Chinese are not all that bad, but possess some good qualities also. Some have established societies for the welfare of the Chinese.

People of the Irish, German, Scandinavian, Italian, Russian, and other races come here to escape the ruling power, oppression, or poverty in their own countries. They are also hated by most, but not considered utterly worthless like the Chinese, because their skin color and facial features are similar to the color and features of the red-faced English. They also have the habit of finding fault with each other. If there is a disturbance in their State, some say that the Irish are the root cause. If their State has an excess of liquor and intoxicants, some say it is because of the Germans, who are naturally addicted to drink! If immorality prevails, the poor Chinese receive all the blame. If mean-spirited officials are elected, it is rumored that the Negroes have accepted bribes and voted for them, which is why such officials have come to power. Thus many different kinds of racial prejudices can be seen everywhere, the reason being none other than mutual ignorance and wicked beliefs arising from ignorance.

There are many sensible people who believe that such racial discrimination and prejudice, which are prevalent among the common people in the United States, are very detrimental to the unity and prosperity of the country; and strive to remove them. Many good people consider the much-hated Negroes, Indians, Chinese, and others to be people like themselves; moreover, they are convinced that, under favorable circumstances, they would equal them in all things. But it is not easy to change old customs. The belief in the inferiority of the non-White races, such as the Negro race, has been deeply ingrained. Even so, there is no fear whatsoever that racial discrimination and prejudice here would reach the level of the caste discrimination and prejudice in India. Day by day, with increasing progress and increasing knowledge among the people, racial prejudice stemming from ignorance is on the decline. Those who impart religion, morality, and knowledge, and are desirous of the country's welfare, preach by word and deed to small children in schools and to adults in religious assemblies, so as to impress upon them that mutual civility and equal treatment alone will be beneficial to themselves and to the country. As a result, racial discrimination and prejudice have declined day by day; and mutual love, civility, and respect have increased. Customs and beliefs are changing with the changing times even in the Southern States, where the common people once regarded the Negro as a donkey, or an even more inferior animal. Twenty-five years ago a Black and a White man would not dine at the same table; moreover, a Negro was not allowed to travel in the same railroad car or streetcar as a White man. Now the Negro has started to travel in the same streetcar and railroad car as the White man. A well-bred White man does not consider it demeaning to get up and offer his seat to a Negro woman in a crowded streetcar. Occasionally, if the dining hall of a railroad station is very crowded and there is no vacant seat anywhere else, a Black man even gets seated at the same table as a White.

Personal Characteristics

The characteristics usually found among the Americans are very good and worth emulating. On the whole, these people are truthful and respectful of religion, but not excessively religious or obsessively truthful. They have great affection for their children, and also dearly love their parents. Parents take great care and trouble to ensure the welfare and advancement of their children. They do not hesitate to spend any amount of money and effort on giving their children a useful education. They do not deprive their children of freedom by wielding too much power over them. Nor do the children fail to extend due respect to their parents. Sons, and especially daughters, are eager to serve their parents and earn their love. I have seen many cases of girls who have refused to marry, even after receiving offers from suitable men who were rich and educated, for fear of having to leave their parents alone and unattended in old age. Many have refused good positions with high salaries. Such cases of self-sacrifice are seen mostly among women. Men do not refuse to leave their parents and go away for work; nor do American parents think it fair to detain their sons and hinder their advancement. (Parents in India who refuse to let their sons go to England for higher studies or for work would do well to keep this in mind. The excessive attachment which makes them wish that their children would never go away and which thus hinders their children's advancement is not love; it is a form of selfishness.) American parents raise their children well, educate them, and get them some work. But the parents do not unduly pamper the children once they are able to start working. Twenty years ago, the American system of dividing inheritance among the children was somewhat similar to that of savages; daughters received a very small share of their parents' property. But now the U.S. laws of inheritance are undergoing great improvement. The practice of bequeathing property equally to sons and daughters is becoming prevalent. The responsibility of parents toward their children usually extends only to educating them well and getting them work. Once the children are grown up and able to earn a living, the parents do not worry too much about them.

These days respect for women is on the increase among the people of the United States. Proof of this is the fact that, in earlier times, men would treat women as quite ignorant and unfit. Men would, at the time of death, appoint some man as the legal guardian and trustee of their property and young children to ensure that they would be well protected. But now many rich and middle-class people have begun to appoint their wives or sisters as guardians of their children and property. Many experienced and knowledgeable Americans say that their women are more upright than their men. Women are generally modest, virtuous, and devoted to their husbands. But one hears that most men are not as devoted to their wives as they should be. My considered opinion is that, on the whole, Americans are compassionate, civil, generous, upright, industrious, and progressive.

Seasons

In keeping with the Anglo-Saxon custom, the Americans divide the year into only four seasons.[26] The spring extends over March, April, and May; the summer spans June, July, and August; the fall comprises September, October, and November; and the winter extends over December, January, and February. The state of the ground and climatic factors, such as heat and cold, undergo a complete transformation during these four seasons; likewise there is a corresponding change in the people's attire, festivities, the furniture in their houses, and their diet. At the beginning of each season, stores keep a large stock of things which are appropriate to and essential for the season. Newspapers, dilapidated walls of old houses, street corners, and some shop windows are covered with advertisements of various kinds; and railroads, railroad stations, and the portion above the windows in railroad cars are crowded with advertisements. These people are very skilled in the arts of advertising and extracting money from people's purses. In order to attract people's attention to a particular item, they publish verses about it, write excellent stories, or inscribe only its name in large, stylish, colorful letters on a sheet of paper and paste it on a wall. They write its name on fence posts, rocks, rooftops, or trees. Although advertisements cost an enormous amount, they are also very profitable. I first saw a specimen of the advertisements here on the night I arrived in Philadelphia. While traveling in a public streetcar, I saw a sheet pasted above the widow in front of me, with writing in large letters. I read the first line, "God helps those who help themselves," and thought to myself, "Oh, how moral the people of this country must be! It seems that they write such moral aphorisms and place them everywhere in order to turn people's thoughts in the right direction, and to cultivate in them a taste for morality." But on reading the second line on the sheet, I began to entertain doubts as to the accuracy of this. It said, "Soppolio (a soap of that name) is the best means of helping oneself!" The advertisements in newspapers and magazines contain many catchy verses, lovers' conversations, and other amusing stories about hundreds of things like Soppolio.[i]

At the onset of every season, there is a great rush to change over to a new style of dress, and to turn around everything in the house and rearrange it. All big and small stores are crowded with women making their purchases. It is the women who make household purchases here. It is not customary to bargain in the stores; most articles are sold at fixed prices. Instead of the problem of bargaining, the storekeepers here are faced with another similar difficulty: that of customers making a choice. Although nothing should be bought without proper scrutiny, it does not help if the customer visits several stores, or makes the storekeeper go back and forth several times, and unroll bales of material, when only a small purchase is to be made. Neither party gains anything from this; moreover, it is tiresome and wastes a great deal of time. Besides it is harmful to people. In this country, the storekeepers and their salesmen or -women do not conduct their business while sitting comfortably [on a mattress on the floor], leaning against a bolster or a wall. They have to stand behind tall counters in front of cupboards and shelves where the goods are stocked. There are many women who work in stores here; sometimes they are unable to sit down for ten hours at a stretch. To make these women walk back and forth several times for small items is very bad and troublesome; but there are many who do not realize this. It is customary to give gifts to friends and relatives on holidays and birthdays. All the stores are filled with splendid wares on holidays.

Summer

The spring is considered to be the best of all seasons (and is described briefly at another place below).[27] When I arrived in the United States of America in March 1886, the winter was on the wane and the spring had started, so I could not see the winter in its true manifestation. It rained several times and snowed occasionally during the last part of March and in April. It is very hot here from May to September. Sometimes the mercury rises even to a hundred and ten degrees, but such days are few and far between. Normally the summer temperatures reach eighty to eighty-five degrees. The houses here, and their interiors, are designed for the winter, so that it is more difficult to endure the summer here than in our country. Moreover, the customs of these people are different from ours, which causes us a great deal of inconvenience.

An amusing incident occurred in the house of the lady with whom I stayed as a lodger in Philadelphia. Although no one stopped me from doing anything I wanted in my room on the third floor, I had to be very cautious when I went downstairs and was in the company of others at mealtime. One particular day in June happened to be very hot, with hardly any breeze. In the afternoon the whole house was quiet, so, instead of being cautious as usual, I went down to the kitchen barefoot to fetch a glass of water. As ill luck would have it, the very thing that should not have happened, did happen. I was about to go upstairs with the water, when I ran into old Dr. B.! Who knows what the old man thought at the sight of my bare feet, but his face fell and his expression showed chagrin and surprise as though at some shameless conduct. I just rushed off to my room without looking at his face too long! A couple of hours later I was reading in my room and had almost forgotten the incident, when there was a knock on my door. As soon as I said, "Please come in," a twelve-year-old boy, grandson of old Dr. B., entered and left me a short note which I opened and read as follows:

"I know that it is the custom of your country to walk about barefoot without shoes and stockings; but it is considered immodest in our country. The members of my family are shocked to see you walking barefoot. Be kind enough to wear your shoes and stockings when you come down.

"Your friend,
"Mrs. B."[ii]

After this incident I vowed never to commit the offense of walking barefoot in anyone's presence as long as I was in this country.

During the summer there are visitations from flies, gnats, and other insects here, just as in our country. The mosquitoes in the State of New Jersey are not inferior in the least to our mosquitoes in Mirzapur or Calcutta. I had occasion to spend three or four nights at the summer resort (a place visited by people in the summer for rest or a change of weather) of Lake Bluff on the banks of Lake Michigan near Chicago. During the day and most of the night, it was excessively hot, with no breeze at all. Moreover, the place had an abundance of mosquitoes. After I left Assam[28] in 1882, I had not set eye upon the "Dark Hell"; but I did so on the banks of Lake Michigan in 1887. In the fifth section of the Shrimad Bhagavata, this Hell has been described thus: "He who destroys insects, such as flies, is dispatched to the Dark Hell. He is in total darkness there, but can never sleep or rest. Mosquitoes, lice, flies, bugs, and whatever other insects he might have destroyed, bite him incessantly in revenge." Whoever wishes to catch a glimpse of this Hell should visit Mirzapur, Calcutta, Assam, and such parts. Not that our Maharashtra is inferior to other parts of India in this regard. When I met these old and close friends in a foreign country like America, I realized their true worth. Never before had I understood so clearly the meaning of the verse "Besides extracting blood, a mosquito afflicts one by humming in the ear."[29] Although flies and other insects create such havoc in this country, the clever people of America protect themselves by employing several methods of killing them and by using other stratagems. As the summer approaches, they put wire screens on windows and doors, which keep out the insects to a large extent. Around May there is a general rush to remove and clean the carpets and mats on the floors and staircases, to put fresh paper on the walls, and do other similar chores.

All the people connected with education get a vacation in June, July, and August. Many government employees get a vacation for a few days in the summer. Other working people also take rest for a few days in this season. The rich and the idle have holidays throughout the year; but even they feel the desire to leave home and visit a summer resort. Anyone who has a little money spends a few days' vacation at a summer resort nearby or far away for recreation, either with or without his family. The main purpose of visiting a summer resort is to leave work and household cares behind for a few days, and enjoy rest. But, like many other customs started with a good intention, this custom also becomes oppressive. There is no sign of rest in these resorts. They may more aptly be called large fairs. During the three summer months, the famous, scenic places like Saratoga, Cape May, Niagara, Chautauqua, and Lake Bluff are very crowded. There is a round of balls, music, plays, and banquets. All these places have large and small hotels for the accommodation of visitors.

One cannot but be amazed at the magnificence of American hotels.[30] The hotels in cities like Chicago, New York, Philadelphia, and Boston are like paradise.[31] The famous hotel in Chicago, called Palmer House, is worth more than $2,000,000, if its building is taken together with the gold, silver, and other valuable decorations inside.[32] Fifteen to sixteen hundred people take rooms there, with another five to six hundred men and women servants to wait on them. The hotel has adjoining stables which house four to five hundred horses, about two hundred and fifty carriages and buggies, and also coachmen, grooms, and attendants whose numbers and salaries are astounding. There are many such hotels in this country. Rich people, and even many middle-class people, stay at these hotels. Staying there for any length of time does not ensure enjoyment or rest at all. But many people spend beyond their means to stay at a famous hotel at least for a week, only in order to get their names mentioned in the newspapers. Praise be to human ambition! The kind of hotel mentioned above costs a minimum of three to four dollars a day per person. A medium-grade room costs four to six dollars, and the very best room over ten dollars. The cost of laundry, carriages, etc., and other expenses are extra.

A friend of mine from Chicago warmly invited me to spend a week with her in Saratoga, so I went there with her in August 1887.[33] Saratoga is a truly lovely place, with very scenic environs. It has several mansions of wealthy people, and lovely gardens. Bands play in parks every afternoon for the entertainment of the visitors. Thousands of men, women, and pretty children dress up in their finery and go out to take the air and enjoy the scene. There are a number of marvelous springs in Saratoga; their mineral water has an extraordinary taste like soda water. This spring water is said to possess great curative powers; there is no illness or disease—constipation, consumption, asthma, or any other—which it does not cure! It is rumored that a rich countryman of ours had vowed to drink nothing but Ganges water[34] every day. He is said to have employed a number of Brahmins in his service, to bring the Ganges water from a distance of hundreds of miles. The rich and fashionable people in America use spring water from places like Saratoga, brought from a distance of hundreds of miles. But, just as a person living on the banks of the Ganges regards it as lowly and goes on a long pilgrimage to bathe in another holy river, so do the fashionable people living near Saratoga consider the water of its springs as nothing special, and drink instead water brought from distant countries like Germany. It is not at all true that a person who drinks the Saratoga water does not suffer from constipation, consumption, or disorders of the blood; but people have a habit of exaggerating. In sum, the habit of blindly following others exists everywhere.

While in Saratoga, my friend from Chicago took me along to the park to take the air one morning before breakfast. It was a very calm and pleasant day, and the morning was cool, so that everyone in the park was happy. Our stroll brought us to the edge of a spring. It was bounded by a brick wall, a foot or more in height; and the gate was manned by a lad. He charged us a fee of six cents each and let us in. A number of men, women, and children were eagerly drinking their fill of the spring water at four cents a glass. My friend drank two glassfuls, and asked me to drink it too. When I refused, she said in great surprise, "Why do you not drink this medicinal water? It will purify your blood and cure dysentery and other problems at once." I said, "Yes, Madam, that is true. But hundreds of people have put these glasses to their mouths and sanctified them with their saliva; others are drinking out of them without rinsing them properly. And this is the kind of holy water which I will be offered. The very thought of it has cured me of dysentery.[35] Now there is no need to drink this holy water."

Fall

The United States is such a lovely country that its beauty does not diminish in any season. Each season has its specific attributes which decorate Nature with distinctive ornamentation. But the fall has neither the intense cold of the winter, nor the excessive heat of the summer, and is pleasing to all mankind. Its arrival infuses the golden land of the United States with very appealing and ethereal beauty. Leaves change color everywhere. A Nature-lover would realize the truth of my words if he wandered through the woods and forests of the United States at the tail end of the fall, prior to the onset of the winter, when trees shed their leaves. There are many varieties here of the tree called maple; one of them, the silver maple, turns bright red in the fall. There are many other similar trees whose names I do not know. There are various types of oaks also, which turn many lovely colors. The forests of the Adirondack range in New York State and the Allegheny Mountains in Pennsylvania are indescribably beautiful in the fall. Many enthusiasts make a point of traveling in these mountains just to enjoy the fall scenery.

I, too, had occasion to travel by railroad through these lovely parts. A river called Susquehanna winds its way like a snake through the Allegheny Mountains, and is lined with maples and other similar trees on both banks. The beauty of Nature reaches its zenith between Mauch Chunk and Watergap (which are two railroad stations), and a few miles beyond. Had there been a mechanism to capture the colors of the sky and the woods, like the photograph which reproduces the human figure, it would have been possible at least in some measure to convey an idea of the beauty of these parts in the fall, to those who have not been there. Just imagine that you are traveling slowly through this region in a palatial railroad car, seated on lovely chairs upholstered in velvet. The day is pleasant, the sky clear, with just a cloud or two moving about in the heavens. Very tall mountains, with their peaks touching the sky, are seen in all directions, as far as the eye can see. A wide variety of pine trees have draped the mountains with their sapphire foliage, as if covering them with blue clouds. Scattered among them like so many gems are birches, maples, oaks and many other trees, different types of creepers, and small bushes coloring the forests with their leaves of red, yellow, green, violet, brown, and myriad other hues. Along the foot of the hills in the mountain range ripples a crystal-clear river; its water reflects the rays of the sun and appears in places like molten silver. The sight of such a landscape spontaneously suggests the fancy that one has arrived in the Nandan or Chitrarath forest on Mount Meru,[36] described in the Puranas. All the inhabitants of the United States, young and old, are very eager to watch the beauty of this season.

This season brings something else, besides the forest scenery, to add to the general cheer: harvest and fruit picking. This is an occasion of great joy to farmers everywhere. Children cannot contain their enthusiasm as apples and other fruit pile up all around. At the end of November the holiday of Thanksgiving is celebrated. On that day, churches are decorated all over with ears of corn, vegetables, fruit, and flowers; and all the people, young and old, praise God in sweet songs and thank Him devoutly for their plentiful harvest. This scene is delightful and well worth seeing. November, the last month of the fall, and December, the first month of the winter, are the two months when it rains most heavily in the United States. This can be called their rainy season. In addition, there are occasional showers during the winter, spring, and summer.

Winter

Brrr! Brrr! The limbs are cramped from cold, teeth chatter and speech is slurred. People have started walking freely on river water; a great deal of effort is required to cut through butter even with a very sharp knife; at times it becomes necessary to stop drinking milk and start eating its solidified pieces instead. Such is the power of the cold! Everything is great in a great country like the United States. During the summer, one is utterly distressed by the heat, the body is almost on fire, at times one perspires so profusely that the whole body seems to melt. But let the winter arrive and it seems as if the summer is a totally unheard-of phenomenon. The simple, thin, white cotton garments disappear like an illusion in a dream; in their place appear thick woolen coats and jackets, shawls, thick double-lined boots, warm caps with ear-flaps, stockings, gloves, and similar items of winter clothing. One who has never experienced the force of the winter in the north of this country cannot even begin to imagine the cold here. Sometimes in the winter the mercury in the thermometer dips to ten or twenty degrees below zero; rivers, streams, and lakes freeze over, and their water becomes hard like rock.

It is difficult to estimate the extent to which the city folk and even villagers make use of ice instead of drinking water. When rivers and lakes freeze in the winter, ice is stored for use in the summer. Ice-houses are built at isolated spots on the banks of every large river and lake. These ice-houses are shaped like square houses but have no doors. At the top of their wooden walls, near the roof, are a few small windows to which ladders are raised. Blocks of ice, about two feet in length and breadth, and a little less in thickness, are cut out of the frozen river water at an appropriate time and skillfully carried and stored in the ice-houses. The blocks are well covered with sawdust and protected from heat and air in order to prevent the ice from melting. During the summer, ice is taken out of the ice-houses in hundreds and thousands of carts, and sold in cities. Every morning the ice vendors go from door to door in their carts, selling ice. Some buy one slab, others two or more; some buy half a slab, others a quarter or less. Every house has a large vessel of drinking water which is half filled with clean tap water to which are added large pieces of ice; this ensures that cold drinking water is available to all in the summer. Although this water tastes very good, it is very harmful if not drunk in moderation and with caution. A person who comes in from the heat outside is driven by thirst to drink his fill; it does cool him down and slake his thirst, but the extremely cold ice water has an adverse effect on the heated intestines. Therefore, it is best as much as possible not to drink ice water. And if that is difficult, one should at least keep the water in the mouth for a while and swallow it after its iciness has diminished. This will avoid any harm.

During the two months of January and February it becomes difficult to walk in the streets. Someone who is unaware of this fact leaves home feeling pleased with the clean and shiny sidewalks, and takes barely a stride or two before he comes crashing down. Anyone who happens to be around inquires sympathetically whether he is hurt. But the person concerned, even though aching all over from his fall on the hard pavement, says in a confused manner that nothing is amiss. Many such strange scenes are witnessed in the streets in the winter. Some people have the strange tendency to feel ashamed at having slipped and fallen—although it is nothing to be embarrassed about. But habits are strong. The moment they fall, they get up fearing that some one is laughing at them, and rush off without even glancing around, with a strange expression on their faces.

In March of this year (1888), I traveled from Philadelphia to New York City. The sky was clear, the sun shone brightly, and the weather was quite hot. The weather changed the day before I left, and it started to drizzle. That afternoon I delivered an address at the invitation of the Rev. Dr. Heber Newton[37] in their large church, which was terribly crowded with men and women. I had planned to deliver two more speeches in the same city and establish two circles (in aid of my cause[38]), and then go on to Boston on Wednesday morning for some urgent work. When I woke up the next morning, my windowpanes looked very strange. They seemed to be thickly coated with a whitish substance in which someone seemed to have traced a very beautiful and intricate design. When I went to take a closer look at this marvel, I saw the street, rooftops, windows, and doors covered with snow which was whiter than moonlight. The New York I had seen the previous day was totally transformed now; it was difficult to believe that the two cities were one and the same. Lovely, broad streets like Madison Avenue and Fifth Avenue were covered with snow, and appeared quite narrow. As if to accelerate the snowfall, a strong wind was blowing that day, and the mercury had dipped to four degrees. The cold was overpowering; water in the taps was on the point of freezing. At breakfast time the cook brought me a glass of milk as usual; before swallowing it I had to crush each mouthful as if it were a lump of sugar! Even the fire had lost its warmth because of the cold. The snowfall had prevented people from going out into the streets. No stores were open in the city. It seemed doubtful whether any unfortunate man or beast caught in that dreadful snowfall would reach home alive. The tramway, buggies, overhead railroad, all of which plied regularly, had come to a complete standstill. The snow falls soundlessly. When fine flour is being sieved, it falls lightly to the floor without a sound; snow falls just as silently. When snowflakes come down from the sky, they look beautiful, like minuscule, happy fairies, dancing and frolicking like delicate jasmine petals, flying and falling in confusion, and rushing about at great speed. Snowflakes caught on a black or dark cloth display very beautiful and strange patterns. The beauty and strangeness of snowclad earth, trees and vegetation, open grounds, streets and housetops cannot be conveyed adequately in words to one who has not seen them. The beautiful scene can be adequately described only by a Kalidasa[39] or a Shakespeare, or by Goddess Saraswati herself. It would be folly for a person like myself, possessed only of a modest intellect, to even begin to describe it.

Although snow is so white and lovely, and arrives on the earth silently and wordlessly like an excessively shy woman, its might is so terrible that no one who has witnessed it can ever forget it. Should a snowflake fall on the hand, it is seen to be no larger than a tiny lentil, and no thicker than a fourth part of a thin petal of a mustard flower. The flake melts away the moment it touches the hand, because of body heat; there is no need to even lift a finger to crush it. What a light and delicate substance it is![40] But let these atomlike flakes shower down, and it would not take long to understand what can be achieved by a number of negligible small flakes together. They created total havoc in New York City and its vicinity. They fell all over the streets in drifts like sand dunes in a desert. They outwitted the smart American who had harnessed to his service Fire, Water, Lightning, Wind, and other elements. They brought to a standstill the extraordinarily speedy, fiery horses of railroads; they fell onto people in the streets and onto animals, and smothered them to death; they devastated railroads and bridges. It is not possible to estimate what else they did. There was such an excessive amount of snow in the city that even the most essential commodities like milk and coal were impossible to obtain. The railroad track between Boston and New York was closed. The telegraph poles fell, their wires snapped, and no one could find out what was happening in the two cities. The news that this kind of snowfall had occurred in New York on Monday was sent to England through oceanic telegraph, and was cabled back to Boston to reach it in this roundabout fashion! The fifty-odd railroad trains running between Boston and New York were stranded on the way for two or three days, because the engines could not make headway through the drifts of snow covering the iron tracks. Many of these trains had derailed, killing a lot of people. Several people paid fifty dollars (about Rs. 150) per carriage to travel from the railroad station called "Pennsylvania" to the center of New York City. I had to attend a meeting on Wednesday at a place about a quarter of a mile from my lodgings; I had to pay ten dollars (about Rs. 30) to hire a carriage for that distance. On Wednesday I went to a railroad station called the "Grand Central" to make inquiries, and learned that the route to Boston was not yet open. I had to go urgently that day to meet the organizers of our Association.[41] Because the railroad was out of the question, I inquired whether ships were still sailing along the coast; but that route was also closed, and I decided to return to Philadelphia.

The distance between New York and Philadelphia is a hundred miles, and can be covered in two and a quarter hours by the fast train. But the snowfall from Monday to Wednesday morning had closed that route also, and caused several accidents. Our train left New York at 11 A.M., but did not reach Philadelphia until 8 P.M. The entire route and the area around was covered with snow, and sunlight falling on it dazzled the eyes of all the passengers. The train encountered several obstacles. Thousands of men were shoveling snow to clear the tracks. Two large engines had been attached to our train. At least thirty delayed trains passed us on their way to New York, each with two or three engines attached to it; even so it was not easy to pull the train through that vast desertlike stretch of snow. The tracks were lined with tall heaps of snow on either side. While pushing through the snow which covered the tracks, our train would at times half disappear in the drifts of snow. The area where a strong wind was blowing had ten-foot-tall drifts of snow which covered houses, fields, orchards, etc.

A couple of days after the incident, when I had reached Philadelphia, a letter arrived from a friend. She had written that this type of snowstorm was very rare on the East Coast, but it was nothing compared to the snowstorms of the West and the North! There the mercury descends to sixty degrees below zero, and the snowdrifts reach a height of twenty-five to thirty feet. For lack of shelter during such a disaster, millions[42] of cattle on the Great Plains of the West succumb to the dreadful cold and die. Last year and the year before, over eight million head of cattle died of such severe cold. One shudders even to imagine the agony of the poor creatures. No one knows how many thousands of people, and also animals and birds, die of cold there every year.

Although the winter here is so dreadful, people can derive some benefit from it. When the rivers freeze over, some people store the ice and sell it. Also, hundreds of thousands of men and women enjoy sports such as "skating" and "tobogganing." [iii] In many severely cold areas, especially in Canada, fun-loving people cut huge blocks and bricks of ice and build large castles with them. When walls are built with ice bricks at a suitable spot on the bank of a river or lake, water is used instead of lime. When ice bricks are placed one on top of the other, and water is poured on them, it freezes in the cold and makes the ice walls very strong. Large ice castles are built in this fashion and are beautifully illuminated. Then some people pretend to be soldiers of two warring factions and fight a mock battle. Brilliant fireworks are used instead of gunpowder in this battle. The illuminated ice castles and the fireworks above them look indescribably beautiful at night. Thousands of men, women, and children come from afar to enjoy the spectacle. The cities of St. Paul and Montreal are famous for their ice castles.

At the end of January 1888 I traveled from Philadelphia to Indianapolis, capital of the State of Indiana. The city lies about twelve to thirteen hundred miles to the west of Philadelphia. The route is very scenic. After leaving Philadelphia one has to travel for hundreds of miles through the mountain range called the Alleghenies. The Allegheny Mountains are extremely beautiful and imposing, like the foothills of the Himalayas. Pines, oaks, birches, and many other trees grow there. Everywhere woods and forests are seen in the youthful bloom of their natural beauty. The great Susquehanna River snakes its way through these mountains. The railroad keeps to the riverbank for the most part, so that the traveler on this route can watch the entire beauty of the Earth. I traveled on this route two or three times. Once I traveled during the winter when snow had turned the peaks and the area near the foot of the Allegheny Mountains a bright white. The enchanting scene of the snow-clad mountains, whiter than moonlight and shining bright in the sunlight, made one feel that one's faculty of vision had reached its ultimate fulfillment.

At the beginning of February I had gone to a village called Farmington, near the city of Hartford in Connecticut, to visit a girls' school. The village is quite far from the railroad, and was reached not by a four-wheeled carriage but by a vehicle known as the "sleigh" which has no wheels. It was in a sleigh that I went to Farmington with a woman friend. Snow on the ground is like the desert sand on which it is difficult for horses to pull wheeled carriages; but sleighs are much easier to pull. It is a great pleasure to ride in a sleigh. The people here, young and old alike, are eager for sleigh rides. On the way to Farmington we saw the entire surrounding area covered with snow. The mountains around, the trees, roof-tops—all seemed to be snugly asleep under the white blanket of snow to keep out the cold.

National Holidays

New Year's Day, Washington's Birthday, Christ's Death Anniversary, Decoration Day, Independence Day, Thanksgiving Day, and Christ's Birth Anniversary are considered to be national holidays in the United States. All stores, offices, factories, schools, etc., are closed on these days and everyone gets a holiday. New Year's Day means the first of January. This is a very old public holiday which these people have taken over from their ancestors. Christ's Death Anniversary, that is, Easter, and Christ's Birth Anniversary, that is, Christmas, are considered holy days in honor of the founder of Christianity. The twenty-second of February is George Washington's Birthday. During the last century, the Americans declared their independence and severed their ties with England. That naturally led to war between them and the English, in which George Washington defeated the English and led his country to victory. This pleased the American people so much that they made him their President and began to regard him as the Father of the Nation. In his honor people celebrate his birthday in any way they like; and meetings are held to deliver speeches praising him. Decoration Day is the day for decorating graves; it is described later in this book.[43]

Independence Day falls on the fourth of July. On the fourth of July 1776, thirteen old colonies of America became thirteen independent States, and severed their connection with English rule. They not only declared themselves an independent nation from this day on, but also fought a powerful country like England and won their freedom. This national holiday is very important, and is celebrated by all the people in every city, town, and village of this country. The glory of national independence and the country's success are lauded in public meeting halls, and patriotic speeches are made. The Star-Spangled Banner of the United States is raised everywhere. There are illuminations and fireworks in public places like markets. Children are indulged with sweets and fireworks. The Fourth of July may be said to be the "Diwali" of this country.[44] In our country the real significance of Diwali is as good as forgotten. It was regarded as a political holiday because Krishna killed the demon Narakasura on the fourteenth day of the waning lunar fortnight in the month of Kartika, and conquered and occupied the kingdom of Pragjyotishapur. These days Diwali is regarded as a religious holiday. Even if Diwali is assumed to be a political holiday, it is poles apart from the Fourth of July. On Diwali day, a sovereign king was killed and his son deprived of his independence. On the Fourth of July a small nation decided that it would no longer be subjected to an oppressive and greedy nation, and won its freedom; and vowed—at least in words—to confer that freedom on anyone who came to live there.

While I was staying in Philadelphia, I was able to witness the excitement of this holiday. The Independence Hall there is the birthplace of the Goddess of Liberty. Many great speakers made excellent patriotic speeches. The Star-Spangled Banners were flying everywhere in the city. The doors of large stores and the porches of buildings in the central market were decorated with wreaths and red, white and blue cloth banners. There were illuminations everywhere at night, and there were excellent fireworks on the bridge over the Schuylkill River. Men and women, along with their children, had come from afar to the large public park known as Fairmont Park to see the spectacle. Joy, expectation, and pleasure were in evidence everywhere in that crowd of thousands of people.

In November comes Thanksgiving Day, or the day for expressing gratitude. All crops are harvested in this month, and there is an abundance of fruit, vegetables, and grain. The President of this country selects a suitable day in November and conveys a written "message" (not order!) to his fellow citizens to the effect that that particular day should be celebrated as Thanksgiving Day, and that they should join him in prayer to humbly thank the Lord for His blessings upon the country and for the plentiful crops harvested during the year. Then all stores, offices, etc., are kept closed on the day appointed by the President. All men and women, young and old, go to church and prayer-houses to offer prayers. A lot of alms and charity are given to the poor on that day.

It is not customary to invite people home to a meal on these holidays. Sometimes relatives and friends are invited to dinner. The manner of celebrating a holiday is for each family to eat especially well, go out to see some entertainment, and enjoy the day.

There are many other holidays in addition to these public holidays. People of different religious denominations observe holy days in accordance with their beliefs. Roman Catholics consider the birth and death anniversaries of a number of saints to be holy. Hundreds of thousands of Irish people have left their country because of oppression by the English, and come to this free country; they have great celebrations on the special days of their community and religious denomination. On the birth anniversary of their patron saint, St. Patrick, they hoist green flags on their houses. Similarly, the diverse peoples of Europe—German, Scandinavian, Italian, French, Russian, etc.—who have settled down here celebrate their own holidays.

Just as we make special sweetmeats on holidays, so do these people busily engage in making sweetmeats in their own style. But their holidays are marked by a great deal of killing of animals. Just as we plant vegetables in gardens and fields, and save them for special days, so do these people "farm" turkeys and hens. They consider turkey meat to be very tasty. When a guest arrives, he is treated to a real feast with a whole cooked turkey.[iv] An excessive number of animals are killed in this country because of the general practice of eating meat. In the Middle West, that is, to the west of the States of Illinois, Ohio, and Missouri, lie the Great Plains, which have only a sparse population. Some up-and-coming traders there cultivate large "farms" and "orchards" of cattle and pigs, and supply these living and moving "vegetables" to cities thousands of miles away. These heartless butchers are too concerned with filling their purses to care about the well-being of these creatures. Hundreds of thousands of cattle on the Great Plains are scorched by the sun, drenched in the rain, frozen in the snow; and die in agony. They are not even provided with shelters under which to stand or lie down. The principal branches of the Society for the Prevention of Cruelty to Animals in the States of New York and Massachusetts are trying hard in their own way to reduce the oppression of these creatures. The statistical information published by them shows that during the last two years more than 8,000,000 head of cattle, kept in the open, shivered to death in agony in the winter snow of the Great Plains.

I still shudder at the very memory of the distress suffered by the cattle which I saw while touring through the States of Iowa and Nebraska during the summer. Hundreds of head of cattle grazing in the treeless plains, the sun beating down mercilessly at midday, and no shade anywhere for the poor creatures to rest in. Any small pool filled with rain water would have cattle standing in it. Little, tender calves, unable to bear the heat of the sun, would be crouched near a fence, their heads pushed into the meager patches of shade from its two-inch-wide boards. The occasional small bush would be surrounded by a dozen cattle, shoving their heads under its inadequate shade. In places lacking a fence, bushes, or pools of water, the helpless creatures would be lying in the grass, utterly distressed by the heat of the sun. But compared to the dire fate in store for them, this distress cannot but seem like the pleasures of heaven. These hundreds, thousands, millions of cattle grazing in the pastures are intended only for the satisfaction of man's hunger! These pastures are the vegetable gardens of the Americans. Cattle, sheep, and pigs are bred here, and at the specified time these living and moving vegetables are loaded into railroad wagons and sent across thousands of miles. Sometimes these incarcerated creatures do not get fodder or water for five or six days at a stretch. When they are unloaded, they are fed a little and handed over to the butcher. I have never seen their slaughterhouses, nor do I wish to. But, from the descriptions I have read, they seem to be Hell itself, and the butchers and traders living off this cruel trade not just human demons, but a species of whom one can say "We know not who they may be."[45]

On the whole, the people of this country are very kind and compassionate; but they seem not to care for the well-being of creatures other than humans, either because of their habit of eating meat, or for some other reason. A couple of years ago, I remember having read an excellent essay in the monthly magazine called *Balabodha Meva*,[46] published by the American Mission in Bombay. The essay had an illustration showing a woman and her children patting and feeding a cow. The author of the essay had proudly penned a sentence purporting that the people of India torment cattle and other animals, but that Americans treat them with great kindness. This contains a degree of truth, but its accuracy cannot be universally proven. It is true that poor oxen and horses have to suffer a great deal in our country; but it is not as if they receive no kindness. In villages, and sometimes even in cities, there are families which keep milk cows; the women and children of these families love the cows and calves as if they were family members. It is terrible that traders, milkmen, and butchers ill-treat cattle; and all must strive to put a stop to this ill-treatment. But it is not true that such ill-treatment does not exist in America. Anyone who has been to the city markets and factory towns and seen the state in which heartless carriage drivers keep their horses would be inclined to disbelieve that it is not customary to ill-treat animals in this country.

Twenty-five years ago a compassionate man named Henry Bergh[47] started to address the people of the city of New York, espousing the cause of these dumb animals. It would be impossible to describe the way the people tormented dumb animals in those days. Most people ridiculed Henry Bergh when he began to champion the cause of animals. Some said he was insane. Some pious people said that the heterodox fellow was speaking against the Scriptures, because the Scriptures say that God has given Man mastery over all animals, which means that they are created solely for the use of Man. Supported by such scriptural evidence, all people began to harass Henry, the champion of animals. They defended their belief by pelting him with stones, and throwing garbage at him, hundreds of times as he walked about the streets of New York. But Henry Bergh was a very sincere and determined man, and did not abandon his humane cause even in the face of thousands of obstacles. After a few years' effort, he succeeded in getting a law passed to forbid the ill-treatment of animals. One evening it was as if New York city woke up from its sleep. Someone stopped five hundred carriages plying in the streets of New York, and examined the horses harnessed to them. The horses found to be sick, lame, or very weak were unharnessed and led away without their owners' permission. This made everyone comprehend who Henry Bergh was, and also understand that the owner does not have the right to ill-treat dumb animals at will. Henry Bergh's efforts were crowned with success.

Nowadays public opinion is favorably disposed toward animals. The Society for the Prevention of Cruelty to Animals in Massachusetts is engaged in strong efforts in this cause. Its president, George T. Angell,[48] is aged, but exerts himself day and night for the welfare of dumb animals purely out of charity. His efforts, and those of many other good men and women, have led to the establishment of Societies for the Prevention of Cruelty to Animals in the principal cities of this country. A number of laws have been passed to prevent ill-treatment of animals and birds. "Bands of Mercy" have been formed in order to propagate kindness to animals among children. More than six thousand such bands have come into existence to date, and are actively engaged in propagating kindness to animals. Our country has a great need for such societies. It is essential to teach children benevolence, kindness to animals, and the proper use of all things, from an early age.

Although such efforts for promoting the welfare of dumb animals are being made everywhere, there is still a great deal of cruelty to creatures other than human beings. Fashionable women lead to the sacrifice of countless lovely birds every year, for decorating their bonnets. One can find many people in this country who cite scriptural evidence and say, "Animals and birds are created for the use of Man; why then should we not use them as we wish?" It seems that the people who buy a live hen to put in a stew, and carry it upside down by its tied-up legs with its head dangling below, do not have an inkling of the agony suffered by the creature. One day, while waiting for a streetcar in a Philadelphia street, I saw a boy of about thirteen or fourteen holding a hen by its legs, with its head dangling below, standing at a distance. I approached him and said, "Brother, why do you not hold the hen with its head up?" He smiled and said, "It is more convenient to hold it by the legs." "Oh, is that so? I thought you might not like it if someone carried you upside down. Am I right?" The boy laughed at this and held the hen with its head up for a few minutes, out of regard for me. When I went home that evening and narrated the incident, a young female teacher said that it was the accepted custom to hang hens upside down, and that it was quite right to do so. But I had my doubts about this, because we have not inquired and ascertained the opinion of hens as to whether it is good or bad to hang them upside down. (Needless to say, the cruel custom of hanging hens upside down exists in our country also.)

Sometimes dining room walls are hung not with pictures but with dead and stuffed peacocks or pigeons, upside down. It is also customary to hang on the walls paintings of freshly caught, bloodied fish dangling from a peg, or hares killed in a hunt. Needless to say, it is not a good custom. Such cruel pictures harden the hearts of children. Some of the sports of children, and even grown-ups, are very cruel. Lovely young ladies, tender children, young men, and even middle-aged scholars go fishing to amuse themselves. A long slender rod is tied with a long string at the end of which is an iron hook. Pieces of meat are attached to the hook and dropped into the water. The poor hungry fish are lured by the meat, and when they try to swallow it, the hook pierces their throats and kills them. These cruel people then say, "Ah! I have caught a fish!," take it out of water, and feel delighted at the sight of the fish in the throes of death. These customs cannot but make one feel that it would be a good thing if missionaries of some compassionate Buddha came to this country and converted the people here.[v]

The Americans have various types of amusements. These people are largely industrious and diligent, so that it is appropriate for them to have some amusement after their work is done. A game called "lawn tennis" is very popular among the native men and women. On winter[49] and spring days this game provides a good deal of exercise. Men play a game called "baseball," do boxing, and row boats. Women also row boats sometimes in the summer. In the winter it is customary to skate on frozen rivers and lakes. In addition it is also customary for men and women to sing and dance together during festivals and holidays. It is excellent that men and women should make good use of the priceless God-given gift of music and enjoy it, but their manner of dancing is not proper. There are theaters everywhere in cities and even in small towns. These people are very fond of seeing plays. Sometimes concerts are held in music halls. The arrangements there are very good, and numerous respectable men and women go there to listen to vocal and instrumental music. In the evening or during spare time men and women of all ages go to public parks and enjoy the fresh air. It is true that the Americans are fond of seeing plays and watching sports. But they do not waste their money and their life only in seeing plays, as so many idle people in our country do. They play sports for amusement during their leisure hours after the day's work is done; and during working hours they exert themselves to the utmost to do their work.

Notes in the Original Text

i. It is worth remembering in this context that no one is allowed to advertise questionable or objectionable goods in newspapers or at public places in this country. It is regrettable that there is no such restriction in our country. Everyone should feel ashamed that our newspapers are filled with many vulgar advertisements (see, for example, the advertisements for potency pills).[50] It is shocking that respectable gentlemen who publish great and famous newspapers allot space in them to such bad advertisements. These newspapers are seen and read by respectable women and tender children; even pure-minded men have occasion to read them. It is difficult to assess the extent to which this saddens the minds of good men and sullies the minds of children. Why do the upright gentlemen of our country not put a stop to this? Why do our great big societies for the propagation of morals not do so? It is shameful indeed that the gentlemen who belong to the profession of newspaper editors, which is devoted to public welfare—and especially the editors who call themselves respectable and highly religious—should allot space for such advertisements in their newspapers and thereby impress immoral ideas upon the minds of immature children and pave the way for the ruination of our future generations by allowing them to hear, think, and ponder over immoral things! It would be better if they themselves decide not to give space to immoral advertisements and vulgar words, and act accordingly, before the Government enacts a law and imposes it on them. This would at least justify their advice to people not to appeal to the Government to enact laws for everything.

ii. After my return to India, I received a letter from Mrs. B. in which she has asked me whether or not I wear shoes now.

iii. "Skating" is a sport in which one goes sliding over the frozen surface of a river or lake, wearing clogs called "skates," and moving in different patterns. The skating clogs are fitted with thin and sharp iron strips on the soles, stretching from the middle of the heel to the middle toe. It is not possible to stand still when wearing skates. "Tobogganing" was originally a sport of the Indians here. It is very amusing to come sliding down a slope after a heavy snowfall, and this sport is called the "toboggan slide." The toboggan is a wooden vehicle without wheels, like a flat-bottomed boat.

iv. About two thousand years ago, even Brahmins ate meat in our country. It was customary to kill a healthy young fatted cow or calf if one received a visit from a Shrotriya Brahmin, a son-in-law, or a king. There are sayings in sacred books to the effect that the ancestral spirits are satisfied for a specified number of years if Brahmins are fed with fish and other types of meat during funeral ceremonies. In North India the Panchagaud Brahmins usually honor their guests by killing a goat. Bengali Brahmins eat fish, lamb, and other meats which are not prohibited. The killing of animals decreased considerably in our country because of the teachings of the Buddha; even so, there are still many who do not hesitate to eat meat if they get an opportunity.

v. India and America are located on opposite sides of the earth; therefore it is natural for the American people to think that we walk upside down, and for us to think that the Americans walk upside down. Our method of showing kindness to living creatures is the opposite of the American method. They torment creatures other than humans. We open cow pens and asylums for animals; we very compassionately supply human blood to bedbugs, lice, mosquitoes, and ants, and nourish them; we feed snakes with milk and worship them; but we care nothing for human life. If there is a death in a neighbor's house, we shut our doors. If our neighbors contract cholera or some other epidemic disease, we find it difficult to visit them to inquire after their health. Our women die of numerous diseases, but we do not open hospitals for women unless the British compel us to. We venerate the cow like a mother and prostrate ourselves before it, but we beat to death our wives, the mothers of our children. Our princes spend millions of rupees to entertain English officers and boys from affluent English homes; but they can never conceive the idea of opening orphanages for the country's destitute children, or industrial schools for the country's poor! Truly, the Americans do possess a higher degree of kindness to living creatures!!

6 Education and Learning

The independent nation of China is more ancient than all the nations in the five continents of Asia, Europe, Africa, America, and Australia, and has lasted for four thousand years now. The Egyptian, Hellenic, Roman, Indian, and other ancient nations suffered a decline. Some of them are now being trampled underfoot by foreign enemies, some are living in subjection under strong foreign rule, and some have left behind no sign other than their names. But China is still an independent country; it enjoys self-rule. Although it is compelled at times to bow down before a strong Western enemy, it is capable of achieving the advancement of its country and people, and of developing the power to resist Western nations; and it is improving itself accordingly. The Americans, the English, and other Europeans may show disrespect to the Chinese, or ridicule or censure them as much as they like; they still treat the Chinese with caution. Today China has no reason to fear foreign domination. It appears certain that if China introduces changes conducive to the modern human conditions in keeping with the changing times, and strengthens the nation from within, it need fear no danger from without. What is the reason why this nation has acquired such strength, such stability and such prominence? Confucius, the teacher of the Chinese people, said that education eliminates class differences. Following his advice, the Chinese people decided not to treat any particular class as the highest, but to accept that a person's education and good morals are the true criteria of his superiority; and they established the practice of appointing a person to an office which was suited to his education and conduct, instead of entrusting the administration of the country to the nobility or a special class of people. Therefore even a person born in a poor, unknown, and lowly family in China cherishes hopes of rising to a high status on the strength of his education and good morals. Education enjoys pre-eminence among the menfolk of China. Even an ordinary laborer or servant there can read and write. Rare indeed is an illiterate man. Why then would a country whose administration is founded on education not be strong? It is not surprising that a country whose inhabitants are ever ready to work, who do not pamper idle beggars, and who appreciate education should be independent; it would be astonishing were it not so. The learned Plutarch has said that "The fair fabric of justice raised by Numa passed rapidly away because it was not founded upon education."[1] What other reason can there be for the decline of a kingdom which has all other good things? What stronger reason can there be for its downfall than that its political philosophy was not supported by the firm foundation of education? It would be surprising indeed if a nation were not destroyed, when only a few of its people get an education—and those too belonging to a particular class—and where thousands and millions of its inhabitants are immersed in the darkness of ignorance, without even a hope of obtaining a high position.

As in China, the political and moral leaders in the United States have realized the importance of education. They know well that all the inhabitants of the nation need to be at least literate if their independence is to last. And these days they consider it absolutely essential to open the avenues of education to women as well as men. In this matter they have surpassed China. Gradually all nations, including China, will come to realize the importance of women's education. The national might of the United States does not lie in its standing army, cannons, and swords; it lies in the educational advancement and diligence of the nation's inhabitants.

Schools[2]

People belonging to the Puritan sect found that they were unable to freely follow their own religion in their country, and crossed the Atlantic Ocean to settle in the United States. They opened schools right from the beginning, because they considered education to be essential for their children. Four hundred years ago, Martin Luther tried to free Christians from their subjection to the Roman Catholic priesthood; since that time it has come to be generally accepted that the common man in Europe needs to have some education. Luther understood that ignorance was the reason why the scheming priests could deceive millions of poor gullible people and shackle them with the chains of heterodoxy. He therefore translated the Bible into a commonly understood language, and advised all to read it and to practice their religion independently, after due thought. Luther realized that the position of a teacher is more important than that of a preacher, and said that had he not been a preacher, he would certainly have become a teacher. People need the ability to read the Scriptures so as to practice religion according to their independent thinking; and they need the ability to read and understand the laws of the land in order to ensure that their conduct would be lawful.

A few years after settling in America, the Puritans made a rule that there should be one teacher for every fifty families, in each of the towns of fifty or more families in the Puritan settlement. They stipulated that the teacher should teach the children and servants of the families to read and write, and that the townspeople should maintain him. Subsequently other settlers followed the model of the settlers of Massachusetts, and made similar rules in their own colonies. In 1665 the people of Massachusetts established schools in their State, and passed an order that all its inhabitants must send their children to school. Subsequently other settlements in New England passed similar laws. But the condition of the State of Virginia in the South was very different. It had no free schools, nor printing presses. History is witness to the ill effects of the lack of education in that State and other similar Southern States.

Although the system of education in the United States is government-run, it has no connection with the Federal Government. Each state government assumes the responsibility for educating its citizens and their children, and establishes and pays for schools, colleges, etc., according to its own convenience. Thus all States and Territories have their own systems of education. In twenty-eight out of the thirty-eight States, there are a total of ninety-eight large normal schools for training teachers. The male and female teachers trained there teach the children in all the government-run or private schools. The United States Government realized that it was essential to educate its citizens and their children, and that it is the Government's duty to provide funds for public education; and immediately after the establishment of the Republic, the United States Government made laws to encourage education. In 1785, that is, immediately after the end of the War of Independence with the English, the United States Congress passed an act that in each State one-sixteenth of the public lands should be reserved for defraying the expenses of public education. In 1848 the Congress passed a new act and gave another 68,000,000 acres of land to the twenty-seven States in order to further encourage education. In addition, the Government has also allotted vast areas of land for the establishment of state universities. In 1862 much more land was given for the establishment of schools of agriculture and the mechanical arts in all the States. The land in the States and Territories allotted by the Federal Government as educational endowments since 1886 amounted to 78,000,000 acres, that is, more than the combined area of England, Scotland, and Ireland.

Among the nations of Europe, Germany is in the forefront of public education. It spends \$34,500,000[3] annually on education. The United Kingdom ranks immediately below Germany; it spends \$33,425,000 annually on education. The United States Government expends \$96,000,000 per year on providing education to its citizens. The same Government spends about \$47,000,000 every year on its army. The United Kingdom is said to spend \$144,500,000 per year on its army. This will show that the British Government spends on its army alone three times the amount of money required by the United States Government for the same purpose; and that the United States Government spends on educating its citizens two and a half times or more the amount of money spent by the Government of Great Britain on its department of education. The reason why they are poles apart in this manner is that the monarchies of Europe depend for survival on their armies, and the Republic of the United States draws its life and strength from education. There is only one single nation on earth which incurs a higher expenditure on education than on its army, and it is this republic.

The government-run public schools are forbidden to provide religious instruction, that is, to teach the beliefs of the different religious denominations. Before school starts every morning, the principal teacher, male or female, reads a passage from the Bible, but without commenting on it. This practice meets with general approval. All people, with the exception of orthodox Roman Catholics, want education for their children and for the common people. The Roman Catholic bishops have always been afraid of education, because they know very well that educated people will not blindly accept their preaching. But the ordinary Roman Catholics in the United States have also come to appreciate education; they too send their children to public schools. No one asks them about their religious affiliation there. As a result, even the papal orders forbidding this irreligious general education no longer have any effect. If a hungry person is offered a plate heaped with delicacies, such as nectarlike education, and told not to touch any of it, why would he listen?

It has been mentioned above that the United States Government spends its own money on providing people with an education; but this Government is a body of elected administrators, and spending its own money means utilizing the money collected from its citizens. Also in our own country, which is under British rule, the subjects pay tax for education. But the Government does not consult them about the expenditure of that money; on the contrary, even after collecting tax from its subjects, it charges a monthly fee for giving education to their children. In the year 1880, four-fifths of the total educational expenditure of the United States Government was defrayed by taxes, the remaining amount was met by selling or leasing lands attached to schools. That the citizens of this country are happy to pay the tax for education clearly shows their strong appreciation of education.

In addition to public schools there are thousands of colleges which are by and large independent and privately established. Their expenses are defrayed by fees paid by the students and donations from generous people. Many receive government aid. Most colleges are accredited by the Government, so that their managing bodies can award appropriate degrees to their students. There is a great deal of unevenness in the standards of the colleges; while one may be termed a university, another will be included among colleges. Harvard, Columbia, Cornell, Princeton, Michigan, Oberlin, and other similar colleges are known as elite universities; other universities do not have the same status as these. In this country there are 3,550 high schools (higher than the public elementary schools), colleges, and universities, in which there are about 500,000 students. Of these, 364 are colleges and universities, and the number of men and women studying in them is 59,594.

The last census shows that in the year 1880–81, there were 180,750 schools (including both public and private schools) in the United States; and 273,000 teachers taught in them. Of these, 154,375 were women! (Detailed information about the education, etc., of native women is given in the chapter entitled "The Condition of Women.") The United States troops do not exceed twenty-five or thirty thousand; but the troops of teachers working day and night to fight and defeat ignorance amount to 273,000. How then will the fortunes of this country not be ever brilliant? When these vast troops are ever ready to protect the prosperity of the country and the freedom of the people, it is no wonder that the country and the people will shine like the most brilliant gems in the necklace of the nations of the world.

When I arrived in Philadelphia at the beginning of 1886, I had planned to spend only two or three months in America. But when I had occasion to visit the public schools in the city, I was so impressed with their management, their teaching methods, the ability of the teachers, and so on that I decided to spend some more time in the country to acquaint myself with the system and methods of education; and I stayed on longer. In this manner, during a period of nearly three years, I made a practice of visiting most of the elementary and high schools at every place I went to, and getting acquainted with the system of education. Germany, England, and other great nations of Europe perhaps have an excellent system of higher education; but one can safely say that the United States is the most advanced in terms of general public education.

I find the American teachers to be excellent on the whole. The female teachers are usually modest, unassuming, self-controlled, diligent, firm, but affectionate, and they keep excellent order in their schools. They take pride in their position and their schools, and exert themselves day and night to raise the standard of their schools. They believe that it is more creditable to win the affection of the children, give them an excellent education, and win the respect of their parents than to extract forced obedience from the children by threatening them. Corporal punishment has stopped in most of the schools here ever since women were put in charge of education. Educated women are able to extract good work and obedience from the children without beating them. The female teachers of this country are totally unacquainted with cruel punishments like caning, sit-ups, pinching, ear-pulling, and slapping. I had occasion to see an obstinate child being punished in some of the schools I visited. The punishment would be to sit quietly on a high chair for a quarter or half an hour. The very worst corporal punishment is to make a child stand in a corner for a while. The style of teaching is excellent and captivating enough to make children eager to learn. I have heard many children say that they were waiting for the vacation to be over and for school to start. If the education imparted by the teachers is so enjoyable for the pupils, it is no wonder that the children find it a terrible punishment to sit quietly on a high seat instead of learning lessons. Most of the naughty children begin to behave themselves out of fear that they would have to sit idle instead of learning a lesson, and that all the children in the school would point at them and laugh inwardly. Of course one must not forget that even in America there are a few surly teachers and obstinate children!

The subjects taught in the general elementary schools are reading, writing, English grammar, history of the United States, arithmetic, geography, mapmaking, drawing, sewing, physical education, and health and hygiene. Some of the science subjects are also taught in some schools, according to the inclination of the teachers. The high school curriculum is similar to that in our own English high schools and colleges. However, the rote learning common with us is not found here.

Singing, playing the piano, sewing, drawing, and other useful accomplishments are ordinarily taught in girls' schools, in addition to the other subjects. Boys and girls study together in the public elementary schools. This is mostly the rule also in high schools; but in some places there are separate schools for boys and girls. In elite universities also it is getting to be common to give men and women the same education, and together. In many universities, such as Oberlin, Michigan, and Cornell, women study along with men. This is very beneficial to the students, and propagates good morals in society. The student body started to observe decorum after women gained entry into colleges which were earlier reserved only for men, and indecorous conduct is now on the wane. After having had this experience year after year, the presidents of the great universities, who are pre-eminent scholars among the native teachers, have now expressed an opinion favorable to women. The presidents and professors of universities such as Michigan, Cornell, and Oberlin support this idea.

In 1884 the famous General Armstrong,[4] of the excellent industrial school at Hampton, wrote in his historical account of the Hawaiian Islands that the best way to strengthen the morally weak is to monitor them constantly.[5] It is essential to give them a good upbringing by dispelling their prejudices regarding the relationship between the two sexes, and by replacing them with a proper understanding. This would have an effect only if education is given by setting a concrete example, instead of citing imaginary cases and preaching. If the two sexes are kept apart, they are not able to deal appropriately with situations where they come into contact with each other later in life. It is like teaching a boy how to swim while keeping him away from water. If anyone finds that it is morally undesirable to teach boys and girls of a community together, even after proper arrangements have been made by schools, it means that there is no hope for the advancement of that community. It is certain that the community is doomed to immorality and destruction. It is true that coeducation requires resolute, upright, and excellent teachers as well as superior schools. But if we hope to strengthen a community in body, mind, and morals, and to ensure its survival, we are likely to succeed only if we combine decorum, religious conduct, and interaction among family members, not otherwise. A coeducational school is a place where women and men have constant opportunities to enjoy equal rights and opportunities to display their abilities; and it is a good means of getting acquainted with one another and observing one another's abilities. The experience at Hampton has made them think deeply about the various kinds of future interaction among young men and women, and they have increasingly come to prefer the coeducation of men and women interacting like members of a morally upright family.

Some years ago, only men sat on the managing committees of public and private schools. But women are very helpful in educating children, and mothers are more concerned than fathers about the type and level of moral instruction their children receive, about the morals of the teachers, etc. This realization has made the discerning and farsighted men and women in some States support women as managers and inspectresses of schools; and these women managers are engaged in greatly improving the system of education. If women are given an opportunity to work in education and other departments side by side with men, the management of each of these departments will improve and the entire country will benefit. Such is the belief generally gaining ground everywhere; and it appears that it will soon be put into practice. May God let this happen! Because it is obvious that the country can achieve its welfare only if both wheels of the carriage—which society can be imagined to be—run together and on the same path, and not if each goes in a different direction. It is not right to think that men alone are wise and have a deep understanding of everything. Some years ago it was customary for people of the Conestoga tribe (with whom the great William Penn made a treaty of everlasting friendship), who were among the original inhabitants of America, to appoint also women as their leaders to speak for them in assemblies. The Englishmen of the time found this custom very strange. When they asked the Conestogas why they allowed women to speak in assemblies, they answered that some women are wiser than men. Two or three hundred years ago a savage tribe knew this truth to be self-evident; it is only now that a civilized and advanced race like the Americans is beginning to realize it. But the Americans have still not fully comprehended its import. The chief reason why education and other matters here are improving day by day and attaining excellence is that educated, cultured women are concerned about them and are exerting themselves day and night. The nonpartisan and farsighted men in this country support this belief.

Among the White inhabitants of this country, there are very few who cannot read and write. Ninety-three percent of the men and 89 percent of the women are literate. The reason why the proportion of literate women is lower than that of men is not the inferiority of their intellect or brains, but that general education has been made available to them for less than sixty years, and higher education for less than four decades. And the avenues of education had been open to men for hundreds of years before the founding of this nation. Women have endured many kinds of calamities, struggled against public censure and against thousands of obstacles within such a short span of time (of fifty or sixty years), and reached the same level of education as men; this clearly shows how genuine are their qualities of sharp intellect, diligence, and intrepidity. The number of schools for the superior instruction of women was 175 in 1870 and had increased to 227 by 1880; during the last eight years, hundreds more colleges have been established only for women. This will show how eager women are to obtain an education if they get the opportunity. Who can even begin to estimate what brilliance and strength the republic of the United States has gained and will continue to gain on account of this excellent growth in women's education?

The details of people studying in different branches of education in 1880 are as follows. Of all the inhabitants of the country, one in five attends public school at the elementary level, one in every 455 receives a secondary education, and one in every 842 receives higher education in a college or university. One in every 1,848 is given a commercial education, one in every 4,321 receives a scientific education, one in every 9,568 persons is taught theology, and one in every 16,000 is trained in law. This clearly shows how interested the Americans are in education, and how firmly they believe that their level of education will determine whether their country will progress or regress.

For some years now, many farsighted men and women have realized that education does not mean mere literacy, but that pupils need to be given vocational training along with book learning for education to be a complete success. This alone will ensure that the thousands of rupees spent on education and the labor of millions of people bear fruit. These people have therefore started offering industrial education in general schools. Great philosophers of education in Germany also shared this belief. Froebel,[6] the famous teacher and inventor of the "kindergarten" method of education, maintains that one should receive an education from early childhood, and that this education should be such that one makes equal use of one's hands, feet, intellect, sight, hearing, speech—in other words, the whole body and mind, which thus gain strength in equal proportion. When an infant begins to identify objects by sight, its parents should pay heed to training it well while talking to and playing with it, and to giving it a physical and mental education. And man's real progress depends on receiving such a well-rounded education from infancy on; which is why Froebel said that children's education depends entirely on their mothers. It is futile to hope that children will achieve excellent, general, and balanced progress as long as their mothers do not receive an education and moral instruction.

The natives call the famous Miss Elizabeth Peabody[7] of Massachusetts, a highly respected elderly lady, the Mother of Child Education. This good lady suffered many hardships, struggled against obstacles and public opposition, made persistent efforts for many years, and propagated Froebel's kindergarten method of education in this country. I met this lady about two years ago. She is now about eighty-six years old, and has become feeble. But although old age has rendered her body infirm, her mind and intellect remain young. Her face expressed pleasure when she talked about education. She told me of her childhood experience. Her mother was a very good-natured, thoughtful, and affectionate woman; and she educated her daughter mostly at home. It was due to the kindness of her loving mother that Elizabeth has acquired this stature today, and is counted among the chief architects of education in this country. The face of the elderly Miss Peabody became radiant when she talked of her mother, and for a moment she looked very pretty, as if she had forgotten old age and re-entered childhood. Elizabeth was compelled to earn her livelihood from the age of about fifteen, and she started teaching children. After a few years, when she had saved some money, she studied hard and went to Europe to acquire a knowledge of the best methods of education there. When she went to Germany and studied the Froebel method, she was convinced that it would be best to train children by this method from an early age, and to lay a firm foundation for their morals, education, and general progress. Without all these, hollow book learning would be useless. Then she returned home and delivered innumerable lectures on this subject at different places. She trained thousands of women in the kindergarten method, and taught children herself. Her labors have begun to yield results now, and she feels contented to see that the fruit of her efforts is available to her countrymen and -women during her lifetime. This affords us great happiness indeed. Few people in this world are blessed with the great good fortune of seeing the results of their labors.

The kindergarten method has been adopted in the public education system in famous educational centers like St. Louis, Philadelphia, and Boston. It seems likely to be introduced soon in other cities also. The Department of Public Education in St. Louis has used this method for twelve years now, as a result of which its public schools are superior to all other public schools in the country. The National Education Association, which met in Chicago in 1887 and in San Francisco this year (i.e., in 1888), had organized an exhibition of sketches, drawings, maps, etc., drawn by schoolchildren, in which the schools of St. Louis won the first rank and the award.[8] This showed everybody that the Froebel method is excellent and serves as the foundation for all knowledge. The method has not been accepted as much in public schools as in private ones, but it is expected to be more widely accepted soon. Following Miss Peabody, teachers like Professor Adler,[9] Colonel Parker,[10] and others began to demonstrate the principle that it is necessary to impart vocational training together with book learning. Dr. Adler has opened an excellent school in the city of New York, in which children receive both kinds of education, which they greatly enjoy. Colonel Parker is the principal of the Cook County Normal School near Chicago; he teaches thousands of male and female teachers how to give vocational training to children. His method is truly laudable.

What is meant by vocational training here is not training in industries like carpentry or the craft of the blacksmith, etc. Many public and private schools have been established for teaching such industries. This vocational training means teaching children to work with their hands, to draw or sculpt in clay any object they see, to handle tools, etc., in order to strengthen the muscles in their limbs along with their brains, while teaching them to read and write. This does not merely strengthen muscles, but also provides children with amusement; it also helps to assess a child's aptitude for a special type of education and makes it easy to send him to the right place and give him the right type of schooling or industrial education. A boy who has no aptitude for mathematics might learn drawing or a craft very well, and one who cannot draw might be able to read excellent books. Vocational education is very useful for ascertaining such things. Special schools for giving such education have been established in Boston, Philadelphia, New York, Chicago, St. Louis, and other cities. In Quincy, Massachusetts, there is a large school with such an excellent method of education that children of all ages acquire theoretical as well as practical knowledge, and develop an interest in industry. This method is known as the "Quincy Method." In Hampton, Virginia, an agricultural school has been established through the efforts of General Armstrong. It gives a theoretical and industrial education to the boys and girls of two races—savage Indians and half-savage Negroes newly freed from slavery. The school at Hampton is "agricultural," but it teaches other useful industries also. The children trained there emerge from their savage state as if reborn, with good breeding and industriousness; and they become fit to go into respectable society. This clearly shows the combined power of theoretical and industrial education.

Newspapers and Books[11]

Merely spending a few years in school does not make children experts in managing household affairs. School education indicates the direction of future duties. Just as the alphabet opens the door to the storehouse of knowledge for one who will one day study philosophy, so does school education open the door to practical and scientific knowledge. One should be ever ready to enter through that open door and seek the gems of knowledge. The means of acquiring these gems are quite different. There are two chief ones: reading newspapers, and perusing old and new books. Just as the people here have the facility of acquiring an education at school, they have the means of acquiring a variety of useful knowledge through books after leaving school. Immediately upon settling here the Puritans started the practice of reading newspapers. They were by nature interested in politics, and had an intense desire to understand the political events and developments. Later, when a political transition was about to occur, the men and women, and even children, of New England eagerly awaited news about further developments in the country, about who won or lost the war, who delivered what kind of address in the Congress in Philadelphia, etc. The first newspapers in this country were handwritten; then came printed sheets. In a republic, every person is well aware that it is his nation, that he is closely connected with its welfare, that he is able to participate in making the laws which are applicable there and in bringing about new developments which will advance the nation. It is quite right that in such a republic the people should have a strong desire to understand the events taking place there, and to decide where their duty lies. There are no other means as excellent as newspapers to convey these essential matters to the people.

At no time did this country have the "Press Act," which is in force in Russia under the tsars or in India under sahibs like Lytton—that is, a prohibition on expressing one's opinion freely through newspapers.[12] And such a prohibition will never be enforced as long as this country remains a republic. If the people themselves cannot speak their minds freely and express their opinions about matters which closely concern all, who can? It is only those who want to extract forced obeisance and make profits at the cost of their subjects who feel the need for detestable laws like the Press Act. Everyone in this country expresses his opinion freely. If President Cleveland wants to abolish tariffs on imported goods, any street sweeper or cobbler who does not approve of this boldly corrects the President Sahib and does not hesitate to fault Mr. Cleveland just because he is President.[13] Daily, weekly, biweekly, and monthly papers are seen in people's hands everywhere—in every house and street, lane and alleyway, in every store, in the mansions of the rich and the huts of the poor. If a carriage driver has to keep his carriage waiting for someone, he immediately takes a newspaper from his pocket and starts reading. Cooks, maids, launderers, tailors, sweepers, coal sellers, chimney sweeps—all these people read newspapers in their free time. Every morning, noon, and night, people come down to breakfast or other meals, newspaper in hand, and read while they eat. An incident which takes place three thousand miles away is conveyed from one coast of this vast country to the other by telegraph, printed immediately in newspapers, and made available for all to read within twelve to fifteen hours. It is rare to find a town or village which does not have at least one local newspaper. Also, newspapers cost very little, just a few cents. In 1880 this country had a total of 11,314 newspapers, magazines, etc.; four-fifths of them published political, social, and commercial matters, and one-fifth dealt with professional and scientific subjects. Hundreds of additional newspapers and magazines must have started during the following eight years.

It is worth remembering that 10,515 of the above-mentioned 11,314 papers and magazines are published in English. A common language is essential for national unity and for enabling the people of one region to know the thoughts of those in another. People from almost all parts of Europe, such as the French, Scandinavians, Spanish, Dutch, Italians, Welsh, Bohemians, Poles, and Portuguese, come and settle down in this country; they speak their mother tongue at home, and together they publish almost a thousand papers in their own languages. But they have to deal mostly with English-speaking people everywhere. Only English is taught in public schools, the administration is conducted in English, and all the things like trade and commerce, accounts, etc., have to be carried on with the help of the English language. Therefore they cannot manage without learning English. And it does not require too much effort to learn the language in a place where one hears only that language spoken all around. About a hundred million people who have settled down in different parts of the world are born in English families and speak English. On the strength of this figure, the supporters of that language have started claiming that English will become the language of all the people in the world. It is difficult to say how far this will come true; but certainly the growth of this language is quite marvelous.

Now, why should our people not give a little thought to this matter? When our National Congress[14] meets in Calcutta, Madras, Bombay, or the Punjab, the words of the speakers from one part of India cannot be understood by the people from another. Then they deliver long orations in English; but what use are they to the common people? Erasing all the existing languages of our country and putting English in their place is like drowning India in the sea and installing the British Isles in that spot. If our learned, intelligent, thoughtful people are attempting to elevate our country and people, how is it that they do not consider the fact that it is essential in our country to have a single language—and an Indian one—which can be understood by all?

There is a language in our country also, similar to the English language which has now become the language of a hundred million people. Almost all the people in India understand Hindi. Braja or Mathuri, Avadhi, Punjabi, and Madhyadeshi are all dialects of Hindi,[15] and the slight difference among them is not greater than the difference among the Marathi of Poona, the Konkan, and the Deccan.[16]

The Hindi language, including all the above-mentioned dialects, is today the mother tongue of a hundred or a hundred twenty million people in India. The language of our neighbors, the Gurjars,[17] is half Hindi and half Marathi. Then what is the objection to granting a great language like Hindi the status of the national language? During their reign, the Mahommedans had dealings with the people in Urdu. Urdu is not a separate language, but is half Hindi, mixed with words from languages like Arabic, Persian, Marathi, and Kanarese.[18] Besides it does not require much effort to learn Hindi. Like English, Hindi can also accommodate all the languages of the world; therefore there is no hindrance to its growth. Hindi grammar is also very easy. Words from Arabic, Persian, Sanskrit, English, and even the language of the Demons[19] can be transformed into Hindi. We have such an invaluable, beautiful language available to us, and it is so easy to make it the national language. But our learned brethren discuss the public matters of India in the English language, which has come from beyond the seven seas, and which is as unintelligible to the common people as the ancient Egyptian hieroglyphs. Will they explain why?

If our National Congress and other public bodies take this matter seriously, all farsighted well-wishers of the country—from Kanyakumari to the Himalayas, and from the mouth of the Indus River to the frontiers of Manipur[20]—will exert themselves in their own ways to promote Hindi. Newspaper editors and authors of books will receive encouragement. It will not be difficult for the brethren from Madras and those from the Punjab to talk to one another when they meet. And how many languages can there be in this world which cannot be written in the Devanagari script? This alphabet contains the essential sounds in all the languages in our country. Therefore, even if we take words from all those languages and put them together to make an admixture of Hindi, it can be written in Devanagari letters. I humbly request the National Congress to take up this matter for consideration during their next session.

Not all the newspapers in the United States are good, and not all the topics covered by them are excellent. There is bound to be a mixture of good and bad wherever people enjoy the liberty to make their views public. But if one investigates the matter with due thought, one will find that the good emerges victorious. The reason for the existence of newspaper editors is to provide knowledge about religious, commercial, and scientific topics to the general public in a simple manner and at a low cost; and this purpose is fulfilled in this country. The great, influential newspaper editors do not content themselves with publishing only the matters of their own country. The proprietor of a newspaper called the *New York Herald* provided money and other assistance to Henry Stanley, who had achieved immortal fame for exploring different parts of the continent of Africa, to enable him to travel in that distant and unknown continent. Since then many other newspapers have also sent their correspondents to many far-off lands to explore new things, and have thus greatly benefited the world. The *Century, Harper's Magazine,* and other American magazines are superior to all European magazines in terms of their range of topics, depth, illustrations, and excellent printing. In Europe, Austria is said to excel in the art of printing; but the owner of the best printing press in Austria congratulated the proprietor of the American magazine called the *Century* on the excellence and superiority of its printing and illustrations, and requested him to reveal the secret of his printing technique.[21]

The essays in the *Century* and other magazines are very good. The magazine proprietors pay the authors one to two hundred dollars, that is, three to six hundred rupees, per essay. The woodcuts of the beautiful and excellent illustrations prepared for printing cost hundreds of rupees each. Evidently a capital of hundreds of thousands of rupees is required to run such a monthly or weekly. But their proprietors are able to make a large profit after paying these vast expenses, the reason being public patronage. A magazine like the *Century* has no fewer than one hundred thousand subscribers.[i] Printing is done by steam power.

At the beginning of each month, these magazines are ready for sale in each city in the United States, and in the large cities in Europe. The boys who go around selling newspapers in railway trains and streetcars carry these magazines and local newspapers. In a city like New York, hundreds of thousands of people buy the daily paper; such is the extent of public patronage here. A common language, almost total literacy, and widespread national concern are the reasons for this generous public patronage. It is not surprising that writers and journalists feel encouraged to perform their duties with zeal, and that the people appreciate their sincere work and support it. But, for all this to happen, it is essential for people to have the freedom of expression, courage to express their views, and patriotism alive in their hearts.

Like newspapers, new books are published here all the time. Different kinds of books are published—old English books and books by modern authors, translations of good books from foreign languages, etc. Their prices are not beyond the means of the common people. The same book is published in various editions—very expensive and quite cheap; in large, medium, and small print—so that they are available to all kinds of people, from millionaires to the poor, to read. Even large volumes like the *Encyclopaedia Britannica* are, like small books, published and sold at a price which is moderate in relation to their size and scope. The *Britannica* is the largest among all the encyclopedias in the world. It costs a great deal in England, but it is available in America for about $75, which is why it has been reprinted several times, and fifty or sixty thousand copies have been sold. A knowledgeable man claims that the number of copies of the *Bri-*

tannica sold in America was four times as high as that sold in England. A bookseller named Appleton has compiled and published the *American Encyclopaedia,* which costs more than $70. It has sold about one hundred thousand copies.

Books written and published originally in England are cheaper in America, and American books are cheaper in England. The reason is that the books copyrighted in one country amount in the other to goods dumped in the street. The two Governments have not yet signed a treaty to protect their own authors in the other country, and to protect the books of these authors from being pirated. As a result, booksellers in England and the United States are filling their coffers by boldly pirating their neighbor's books quite openly. There are upright people in both countries who are engaged in negotiating to stop this daylight robbery; but the booksellers in the two countries are not in favor of a legal arrangement in this regard.

The authors here do not depend on royal patronage for recognition of their books. Public patronage here is greater than any amount of royal patronage. Authors receive the recognition which is their due. The American people are very hungry for books. Every year $90,000,000—that is Rs. 270,000,000 at the current exchange rate—are spent only on books and papers. Every large and small family has the number of books it can afford. An ordinary carriage driver, farmer, or even laborer has a collection of books at home. Rich or middle-class people have proper libraries in their houses. There is also a wealth of public libraries and reading rooms everywhere. It would be extremely difficult to find a village which does not have at least a small public library; large cities have several vast libraries. Men and women who value knowledge exert themselves with great energy and zeal to improve the libraries in their towns. They nurture the pride that their town, like their country, is the best place on earth.

In the United States today there are 23,000 libraries only in schools, holding 45,000,000 books. In addition, there are 3,500,000 books in college libraries. Besides these, the enormous libraries, such as the Philadelphia Free Library, Boston City Library, Astor, Congressional, etc., together hold millions of books, estimated at over 50,000,000. Needless to say, the number of male and female readers who borrow books from these libraries is very large indeed. However, not everyone reads good or serious books; people read good or bad books according to their education and natural inclination. Those engaged in physical labor the whole day, and those who while away their time doing nothing but yawning, are excessively fond of reading novels; at times this borders on addiction. Some people read excellent or medium-grade books and enrich their intellect with gems from the treasure-house of knowledge. Many people here take great care to prevent the publication of bad or obscene matter, and they are largely successful.

On the whole, the American people greatly value education, and there is no fear that their minds or bodies will succumb to subjection as long as the Sun of

Knowledge (clouded only temporarily, once in a while, by Ignorance) continues to shed its brilliant light all around, and to dispel the darkness of Ignorance.

Note in the Original Text

i. Magazines like the *Century* are intended for grown-ups, but the people here are very much concerned about the advancement of children. The famous magazine *St. Nicholas* is published only for children. Its editor, Mrs. Mary Mapes Dodge, is a very scholarly woman, and has equaled the very best and most highly esteemed, learned editors in achievement. They say that even England does not have a magazine as excellent as *St. Nicholas,* which is big, illustrated, interesting, and informative on account of its style of making profound scientific subjects simple. In addition, many other popular magazines, such as *Harper's Young People* and *Youth's Companion* are published for children. They too have more than 100,000 subscribers each. The subscribers here remit their subscriptions to newspapers on time. A diligent man has calculated that about 107,000 tons of paper are needed every year in this country to print newspapers and books. In the United Kingdom 94,000 tons of paper are needed for the same purpose.[22]

7   Religious Denominations and Charities

In England the denomination known as the Church of England is integrated with the power of the monarchy. The King or Queen of England must belong to this denomination, and all the subjects of that country must bear the expenses of its bishops, etc. The Government extracts a heavy tax from them, whether or not they belong to that denomination, and donates it to the bishops of "The Church" and their disciples. This practice of extracting forced obeisance, in a progressive country like England, is very strange indeed.[1] It is said that even the bishops and other clergymen of the Church of England who go to our country to perform ecclesiastical duties for the Government are paid fat salaries from the Treasury of India, although I do not know whether this is true.[2] If it is, then that too is a marvel.

In the United States, no religious denomination is integrated with the power of the people, therefore the people here accept any denomination which agrees with their own way of thinking; and the money they give for defraying the expenses of the churches, clergymen, etc. of that denomination is given voluntarily. The Government does not levy a separate tax on them on account of religion. Even so, religion is not any the less strong here than in England. In England only the Church of England gets high respect, because it is the denomination supported by the monarchy. The adherents of that denomination turn up their noses at the followers of other denominations as "dissenters" (i.e., holding different beliefs). In the free States of America no one publicly accords greater respect to one denomination than to another, because no one has heard of any particular denomination as being especially favored by those in power.

There are many in England who claim that people would become irreligious if the Government did not provide for the support of religion. But this claim of the English is totally false, because in England there are 144 churches per every 100,000 people, whereas in the United States there are 181 churches for the same number of people. This disproves the claim that religious belief is less strong in the United States, where religion is not supported by the Government.

In the year 1880, there were 92,000 churches in the United States, of which more than 80,000 were built by Protestants and the rest belonged to the Roman

Catholics. The total movable and immovable property of all these churches amounted to $350,000,000, or more than Rs. 1,000,000,000. There are a total of 77,000 clergymen of various denominations. About a hundred and fifty years ago, there was strong denominational discord in this country. The Puritans of Massachusetts felt a deep hatred for the followers of other denominations. They persecuted many Quakers. They accused many women of other denominations of witchcraft and burned them alive;[3] they hanged some people and imprisoned others. They whipped some like animals right in the streets, and exiled others after wresting away their property. In the year 1705 the state government of Virginia passed a resolution that whosoever denies that God is a Trinity and that the Bible is a divinely inspired book should be punished with three years' imprisonment. And should he deny these things yet again, it should be made very difficult for him to get government employment, etc.

In the latter part of the eighteenth century, when the American people were trying to sever their political ties with England and become independent, they put aside their internal denominational differences and acted in unison. In the fear that their country would acquire a permanent stamp of English political power and of "The Church" if they did not act in unison at the time, they abandoned denominational differences, put up a united fight against England, and became independent. For the same reason, even now these people disregard denominational differences and act in unison, and will continue to do so. It is not that there is no denominational prejudice in this country. However, because equal freedom is available to all in matters of religion, people prefer not to pay undue attention to or argue about each other's beliefs, and they enjoy a great deal of mutual social intercourse. Therefore one would find more examples in this country than in England of people belonging to different denominations who have friendly dealings with each other. If a religious association is to have a meeting, its members also invite their friends who are opposed to their own belief. Such an invitation is difficult to refuse because of the claims of friendship. Thus people of opposing beliefs come together and have an easy opportunity to understand one another's beliefs. This removes, to a large extent, hatred for people of opposing beliefs, which stems from ignorance. This is a very important thing, worth remembering by all. Chief among the reasons which cause opposition and hostility between two persons is mutual ignorance. Another reason is the tendency to find fault. The people here have largely given up the habit of looking for faults among those belonging to different denominations in their own country and religion. Most of the people in the United States are Christians, among whom there are two chief denominations, Roman Catholics and Protestants, with numerous subdivisions. Their differences may be denominational, but not religious. These denominational differences do not obstruct any work for the national good.[i] One finds cases of husband and wife, or parents and children, in the same family belonging to different denominations, although their natural love for one another remains undiminished.

From the establishment of the nation of the United States to the present day, no single religious denomination has received special patronage from the Government; nor will this happen in the future. The government is concerned with religious denominations to the same extent that it is with medicine, agriculture, or general trade and commerce; and not more. Only if the religious beliefs of a person or group receive interference from others so that they suffer as a result will the Government intervene in religious matters in order to prevent such an eventuality. Similarly, the Government will not allow people to follow a religious belief which violates federal laws. For example, the Mormon sect believes that a man should have several wives at the same time; this violates the federal laws of the United States. That is why the Federal Government has resolved not to allow this and a couple of other similar beliefs to be practiced.

The Anglican Church in England has a custom that bishops sell livings to clergymen. I have heard that the people there sell positions in the army and many other positions in the same manner. The public sale of clergymen's positions is very harmful to the religious sentiment of the country and the people. He who pays a higher price obtains the position, irrespective of his merit. A wealthy person buys a rich living which is on the market, hires one or two curates to do the work, and lives a life of pleasure. This whole business is somewhat like the high priests of our own temples and monasteries. As a result of this system there are many unsuitable clergymen among the Anglicans. I do not claim that all their clergy are of this type; my only point is that there are people there who buy clergymen's positions. If a village has a good minister, the people there are to be counted very fortunate!

Clergymen's positions are not sold in this fashion in America, where the clergy are appointed by the people, with a view to their learning, virtue, and sense of duty. This does not mean that all the clergy here are mines of virtue. A clergyman found to be unsuitable is removed by the people. Because the clergy are learned and virtuous, the people have a greater involvement in religion. The management of churches here runs smoothly like the overall management in the nation. Every church has a committee which manages church affairs. In anything and everything in the United States, management follows public opinion; the same is the case with religion.

In England there is another evil custom that every church owns large landed property, that is to say, land has been assigned to each church. This land is leased out to other people as a source of income; the leaseholder can utilize the holy land for any unholy purpose, as long as the church earns an income. There are many liquor distilleries and liquor stores on such land. How very surprising that the money which is to be utilized for saving people is acquired by destroying people! Here there is very little land attached to churches. Some years ago this country also had the practice of leasing church lands to all and sundry. There was a Methodist church in which people would sing psalms above while the basement was rented for storing liquor. Another strange thing was that, while this country was engaged in the slave trade, these people did not feel ashamed to accept money from the sale of slaves and spend it on church expenditure and on good deeds like evangelization. They were firmly convinced that God had created the Black people of Africa, like cattle, for their own willful use; why then should it matter if the money from their sale was used for religious deeds? In our own country, the upper castes including the Brahmins also believed that the people of the Shudra caste were created by God only to serve them, and that such service was their only means of salvation. People in a state of barbarity always hold such evil beliefs. For a person to make others toil for him mercilessly without payment, and, moreover, to act as if he has conferred a favor on them by allowing them to serve him and thereby opening the way for their salvation— is this not barbarity? Equally barbaric is the utterly demonic practice of selling human beings and using the proceeds for the salvation of other people and for evangelization. It is a matter for rejoicing that such practices have now ceased altogether in the United States.

Here the expenses of the churches as well as those of the clergy are defrayed by charitable donations from the people. The preacher of a church which has a congregation of five hundred gets an average monthly salary of two hundred dollars. In addition, persons appointed to look after the church also have to be paid high salaries. The chairs, pews, lamps, mats, carpets, etc., in the church also cost a great deal. (The churches here are very well decorated.) The congregation pays a contribution to cover all this expense. Every Sunday, after the morning and evening service, the persons appointed by the managing body of the church go around the congregation with plates in hand; it is customary for people to put whatever money they can afford into the plate, to be used for religious purposes.

There is another way of earning money which should be mentioned here, although I do not approve of it. Rent is charged for the pews or chairs in the front portion of the church; they are reserved for those who pay. It is not proper that such trade should be carried on in the Lord's prayer-house, and that only the rich should be in a better position to hear the sermon. A great deal of money is earned in this manner. At pilgrimage places like Gaya in North India, there is a nonsensical belief that only the ancestors of one who pays the priests well attain a higher state; this is a similar belief. It is not to be supposed that all the people who rent the front seats are religious; there are many hypocrites among them. It is considered a sign of gentility, that is, refinement, to go to church every Sunday with one's entire family. So there are many people who go to church, even without piety in their hearts. There are also many here who give to charity only for the sake of publicity. For their generous charitable gifts they may not be awarded lengthy honors by their Government, as Baronet, G.C.S.I., C.S.I., C.I.E., etc., are awarded by our Government in India; however, they do get a great deal of publicity in the newspapers.

Not even all these means can defray all the expenses of the church; therefore the women here employ various means to collect large amounts of money for religious expenditure. Women constitute two-thirds of the congregation, and about half the money needed for church expenses comes from them. I think it is doubtful whether these religious organizations would have continued to function in the absence of women. Men are not as concerned about the livelihood of the clergy as women are. In our country, women are never empty-handed when they attend Purana recitals or go to the temple. They place some money, a betel nut, a flower, some fruit, or at least a handful of rice before the Puranika.[4] (When menfolk go to the temple, they usually content themselves with sounding the bell with their empty hands.) Thus most of the priests and Puranikas are supported by the charity of women. Even so, the pious Puranikas tell people: "Women are inherently evil. The Creator has made them by combining everything that is evil in Creation. They are shackles on men's legs, and the cause of the destruction of religion. Those who desire salvation should avoid seeing their faces. Women should not have the right to study the Shastras, they should not read the Vedas, they should not preach; women alone are the cause of men's destruction in this world."[5] Indeed the conduct and preaching of these Puranikas show the height of gratitude! In olden times, even in the United States men harbored similar derogatory and strange beliefs regarding women. They said that women should never preach. Many people went so far as to believe that women should not even sing psalms. Although this belief has not yet disappeared altogether, it is on the decline. Of the total of 77,000 preachers in the United States, 165 are women. Twenty years ago, there were hardly four or five. At that time it was considered to be highly improper for a woman to preach.

Like Christians in other countries, these people also observe Sunday as a holy day. On Sunday, trading and businesses are closed in almost all places; in the States where they are not, pious people are trying to get them to close. All Government offices, public and private schools, and factories are closed on Sunday. On that holy day, pious men and women go to church, pray to God, and listen to sermons. They consider evangelization to be a part of their religion, and invite everybody to their churches. Although there is no religious education in schools, most people give their children religious instruction at home every day. Children are gathered in church and given sermons on portions of the Bible. The schools held in churches every Sunday for preaching to children and adults are called Sunday schools.

The people here are also greatly concerned about preaching to the new settlers in this country, and about leading them on the right path. The societies which evangelize in this manner are called Home Missions. There are a large number of men and women who work day and night to evangelize with utmost sincerity. They believe that a person cannot obtain salvation except through the Christian religion; therefore they spend a great deal of money on spreading their religion in foreign countries. Hundreds of men and women in this country have left their homes, comforts and conveniences, etc., only for the sake of religion, to travel far and wide for the welfare of people in foreign countries. About a hundred years ago, some American missionaries went to our country. At the time the [East India] Company Government did not allow them to evangelize within their territories. They made no headway in the Bengal and Madras [Presidencies]. Many of them lost their wives, and they suffered great hardships. Then they came to Bombay. Even there the Government did not wish them to stay. But in the end the English Government allowed them to stay for fear of public censure if they drove out of their territory the harmless people who had come to evangelize.[6] The climate of Bombay did not agree with them, nor was the Government favorable to them; and the local people hated and harassed them. They had no protector in that foreign land, and their own country was far away. Also, the means of traveling to and from their country were not widely and easily available as they are now. In spite of all these obstacles, they continued their work. At present they have thirty to thirty-five societies in India. Their efforts are in accordance with the words of Christ: "Go ye into all the world, and preach the gospel to every creature." It would be totally wrong to suppose that all those who contribute money to such evangelical work are rich. It is the poor who help a great deal in this work. Here the rich are not much concerned about religion; or rather, only a few of them have such concern. In New York there is a huge playhouse, known as the Italian Opera House, built by seventy rich local residents. It cost $9,800,000, to which $140,000 each were contributed by those seventy! They spend money on luxuries; help for evangelization comes from the poor.

Although the American people are convinced that those who are not Christians will go to eternal hell, they spend only $5,500,000 on this effort. Today there are at least 10,000,000 people in the United States who listen to sermons in churches and belong to one of the Christian denominations. Their wealth increases by about $310,000,000 every year, and they own one-fifth of the total wealth of this country, which amounts to $8,728,400,000 (that is, Rs. 26,185,200,000). Such wealthy people spend only $5,500,000 per year to support evangelization. This religious expenditure is only one 159th part of their wealth. It is very little compared to the tremendous wealth of the people in this country; and the greater share of it is borne by the poor rather than the rich, and especially by poor women. The women here make great efforts to collect this amount. In this country, 10,000,000 people drink liquor worth $900,000,000 (that is, Rs. 2,700,000,000) every year, and smoke tobacco worth $490,000,000. This shows that tobacco and liquor enjoy greater importance than religion in this country. This is sad and deplorable indeed. The societies for temperance and moral instruction here make great efforts to eradicate both these vices in this country. I pray to God to grant them success and to free this beautiful country from the grip of Demoness Liquor, Fiend Tobacco, and Immorality.

The religious people in our country give alms to everybody who begs. It is good to give to the destitute, but after assessing who is truly deserving; this is not done in our country, with the result that beggary has become rampant. Our virtuous ancestors have said, "Alms given to an undeserving person are wasted; they incur sin." But who pays any heed? Suppose there is a fat *bairagi;* if anybody gives him money, he will spend it on smoking *ganja.*[7] The addiction to *ganja* which has already ruined him passes on from him to children and to other people, because there are many who follow the example of such holy men! Therefore, this is how charity to unsuitable persons promotes idleness and vice in the country, and the country sinks to a lowly state. I have visited many places of pilgrimage myself, and also seen the system of charity there. Alms given to the priests there are undeserved; these priests reduce their patrons to poverty. The priest who extracts the most from his patron in the name of religion is considered learned and regarded as very "clever" and wise.

The people here have a custom of giving to charities, which is very different from ours. Here, nobody wanders through the streets begging. Popular opinion and the laws of the land are openly opposed to beggary. Alms are not given to anybody who comes to the door to beg. Blind and lame, weak and aged persons sit in the street selling matchboxes, strings, mirrors, and other small things. Some good-hearted person buys a thing or two from them and pays a little more than the actual price. These people do not give to those who beg; but that does not mean that they are not compassionate. They are very particular about giving only to the deserving. People in villages and cities collect money through contributions in order to support those who are destitute, crippled, or too weak to work. In addition, the inhabitants also have to pay a small tax for charitable works, which they pay willingly. This money is handed over to the local societies which manage charities, called Boards of Charities. The men and women who manage these societies are elected by the people; they are highly respectable, honest, and pious, and do their work with great care and concern. The management of these boards is similar to that of other societies. Of the money spent on charity in the country, half comes from the people and half from the Government. All this money is spent only on those who are truly crippled and unable to earn a living.

There are many people in our country who never leave home. The people here are very different. They often travel from place to place in search of trade or employment. They are sometimes reduced to poverty after going to another town or province. In addition, there is a great deal of poverty among the people who come from Europe to settle here. Many such people are stricken by poverty, and travel throughout the country. There are also beggars of various kinds. There are many pious people, including women, who try to discover where the poor live, what they do, what their condition is, etc. These good people do this work in an honorary capacity, without expectation of return; even so, the work is sometimes mismanaged. This cannot be helped. No matter what task one undertakes, one is likely to make mistakes sometime or other. It is human nature to be confused. Whoever works will make mistakes. Most people in our country do not do anything themselves, but are very quick to detect the mistakes of anyone who starts anything. The American people do not stop at detecting faults; they devise ways and means of rectifying the mistake, and provide great encouragement to a person who has undertaken any benevolent work.

There are two ways of helping the poor in this country. One is to provide shelter to the destitute, and to provide food and clothing to those who lack them. The other is to find the people who work but are not able to earn sufficient food and clothing, and to make proper arrangements for them, which means to inquire as to who exploits them, what rights they have, etc., and to protect them from their oppressors.

In our country beggary has increased greatly because of the practice of thoughtlessly giving alms to mendicants who have become lazy owing to their addiction to *ganja*, tobacco, etc., and to such others who are capable of work but remain idle. That is why one should not incur sin by giving alms, which results in supporting vice. In the United States, no one who has any capacity to work receives alms. The tenet of their religion is "He who wants to eat, must work." In our country there is no limit to laziness; anybody gets food without doing anything. A person only needs to smear ash all over his body, let his hair grow into long tangles, wear bead necklaces, or don saffron robes. Because he is a holy man, people feed him free of charge. Our people consider it an important part of religion to beg, and to give alms to those who beg. As soon as a man begins to earn well, a number of people suddenly turn up to claim a relationship with him and live off him. But should he fall on hard times, the same people would not hesitate to turn against him! This does not happen here. Everybody works according to his capacity; even small children go about selling newspapers, loudly announcing the important news items. Some shovel snow in winter. Even destitute widows earn their livelihood. Their small children do all kinds of work to help their mothers. Here even begging is turned into a form of work. There are people called Gypsies who are beggars like the *kaikadis*[8] in our country; but they entertain people by playing instruments, etc. Many beggars make monkeys or bears dance in order to amuse people. There are asylums here which give shelter to old people and children who are destitute. Even in these, suitable work is provided.

There is a large number of consumptives here. Drinking and the use of tobacco are among the chief causes of this disease; even so, these people do not rid themselves of these twin vices! Our people are also rapidly imitating these two vices and becoming terribly debilitated. The reason for our Raosahib[9] to be in delicate health, or the reason why Raosahib has a headache and is unable to meet visitors, is liquor! This vice leads to havoc at home, loss of honor outside, and a waste of money; and it carries one to Lord Yama, the deity of Death, quite soon. Even so, our people get addicted to these vices. Great indeed is our desire for imitation! Many people here are sick because of these two vices. Some say that their spleen is affected! Some say that they cannot digest food! Some say that they have no strength! Thus the bodies of many people who are addicted to liquor and tobacco have become veritable lodging houses of numerous diseases, especially consumption. Such sick persons are sent to poorhouses. Going to a poorhouse is considered to be very shameful here; there are many who say that they would rather die than go to one, and who act accordingly. There are some here who would shoot themselves but not live in these homes for destitutes. Even these sick people are made to do light work in these places, such as watering flowering plants. Self-esteem reigns supreme everywhere here. These people sincerely feel that they should not eat at the expense of others. Here nobody gives or receives money without a proper reason. In our country, most people do not even know what self-esteem and self-respect mean. They would accept anything given free, without any qualms, and say that it will tide them over for the next few months. They will borrow and, if unable to repay the debt, say that they will do so in their next life. But they feel no compunction about the fact that they would be compelled to be reborn in order to repay the debt![10]

The number of beggars who come to the United States from other countries is very large. Of all the inhabitants here, one-seventh are foreigners; of the criminals in the country, 30 percent are foreigners.[11] The chief reason is that foreigners do not get work quickly, and are prompted to commit acts which lead them to the "rent-free house." There are not many physically defective people here, who have to be supported by the general public, because those who migrate to this country leave their own only if they are strong enough. In the United Kingdom of Great Britain and Ireland, 33 persons per thousand require public support. In the United States only five persons in the same population require public support, that is, one person in every two hundred, or half a person per one hundred.

This immediately gives an idea of how low the extent of beggary, and how much work, there is in this country. I think that in our own country, the proportion of beggars must be even 150 percent! Now there are a lot of outsiders in the United States. That means that there is quite a mixture of all kinds of people here. There is also a large population of Negroes who were formerly sold here as slaves. Among the Negroes there are very few beggars or persons requiring public support. This is a good example of how a people become industrious once they get the freedom which they had lacked earlier. There are many professionals among the Negroes; some are lawyers, some barristers, some businessmen; others are engaged in some profession or another—all are hardworking. It is not yet twenty-five years since the slaves were freed; but already they have quite equaled other people in every field. This is a perfect illustration of all the advantages which flow from granting freedom to people. The people who favored the traffic in slaves claimed that the emancipation of Negroes from slavery would bring a terrible disaster upon the country, that they would ruin the country, that beggary would become rampant, robberies would increase, peace would be shattered. But happily not one of the things they predicted happened. There are those who are not qualified to do any work in spite of being able-bodied; the religious societies here consider it their duty to make such people work, and to provide them training. One-third of the amount spent on beggars in England, that is, $18,000,000, is spent on beggars in the United States. This figure shows that there are very few beggars here. Some of the reasons why there are very few beggars in the United States are as follows. Only those who are able to work emigrate to another country. There is plentiful land here which can be brought under cultivation. That is why there is a lot of work, and a hard-working person would not ever starve anywhere. Laziness has no prestige here. A person who enjoys the idleness associated with sainthood, claiming that his God would provide for him, would not receive any food here.

In olden times, convicts from Austria, Germany, and England were shipped to the United States, but now the Federal Government has made very strict laws regarding beggars and immigrants. They forbid such criminals, beggars, and persons who are lazy or unwilling to work to enter the country. When I made inquiries about the laws governing foreigners who come here to settle down, people said to me, "Why do you want such information? We do not wish to have the beggars and the unemployed people in your country to come here." This shows that our poverty and idleness have become notorious even here! These people say, "We do not mind if the industrious people from your country come here." I assured them that is exactly what would happen. How would idle people come here? If any idle person comes here from a foreign country and is incapable of, or uninterested in, working and maintaining himself, he is compelled by these people to quickly get up and go back home.

There are very few physically defective people here, that is, ones who are blind, mute, lame, crippled, etc., as mentioned above. There is one blind person in every 2,720 people, and one deaf and dumb in every 2,094. It is proper to give alms to the blind; however, if they receive some education and start working according to their ability, it benefits the nation and reduces poverty.[12]

There are many schools for the blind here.[13] Every State has at least two or three schools for the blind; all their expenses are paid by the state government. In these schools the blind are given an education through the sense of touch. The blind have a very sharp sense of hearing and touch; all their perception is concentrated in these senses. They have a quick grasp. The blind do weaving and many other kinds of work. I have brought with me some articles made by them. They are taught geography; globes and maps are specially made in order to give them knowledge through touch. They are taught mathematics. The kindergarten method of education has worked wonders for the education of the blind! There are many among the blind who sing and also many who play musical instruments. I heard a blind person play the organ in church; the sound was very sweet. The parents here take very good care of their children's eyes, etc. The mothers in our country put drops of oil in the children's eyes and smear them with lampblack;[14] this is not done here. There are also a number of schools for the deaf and mute. Even in the task of educating them, the imaginative people here have made the utmost progress! There is a school for them in New York,[15] which has 500 students. Their education seemed to me to be a marvel. There was a boy in the school who was deaf and mute, and also blind. The man who showed me around the school also showed me this terribly disabled boy. He touched his hand with his own fingers and told him, "An Indian lady has come to see you, talk to her if you wish." In a trice he wrote a few sentences about me on a machine called "typewriter" and brought the paper over. My guide gave me the paper and I have preserved it carefully. On it the boy had written in brief my name, that of my country, and my purpose in coming to this country, and also expressed his pleasure at my visit. I was astounded to see this, and felt that if a miracle could happen in this world, this was it! Besides these, there are numerous orphanages and industrial schools here. There are schools also for feeble-minded children. There are altogether 430 homes and schools of different types for the weak, the destitute, etc. There are 56 schools for the blind and the mute, and 30 schools for feeble-minded children. All the schoolteachers teach their students with great care and understanding.

The people here believe that works such as improving the conditions in prisons, visiting the prisoners, advising them, etc., are pious deeds. In our country people believe that they have no connection whatsoever with prisoners; moreover, they probably think that such a connection would bring shame upon them. Therefore nobody ever goes to a prison to inquire after them. One cannot say that absolutely all the people who go to prison are criminals. (And so what if they are? Why should we not visit them in prison to inquire after them?) An innocent person might also have occasion to go to prison. Who can know with absolute certainly whether or not he will have to go to prison? I have not yet seen a prison in India. Earlier I knew nothing at all about the prisons there, but I got some idea from Mr. Agarkar's *A Hundred and One Days in Dongri Prison* after the affair at Kolhapur.[16] Fifty years ago prisoners in the United States were treated very badly. In most cases they were locked up in dungeons or mines.[17] Even children were tormented in different ways by putting chains around their necks and shackles on their arms and legs. In short, there was a great deal of ill-treatment all around. But since good, pious men and women started visiting them, these prisons have become like our zenanas.[18] I have seen the prisons here. They are clean and have been made safe from fires. The prisoners are turned into useful people. They are advised to conduct themselves properly after being released. There are libraries for them. There are pots of flowering plants. Every Sunday is a holiday, when they pray. Good people treat them with compassion, in the belief that they have come to this pass owing to a lack of proper upbringing by their parents. There are several societies of such good people. There are many reformatories for children. The first such home was established in 1824. In 1874 there were thirty-four such reformatories, valued at $8,000,000. During these fifty years, a total of 91,402 children have been reformed, and about 70,000 children have turned out to be industrious and respectable. Moral education is provided in these homes. Great care is taken to avoid bad qualities being passed on from one to another. The prisoners here do not receive much corporal punishment, but they do get chained. In many States, electrocution is used for capital punishment, instead of hanging. When a prisoner is released after serving his term, he receives all the rights of a citizen.

There are many hospitals of different types here, for those suffering from different diseases, and also many for ordinary patients. The Government pays their expenses, and many hospitals are run at public expense. Pious people visit the patients and cheer them up in many ways. Some women visit infirmaries and sing sweet songs and psalms, and read religious books to the patients. Some tell stories and give the news, some read newspapers out loud, some play sweet instruments, some distribute sweets, some give fragrant flowers. The custom of giving flowers has become popular here. The society which gives flowers is called the Flower Mission. I have seen the pious woman who first had the idea of giving flowers. She has been bedridden for about ten years because of paralysis. Even so, she still performs many such pious deeds. There is real compassion here. In our country nobody knows what real compassion means. There are many patients there, and many hospitals are being built for them. It would be very good if anyone would visit them and speak to them sweetly, inquire after them, give them flowers, etc. We are eager to imitate the Americans and other Western people in matters like drinking, smoking, and talking of atheism. If, instead, we eagerly imitate their good qualities and customs, how greatly it would benefit us and our country!

Note in the Original Text

i. The people of our own country should give this matter serious thought. Although we belong to different denominations and religions, we can and must unite in the work of the national and public good. We may believe that by following a particular religion or denomination we will go to a special, superior place in the next world, and our neighbors who belong to another denomination or religion will go to a quite different place; but such a belief should be limited to the next world. At least in this world we have to live in the same country and on the same earth. At least in this world we do not find that the excellent divine gifts, such as sunlight, rain, wind, and earth, are available only to us and not to those of other [religious] beliefs. We can see that the Divine Grace which is shown to us is shown in exactly the same degree to our brothers and sisters belonging to other religions and denominations; why should we not treat them with friendship, courtesy, and love? Why then should we not unite in the work of national and public good? Hindus, Mohammedans, Christians, Shaivites, Vaishnavites, devotees of Ganapati, Shias, Sunnis, Episcopalians, Presbyterians, Methodists, Unitarians, Trinitarians, and believers in thirty-three *crore* gods—all these should put aside religious animosity and unite themselves in order to serve the country.[19]

8   The Condition of Women

As a child, I took great delight, like all other children, in listening to marvelous tales. Who does not enjoy legends like the Mahabharata, the Bhagavata Purana, the Ramayana, the Adbhuta Ramayana, the Jaimini, the Ashvamedha, and other such ancient literary works popular in our country?[1] And who does not find them inspiring and yearn for the strength to perform similar great deeds? But few are they, children or adults, who do not come to realize, to their disappointment, that such great deeds are beyond their capacity, in view of their lack of strength, general ignorance, and powerlessness; and, besides, that the tales themselves are but imaginary. If we are so delighted and eager to read imaginary tales and marvels, why should we not be eager to read accounts of real events? Seven years ago I had not the slightest inkling that I would really be able to witness strength such as that of Haihayarjuna, who could block the force of great rivers; and to witness goddesses like Sita, who possess similar strength and slay unconquerable demons like Ravana with a hundred or a thousand heads.[2] But, happily, in the course of time I was able to witness such wonderful things and now have the opportunity to present at least a brief account of them to my countrymen and -women.

Some months ago I chanced to see the book *Society in America,* written by the famous and scholarly Englishwoman Harriet Martineau. After visiting America in 1840 and observing the society here, she wrote the book upon her return home.[3] While describing the condition of the native women, she said: "They (the women in this country) receive no higher education at all, moreover, all avenues of acquiring it are blocked for them. The highest reach of their education consists of singing, playing musical instruments, a little reading and writing, and needlework. They enjoy no social or political freedom. Should they suffer the misfortune of widowhood or poverty, they have no recourse but to undertake work like sewing, cooking, domestic service, or similar lowly work; or to marry or remarry against their will. The laws of this country take no cognizance of women's existence at all. Women are mere prisoners of men, like slaves. There is no exception to this in political matters and in the eyes of the law, only in social life might there be an exception, though a very rare one."[4] Harriet Martineau has recorded many such observations in her book; but although very important, they cannot be cited here for lack of time and space. The one sentence, that "women are mere prisoners of men, like slaves," clearly reveals the pitiable and dreadful plight of native women about fifty years ago. The courage, powers of endurance, and unceasing effort which enabled these women to lift themselves out of this condition can be adequately described only by Saraswati, the Goddess of Learning, descended upon our earth; a mortal like me, with her limited intellect, cannot do them justice.

Thus far, kind and philanthropic people have accomplished great deeds (like the abolition of slavery, and promotion of the temperance movement) in the face of terrible adversity; but the emancipation of women was a task far more difficult than them all. Because it is obvious that to purchase slaves like livestock, make them work without wages, and block their worldly and spiritual progress is very reprehensible and cruel. It is also evident that vices like drinking cause physical and mental ruin. The harm done by these things is immediately visible to all; but the harm done by the slavery of women is generally not noticed. Like a mysterious heart disease, it remains invisible even as it continues to destroy the heart of human society. Most people think that women are living not in slavery, but in a state natural to them. The belief that women are not oppressed, and that their condition need not be any different from the present one, is so deeply entrenched in everybody's mind that it is impossible for anybody to even imagine how wretched their condition really is. What is worse, even women themselves believe that their condition is as it should be. In the past, when African Negroes were slaves in America, many of them held similar beliefs: "We may be enslaved, but this alone is our source of happiness; we are low and abject compared to everybody else, and we are utterly dependent on our master, who has the power of life and death over us." In this belief, they silently endured even the worst kind of humiliation. This state of mind is the ultimate in slavery. One cannot even begin to imagine how evil is slavery, which destroys self-respect and the desire for freedom—the two boons that God has given to humanity.

How true is the claim of many Western scholars that a civilization should be judged by the condition of its women! Women are inherently physically weaker than men, and possess innate powers of endurance; men therefore find it very easy to wrest their natural rights and reduce them to a state that suits the men. But, from a moral point of view, physical might is not real strength, nor is it a sign of nobility of character to deprive the weak of their rights. Even among the barbaric or semibarbaric people of the past and present, physical strength is seen to be generally supreme. "Might is right" is their creed; if, in accordance with it and in complete disregard of the principles of justice, one who has physical strength captures another's kingdom, he becomes the king. From this very morality has arisen the ancient and even current practice of revering brave warriors as if they were divine beings. It is the followers of this very morality who find war more palatable than peace. For them, what can be accomplished by the use of arms and physical strength is both an established dictum and justice. But, as a country advances in knowledge and civility, brute strength declines in importance and intellectual strength comes to be recognized as superior; and people begin to accord a higher status to venerable customs and common wisdom than to the pompous scriptural precepts of self-proclaimed scholars. Such people do not regard it as justice to grasp the property and rights of others just because they are weaker. For them justice means protecting the weak, forgiving those who harm them instead of retaliating, and being modest rather than arrogant about their natural strength. Thus, as people progress and expand their knowledge, they naturally develop greater innate civility and better morals. For the same reason, the tradition which believes in exercising arbitrary power over women on the grounds of their weakness is considered barbaric; and as men gain wisdom and progress further, they begin to disregard women's lack of strength, to honor their good qualities, and elevate them to a high state. Their low opinion of women and of other such matters undergoes a change and gives way to respect. Thus, one can accurately assess a country's progress from the condition of its women.

According to the natives, the social condition of England and of the Americans who have emigrated from that country is absolutely the best, because their women are honored everywhere and because they treat men and women as equals. And those who profess the Christian religion claim that women acquired a high status because of that religion, since the people of other religions do not respect their women at all; and also that when a community embraces Christianity, its women begin to progress immediately. Both these claims contain a great deal of truth, but also a great deal of falsehood, as will be apparent after some thought. The condition of women is not identical among all the communities which call themselves Christian. All peoples, like the Russians, Italians, Greeks, French, Swiss, Finnish, English, and Americans, are Christians; but there is a wide difference in the condition of their women. To claim to be the follower of a religion and to actually practice that religion are two very different things. Almost all the people in this country call themselves Christians, but not all of them practice the teachings of Christ. The doctrine which Christ taught and the practices He propounded did not differentiate between men and women; but that egalitarian view is not acceptable to everyone here. When it comes to recognizing women's worth and treating them accordingly, people show through their conduct that they regard as acceptable the doctrine of Christ, St. Paul, Moses, or even Satan, although they all claim that they find the Christian doctrine acceptable. The doctrine of Christ, and that of St. Paul who conformed to it, states that there is no difference between men and women in Christ, but that all are the children of God; whereas most of the doctrines prevailing in this country consider women to be inferior to men. Women do not have the right to climb onto the pulpit and preach like men, or to conduct religious services and rites; they have to take a vow of obedience to their husbands during the wedding ceremony; (male) preachers maintain that a husband has supremacy over his wife. This falsifies the claim of all self-styled Christians, that their religion is the cause of the freedom, high standing, and honor enjoyed by the women of England and of this country. The religion which has led to women's high state should properly be called, by these adherents of different denominations, not "our" religion but simply "the holy doctrine" or "the doctrine of Christ" (which is not the prevailing form of Christianity). The prevailing form of Christianity continues to change according to the inclination of popular opinion. From olden times, the religious heads of different denominations have followed the tradition of shaping religion in the manner of kneading a ball of wax and molding it into the shapes which appeal to them and to popular opinion. What different shapes these clergymen have given to the Christian religion and how they have changed its essence is clearly seen from the history of the native slaves and women.

The sect known as Quakers, which was founded about two hundred years ago, does not discriminate in this fashion, at least in matters of religion. According to them, God loves men and women equally. God sends a call to people according to their worth, whether they be men or women; therefore they believe that a man or a woman who has received a call from God should preach. But in other matters even Quakers considered women to be inferior to men. In the year 1840, the World Anti-Slavery Convention was held in London, and was attended by Lucretia Mott and many other eminent women as delegates of the American Anti-Slavery Society. The meeting, attended by many Quakers, was presided over by one Joseph Sturge, a famous Quaker gentleman. Even in a meeting devoted to such an altruistic cause, he refused to grant the status of delegate to the women who had dedicated themselves totally to the service of the Anti-Slavery Society, sometimes at the risk of their own lives.[5] The reason advanced was the "British tradition."

The other day (in May 1888), there was a Methodist meeting of the clergy and laity in New York City, to which many local Methodist societies had sent their representatives, including five well-known women. But they did not receive due recognition at the meeting, the reason being none other than that they were women. One thing worth remembering here is that two-thirds of the Methodists are women, and that on their support depends the livelihood of most of their clergy and the charitable works of the denomination. The same thing applies to other denominations. When it comes to religious and charitable works, the task of collecting money for them falls to the women's lot. After completing their housework or the paid work they have undertaken to earn their livelihood, they do sewing and embroidery and make beautiful articles; go from door to door and plead with people; and collect money and other things for charity and philanthropy through all such possible means, thus getting together large sums of money. But then, how to disburse this money is decided upon by men; and the presidents, vice presidents, and other members of the committees appointed for managing the charitable works are all men. All those doing secretarial and other slow, tiresome work are bound to be women. This is the fairness of the Methodists—how beautiful it looks in the clear sunlight of the nineteenth century reform! Among the Christian sects, except for the Congregationalists, Quakers, Unitarians, Universalists, a progressive branch of the Methodists, and such others, women lack the freedom to preach in church, the only reason being that they are women![6] In his Epistle to the Corinthians, St. Paul says in one place, "Let your women keep silent in the churches." Therefore women—who may be pure, educated, effective as speakers, possessed of other excellent qualities, and much more capable than male preachers, but whose only fault is that they are women— are ordered by men to shut their mouths and sit quietly even if they have received a call from God to preach.

It is not yet sixty years since the condition of native women started to improve, but even within such a short time they have begun to taste many excellent fruits of their industry and persistent effort. Even at the time when Harriet Martineau wrote about these women that they were men's slaves, and that there was no exception to this rule in political matters or in the eyes of the law, there were one or two women who had already noticed the disrespect shown to their sex and attempted to bring this injustice to the notice of American society. A hundred years ago, the sister of the famous Robert Lee in the State of Virginia and the wife of John Adams in the State of Massachusetts told government officials clearly that they would not pay taxes because they had no right to vote in political matters.[7] But nobody paid much attention to those things at the time. Later, in 1830, an opinion began to be created in this country in favor of abolishing slavery; since that time the matter of improving the condition of women has also taken shape. In 1832 William Lloyd Garrison first established the Anti-Slavery Society. He, Wendell Phillips, and many other eminent speakers gave hundreds and thousands of speeches propounding the injustice of enslaving Negro men and women. The arguments they advanced against the slavery of Africans were also applicable to the slavery of women. Realizing this, some brave and adventurous women started delivering speeches in public meetings, espousing the cause of their sex along with that of the Negro slaves.

The year 1832 should be called a golden year.[8] That year the chains of the slaves received a severe blow, and began to break. Similarly, ignorance, which was the root cause of the slavery and inferior status of women, began to decline. In this auspicious year a very famous college, known as Oberlin College, was founded in the town of Oberlin in the State of Ohio. The founders of the college made a rule to generously impart education to all who were interested, without judging their suitability by criteria such as skin color—whether black, white, yellow, or any other—or sex.[9] Not many years have passed since the condition of native women began to improve, but the Sun of their good fortune has begun to acquire greater brilliance with every passing day. Favorable signs are visible that within a few years they will obtain all the rights that men enjoy, and that this nation of the United States will become a full-fledged democratic nation. Every day women are making great strides in social and political matters. The topic to be discussed in this chapter is the matters in which they have made strides during the last fifty years or so, how society has benefited from this progress, and their current state.

Education

Education, which is the root cause of progress, began to be made available to native women in a small way about sixty years ago.[10] It is almost a hundred years since the Englishwoman Mary Wollstonecraft said publicly that women of England should receive an education.[11] In the year 1789 this woman openly claimed that the lack of education was the biggest obstacle to women's advancement in England at the time, and that it was not proper to prevent women from studying. In 1799 a woman named Hannah More wrote several books to publicly express her opinion that it was appropriate for women to be educated.[12] In 1809 a gentleman called Sidney Smith presented before the people his favorable opinion of women's education, through his books.[13] The two decades from 1789 to 1809 may be called the preface to the history of Western women's education. During these twenty years, the desire for a wide dissemination of women's education took root in the hearts of many men and women, and gained strength day by day.

In 1819 the American woman Emma Willard made the first attempt to make education available to her countrywomen.[14] That year she presented an address to the Senate of New York State with a request to establish a female seminary. The history of American women's higher education can be said to have started from this date. However, women's higher education itself did not start at this time. Until 1831 almost all the supporters of women's education said that women should get only a general education, because higher education would not only not benefit them, but would destroy their natural modesty, beauty, and usefulness to society, and make them arrogant, careless, and thoughtless. In 1832 Oberlin College in Ohio made higher education available to women along with men. The founders of Oberlin College set the world an excellent example by dismissing the prevalent, barbaric belief about women's inferiority. The city of Boston, capital of the State of Massachusetts, is famous as an old center of learning in the United States; and Boston scholars are popularly believed to be most superior and pioneers in matters of progress and public welfare. But not a single high school for girls was established in Boston until the year 1878. It was only a hundred and twenty-five years after the establishment and advancement of Harvard College (at Cambridge, Massachusetts), regarded as the jewel in the crown of America's best universities, that permission was granted for Boston girls to enter even the most inferior schools. If, keeping this in mind, one analyzes the history of native women's education (which started very recently), one is amazed at the feats achieved by women in the sphere of education in such a short time.

Now, one should not assume that the general progress in female education in the United States, which one sees today, was achieved without meeting obstacles.[15] As soon as women began to read a new book, or declared their intention to learn a new branch of knowledge, they would immediately be subjected to curses, censure, criticism, wrinkled noses, and meaningful glances everywhere —from newspapers, preachers' pulpits, the mouths of public speakers, declarations of religious meetings, and from the eyes and tongues of neighbors; and this continues even now. Only a cause which was naturally pure and had the support of eternal truth could hope to endure such a shower of stones and thunderbolts, and still survive to this day. During the last fifty years, female education has been considered in all possible ways and tested by all kinds of big and small religious leaders, medical doctors, scientists, philosophers, male teachers, college presidents, newspaper editors, and leaders of public opinion to see whether it is in accordance with the gospel, the science of anatomy, philosophy, popular custom, economics, etc., and whether it would be beneficial or detrimental to the nation. Then they found it difficult to challenge the truth, and therefore declared very reluctantly that women may be given some education.

There is a State called Colorado in the western part of the United States, in which a solid, stony, immovable range of mountains known as the Rockies has spread across the land of America since time immemorial. It seems impossible to break through it in order to cut a road and cross it. How would a river, almost a tiny stream, possess the strength to penetrate the mountain? But behold the marvel! The Arkansas River started quietly to make a way through the Rocky Mountains. Its unshakable resolve must have caused regret and surprise to the sea, the lakes, and the rivers of the plains; and the sky-high range of the Rockies must have pitied it. The smaller mountains must have censured and condemned it for this risky venture. But the Arkansas River ignored them all. It was only a small, weak rivulet, but its resolve was strong enough to lift even the mountains in its path and fling them away. With persistent effort and strong resolve it defeated even the Rocky Mountains. The tiny Arkansas clashed against that impenetrable, unbreakable stone range and carved out a way for itself right through the Rocky Mountains! Bravo, Arkansas! And bravo, American women! Even though weak like this rivulet, and lacking the support of Scriptures, money, popular opinion, or religious tradition, they clashed, only on the strength of persistent effort and resolve, against thousands of obstacles a hundred times more difficult, more impenetrable and unbreakable than the Rockies, bored tunnels right through them and cut a trail for themselves. I say once again, bravo American women!

The arguments against female education which were advanced and accepted by all, not just twenty-five but even ten years ago, are beginning to fade now. That educated women will become arrogant, neglect housework and the care of children, be unable to cook; that they lack the necessary physical, mental, and spiritual strength to study hard, pass college examinations, and complete their education in good health; that men will have to sit at home if women get educated and enter the professions or get jobs; that men will lose their livelihood; that the world will see an apocalypse—all such objections are now dead, and their corpses are being buried in deep graves. The ghosts of one or two of these objections still appear occasionally before the people and terrify the fainthearted; but, lacking bones and muscles, brains and life, [these specters] soon dissolve into nothingness and disappear!

The foremost among the institutions for women's higher education in the United States now (in 1888) are the colleges; below them rank the four secondary arrangements: (1) clubs for the promotion of education, (2) lectures, (3) correspondence societies, and (4) university examinations. The details of colleges offering higher and professional education to women in 1886 are as follows:

Colleges for women only	266
Coeducational colleges	207
Other institutions admitting women	
Agricultural and mechanical	17
Scientific	3
Medical	36
Total	529
Women registered in institutions for women only	27,143
Women registered in coeducational institutions	8,833
Total women in higher education	35,976

In addition, most schools offering middle-level education admit girls. They include 117 state-run teacher-training colleges and 36 independent (privately established) teacher-training colleges, which have a combined strength of 27,185 female students.

The primary and general public schools as well as most state-run high schools provide coeducation.[i] Seventy years ago, primary schools for girls had not been set up, whereas men had free access to education. Men could not only study in primary schools, but could also get an excellent education and vocational training in high schools, colleges, and technical schools. Today women of the United States are trying to equal men in education, in spite of popular opposition to female education and many other obstacles. This is cause for not a little surprise. The census of 1880 shows that in that year, 8 percent of all men (i.e. White American men, excluding Negroes) in the United States were illiterate, while 11 percent of White American women were unable to read and write. This proves that women are not very far behind men in general education.

A truly large-hearted woman named Mrs. Emma Willard had appealed to the legislature of the State of New York for a subsidy to a middle school for women, called the Troy Seminary, established in 1821; but the government refused to support this good cause. Mrs. Willard then regretfully wrote: "Could I have died a martyr in the cause (of female education) and thus have insured its success, I should have blessed the fagot and hugged the stake." Hundreds of large-hearted women enthusiasts of education like Mrs. Willard, knowing that government and popular opinion would not support them, dedicated themselves body and soul to the cause of emancipating their sex, saying that they were prepared even to die, and that death in such a cause would mean immortality. Like the Arkansas River, their firm resolve cut through impenetrable and unbreakable mountain ranges of great obstacles like the Rockies, and opened a safe path to women's education. Today women are provided with advanced education equal to that of men by many colleges (of which the coeducational ones are indicated by an asterisk): Oberlin College,* Vassar College, Michigan University,* Smith College, Wellesley College, Harvard Annex, Ingham University, Bryn Mawr College, Cornell University,* and many others.[16] This progress in women's education in the United States was achieved not through empty chatter, wishful thinking, and meaningless arguments, nor through lounging on soft beds with feather cushions. This golden age for the native women was ushered in by the women champions of education and some liberal-minded men by facing unpleasant allegations, enduring endless hardships, and making persistent efforts.

In the past, many people worried whether women would be able to manage the same education as men.[17] In 1858, an American man named Matthew Vassar decided to found Vassar College for women, and consulted William Chambers, the famous, learned philanthropist of Edinburgh in Scotland, on the matter.[18] Mr. Chambers expressed his astonishment and dismay at Mr. Vassar's plan, and gave him the excellent advice not to attempt to establish a girls' college because it was sure to embarrass and disappoint him, but instead to set up a school for the blind, deaf and dumb, or an asylum for the insane. Today the number of skeptical scholars like Mr. Chambers has declined considerably. On hearing that Michigan University gave women an excellent, rigorous education along with men, many institutions in different parts of Europe and the American South sent their representatives there to decide whether such an arrangement was beneficial or harmful, whether women's constitution was strong enough to stand the strain of such coeducation, and whether women's intellect could comprehend the profound knowledge imparted to men. Nowadays, perceptive men and women who have given the matter deep thought entertain no doubt whatsoever about the benefit of women's education and higher studies. The advantages of women's education to the United States and its contribution to social progress are reviewed below.

Before completing this section, I would like to cite two passages to show how public opinion regarded female education forty years ago and how it has changed since.[19] In 1850 the influential leaders of public opinion said: "Culture for women should never develop into learning. Only an unwomanly woman could try to become learned, and she would try in vain, as she has not the mental ability of a man." The leaders of public opinion in the 1880s say: "The admission of women into schools heretofore exclusively open to men is the straw on the moving current to tell us what is coming. It is in accordance with the spirit of our institutions that women shall be treated as self-determining beings."

Fifty years ago, the United States had barely four or five institutions of higher education for women. Today, it is doubtful whether one can find four or five such institutions of academic excellence in the whole country which refuse admission to women to study along with men. There was a time when people labored under the absurd misapprehension that "learning was a very dangerous thing for women; it would draw them from their domestic duties, and, therefore, it would be very pernicious for the interests of the State and society."[20] It was then that some farsighted, nonpartisan, and perceptive men and women embarked upon the great adventure of floating a small boat of their own opinion in the great river of popular opinion, and rowing against the current, said: "That women are capable of the highest culture, the generation to which Mrs. (Mary) Somerville and Mrs. (Elizabeth Barrett) Browning[21] belong will hardly deny. All must admit that it would be a great gain if we could secure to every young woman who desires it an education as thorough, generous, and stimulating as our colleges afford to young men."[ii]

Many avenues of acquiring an excellent education have recently been opened to women, and the above prediction is proving to be true. Nobody, except a half-baked and inexperienced person, dares to claim that women's intelligence is not equal to that of men. Of the elite universities in America, Columbia and Johns Hopkins have crossed the old traditional boundaries and allowed women to pass their thresholds and enter their portals. These universities have conferred their very highest degrees on two excellent women graduates—out of either generosity or lack of choice—and achieved a rare miracle which could be witnessed "neither in the past, nor in the future."[22] Harvard University at new Cambridge in the State of Massachusetts followed the model of old Cambridge[iii] and denied women the nectar of knowledge which was gathered from the inexhaustible vessel of Goddess Saraswati, and which was served to men all the time. Therefore some industrious women attempted successfully to establish an independent college and obtained the nectar from the same inexhaustible vessel, if not inside Harvard, then outside its portals.[23]

In the Eastern States, women have gained entry into the best universities, such as Michigan and Cornell; and women's colleges which vie with them, such as Wellesley, Smith, Vassar, and Bryn Mawr, have been and are still being founded. In the Western States almost all the colleges and universities admit women as well as men, so that there is no need for establishing separate colleges.

Nowhere does one see evidence of higher education having impaired women's health or beauty. Let alone small or middle-level colleges, even colleges like Cornell, Vassar, Wellesley, Smith, and Bryn Mawr have thousands of young women in higher education. I have visited each of these places and spent a few days there to investigate these and other such matters, and I have become convinced that women are well able to cope with higher education. It does not impair their beauty, nor does it change their delicate, modest disposition and make them unnatural. Many women graduates of these colleges have married and are managing their domestic life very well. They do not neglect their children or housework because they are educated; nor have the husbands of these educated women suffered or been reduced to dire straits, or their homes ruined! I visited many women graduates of the said colleges, saw their homes, and made inquiries with their husbands. I was satisfied when the husbands repeatedly said that women should have a good education.

Two years ago Miss Alice Freeman was President of Wellesley College.[24] Before she took up this position, the whole world believed that a woman would never be able to manage even a small school as its principal, let alone a college. But Alice Freeman accepted the presidency of a large college with six hundred young and promising women students and managed her duties extremely well, to the surprise of the whole world. Her learning was suitably honored by Columbia University, which, after duly examining her, awarded her the Ph.D.—the highest of all university degrees. A skeptic was worried that this president of a large college, having spent a lifetime (thirty years) in education, would be lacking in the knowledge of domestic duties and would not find a husband. It is true that she is able to run a college or organize large meetings, be a good teacher, debate with renowned scholars on scientific subjects—but what use is all this? If she cannot marry and manage her husband's home, what is the use of her education? But calm down, all ye skeptics! A learned woman like Alice Freeman could and did find a husband who is himself a scholar of no mean repute. Alice Freeman, the great Ph.D., is now an excellent housewife. She is knowledgeable about big matters related to the college, but also about small domestic matters. There is no doubt whatsoever that she is able to manage her household as well as a college with six hundred women students! Now if you ask me what happened to our leading skeptic and faultfinder, let me just say, "One who doubts is doomed to destruction; for the doubter there is neither this world nor the next, nor even happiness,"[25] and conclude this section.

Employment

The history of women's education during the half century from 1828 to 1888 is quite extraordinary, interesting, and instructive.[26] It has been mentioned above that about sixty years ago Mrs. Emma Willard presented an address to the Senate of New York State for a government subsidy to women's schools. Therein Mrs. Willard clearly explained, in keeping with the prevalent popular belief, that higher education was not necessary for women, but that general education was essential. The learned Senators of New York disapproved even this moderate request, and refused any encouragement even to women's general education. A very learned statesman won immortal fame by saying that "learning was a very dangerous thing for women; it would draw them from their domestic duties, and, therefore, it would be very pernicious for the interests of the State and society."

Some were of the opinion that the study of mathematics and law would derange women's brains and make them ill, that a study of the sciences would make them lose faith in religion, that a knowledge of Greek would destroy their womanliness and make them unruly like men. Some said that no matter what else happened, educated women would deprive men of their employment; that men would be compelled to sit at home, mind the babies and sing them lullabies, or do the cooking, because educated women would grab their jobs. Other thoughtful men said that there was absolutely no fear that women would grab men's jobs because they simply lacked the brains to acquire scientific knowledge and put it to use. A headache presupposes a head, and fear of an educated woman would arise only if she possessed the brains to acquire a good education; but where would women get the brains?[iv] There were other intelligent and experienced men who wondered how women would find the time for studies; and if they did, to what use they would put them.

There is hardly any point in discussing how far these doubts were real or imaginary. A hundred years ago women in the United States were not able to work as teachers in government schools because men believed that women lacked the strength to control rowdy children and discipline them. But in 1789 the male legislators of Massachusetts made a new law allowing women to be employed as teachers in the state-run public schools—whether to test women's ability to teach in schools or to get the job done at low salaries, it is difficult to ascertain. At that time women were unable to teach anything other than "A, B, C" and "1, 2, 3," because the kind, thoughtful, and learned men had, for fear of women's falling ill from studying too much, taken the precaution of drawing up a curriculum of the "ladies' courses." It is difficult to say whether those who studied this curriculum were able to even write a short letter in grammatically correct language, let alone prepare children for higher studies or impart higher education themselves. In due course, women expanded their knowledge by studying at home, instead of giving up in fear when confronted by a mountain of obstacles and the Chinese Great Wall of popular opposition. When the status and influence of women teachers and their usefulness in imparting general education was widely recognized, some wise people favored giving them an education somewhat higher than the curriculum of the "ladies' courses" to help them to perform their job well. Even after women were able to get higher education, the positions of college teachers were not open to them until Michigan University opened the golden gates of its Temple of Saraswati and invited them, along with men, to worship at her throne. Ever since, women have had the opportunity to occupy the positions they are qualified for, as teachers, professors, college presidents, and others (which had earlier been reserved for men), to give a good account of themselves and demonstrate the extent of their capability and intellectual strength. Now nobody doubts that women will be able to manage schools and train children properly. The triumvirate of local, state, and federal governments in the United States is so impressed by women's performance that it has entrusted women with the primary and middle-level education of almost all children. Now women teachers are beginning to handle higher education also. In the country's public educational institutions (i.e., higher, middle, and lower grade schools and colleges) a total of 273,000 teachers impart education; 154,375 of them are women. In addition, there are women teachers in many private and public high schools, teaching mathematics, chemistry, botany, astronomy, anatomy, physics, and other difficult scientific and philosophical subjects, and performing their duties well. Some are college presidents or vice presidents, some are chiefs of all city schools, some are headmistresses, some deans and some teachers of moral science. Some are engaged in writing instructive books on politics, philosophy, history, and other difficult subjects.

Some scholarly women are studying not only in the United States but also in the old universities of Europe, and earning praise from the learned people there. Professor Maria Mitchell,[27] professor of astronomy at Vassar College, has gained high proficiency in astronomy just like the scholar Caroline Herschel;[28] she has discovered new planets, won praise and an excellent prize from the Government of Russia, and made her name immortal among Western astronomers. Professor Jane M. Bancroft[29] has written a thesis on the politics of France, entitled *The Parliaments of Paris,* which has been adjudged the best book on politics by great scholars at universities such as Johns Hopkins and Cornell. The famous Professor Louisa Reed Stowell of Michigan University has gained such proficiency in microscopy that she has been made a member of the great Royal Microscopical Society of London.[30] Women scholars gain membership in all the well-known and influential scientific societies in America today, as equals of their male colleagues.

If it had been prophesied to the learned but somewhat shortsighted Senators of New York sixty years ago that the following half century would witness women entering the academic field and achieving great feats, and that half the task of imparting education and moral instruction to the countless sons of the United States would be entrusted to women, it would have seemed utterly impossible not only to the politicians of New York but also to the whole world. The extent to which educated women have advanced national education in the United States after entering the Department of Education cannot be described or praised enough. To women goes the credit of making the great effort to start the kindergarten or "children's garden" method of education which today benefits thousands of children, and which has put a stop to corporal punishment for the tender ones. Elizabeth Peabody and her students taught the kindergarten method to thousands of women; and wealthy ladies like Mrs. Shaw and Mrs. Thompson provided financial assistance to teachers like Elizabeth Peabody and helped them with the proper means to put this method into practice. When the local government of Boston refused to grant premises or expenses for kindergarten education in its Department of Public Education, Mrs. Quincy Shaw, a wealthy and philanthropic lady of Boston, resolved to help in propagating kindergarten education in her city.[31] She established many kindergarten schools in Boston in a spirit of charity, and has followed the practice of spending $36,000 (about Rs. 108,000) on their development every year continuously for the past twelve years. Now the government has realized the value of this educational method and granted permission to start it in all the public schools. The famous philanthropist of New York, Mrs. Elizabeth Thompson, spends up to $67,000 every year on child education and vocational education.[32] She spends most of her income on children's education and lives the simple life of a nun. It is because educated women like Elizabeth Peabody, Mrs. Shaw, and Mrs. Thompson have devoted their energies and money to this noble cause that the system of education in the United States has progressed thus far.

Educated women of the United States serve as teachers in two ways: one is to teach in educational institutions, and the second is to improve people's minds by giving them a moral education through newspapers. Women have taken to the journalistic profession for the last twenty-five years or so. The earlier practice, by and large, was for anybody to write whatever he wanted in the newspapers. There was no special restriction on the use of vulgar language in newspapers. Educated women did not approve of this, because the papers were read by young boys and even girls; therefore they began to bring all sections of the newspapers, one by one, under their purview. This practice still continues today, and is very beneficial. Every newspaper which has a women's section is very careful to avoid reports unfair to women or articles violating morality. Besides, these newspapers acquire a greater interest because of the sweet language and style used by women. Prominent newspapers such as the *New York Herald*, the *Philadelphia Ledger*, the *Boston Transcript*, the *Boston Herald*, and the *Chicago Inter-Ocean*[33] enjoy strong support from women journalists. Every reputed newspaper invariably has a women's section. Now vulgar language is usually not seen in newspapers. Women are able to discuss matters such as their own and their children's needs, what should be done for the benefit of children and society and which customs should be changed, the ideal school curriculum, the kind of laws necessary for ensuring equal justice for men and women, and so on. From the time of Creation, strong men, in the arrogance of their physical might, had lost their sense of duty and shut women's mouths. But they have opened now, not to the detriment of society but for its good, as people have realized.

Now women are no longer content to run only a section of a large newspaper, but have started independent newspapers themselves. There are hundreds of newspapers managed entirely by women. The *Boston Woman's Journal, Chicago Justicia*, the *Union Signal, Beatrice Women's Tribune, Women's Work for Women, Children's Work for Children, St. Nicholas, Women's Magazine*, and many such papers and magazines are doing very useful work in improving social and political matters as well as public education. The weekly paper the *Union Signal* grew in a novel manner. It was started about seven years ago by four or five women with capital of $2,500. At that time temperance was not a popular subject—nor is it so today—but this paper was started by the officials of the Woman's Temperance Union,[34] and it was doubtful whether it would run. Even so, it seems to have become popular now. It now has capital of $50,000 and over 40,000 subscribers. The same women's union which runs this newspaper has started four or five other newspapers to spread the message of temperance. In 1888 this society published 52,000,000 printed pages' worth of material and provided great support to temperance in the United States. During the same year they received $93,000 for their work of printing. The future of the *Boston Woman's Journal* was also in doubt, because it supports the view that women should obtain the same political rights as men. Just as the people of the United States opposed women's education thirty years ago, they oppose women's political rights today. But just as women, through ceaseless effort, changed public opinion with regard to education, they are resolved to change it also in this regard; and there are signs that their resolve will lead to success. In some places women are found to be even more suitable in the field of journalism than men. Now there is no need for pure-minded men, women, and children to unwillingly read shoddy newspapers for lack of an alternative.

The greatest benefit arising from women's entry into diverse professions comes from women doctors. Ignorant women are unable to protect their own health or that of their children. This ignorance is very harmful to mankind, which makes it essential for women to possess medical knowledge. But people of the United States used to hold very strange beliefs in this regard. About thirty years ago, when a medical college for women was opened in Philadelphia, people persecuted its founders because they believed that women would be ruined by medical studies, lose their innate delicacy, and become useless for domestic work. Lack of knowledge breeds strange beliefs. Half the people in the world hasten to deliver their opinion about something without getting adequate information first; this creates doubt in the minds of the other half. If only they would inform themselves adequately before giving their favorable or unfavorable opinion, it would prevent the untold harm which the world suffers—harm which results because new customs cannot be started or new innovations put into practice. Now, thirty years after the founding of the Woman's Medical College, the people of the United States have realized that women doctors are very useful to society. Today there are over one thousand licensed women doctors in the United States; their annual net income ranges from $100 to $50,000.[35] Now women doctors are greatly appreciated everywhere, and people are thoroughly convinced that women are more skilful than men in treating patients.

Let me cite an example of the change in public opinion in this regard. About twenty years ago a famous society of male doctors, known as the Philadelphia County Medical Society, had boycotted women doctors, and resolved not even to look at their faces. The reason they gave was that a woman's pure mind would be sullied by the study of medicine and she would engage in unnatural conduct; also, possessing brains lighter than a man's, she would be unable to gain mastery over a difficult science such as medicine, and would be likely to destroy life on a large scale. While boycotting women doctors for the last-named reason, these brethren of ours seemed to have forgotten that they themselves were the elder brothers of Yamaraj, who was known to have killed many more people than Yami ever did.[36] In 1888 there are signs that the muddy brains of this County Medical Society have cleared up a great deal. They have not only withdrawn the boycott of women doctors but invited them humbly to accept membership in their famous society. Twenty-five years ago, not even one or two well-known medical societies had women members; now there may not be even one or two reputable medical societies which lack women members.

Whether or not women's brains function competently in difficult scientific subjects like medicine will become clear from the following anecdote. There is a prestigious medical society in the United States which gives substantial awards to doctors who write excellent essays on a topic specified by it. On one occasion, the society had invited essays on the topic, "The Question of Rest for Women during Menstruation."[37] One of the essays, among the four or five written by candidates at the time of the examination, was adjudged to be the best, and it was resolved to give an award of $500 to the author. This author had cleverly signed with only initials rather than the full name. The society was deeply prejudiced against women doctors and had not imagined that women would write such difficult papers. But after the prize was announced, it was discovered that the author was a woman, the famous Dr. Mary Putnam Jacobi of New York. After realizing this, the partisan medical association found it very difficult to admit that a woman had written such a good essay and was awarded the prize. But what could it do? Having already declared its decision, it was compelled to reluctantly give the prize to Dr. Jacobi.

New York City has a medical college known as the New York Infirmary which is considered to be very prestigious among the best governmental or independent medical colleges in the United States.[38] Needless to say, its founder is a woman doctor who is counted among the best doctors in the United States. When Elizabeth Blackwell, founder of the New York Infirmary, returned home in 1850 after studying medicine and obtaining medical experience in Europe, she saw the acute need for women's hospitals.[39] In the large public hospitals under the supervision of reputable male doctors, women—who were thought to possess inferior brains—were not allowed to study how to treat patients, perform surgery, etc. In 1857 this industrious lady, together with her sister, founded her famous hospital, with a medical college attached to it. She was assisted by other equally industrious and altruistic women. Her example was followed by the women of Boston who founded the New England Hospital for Women and Children in 1862.[40] Newly graduated women work here as well as in the New York Infirmary to gain valuable experience of medical practice by treating patients, performing surgical operations, etc., and by watching the other doctors. Our dear countrywoman Dr. Anandibai Joshee spent some time as an intern at this New England Hospital, after graduating from Philadelphia. Following Boston, the women of Philadelphia established a hospital for women and children, attached to the women's medical college there; it also offers internships to newly graduated women doctors. Similarly there are the Chicago Hospital for Women and Children in the city of Chicago, the Pacific Hospital for Women and Children in the city of San Francisco, the Ohio Hospital in the city of Cincinnati, and the Northwestern Hospital in the city of Minneapolis. These seven excellent hospitals and colleges in the Northern States, established by women and also run by women, shine with extraordinary brilliance like the seven stars in the constellation of the Pleiades in the northern skies, and are a source of great happiness to the men and women who look to them with hope and expectancy. It is good news that the women of England are following the example of the women of the United States, by establishing colleges and teaching hospitals.

To date there are thirty-six medical colleges in this country, established only for women. Most of the teaching there is also conducted by women. Many women doctors work as teachers even in coeducational colleges. This proves that the prevalent belief in the United States, that medical education will ruin women, has undergone a change. After women started studying medicine, medical experts began to regard the human body and anatomy as sacred. Before women were admitted as students, anatomy lessons led to vulgar practices which have now ceased altogether, because the modesty and very praiseworthy morals of the women students made the male teachers and students ashamed of their vulgar behavior. Now the presence of women has improved the teaching style and language of anatomy to such an extent that people want to teach it even to young children of eight or ten.

Another useful profession undertaken by women is the practice of law.[41] In the year 1868, Washington University in the city of St. Louis agreed to teach women law. In 1869 Arabella Mansfield became the first registered lawyer and began to practice law;[42] since then most large universities have allowed women to study law in their schools. The doubt entertained by many as to women's ability to study a difficult subject like law has almost completely vanished now. Their capability has been proven by their clear legal arguments, competence equal to that of famous male lawyers, and most of all, their modest conduct in the courts of law. There are hundreds of registered women lawyers in the United States, who work through small firms as men do; there are twenty-one such firms started by couples where both husband and wife are lawyers.

There were many who objected that it would be difficult for women to protect their modesty and decorum in law courts where all kinds of cases, good and bad, would be tried. But the objectors should have realized that court cases involve not only men but also women. Although womankind does not produce as many culprits as mankind does (which is indeed praiseworthy and creditable to womankind), some of the culprits do happen to be women. Their true feelings can be better understood by a lawyer of their own sex than by a man. Every thinking person must realize how difficult it is for a woman to be in a place which is full of men, without a single woman around. Moreover, it should not be difficult for a respectable woman to go where respectable men are present—and men in the position of judges and lawyers are bound to be respectable. The probability of getting due justice for women offenders increases with the advent of women lawyers. Be that as it may, experience shows that women lawyers of the United States have not lost their natural modesty and dignity in any way. All the men in the law courts where women lawyers are present treat them with due respect; moreover, the rules which prohibit smoking, bad language, and improper conduct in the courtrooms are being more closely observed since women entered them. Nobody can assess women's proficiency in law without seeing for themselves their work in the Supreme Court and other courts of the United States. Men have been practicing law for hundreds of years in the United States, and women obtained the right to pass law examinations only twenty years ago. Within this short span of time, these brave women have caught up with highly reputed male lawyers. Women have not yet produced famous lawyers like O'Connell, Curran, Webster, and Choate; but they may very well do so in the future.[43] Besides, it is not as if all male lawyers are so famous.

Since 1868, a monthly legal journal called *Legal News* has been published in Chicago, edited by Myra Bradwell, president of the largest publishing house of legal books in the United States.[44] The massive volume known as *Bradwell's Appellate Court Reports,* prepared under this lady's supervision, is very famous and is consulted by most lawyers. Another woman, named Catharine Waite, publishes the fortnightly *Law Times* of Chicago, which is also reputed among the legal community for its excellence. In 1886 the women graduates and students of law at Michigan University formed the "Equity Club" with the objective of establishing friendships among women lawyers not only in the United States but in all countries where women have the right to practice law, thus achieving the general advancement of women through mutual help. Although men have been practicing law for thousands of years, one has never heard of their having formed a similar association for the common good of the male sex, irrespective of the distinctions of class and nation. This is an excellent example of how women make good use of any power they acquire.

The fourth important profession which women have entered is preaching. During the initial years after the founding of Christianity, Christian women had the same right to preach as men did. The rule at the time was that only a person—whether a man or a woman—who was chosen by God and endowed with this holy power should preach. The Christian doctrine preached by Christ is simple and its rules apply equally to men and women. The God of Christ imparts His Holy Spirit equally to men and women without distinction of sex. He is not partisan like man and does not entrust the task of preaching only to men. He gives the right gifts to the right person, and distributes such gifts to men and women in many different ways. As regards qualities like civility, artistic skills, intelligence, and devotion, it cannot be said that some belong only to men and some to women as typical of their sex. But when the Christian religion came under the control of the Romans, who regarded women as inferior, they incorporated their own beliefs and prejudices into it. The Roman Catholic bishops and monks regarded women as an enemy like Satan; it was they and others like them who deprived women of their right to preach. Until recently, women with a divine call to preach had to refrain from speaking because of the restriction imposed upon them by partisan men, and had to listen quietly to what men said. But the light of Reason in this nineteenth century has shown men their mistake. Many nonpartisan bishops in most Christian countries have begun to say that women should have the right to preach. In the United States one hundred and sixty-five women of different denominations are registered preachers. The people of this country are beginning to see that on many occasions women preachers are more easily able to evangelize than male preachers. This and other reasons have strengthened the public desire for more women preachers.

Stenography, that is shorthand writing, is another occupation taken up by women. They have become so skilful at it that these days great and famous newspaper editors and lawyers in the United States are eager to employ women stenographers in their offices, and entrust them with great responsibilities. The women in this occupation earn much more than average women schoolteachers. After learning the system of shorthand writing for a year or so and after completing a short apprenticeship, these women are able to copy down verbatim entire speeches made in law courts and in public meetings. For this work they earn wages ranging from five to twenty dollars per hour.

When the learned Englishwoman Harriet Martineau visited the United States in 1840, women here were free to engage in seven low-level jobs, namely: (1) teaching children the alphabet and mathematical tables, (2) tailoring, (3) running boardinghouses, (4) domestic service, (5) working as compositors in print shops, (6) folding pages and stitching them in book binderies, and (7) working as operatives in factories. But times have changed.[45] Women have become educated, and those who are qualified to do better jobs are no longer content with these. Although they do not receive much help or encouragement from the United States federal and state governments, they develop their God-given imagination aided by a sharp intellect, firm resolve, and hard work. The census of 1880 shows that the women of the United States were engaged in three hundred different occupations. In Massachusetts alone there were 251,158 women engaged in 284 different occupations, earning an annual income ranging from $150 to $3,000.

Some say that women are lacking in imagination because their brains are smaller, that all the inventions to date are men's. We say that women did not invent things because nobody gave them scope and encouragement to develop their inventiveness, and not because their brains are smaller. It has also happened that women have had new ideas, but, true to their natural generosity, have allowed men to take the credit. For example, the sister of the famous European singer [sic] and musician Beethoven composed many excellent and extraordinarily melodious musical pieces, and allowed them to be made public under her brother's name.[46] They have helped to immortalize Beethoven's fame, but very few know that the compositions were his sister's. Similarly Caroline Herschel, sister of the astronomer William Herschel, discovered several planets and provided able assistance to her brother in his astronomical observations with her extraordinary mathematical abilities.[47] But Caroline Herschel, whose ceaseless efforts and selfless assistance made William Herschel famous, was not credited by the world with a share in her brother's success. One reason why women like Beethoven's sister allowed their own inventions and discoveries to be made public under the names of their male kin or friends was their natural generosity; another reason was the barbaric belief in most countries in the past that it was shameful for women to attract notice either through an invention or any other act. We still hold this belief in our country. In the United States women's ideas are just beginning to receive a little encouragement. Even in such a short time they have made 1,935 inventions and discoveries which they have patented with the United States Government. They are not minor inventions, but ones of a kind which clearly displays women's deep scientific knowledge. For example, in 1845 a woman invented a submarine telescope, another invented life jackets and rafts for seafarers, yet another constructed a steam generator. A woman made improvements in the steam engine of the locomotive, another found a way of reducing the sound of elevated railways, a third thought of a scheme to prevent the loss of standing crops due to flooding, and a fourth made a non-inductive electric cable. Women have made many useful machines for lifting grain onto barges, for winnowing grain, for harvesting fields, etc. Thus there is no room for the charge that women are not inventive.

It must be known to many that in China and in some parts of India, women work as boatmen. It is not customary for women in the United States to work in this capacity, but they are likely to do so in the future. Of the numerous steamers on the large rivers Hudson and Mississippi, some have women navigators as captains who perform their duties efficiently and systematically. It would be difficult to find many occupations in the United States in which women are not engaged. During the last forty years, when they have been allowed into different occupations, their means of earning a livelihood have multiplied. Of all the farmers in the United States, 7 percent are women who manage their own farms. Sixteen percent of the artisans are women; over 600,000 women support themselves through handicrafts. In addition, there are 60,000 women who are independent traders or their agents. Thousands of women are telegraphists, railway ticket clerks, and post office workers. About 1,370,000 women work as cooks and domestics.

Legal Rights

It is both surprising and regrettable that for all the progress in the United States, women have been granted very few legal rights.[48] The social restrictions prevailing in the United States stem mainly from ancient English law, which in turn is founded on the Commandments of Moses and Roman law. Keeping this in mind enables one to solve the riddle as to why women are treated as greatly inferior in American law. In the new States in the West, there are several changes in laws pertaining to women; for example, the law stipulates that the house in which a married man lives with his wife should be treated as hers and not his. But in most of the Eastern States a widow is not allowed to stay in her late husband's house for more than forty days after his death without paying rent! The compassionate and learned men in the State of Maine have taken pity on the grieving widow and allowed her to stay in her deceased husband's house for ninety days! These days many States have granted married women the right to dispose of their self-earned property according to their wishes. The law states that they do not have a right to money earned by doing work at home, such as tailoring, drawing, and painting, but only to money earned by gainful employment outside the home. In several States women have a full right to the movable and immovable property gifted by their father or brother, and married women have a right to a third of their deceased husband's movable assets. But in many States they have no right to self-earned assets or those inherited from their father, and no share whatsoever in their husband's property.

In New York and many other States, a mother has no right over her minor children. A father may give guardianship of his children to whomever he wishes during his lifetime or through his last will and testament. Thus the husband has the right to give away the children his wife has borne, against her will. Only if he is of unsound mind or dies intestate does the mother obtain custody of her minor children. The children born to legally wedded couples are the father's children by law; the mother can claim no right to them. Only the children of unmarried women or prostitutes are regarded as their mother's. A couple of years ago, there was a respectable woman whose heartless husband tried to give away her tender babes against her wishes. The poor mother could not endure the separation from her own flesh and blood. Then, in order to get guardianship of her children, she set aside her modesty and took a false oath in the court of law that they were not her husband's children. Only then did she get her children back. See how the laws of so-called civilized countries insult women's modesty, maternal love, and God-given natural rights! Though not quite human demons, the makers of these laws probably belong to the class of whom it has been said "We know not who they may be!"[49] Only in the three States of Kansas, New Jersey, and Iowa can mothers obtain custody of their children.

A few years ago, in Massachusetts and some other States, women did not have the right to be buried in graves next to their husband's; now this law has changed. Immediately after getting married, a woman becomes her husband's prisoner. The priest makes her take the vow of obedience to her husband. The movable and immovable property gifted by her father or brother, her jewelry, and such other possessions go into her husband's hands.[v] A few years ago a woman could not claim a right to the clothes she stood in, but now the law has forbidden husbands to sell or pawn their wives' dresses in order to fill their own pockets.

The laws governing marriage and divorce differ widely throughout the United States, which causes a great deal of confusion in the social order. The good people of this country, especially the Woman's Temperance Union and its supporters, have been striving for a long time to ensure that laws regarding marriage should be just, and that they should be uniform throughout the country.

There is a law which entitles citizens of the United States to obtain justice in a court of law through a jury of twelve men who are their peers. But women do not have the right to trial by a jury of their own sex, who are their real peers. Men—even though they be a hundred times more foolish than women, or riddled with vice—do not allow the legislature to lift a finger without consulting them while enacting federal or state laws. But women—no matter how learned, intelligent, thoughtful, and moral—have no right to vote for the federal or state legislatures. This makes men far superior to women in the eyes of the law; therefore, if they as jurors try a case involving a woman, it does not mean that the woman defendant is tried by a jury of her peers. Except for the Territory of Wyoming, every other part of the United States has denied women this important right of an ordinary citizen, solely on the ground that they are women. Even so, these diligent women are trying to win political rights, and there are hopeful signs that their efforts will be crowned with success in the course of time.

Collective Effort and National Organizations

When the democratic republic of the United States was founded, Benjamin Franklin suggested that the national seal be inscribed with the motto "E pluribus unum" or "One out of many." Now one can see this motto on the national seal everywhere in the United States. Furthermore, we can see, hear, and experience it at every step in the actions of these people. The power of the United States lies not in its artillery, cavalry, or vast army, but in the people's wisdom and in the truth of the motto "One out of many." When women were uneducated and generally inexperienced in worldly matters, they were ignorant of this truth, and therefore did not accomplish great things. With the increase in their education and knowledge, this eternal truth has awakened in their hearts and shines with greater brilliance with every passing day.

Though famous throughout the world for its progressiveness, the United States did not have a single important women's association fifty years ago. Women would just sit at home or gather at a neighbor's house to gossip, or do some sewing in aid of churches, priests, or the poor. Nobody even imagined that women were capable of doing anything more important than this. Women themselves, apart from men, had no idea of their real worth, capability, and mental powers. Fifty years ago women supporters of education in England founded an association called the Bluestockings Club, with the aim of promoting general education.[50] It became the laughingstock of the world at the time, and "Bluestockings" became a derogatory word. Self-styled modest women would quake and tremble at the thought of a women's association and of women attending its meetings to discuss educational advancement. Everybody thought it sinful for women to attend public meetings or to address them. But the light of this progressive century has dispelled the darkness of such a belief.

The learned American woman Frances Willard has said that this glorious nineteenth century has seen many wonderful scientific discoveries; but the most wonderful of them all is Woman's discovery of herself. This is borne out by considering the history of women's collective effort during the last forty years to promote their own welfare and that of their society and country, by forming a number of associations. In 1848 a few courageous, progressive, and learned women like Lucretia Mott and Elizabeth Cady Stanton established an important women's society to work for women's equal right to education and employment, as well as for their political rights.[51] Women's collective effort can be said to have started from this date. From that time until 1869, perhaps a couple of small women's societies were established, but there is no record of their having done anything special to achieve national stature. No "National Convention of Women" had come into existence before 1858,[52] not only in the United States but anywhere in the world. Until that time nobody imagined that women could establish a national association and manage all its work smoothly.

About 1860 signs of a terrible civil war became visible in the United States. A controversy arose between the Northern and Southern States over the slavery of Negroes, and it flared into enmity. In 1860–61 the Southern States declared war against the Northern States, and the terrible war which was fought between the two until 1865 devastated American families everywhere. Initially the Civil War caused untold misery, poverty, and suffering; however, they were immediately followed by great good, just as the deadly Poison was immediately followed by Nectar and other marvelous and brilliant Gems.[53]

President Lincoln became the leader of the Northern States, abolished African slavery, and called upon strong able-bodied American men to volunteer for the army to quell the Southern rebellion and protect the country's honor. When the brave Northern men went to war, honoring President Lincoln's call, they did not have any uniforms (trousers, jackets, socks, etc.). Nor were there any organizations to supply these or other materials for war. When the war started and news came that the soldiers needed uniforms, the women of almost all the towns in the Northern States gathered in the churches and started sewing uniforms. Initially they supplied uniforms to last the soldiers for three months. This event showed the women the result of collective effort and its tremendous benefit to society and the nation.

A little later, the American Civil War assumed terrible proportions, and the fighting spread everywhere. The Northern States established a committee called the Christian Commission, with the aim of providing spiritual solace to the soldiers by sending clergymen to the battlefield to preach to them and to administer the last rites. The task of collecting money for the expenses of the commission fell to the women's lot, while men occupied the positions of president, vice president, and so on. Women worked very hard to collect large sums of money, which they delivered to the commission, and with which the commission sent hundreds of clergymen to preach to the soldiers. The commission's intention was undoubtedly very praiseworthy; but the soldiers, wounded on the battlefield, dying of hunger and thirst, and suffering agonies, did not have much interest in listening to sermons. On the other hand, the clergymen who had gone there to ensure the soldiers' spiritual welfare did not know how to achieve their physical welfare by alleviating the suffering of their "temporal" bodies. The poor wounded soldier could not be blamed for not tolerating the chatter of the clergymen, who started preaching instead of providing physical aid when he was severely wounded in the arm or the leg. This made many people realize that it was necessary to create a separate organization to give physical aid to wounded soldiers, and that it was desirable for this organization to appoint women to nurse and look after them. This led to the establishment of the Sanitary Commission.

The very existence of this commission and its great achievements were impressive; but what astonished the world even more was the feat of the American women who supported it, supplied it with all the requisite equipment from beginning to end, and managed it. The commission sent not hundreds but thousands of male and female nursing staff to the battlefield. They made proper arrangements for the regular meals of the wounded soldiers of the allied army (and also of some destitute enemy soldiers), set up hospitals on the battlefield, buried dead soldiers, and gave succor to the poor and the helpless. It was difficult for the commission to find the large sums of money and supplies needed for these numerous tasks. The Government treasury had no money, and there was not a single person who possessed the wealth to finance the commission's formidable expenditure, or at least the generosity to donate it. That was when the prominent women in the working subcommittee of the commission thought of a clever plan. Mary A. Livermore[54] and a couple of other women proposed to put the plan into practice, and sent an appeal to many people in Illinois and other States to inform them of their aims and their plan of action. Shortly, all the newspapers in the Northern States published the news that some industrious women of Chicago were proposing to hold a charity bazaar where articles gifted by generous people would be sold at a high price and the proceeds donated to the Sanitary Commission; and that those interested in supporting this admirable enterprise should send whatever they could to the address of a certain lady in Chicago.

The women organizers of the charity bazaar had estimated that, if properly managed, it would yield a profit of at least $25,000. This made learned men and respectable newspaper editors laugh. They thought that not only did the women lack sense enough to earn $25,000, but they were sure to end up ruining the whole charity bazaar. Some sneered contemptuously and said that there would be a "potato parade" in Chicago on that day. But the brave and diligent women ignored public denunciation and ridicule, and started working day and night to make their effort a success. Women of Illinois and many other States sent clothes, novelties, many kinds of preserves and pickles, sweets, and numerous other things to Chicago. The bazaar opened on the appointed day. Some good farmers around Chicago, perhaps with the intention of teaching a lesson to the critics of those benevolent women, loaded their carts with vegetables, flowers, potatoes, and other things and brought them to the bazaar with great fanfare. The intelligent women who had organized the bazaar had made excellent arrangements. Thousands of people visited the bazaar with diverse motives, but were pleasantly surprised to see the excellent arrangements, the civility of the organizers, and similar things, and ended up making some purchases. After the bazaar was over, people discovered that the sale proceeds, after deducting all expenses, yielded a net profit five times higher than the organizers' estimate. The hardworking women of the Sanitary Commission made a profit of about $125,000 (about Rs. 375,000) and dispatched it for the commission's use. Many such bazaars were held after that in aid of the Sanitary Commission. The last two were held at New York and Philadelphia, where the profits amounted to $1,000,000 (Rs. 3,000,000) and $1,200,000 (Rs. 3,600,000), respectively. It was women who thought of the idea of the bazaar, they who managed it from beginning to end, and they who made all the big and small articles which were sold. This capability, organizational ability, political insight, foresight, and perseverance astonished the men, who had arrogantly thought that they alone possessed these qualities and who had babbled that women had no capacity for practical work; while the good people who had recognized women's true worth applauded them.

The Sanitary Commission was a kind of national benevolent association, and it gave women the first opportunity to work alongside men, in high and low positions. The fetes and bazaars organized in aid of the commission yielded innumerable benefits and allowed massive tasks to be undertaken and carried through to completion. All this made the women realize the truth that great aims can be achieved if many work together collectively, smoothly, and in an organized manner. It also showed the world what mighty deeds women are capable of when they are given the education, freedom, and opportunity to work. The famous and benevolent Englishwoman Florence Nightingale set aside the English-style seclusion of women, went to the Crimean War, nursed wounded soldiers, made proper arrangements for patients on the battlefield, and set an excellent example for all the compassionate women of the world.[55] How well Miss Nightingale's example was followed by the American women is shown by the American history of the years between 1860 and 1866. While the Civil War lasted, women of the Northern States managed not only their homes but also the jobs and tasks of men; they collected large sums of money and innumerable things required by charitable associations like the Christian and Sanitary Commissions. Moreover, thousands of them went to the battlefield and worked day and night to nurse and serve the tired and weary, wounded and half-dead soldiers. At high noon or in the middle of the night, they went personally and in the nick of time to help wherever help was needed, even in the thick of battle, ignoring hunger, thirst, and physical discomforts. Hundreds of millionairesses left their wealthy homes and went into self-imposed exile to alleviate the suffering of their countrymen on the battlefield, and risked their lives doing a variety of good deeds; at times they lost their physical strength, movable and immovable property, and even their invaluable lives! Blessed indeed are these saintly, philanthropic matrons!

From 1865 to date, a number of women's organizations have been established in the United States, with many more to come. Not only in the United States but also in England, France, Germany, Finland, Norway, Italy, and other countries, local and national organizations have been set up, with a variety of aims. The reason for the existence of these women's national organizations was that women's innate capability was seen by the world through associations like the Civil War Sanitary Commission; and that women recognized their own worth and strength, and realized that enormous tasks could be accomplished if many undertook an enterprise with a single aim and collective effort. Women then began to put this newly acquired knowledge to good use. During the last twenty-five years or so, at least forty women's national organizations have been founded and are functioning very smoothly. After the end of the American Civil War and the dismantling of the Sanitary Commission, hundreds or even thousands of women's organizations, big and small, came into being. The words "women's organization," which women were ashamed to utter fifty years ago, have become universally acceptable today. Now it would be difficult to find a town of a thousand inhabitants which does not have at least one women's organization. In every town and city, one finds a variety of women's organizations—for the Promotion of Education, Mutual Improvement, Aid to the Poor, Temperance, Protection of Orphans, Protection of Children, Rehabilitation of Fallen Women, Promotion of Music, Charity, Demand for Legal Rights, Social Progress, Advancement of Women, and so on. Hundreds of such women's organizations are ever ready to devote all their energies to good deeds, for the elevation of society and the nation. Fifty years ago women were ignorant and unable to appreciate the greatness of collective effort; so they did their religious and philanthropic work separately, and failed to achieve anything substantial. Now Ignorance has lost its sway and Reason has taken command. Women have realized the tremendous advantages of collective effort undertaken by many with a single goal in mind and after mutual consultation. Now women are equal partners with men in undertaking good works for national progress in the United States. I cannot describe these women's organizations in detail for lack of space, but let us consider the nature and salient achievements of some of them.[vi]

In every country we see that women are the guardians of religion and morality. In all countries and all communities, women are the ones who protect their religion by their pure and pious conduct, charity, devotion to God, and total sacrifice of everything in defense of religion. During the last forty years, these invaluable qualities of women have been discovered in Christian countries, and women have been given the opportunity to conduct religious services independently in the light of their own conscience, which is of great benefit to the world. About twenty-five years ago, the first women's missionary society was founded in this country. Now most Christian denominations have established women's missionary societies of their own. Together these societies have a total of about 1,500,000 women as members; they pay over $2,000,000 (Rs. 6,000,000) annually as membership fees; and they utilize this money, through their representatives and presidents, for evangelical activities and for aid to the destitute. All these women's missionary societies taken together publish over 125,000 copies of evangelical newspapers and magazines, and distribute them widely. In addition, they publish and distribute numerous small religious tracts. The women of these societies organize 500,000 meetings per year, where they give religious sermons, read papers, and arrange lectures by famous and learned speakers. All the work of these societies and meetings is managed by the women themselves. All the officeholders, such as president, vice president, secretaries, superintendents, speakers, preachers, treasurers, and editors of newspapers and magazines, are women; and they alone manage all the work. They are not content with doing charitable work themselves, but also take along their sons and daughters, from a very young age, to attend evangelical meetings; often they arrange meetings only for children, in order to inculcate in them a taste for charitable work. In this manner they impress deeply on the tender, pure hearts of the children the truth that an endeavor undertaken collectively by many, with but a single thought, acquires great strength, and that mutual friendship and respect yield untold happiness. A very highly respected, learned American woman has said in her description of missionary societies that twenty-five years ago it would have seemed much easier for the women of this country to fly to the moon than to speak at public meetings, present papers, preside over meetings, deliver sermons, run newspapers, and so on.

Since this large body of missionary women came into existence, women have realized their own worth and strength. In the past, only male preachers went to evangelize in other countries as representatives of missionary societies. Only if they were married to missionary men could women serve abroad—without, however, the permission or leisure to preach. The general belief at the time was that women were not capable of preaching, let alone of traveling by themselves to far-off lands to evangelize. The orthodox Christian societies still do not ordain women as clergy; however, hundreds of unmarried or widowed women belonging to these societies, who are educated and devout, are ever ready to travel long distances, even alone, within their own country or abroad. Their aim is to emancipate the women there, both rich and poor, from the clutches of falsehood and ignorance. The domestic societies of missionary women bear the expenses of these evangelical women, finance and manage the boys' and girls' schools they have started, and send them all the necessary supplies and aid.

Women's Clubs

After women's missionary societies began to be established in this fashion, many learned and farsighted women developed a strong desire to start women's clubs. Although societies and clubs are generally similar, there is an important difference between them. A society is an association established with a single chief aim, and only those who subscribe to that aim can join it as members. A club is not established with a sole object; it assembles people of diverse beliefs, so that a single club can undertake different types of activities. Because of this diversity of opinions and ways of thinking among the members, each member gains a wide general knowledge from the numerous views expressed on any topic being discussed. Realizing that women need such wide knowledge, some diligent American women founded the first American women's club twenty years ago, under the name Sorosis.[56] The word "Sorosis" is derived from the Greek and means an assembly or coming together of many. When the Sorosis Club came into being, many expressed reservations about its usefulness, considering that women's missionary societies were already in existence. There was no prior model for this club. Although the founders of the Sorosis Club did not acknowledge a specific aim, they had a grand design in mind. At the time, women did not have practical wisdom like men, nor did women of different views communicate with each other; therefore they remained narrow-minded (like frogs in a pond), and were prejudiced and ready to detect and criticize the faults of others. The founders of Sorosis knew that a familiarity with diverse opinions in large gatherings would dispel the prejudices born of ignorance, and that women would be able to act with a single aim and achieve great things.

The establishment of Sorosis showed everybody the numerous advantages of a club; and it soon assumed a variegated and universal character by promoting knowledge and friendship, undertaking charitable work, helping the destitute, and so on. The club surveyed the condition of orphaned and abandoned infants, and of infant asylums, in New York City, and published the information. The club also reformed existing infant asylums and earned credit for founding two new ones. It also surveyed the condition of women factory workers in New York City, their treatment by the factory owners, and the reforms necessary in their condition; and presented these findings before the public, thus greatly benefiting the women workers. The club was the first to petition the management of New York University and of Columbia University to admit women students along with men. Due to lack of space it is not possible to give a description of the hundreds of important and beneficial undertakings of this club. Sorosis prohibits a discussion of three topics: religion, politics, and women's political rights. This has been done so as to prevent discord among the members while discussing religion and similar topics, because the club has been established mainly in order to disseminate knowledge to ladies and to engage in philanthropy. But this does not mean that its members have no interest in these topics. Numerous other clubs, such as the New England Woman's Club and the New Century Club, which are the "daughters" of Sorosis, not only discuss these topics but have vowed to propagate progressive ideas by inviting women of diverse opinions to address them and explain their views, without causing any disagreement.

Some useless fellows say that these women's societies and clubs are but an imitation of men's; but the women's societies and clubs which I saw in large numbers in the United States had no connection with men's. Women's missionary and temperance societies and clubs were founded and developed solely by women.[57] Men usually establish clubs only with the intention of discussing politics, chatting, or amusing themselves by playing ball games. Men's clubs are not much inclined toward charity, promoting education, helping the destitute, comforting sufferers, and so on. Because these men's clubs do not allow ladies, they are infested with harmful and bad habits like drinking, using vulgar language, etc., as I have heard many people say. If this be true, I am happy and proud to say that women's clubs show not the least sign of imitating men's clubs.

Soon after the creation of the Sorosis Club, another very important club, known as the Woman's Congress, was established. It makes strong efforts to promote women's education, and is therefore also known as the Society for the Advancement of Women.

Its members include women from many parts of the United States who are very learned, farsighted, experienced, and interested in education. There are many local branches of this club, and once every year the members meet at an appointed place. On this occasion scholarly women read well-reasoned and thoughtful papers on serious subjects such as politics, social reform, social conditions, education, arts, sciences, poetry, and history; and also deliver lectures. This club enjoys great prominence because of the prestige, learning, and fame of its members.

There is another famous club, known as the New England Woman's Club, in Boston,[58] which also aims to promote education, as is the case with the Woman's Congress. These clubs for promoting education do not merely propagate book learning. As soon as they were founded, the members decided to undertake practical tasks after mutual consultations about the shortcomings of the female sex and the measures necessary to rectify them. They acquired practical knowledge, studied the management of other societies and associations, and made use of this in improving the conditions of the women toiling in different occupations and in alleviating their misery. They are still engaged in this task.

The New Century Club of Philadelphia is famous for its valuable qualities of progressiveness and philanthropy. Its efforts have led to the formation of the Working Woman's Guild, which has over seven hundred working women as its members. Only self-supporting women who work in factories, shops, etc., can become its members. For an hour or two every evening, classes on different subjects are held in its meeting hall. Hundreds of women are able to study subjects of their choice every day in about six different classes. Ordinarily every woman has some interest in cooking, sewing, embroidery, knitting, exercise, and so on; but the subjects of special interest among these members are poetry, history, and languages. These women have a special class, known as the "thinking class," in which they discuss abstruse subjects like philosophy. The intellectual capability and insight displayed by these women astonishes even highly educated audiences. Women who earn their livelihood through menial work are able to get an education, good company, and refuge in times of need, because some industrious and philanthropic women decided to establish this club. These days the example of the New Century Club has been followed by respectable, educated women in many other places, who have established organizations like the Working Woman's Guild for the advancement of working women and for the welfare and moral protection of misguided, destitute young women. Nobody will be able to assess the extent of the benefit of such clubs to working women and society at large.

Boston has the Woman's Educational and Industrial Union, which is managed by educated, experienced women of good families, who take turns visiting the union and supervising its working.[59] Currently the union has four committees; more may be added as and when necessary. The Entertainment Committee holds weekly receptions for the members, their friends and well-wishers, which is open for anybody. In addition to the management, several knowledgeable ladies assist in whatever way they can by investigating the problems of the women who approach the union for shelter and help. The Industrial Department arranges to take in articles made by poor women wishing to work; it sells them at a good price, and passes the money on to the women. More than seven hundred women bring some homemade things. Last year this department sold goods worth $26,000 (Rs. 78,000). The Employment Committee arranges to find suitable wage work for poor women seeking a job, or for educated women seeking a teaching position. Attached to it is a lunchroom, where food and drinks can be bought at moderate prices. If women servants, workers, and others are made to work without due payment, they can lodge a complaint with the Protective Department, which obtains justice for such women. The Protective Department is not only famous throughout the city of Boston, but strikes terror among the unjust. On its behalf, famous, learned, and altruistic lawyers fight poor women's cases free of charge in the courts of law. An iniquitous employer who refuses to pay due wages for work needs only to be told that a complaint would be filed before the Protective Department of Boston; that is enough to bring such persons back to their senses.

There are many other societies modeled on this one all over the United States, known as Woman's Exchanges. They are all run by women. Their objective is to help the poor, destitute women who work for a living, by selling their homemade goods at a fair price. In some places a boardinghouse is attached to the Exchange, to accommodate women visitors who come from other towns for work. These houses are under the supervision of respectable, influential women of the town. The entire management of the Exchange is entrusted to women's societies, which are of great help to the working women of the United States.

The Young Women's Christian Association is an excellent philanthropic organization in this country. It has branches in almost all cities, and has hundreds and thousands of young women as members. It has been formed to achieve several praiseworthy and important aims (in which it has been very successful), such as explaining and propagating Christianity among young women, preaching to ignorant women and leading them on the right path, arranging for good and reasonably priced accommodation for self-supporting women, and making education available to anyone who is interested in learning languages, or in getting scientific or vocational information.

In 1848 several active women held a Woman's Rights Convention at Seneca

Falls in the State of New York, as mentioned above. This was the very first association established for protecting women's rights; all other women's societies have come into being after following its example and with its assistance. The whole world ridiculed the convention when it was held. So-called gentlemen slung mud at the women who spoke on its behalf, and cursed them; the yellow newspapers drew cartoons of them; public leaders and opinion builders denounced and ostracized them; preachers honored them with epithets, such as "irreligious," "immoral," "heretical," "evil," "witches," "Satan's messengers"—epithets which served to expose their own breeding. But the women did not abandon their determination although the circumstances and public opinion were so unfavorable. They sacrificed their happiness, dedicated themselves with all their energies and wealth, and even shared the oppression of the women they helped, in order to continue their work for the abolition of women's slavery. Now the convention has become the National Woman Suffrage Association[60] with branches in hundreds of places in the United States and headquarters in Boston. It publishes weekly, fortnightly, and monthly newspapers as well as books at several places. The American Woman Suffrage Association publishes a famous weekly paper, the *Woman's Journal*, in Boston.[61] Its example has been followed by women in England, Canada, Australia, France, Denmark, Finland, and other countries, with the establishment of similar societies.

The efforts of the National Convention for Woman's Rights in the United States have led to several changes and improvements in the laws pertaining to the women of this country. In the State of Kansas women have obtained all the important rights of representation in municipalities. In the Territory of Wyoming women have received all the political rights which men have,[62] with a clearly beneficial effect. (Also in Canada, England,[63] and the English territory in Australia, unmarried and widowed women have obtained rights in municipalities.) The efforts of these societies have succeeded in large measure, and there are favorable signs that they will be entirely successful in the near future. This important women's convention was founded forty years ago at Seneca Falls. It made a small breach in the ramparts of the impenetrable fortress of custom which society had erected around the female community in order to imprison them and block their progress; and it made a small path for women to escape this terrible fortress. Thousands of women are leaving the fortress in groups in order to reach freedom, and more will continue to do so. This convention has now become international. At the end of March 1888, women of about ten civilized countries had come to the city of Washington at the invitation of the American Woman Suffrage Association. At that time the association called a convention of the International Council of Women[64] and resolved to establish branches in each member country. In some cases this resolution has already been carried out. This International Council of Women has been established not merely in order to obtain political rights for women. It has come into being in order to achieve very important and laudable aims, namely, to establish friendly relations among all kinds of women's societies everywhere in the world, to provide mutual help when necessary, to provide mutual encouragement, and to create friendship among women of all nations. More information about it is given at another place below, which is why nothing more is added here. There are many other important women's societies in this country, which are not mentioned here because information about all of them would take up considerable space. However, this essay will remain incomplete without at least a little information about the Woman's Temperance Union in this country, which I give below.

In November of last year (1887) the National Woman's Temperance Union of the United States held its fourteenth annual convention at the town of Nashville, in the State of Tennessee. The society's president had invited me to attend it. I traveled two thousand miles, all the way to Nashville, to see the great convention and the gathering of eminent women from all the States. For a whole week the city was crowded with women. About three hundred leading women had come there as representatives of the Woman's Temperance Unions of all the States in this country. Besides, many men and women had gathered there to see the convention.

The State of Tennessee is situated in the South of the country; and independence, education, and diligence are not seen among the women in these parts to the extent seen in the North. Some years ago, nobody there approved of a woman addressing a meeting, and nobody had even dreamt of the words "women's societies." The female sex has not advanced there as much as it should, nor are the means of higher education available to it. On the way to Nashville, I had occasion to stop at the city of Louisville in the State of Kentucky, and to address a meeting at the insistence of the people there. On that occasion, the minister of the church where I was to speak insisted on my sitting on the dais. It was my intention that if I was to sit on the dais, some of the eminent women of the town should also sit there with me. But the women said, "We have never done such a thing in our lives, how can we bring ourselves to do so now?" I said, "Ladies, you have never sat on the dais before, but what is the harm in making a beginning now? Just sit there with me once; if it bothers you in any way, don't do it again." After much hesitation, five or six women agreed to sit on the dais, and stayed there until I finished my speech. Needless to say, they came to no harm. Although women in the South do not live in seclusion, very few of them seem to possess the necessary independence and confidence to move about in society.

On hearing the above-mentioned news that the annual convention of the Woman's Temperance Union of the United States was to take place at Nashville, many people there made many kinds of speculations about it. Nobody really knew much about the society or how it worked. Many thought that it would be some kind of playacting or spectacle produced by the unimaginative ideas of half-sane and half-crazed women. Many clergymen refused them permission to hold meetings in their churches on the grounds that it was an irreligious act, and that the women were engaging in unwomanly conduct in contravention of biblical injunctions. At last it was decided to hold the meetings in the hall of a public library. The local Woman's Temperance Union of Nashville exerted itself extremely hard to coax the local women to help with the convention. These generous women invited to their homes the women who had come from afar, and entertained them very hospitably.

The marvelous convention began on the morning of November 16. Seven hundred chairs had been arranged in a semicircle in the meeting hall; there was no room for more. All the walls of the hall were decorated with the flags of different States and the colorful banners of the Woman's Temperance Unions of each State, embroidered and inscribed with their mottos. The spot where the president and other prominent women were to sit was decorated with the Star-Spangled Banner of the United States, flower bouquets, and green wreaths.

By nine in the morning, the meeting hall was filled with the Woman's Union. The audience also included a number of men. Then the president, Frances E. Willard, called everybody to attention and started the meeting. On that occasion, some eminent women said excellent, absorbing prayers, sang sweet songs, gave touching advice, and Miss Frances made an unparalleled, absorbing, deeply meaningful and beautiful speech. A great poet should have been present to do justice to all these things.

Before the first day's meeting was concluded, many clergymen in town changed their minds and sent invitations to this unparalleled Woman's Union, insisting that they should oblige them by holding meetings in their churches, and making speeches. The men in the audience stopped ridiculing the Union and began to show respect for it. Then, throughout that week, prominent women in the Union went to half a dozen different places every morning, noon, and night, to make speeches and give advice; even so, the people were not content. During that week, people saw resolutions being passed in the meeting, reports of the previous year's activities being read out, and proceedings being conducted in an efficient manner. The overall beauty and excellent management of all this would have made even the British Parliament and the United States Congress envious of this Temperance Union. Those who witnessed, on that occasion, Miss Frances Willard's talent for public speaking, leadership, managerial skill, organizational capacity, and extraordinary knowledge of the old rules of parliament, undoubtedly thought that she was the very image of the three goddesses of Learning, Statesmanship, and Government!

Many egotistical men probably think that women are not able to manage any task properly; but those who saw this Woman's Union and its well-organized functioning at Nashville probably also thought that the two world-famous political assemblies, namely the American Congress and the British Parliament, which often show confusion and lack of organization, would profit from following the example of the said Union.

On the evening of November 24, the convention was concluded. On that occasion, while bidding farewell to the women gathered there, prominent men and clergy of Nashville recounted how they had changed their minds about women and how the procedure and excellent organization of the society, its good advice and benevolent moral philosophy, surprised and gladdened them; and, with high praise and great respect, they bade the National Woman's Temperance Union of the United States farewell and invited it to come there again the following year.

The whole convention passed off happily. Never before had I seen such a marvelous, charming, and vast scene in my life; and it made me feel that my life was now fulfilled.[65] This great convention and this great Union cannot be compared to any association or convention other than the convention of the International Council of Women at Washington, at the end of last March.[66]

Woman's Crusade

The Demoness Liquor and her brother Tobacco had forced their way into people's houses and caused terrible devastation. Almost every single man began to give imaginary justifications, such as "I am a man, I can do anything with impunity; liquor helps to ease tiredness; chewing and smoking tobacco relaxes the brain; it is scientifically proven that a small drink, taken for medicinal purposes, or to help digestion, is perfectly harmless"; and began drinking and using intoxicants to his heart's content, and squandering money on them. Saloons, which are the gateways to hell and the causes of total ruin, sprang up everywhere. Their stained-glass windows and decorated doorways beckoned temptingly to men. Saloonkeepers, who filled their pockets by exploiting others, invented thousands of ways to increase their business by luring the young and the old, the ignorant and the wise, in many different ways. Day by day, more and more men were caught in their noose, lost all they had, and forfeited their happiness, respectability, and sometimes life itself. Because of them, their poor wives and their tender newborn babes were reduced to misery. Thousands of devoted wives suffered inwardly as they watched their husbands being totally ruined by the vice. Millions of mothers were sick at heart as they saw their sons, dearer than their own lives, abandoning religion, morality, and happiness in this world and the next, and heading for eternal hell because of their addiction to liquor. Even so, all those poor women endured their agonies in silence. Scripture and custom—the two arbiters of society—have served women with an order to sit at home and put up with everything quietly; in obedience to this order women have endured endless, intolerable agonies and mental suffering without as much as a whimper, until today.

But there is a limit to everything in this world. When oppressed too heavily, even a worm turns once in a while and prepares to fight the enemy in self-defense. It is not very surprising, then, that a time comes when human beings—even women, who are accustomed to enduring oppression patiently—are driven to put up resistance against oppression when the oppression reaches a limit. Such an occasion arose in the case of women in the State of Ohio, when they dispensed with their seclusion and silence, and resolved in order to protect their babes and their dear ones to fight the saloonkeepers who had heartlessly caught their husbands and sons in their coils and dragged them away. Hundreds of well-born, forbearing, and virtuous women girded themselves and assisted the crusade against saloonkeepers; and vowed not to return from the battlefield until they had defeated the enemy and protected their sons and their homes. In this war nobody slit another's throat or snatched a morsel of food from another's mouth through deceit; nobody's blood was spilt and nobody's heart was pierced by harsh words; nobody terrified another with deadly weapons like guns, swords, or cannons. Even so the mention of this crusade made the liquor sellers and their partisans—those irreligious tormentors and plunderers of others' property—tremble; the crusaders' banner of peace made Satan quake; and their sweet, logical exhortations shook the foundations of Satan's citadels until they crumbled and fell. The Crusades[vii] of the eleventh and twelfth centuries pale before the marvelous and unparalleled peaceful crusade of women in the nineteenth century. There can be no comparison between the two. Men's crusades, during the barbaric times of the past, were aimed at cutting people's throats, sprinkling the whole earth with human blood, and tarnishing the name of religion. The women's crusade of the nineteenth century was aimed at saving people's lives, rescuing them from Hell, and establishing happiness, peace, and joy in their homes. Men's crusades of the eleventh and twelfth centuries destroyed millions of lives; the women's crusade of the nineteenth century employed the means to pull billions of people out of the jaws of death. Those barbaric crusades sullied the religion of Christ, the Angel of Peace; this modern crusade made that holy religion shine like burnished gold.

This marvelous crusade started on December 24, 1873.[67] A man named Dio Lewis had come to the town of Hillsboro in the State of Ohio to make a speech. On the evening of the twenty-fourth, he delivered a lecture on the subject "Our Girls" for the Lecture Association at Washington Court House, Ohio. On that occasion, he described the extent to which the human race was ruined by the use of liquor, other intoxicating drinks, tobacco, etc., and narrated his own experience. His mother, a devout and righteous woman, was deeply grieved at the harm caused in the world by this vice. Dio's father was addicted to liquor and had lost everything. Mrs. Lewis, seeing her happiness and family life ruined, decided to save her husband; and she thought of a new solution to cure the townspeople of this vice. Taking some women friends along, she herself visited saloons which sold liquor and other intoxicants; prayed and preached there; and entreated their owners to give up the wretched and ruinous trade. Her efforts were eventually successful and all the saloonkeepers in the town closed down their saloons. After narrating this story, Dio Lewis said to the women in the audience that if they followed suit, their good efforts would also be successful, and that all the saloons there would be closed down within a week; and that, if the women wanted to undertake the deed, their leaders should indicate their consent. On hearing Lewis's words, about fifty women stood up to show their consent for the undertaking. Then Lewis turned to the men opposed to drinking, who were sitting nearby, and asked how many of them would help the women if they undertook the deed, upon which about seventy men stood up. When it was thus decided to undertake this deed, it was resolved to call a meeting on the morning of Christmas Day, that is, December 25, for this great deed.

On Christmas Day at ten in the morning, a large gathering met at the Presbyterian church there, in accordance with the previous night's resolution. After a psalm was sung and the service held, Dio Lewis made an hour-long speech in which he narrated his mother's story, described how much strength women possess to undertake important tasks, and how their tolerance, diligence, and affectionate nature serve as useful means for accomplishing such tasks. All the people gathered there highly approved of Dio Lewis's suggestion and the Woman's Crusade[68] was launched that very morning.

Like other societies, this crusade also made rules, elected a president, vice president, secretary, and treasurer; all of them were women, needless to say. One committee of this women's society was sent to war. This was a committee of fifty-two women who took a vow to fight to the finish. A resolution was passed to form a Committee of Visitation which would present appeals at hotels and saloons to give up the evil trade and start another respectable business, and which would also offer prayers and sermons.[69] A group of "backers" was set up to help the Committee of Visitation, in which thirty-seven men accepted the responsibility of providing financial aid to the women crusaders. After all these preparations were made, it was resolved that a subcommittee should be formed to write an appeal to be sent to all saloonkeepers.

The Committee of Visitation made Mrs. E. J. Thompson its leader and decided to attack the enemy. Mrs. Thompson describes the first battle as follows:[70]

> On the morning of 25th December 1873, our "band" slowly and timidly approached the first-class saloon (as it was called) kept by Robert Ward, on High Street, a resort made famous by deeds, the memory of which nerved the heart and paled the cheek of some among us, as the seventy entered the open door of the . . . [saloon].

Doubtless he had learned of our approach, as he not only propped the heavy door open, but with the most perfect suavity of manner held it until the ladies all passed in; then, closing it, walked to his accustomed stand behind the bar.

Seizing the strange opportunity, the leader[71] addressed him as follows: "Well, Mr. Ward, this must seem to you a strange audience! I suppose, however, that you understand the object of our visit?" Robert by this time began to perspire freely, and remarked that he would like to have a talk with Dio Lewis. Mrs. Thompson said: "Dr. Lewis has nothing whatever to do with the subject of our mission. As you look upon some of the faces before you, and observe the marks of sorrow, caused by the unholy business that you ply, you will find that it is no wonder we are here. We have come, however, not to threaten, not even to upbraid, but in the name of our Divine Friend and Savior, and in his spirit, to forgive, and to commend you to his pardon, if you will but agree to abandon a business that is so damaging to our hearts and to the peace of our homes!"

The hesitation and embarrassment of the famous saloon-keeper seemed to afford (as the leader thought) an opportunity for prayer; so, casting her eye around upon that never-to-be-forgotten group of earnest faces, she said, very softly: "Let us pray." Instantly all, even the poor liquor-seller himself, were upon their knees.

The scene that followed, in a most remarkable manner portrayed the spirit of our holy religion. Poor wives and mothers, who the day before would have crossed the street to avoid passing by a place so identified with their heartaches, their woes, and their deepest humiliation, in tearful pathos were now pleading with this deluded brother to accept the world's Redeemer as his own. Surely, "God is Love!"

The greatness of that otherworldly love and forgiveness cannot be sufficiently described. The prophecy of Dio Lewis came true. Thanks to the unceasing efforts of this marvelous Committee of Visitation, all the saloons in Hillsboro closed down within a week!

On hearing the report of the Hillsboro Crusade, women of many other places in the United States followed their example. But these crusades were not long-lasting; therefore, some farsighted women decided to make a collective effort. In 1874 some of the successful women crusaders met at a summer camp at Chautauqua and established the Woman's Christian Temperance Union with the purpose of making continuous efforts to eradicate the vice of drinking. Soon it became a national association, thanks to the efforts of some good, diligent, and upright women; and assumed the name the National Woman's Temperance Union of the United States.

The administration of the Union is the very replica of that of the United States. It has four levels—local, county, state, and national—and an excellent system of administration. Each local union has a president, a vice president, a secretary, a treasurer, and a board of management as well as subcommittees appointed for specific purposes. At each annual function the officers are elected, and take office. Similarly, the officers of the county are elected at the annual function of all the Unions in the county. In the same manner, the officers of the state- and national-level Unions are elected annually. The Union has over 10,000 chapters in the United States, and about 250,000 women members. Although the local Union is autonomous, it has to surrender some of its very important rights to the county-level Union in order to gain strength, and maintain unity and friendship with other local Unions; likewise, the county-level Unions relinquish some important rights to the state-level Union, and the latter to the national Union. This helps them to retain independence and unity, and strengthens them. The management, organization, and rules and regulations of this Union are very praiseworthy, and marvelous like the national administration of the United States. The many different capabilities possessed by the female sex had earlier been scattered among individuals and dissipated like vapor in the sky, being un-regulated and ineffective. When they were collected together in this Union, they became activated in various ways like steam concentrated and controlled by a steam engine. Because of this Union, qualities like self-respect, execution, ad-ministration, and leadership, which were hitherto unknown to women, are growing in an extraordinary and wonderful manner among the women of the United States. Thanks to it, the harmful differences of opinion and class ani-mosity among women of different opinions and classes have disappeared, and sincere friendship and sisterhood are growing in their place.

I have no hesitation in saying that this is the best and greatest of all the asso-ciations prevalent among all civilized countries. It would be rare to find a good deed which it had not undertaken, difficult to cite any example of its motherly love being denied to anyone, and impossible to imagine that the virtues of brav-ery, seriousness, courage, and forgiveness can have reached perfection anywhere else, except in God. It is not that the women's missionary societies in this and other countries are insignificant; they have spent millions of rupees and have been selflessly engaged in the task of leading foreign people to the path of the holy religion, for which they cannot be praised enough. But there are denomi-national differences among these societies, which is why they lack unity and are unable to perform as many good deeds as the Temperance Union does. Women's Christian societies include only so-called "evangelical" sects, and do not assist others. All other societies for the promotion of education and philanthropic works may be excellent and beneficial in their own ways, but cannot be com-pared to the union, because their numbers are small and their aims limited. But the aims of the Woman's Temperance Union are many and very important. It has no internal differences of opinion; here women—of all opinions, classes, and types—work together unitedly. It has successive local, state, national, and inter-national levels; it has simple but strict rules which are excellent, acceptable to all, and easy for all to observe; it has extraordinary management, superior to the administration of any country and holding everything and everybody together. Considering all these, one feels that this union is the crown of all the marvelous miracles on God's earth in the present age.

The society now has about forty-five departments, and its activities are as follows:

1. To send representatives and speakers from the Union to different places and to establish temperance unions.
2. To establish international women's temperance unions by sending women messengers to all nations, or by correspondence.
3. To promote temperance among immigrants who intend to settle in the United States.
4. To promote temperance, education, and morality among the newly freed Negroes in the Southern States.
5. To promote morality and temperance among young women.
6. To ensure children's progress by teaching them morality and temperance.
7. To explain to the people the harmful hereditary effects caused by the use of liquor and other intoxicants.
8. To impart health education and to explain to the people the close connection between health and temperance.
9. To consider the changes which are necessary in education and to work toward introducing in all public schools in the country scientific education about the harm caused by liquor and intoxicants.
10. To work toward introducing the above-mentioned type of education in high schools and colleges, and to promote temperance among the young men and women studying there.
11. To give a good education to small children by establishing kindergarten schools for them, and to ensure their proper upbringing.
12. To work for the growth and progress of Sunday schools and to promote temperance through them.
13. To publish books, newspapers, magazines, and pamphlets to propagate temperance.
14. To prevent the publication of books, papers, etc., which are bad, vulgar, immoral, and which encourage the use of intoxicants.
15. To explain the many benefits of temperance to laborers and manual workers.
16. To explain to women and children how to establish large societies, committees, and unions along parliamentary lines, and what their general and special rules are.
17. To establish temperance unions for men and women, manage them, and impart knowledge about their proper functioning.
18. To explain to the people the terrible harm caused by intoxicants, such as tobacco and opium, and their adverse effects on the human body.
19. To work toward preventing the use of liquor extract in medicines, and

to prove through scientific and chemical experiments that it is unnecessary to use medicines containing liquor extract.

20. To evangelize.

21. To read aloud the gospel in public places, and to explain to the people that the Holy Book condemns drinking.

22. To inquire after prisoners; to educate them about the benefits of religion, morality, and temperance; to inquire after and assist prisoners in police lockups and inmates of destitute homes.

23. To promote temperance among workers on railroads and in railroad stations; to teach them religion and morality, and work toward their spiritual progress.

24. To teach religion and morality to sailors and to those serving in the navy and army, and to explain to them the benefits of temperance.

25. To work toward abolishing the use of wine during Holy Communion in churches.

26. To work toward getting all Christian organizations to pray during their special prayer week for the success of the work of the Temperance Union.

27. To work toward increasing the purity of morals among the people.

28. To promote morality, religion, and temperance among Mormon women.

29. To work toward getting the people of the United States to observe the holy Sabbath by abstaining from trading and from committing ill deeds, and by spending time in devotion to God.

30. To visit respectable women in their homes and to promote temperance there with the help of small committees.

31. To give flowers and cheerful gifts to the sick, the ailing, and the aged in clinics, hospitals, and other places.

32. To promote temperance at fairs and fetes, and to make all efforts to prevent the sale of liquor there.

33. To work toward banning the sale of liquor in the United States by sending appeals to the different state governments.

34. To make efforts to obtain for women political rights, such as the right to make laws, in order to assist them in their work of promoting morality and temperance.

35. To raise fallen women and put them on the proper path by giving them vocational training; to protect destitute women who are oppressed at their places of work and who may be in moral danger; to try to prevent the publication of obscene and vulgar books and pictures; and to make every effort to promote morality in society.

36. To work for the progress and increased usefulness of the clinic and hospital established in Chicago by the National Woman's Temperance Union

of the United States, and to train women doctors there through the teaching of temperance medicine.

37. To persuade the different heads of state to establish peace among all nations and to resolve disputes through third-party mediation rather than through war; and to work toward abolishing the cruel and demoniac practice of fighting wars.

38. To assist benevolent societies in different cities and towns.

These are the thirty-eight chief tasks undertaken by the Woman's Temperance Union; in addition there are five or six minor tasks which are not mentioned here.

Subcommittees have been appointed in several places to undertake the activities of these forty-odd departments, and each subcommittee has a woman officer to supervise it. Every year, this woman officer has to submit brief information on the working of that particular department in every State and Territory to the chief officer of the National Woman's Temperance Union. All such information is published in its general annual report. There is a rule which requires the members of each union to pay an annual fee of half a dollar (that is, about one and a half rupees) in order to defray its expenses in different places. In addition, the Union receives many large donations from a number of generous men and women.

Even a brief account of all the activities of the Union and the functioning of all its chapters would mean writing a separate book; so I will not make the attempt. All the activities of the Union are very important; but there is one which is the most important and must be mentioned here. In the United States all adults as well as children are trained in working collectively and unitedly, as mentioned above. It is customary in this country to establish societies for children as well as adults, in order to undertake some specific activity. There are thousands of children's societies in this country—for the promotion of kindness to animals, education, philanthropy, religion, etc.; and hundreds of thousands of boys and girls are doing many kinds of good work. Among them are about 1,500 children's temperance unions established by the National Woman's Christian Temperance Union of the United States, with a membership of about 150,000 children, both boys and girls! They manage the work of their excellent unions very well with the help of their mothers and women teachers, and they have all taken the pledge never to drink. The Woman's Temperance Unions are working ceaselessly to inculcate in them the strength and firm resolve to keep this vow. Through these women's efforts, children are educated about temperance in Sunday schools, and 34,000 children in these schools have taken the pledge never to drink. These extraordinary, hardworking women have been trying incessantly for seven years to get the thirty-seven state governments in the United States to introduce laws to provide scientific education about temperance to children in public schools, and have got them implemented. Over 6,500,000 children receive a scientific education about temperance in public schools in all these States. The scientific education and information, with practical demonstrations, about the harmful effects on the human body of the consumption of liquor and other intoxicants, which are given to these millions of children, is bound to have some permanent, good effect on their minds. Realizing that advice given to adults who are addicted to drink is not going to have much effect, these wise, foresighted women have been exerting themselves ceaselessly to give a sound education to children, for the improvement of future generations.

For many years now, the state governments of Maine and Iowa have passed temperance laws to prohibit the brewing and sale of liquor; but the governments are helpless before the wickedness of the liquor sellers. A clandestine traffic in liquor still goes on there. About two years ago, the women of Kansas won the municipal franchise. The first important task for which they exercised their rights was to put a complete stop to the liquor traffic in the state. About half these women were members of the Woman's Temperance Union; they made efforts to prevent the clandestine traffic in liquor. What the men in the State of Maine, lacking the support of women, were unable to achieve in twenty-five years, was accomplished by the people of the State of Kansas within almost two years, on the strength of the united power of men and women. Senator Ingalls, who represents Kansas in the United States Senate, says:[72]

> Kansas has abolished the saloon. The open dram-shop traffic is as extinct as the sale of indulgences. A drunkard is a phenomenon. The bar-keeper has joined the troubadour, the crusader, and the mound-builder. The brewery, the distillery, and the bonded warehouse are known only to the archaeologist. It seems incredible that among a population of 1,700,000 people, extending from the Missouri River to Colorado, and from Nebraska to Oklahoma, there is not a place which the thirsty or hilarious wayfarer can enter, and, laying down a coin, demand his glass of beer. This does not imply that absolute drought prevails everywhere, or that "social irrigation" has entirely disappeared. But the habit of drinking is dying out. Temptation being removed from the young and the infirm, they have been fortified and redeemed. The liquor-seller, being proscribed, is an outlaw, and his vocation disreputable. Drinking, being stigmatized, is out of fashion, and the consumption of intoxicants has enormously decreased. Intelligent and conservative observers estimate the reduction at 90 per cent: it cannot be less than 75.

When the women of Kansas obtained political rights, some mischievous men of a town in the State elected a well-born young housewife as their mayor, in order to prove that women did not deserve political rights and were not capable of important political work. The very next day, the people who had elected her mayor realized that their assumption, that women were unable to carry on administration or to implement laws, was wrong. Immediately upon assuming the office of mayor, the woman made a search for all the saloons, gambling dens, and other places of illegal activities, and closed them down. The good men and women of the town assisted her greatly in locating clandestine places. The townspeople are very happy with her administration, and she manages her duties in a proper and excellent manner. The members of the National Woman's Christian Temperance Union of the United States used to think that women did not need political rights. But, during the past fifteen years, their intense efforts have not yielded the expected results; and they have realized that the lack of political rights is the sole reason. The liquor traders are almost all men, and they have invested millions of dollars in this trade. There are also many men who support them. All of them have political rights, and they vote against the women's efforts to introduce temperance laws. The law supports the majority vote. In the matter of making laws, women have no power, and men, especially liquor sellers and drinkers, enjoy political rights as well as financial advantage. Many men and women have begun to think that unless women obtain some political rights, they will not be able to defeat the demon of liquor. Therefore they are making unceasing efforts to obtain political rights for women.

The International Woman's Temperance Union has been established thanks to the vision and organizational ability of Miss Frances E. Willard, the respected president of the National Woman's Temperance Union of the United States, and with the help of her friends. Miss Willard had this idea in 1883. Later, all the plans regarding this Union were settled, the ideas about its functioning had matured, and then, in 1884, the International Woman's Temperance Union was established. Mrs. Mary Clement Leavitt,[73] an adventurous, brave, and resolute woman, became its representative, and started on a journey around the world with the intention of establishing temperance unions everywhere. She went first to the island of Hawaii, then to countries like Australia, Japan, China, Ceylon, India, Madagascar, and Africa, and established hundreds of temperance unions. Now she intends to visit all the countries of Europe. When this single, unsupported, helpless woman started on this great enterprise, she had neither money nor a companion; but she was accompanied by her God and her strong resolve to do good. Wherever she goes, she receives the assistance she needs. Now Woman's Temperance Unions are being established in most of the civilized countries. The women of England were also inspired by American women's enthusiasm and sense of duty. They have established a national union, called the British Woman's Temperance Association, and it does a lot of good work. Canada also has a National Woman's Temperance Union; it is making intense efforts to prohibit the traffic in liquor in that country. Similar unions exist in the countries of Australia, the Hawaiian Islands, Madagascar, and Africa. My Indian sisters, why do you lag behind? Such a national union is essential in our country. The

International Woman's Temperance Union proposes to send a strong appeal to all heads of nations, in which women of all nations plan to request them to stop the traffic in liquor and intoxicants. All our Indian women must sign this appeal; everybody must try to circulate the appeal and obtain signatures. May there be no Indian who refuses to assist in this great enterprise, directly or indirectly. This is our prayer to the Almighty.

Miss Frances E. Willard is now president of the International Woman's Temperance Union. Under her leadership, at least one million women are engaged in activities related to temperance, throughout the world. This Temperance Union is the "United Democratic State of Women." These women unite the whole world with a bond of friendship, with the sacred bond of their white ribbon,[viii] a symbol of peace and love. They promote among women of all nations the three precious virtues which are the source of all happiness: peace, love, and friendship. This great deed could not be done by men—men who have been kings and emperors; men who, for thousands of years, have been armed with weapons, have possessed bodily strength, and have been rulers of society. But it has been done by these women who were derided as ignorant and weak. O God, You are great indeed! You make people like these, who are shunned by the world, into the instruments which humble the conceit of the arrogant. In Your hands even a blade of grass becomes immeasurably powerful like a thunderbolt!

Notes in the Original Text

i. In the year 1818, primary schools for girls as well as boys were established in the United States. During the seventy years since then, the native women have made great strides in the field of education; and now thousands of splendid, intelligent, educated women of this country shine forth like brilliant gems. But this should not lead anyone to suppose that all women here have the educational facilities which (all) men enjoy, and that women's colleges receive the same degree of generous public support that men's colleges do. The details of men's colleges in 1886 are as follows:[74]

Universities and colleges	346
Schools of Science	90
Schools of Theology	142
Schools of Law	49
Schools of Medicine, Dentistry, and Pharmacy	175
Total	802
Total number of male students	78,185

The value of grounds, buildings, and apparatus of colleges for men is $62,356,638 (or Rs. 187,069,914); the productive funds of colleges for men are $57,782,303 (or

Rs. 173,346,909); and the income from productive funds is $3,271,991 (or Rs. 9,815,973).

A comparison of these figures with the money invested in women's education reveals a wide disparity between the two. The colleges for women's higher education number 529; their buildings, grounds, and apparatus are valued at $9,635,282 (Rs. 28,905,846); their productive funds are valued at $2,376,619 (Rs. 7,129,857); and the income from productive funds is $136,801 (Rs. 410,403).

In 1886 the local, state, and federal governments made appropriations worth $1,690,275 (Rs. 5,070,825) for the support of the higher institutions of learning for men, but not even a single penny to support women's higher education!

ii. Many years ago, the famous, learned president of the University of Michigan, James B. Angell, presented his above-mentioned opinion publicly.

iii. Some years ago women could not get admission to Cambridge University in England. Now two women's colleges, Newnham and Girton, have been established at Cambridge, and provide a very good education. At Cambridge University women are now allowed to study as men's equals and to sit for examinations. However, the university authorities still retain a residue of the barbarism of their ancestors. They allow women to study and sit for examinations, but deny degrees to the women who pass the examinations—although they have rightfully earned the degrees after years of hard work! Truly unparalleled is the generosity and culture of progressive English scholars, especially those at Cambridge!

iv. Women's education in today's United States was beyond anybody's imagination fifty years ago. It has already been mentioned that a study of mathematics, law, sciences, Greek, and other subjects does not seem to have made women unhealthy, insane, or unruly, or transformed their womanliness and destroyed their love of domesticity and children. It is true that educated women have taken up diverse types of employment for livelihood, but that has not ruined the livelihood of men; on the contrary, the number of trades and industries in the United States has increased a hundredfold and flourished during the last fifty years, as has been shown in the section "Employment."

v. American society still shows vestiges of its ancient barbaric condition, and it may be said that foremost among them is the excessive dependence of married women. American men are shameless, just like the men of our country. They say, "We support our households and feed our wives by our daily toil and the sweat of our brow." Men work for eight, ten, or at the most twelve hours a day; but women have to slog for sixteen or seventeen hours daily, to serve the menfolk, mind the children, and do household chores. The wives of laborers, of farmers, and of men in other occupations look after their homes and children first; in addition, they share their husbands' work equally and help them. In spite of all this, a wife has no right to the family income; whenever she needs a little

money for her expenses, she has to cajole her husband, supply satisfactory an-
swers to a thousand questions he asks, and beg him for it. If he refuses to give
her any money, she cannot claim a right to her hard-earned possessions, either
by law or with the support of public opinion. Nor is this all. On the contrary,
her husband tells everyone how much she is obliged to him; and society—male
society—says, "Men work hard indeed to earn the money to feed and clothe their
wives! Oh, how greatly they oblige their wives!" In the absence of a wife in the
house, at least two or three servants would need to be employed to do the work
which she does single-handedly; and they would need to be paid wages. Servants
are not fed for doing nothing, nor can they be said to be obliged to their master.
But a wife, even if she does the work of ten servants, is under an obligation to
her husband because he feeds her!

vi. All the associations briefly described here are independent, and have been
established with different aims; however, such is the close connection among
them that it would be difficult to find an example of any one of them undertaking an important task without receiving direct or indirect help from the others.
Hence it is difficult to attribute the success of a particular good deed to any single
organization, with any degree of certainty. American women's associations do
not harbor envy for one another if they fail to get sole credit for any achievement; moreover, each is ever ready to help the others and rejoices in the others'
success, which is praiseworthy indeed.

vii. A Crusade is a war fought in the name of the Cross. At the close of the
eleventh century, Mohammedans conquered Jerusalem and prepared to occupy
Christian countries like Spain.[75] The followers of Christianity then fought wars
against the Mohammedans in defense of their religion; these wars are known as
the Crusades. They continued until the thirteenth century A.D.

viii. Women members of the Temperance Union—both the national union of
the United States and the international union—wear its sign, the white ribbon,
on their chest. It indicates that these women do the holy work of the Union with
sincerity and love in their hearts, and that they love all humanity.

9   Commerce and Industry

Commerce and industry is a topic worth considering, and stands next in importance after the system of Government and the condition of women in the United States. The importance which the United States has acquired today derives chiefly from its commerce and industries. Let us consider the various factors which encourage them, before we describe their characteristics.

The public-spiritedness of almost all things here is the chief means of the prosperity of these people. The streets, the means of transportation—that is to say, carriages and streetcars—the method of conducting the sale of goods in shops, colleges, newspapers, libraries, places for obtaining information: all such essential matters are rendered very simple and useful to all, as has already been mentioned.

Public Works Undertaken by Government

From a consideration of the system of Government in the United States it becomes immediately apparent that this system has been intended for the convenience of the people. It is true that the smooth running of the administration ensures peace, and brings happiness to the people. But administration alone does not complete the Government's duties. The United States Government recognizes that it is also a part of its duties to undertake public works which augment the comfort and convenience of all; and it has therefore taken up such works. I shall briefly recount the most important of these.

Department of Agriculture:[1] Approximately ten thousand people work in this department, most of them without remuneration. The department has its headquarters in Washington. The duties of its voluntary workers are to provide information about the state of the farms in their local area and in its vicinity; the cost of exporting produce to other places and other countries; the value of the produce which remains unsold on farms and in orchards, and the value of the same produce when exported to cities; details of goods used in their local areas, where they are imported from, etc. The office of the Department of Agriculture publishes this information in the form of monthly bulletins, and distributes them to traders' associations, newspapers, etc., in important places. This provides great help to commerce, and especially to farmers. (The farmers in this country are not illiterate like our farmers in India. They can read and write, and are able to understand how to improve their farms, and what means are essential for doing so, by reading books, newspapers, and bulletins.) This information enables traders and farmers to know the value of the goods which are to be sold, the prices of goods which are to be bought, the labor charges in different places, etc., so that they can conduct their transactions smoothly.

The United States Department of Agriculture distributes many different kinds of seeds throughout the country. These seeds are then sown in different places, and very detailed information is collected and published, as to the type of soil which is best suited to produce a particular type of crop, the characteristics of different types of soil, etc. Similarly, specialists in biology, agriculture, and chemistry are employed to conduct research on the breeding, sustenance, and extinction of pests and birds which destroy crops in different areas. This information is published and distributed to all the local farmers' associations.

Land has been allotted in the city of Washington, for the use of this department; it is utilized for testing whether the seeds and bulbs of the grains, fruits, and tubers which grow in other parts of the country and in other climates can also be grown here. After ascertaining the parts of the country which are most suitable for growing them, they are planted there. In this manner many fruits, flowers, roots, and grains are grown here, and contribute to the prosperity of the United States. Take the example of the Bahia orange, which was planted in southern California some years ago. It is now regarded as an excellent fruit of this region. Trade in oranges brings great wealth to the fruit growers there. It was from this department that people learned that sugarcane, tea, and other foreign plants can be grown in this country. Now these plantations bring great profit to the whole country.

The officials of this department do not rest content with importing seeds from abroad and planting them in this country. They also conduct detailed research on the characteristics of each kind of food grain, its nutritive value, the diseases it is prone to, and the means of combating them; the different types of trees in this country, their wood and the uses to which it can be put, etc. This information is also published. Similarly, the department informs the people throughout the country about the characteristics of useful animals, such as cattle, horses, sheep, and pigs, about their different breeds and the results of cross-breeding, about their diseases and cures, etc. Thus this department confers great benefits on the nation.

Weather Bureau: The United States Government has established the Weather Bureau, like the Department of Agriculture, to help all the people, and also the country's trade. In this vast country, which is 3,000 miles wide and 2,000 miles broad, there are a hundred and fifty stations of the Signal Service; and its headquarters are situated in Washington. Twice a day it receives information from these hundred and fifty stations about the weather and other atmospheric changes. The United States Government has employed experts in astronomy and meteorology for obtaining meteorological information. They note down all climatic changes at the hundred and fifty stations, and send practical information about them to places throughout the country. This information is sent by telegraph. Arrangements have been made to convey this information appropriately to the offices of the thousands of associations of traders and farmers in cities, towns, and villages; to railroad stations, and to docks in all harbors. This informs the traders, railroad engineers, passengers, ships' crews, farmers, grocers, retailers, etc., about the expected changes in the weather, and how these changes are likely to affect their own work.

Such signal stations reporting on the daily weather have been established at the chief ports on the seashore and riverbanks. They send information about weather fluctuations to Washington. The chief naval officers of the United States then turn this information into a practical form and transmit it to all ports. Similarly, lifesaving stations have been established at all the different spots on seashores, shores of large lakes, and riverbanks, where ships are likely to be wrecked and to cause a loss of life. Small lifesaving boats and all means of assisting shipwrecked people are kept there; also employed there at high salaries are brave and experienced men who are not afraid to jump into the sea even during a storm, to rescue drowning people.

Other Departments:[2] Another very useful department, like the lifesaving department, which has saved hundreds of thousands of people caught in storms, is being run at Government expense, and is doing excellent work. It is called the Lighthouse Board. Until 1880, the United States Government built 900 lighthouses on dangerous rocks in the sea, and erected 1,000 beacon lights on riverbanks; all of them are financed by the Government treasury. Lightships are anchored at reefs in the sea, where ships are in danger of being wrecked. All these lightships are lit up at night, and whenever it gets dark because of fog. Their lights can be seen from afar; ship's captains realize that the light indicates a dangerous rock, and steer clear of it. This saves thousands of ships from being wrecked, and hundreds of thousands of people from drowning. A meteorological survey is conducted every day, and information about possible storms conveyed to every port and harbor. If a particular dock is likely to be hit by a storm and endanger incoming ships, storm signals are raised to warn captains to keep out of the harbor or port. The duty of disseminating information about weather conditions related to the sea, rivers, and lakes is entrusted to the chief of the United Stated Navy. The task of building lighthouses along rivers, improving river traffic, improving seaports and wharfs in lakes and rivers, etc., is entrusted to the United States Army and Navy. The United States Government does not support the soldiers and officers of its small standing army for doing nothing. They have to earn their keep. The army and navy have very few occasions to fight and take life; therefore they are employed mostly on public works and to save life. This is very praiseworthy for the republic of the United States.

The Coast Survey established by the United States Government to survey the seacoast and banks of rivers and lakes is also very important for trade. The officials of this department and their assistants survey the features of seacoasts, gulfs, bays, creeks, lakes, rivers, ports, etc.; and provide detailed information about the places suitable for commerce—grading them as superior, medium, and inferior—and those which are unsuitable; about the measures necessary for making a port more suitable for trade, etc. The officials of this department invented the method for determining longitude; they solved the problem of tides in the Gulf of Mexico, and the reason why the tide comes in only once in twenty-four hours. They discovered ways of rescuing ships from the dangers of under-tow and eddies, and of utilizing the latter in aid of navigation; and thus provided considerable assistance to seaborne trade.

The Federal Government has a Patent Office and museum in Washington, which exhibits specimens and models of all the new discoveries and inventions made, and all the crafts and tools manufactured, since this nation came into being. Patents have been, and are still being, granted to their inventors from this office. In granting these patents for a moderate charge the Government pays attention not to filling its own coffers, but to protecting the rights of the manufacturers, and encouraging arts and crafts. The Patent Office is a place very well worth seeing. A visit paid to it and a look at all these creations is bound to make one feel great admiration for the arts, crafts, and inventions of the people of the United States. Since gaining independence, this nation has spent about fifty years in establishing order, and in recovering from the losses incurred during the war. The inventiveness of these people did not develop much during those years, but grew very rapidly from 1836 to 1880. During these forty-four years, more than 300,000 patents were granted for new ideas, inventions, machines, etc. Forty years ago this office granted not more than 500–600 patents every year; now it grants 24,000 to 25,000 patents per year.

Reports filled with diverse discoveries and many kinds of information are printed at Government expense, and given free of charge to anybody who asks for them, and also to every prestigious society, library, and office in the country. The annual salaries of the workers in the Government press in Washington alone amount to $1,380,000. In this press, 400 typesetters, 50 proofreaders, and 150 printers work round the clock for twelve months in a year. One hundred thousand reams of paper are used for printing here, and at least 750,000,000 pages' worth of matter is printed each year. The report of the Department of Agriculture is printed here, and more than 300,000 copies are distributed free every year.

Similarly, there are many other departments, such as the Geological Survey, Bureau of Ethnology, Commission of Fish and Fisheries, and the National Museum. This is merely a glimpse of the public works of the United States Government. Their names and brief information alone would run into several books; it is therefore best not to attempt it.

It is beyond doubt that the system of Government in this country, and the public works of the Government, are the means by which the people of the United States have become pre-eminent in commerce and industry. But the chief reason for their pre-eminence is quite different. Industriousness, self-reliance, self-rule, and collective effort, which are the excellent root causes of all kinds of prosperity and progress, are visible everywhere among the people. These qualities alone are the chief reason for the importance of these people.

Transportation and Communications[3]

When this nation became independent, and the history of its free citizens' rule began, the United States was a country almost entirely covered by forest. What little human settlement existed was situated along the Atlantic coast, and lacked good communications. There were no proper roads to travel from one town or State to another.

The old belief in our country, that travel is the cause of all unhappiness, and that he who does not need to travel is a happy man, arose mainly from the inconveniences of travel. When streams and rivers are in flood, and there are no bridges, one is compelled to remain on the bank for eight to ten days, drenched in the rain, frozen by the cold, and rotting in the mud. Carriages on roads suffer the same fate. A carriage might get mired in the mud, or dashed against a rock, or stuck in a desert. In addition, there is the fear of wild beasts, thieves, and forest fires. But enduring such discomforts and putting up with harassment from the carriage driver and porter are not the end of one's difficulties. Whichever town one then enters is bound to have an excise collector stationed at the gate when one enters and exits! One then has to undo each bundle which has been tied up, tie up each one that has been untied; have each rag, little box, and tiny bundle searched; have baggage detained and see goods lost, and so on. The poor traveler ends up feeling that it is better to encounter the messenger of Death than the excise official! Where such difficulties abound, it is not surprising that the people think that a person who does not travel is happy indeed.

But the people here have removed all these obstacles with the help of their extraordinary industriousness. The obstacles did not destroy their enthusiasm, but increased it a hundredfold. By 1830 they built roads of a total length of 115,000 miles, in order to facilitate the movement of people and goods throughout the areas under settlement, and also dug canals a total of 2,000 miles in length.[4] Although a number of industries existed at the time, all the facilities were not available everywhere as they are now. The condition of the municipalities was useless. Even after an official sent a notice, house tax was not paid until a man was sent to collect it. The task of removing the dirt in the town and cleaning the streets was entrusted largely to pigs. It was not customary to light the streets. Arrangements for drinking water were the same as they are in the towns in our country—with the exception of cities like Bombay, Calcutta, Madras, and Poona. People managed with water from wells and lakes, and rain water stored in tanks at home. The reason for these poor arrangements was not a lack of industriousness, but the kind of obstacles which are quite unknown in countries like our own, which are settled all over. Land had to be farmed, towns to be settled, communities to be set up, forest to be felled, roads to be built, river and land routes to be discovered, and machines to be invented in order to overcome the shortage of people to do all this work. Because of all these inevitable obstacles, the task of achieving the country's progress was very slow.

Machines and Labor[5]

After 1830, some of these obstacles came to be removed, and the work of progress started with great rapidity. Now all the obstacles have been removed, and the commerce and industry of the American people have assumed gigantic proportions. Machines have now begun to do the work of men and of beasts of burden, such as elephants, horses, oxen, and camels. Just as machines are used for extinguishing fires, pumping water into all the city pipes, printing newspapers, manufacturing cloth, etc., so are many of them used in ordinary houses. These people have risen to fame for producing machines which can do a great deal of work in a short time, and with the help of only a few people. It has become customary for them to do most things by machine. Clothes are sewn by machine; shoes are made and books bound by machine; nails and pins, pots and pans, tools and surgical instruments are all made by machine; lamps are lit by machine; cloth, socks, and vests are woven and knitted by machine. Machines are used for tasks like grinding flour, sowing fields, harvesting crops, binding sheaves of grass and grain; for pounding rice, wheat, and other food grains; for removing the husk from the grain, and separating fine and rough flour and bran after grinding wheat; for slicing wood and cutting it into planks, etc. It is difficult to predict how far these people would carry their practice of doing work by machine. The tasks which everyone considered impossible to accomplish except by human hands are now done by machines, as everyone can see. What is more, machines have even been installed in large stores to convey to the cashier the money which is paid for goods sold. Steam machines can be used for incubating eggs and hatching them. Hens are "farmed" by these means at many places. A diligent man has calculated that the mechanical power used in manufactures in the United States is equal to 3,410,837 horsepower; of this, 64 percent is derived from steam and 36 percent from water.[6] These two chief sources of power are the life force of the machines in the United States, and serve millions of people.

Earth, Water, Fire, Wind, and Sky, which are known as the five primordial elements in the ancient books of our country, are completely at the service of these American people, as one can see. Although there are so many machines here, human labor has not lost but gained in value. A very common type of laborer here earns at least 50 to 75 cents per day. If a person finds himself unable to earn a living by one trade, he is not forbidden to try another. There is no distinction of caste or class in this country, as mentioned above. There is no rule that a priest's son should become a priest, a carpenter's son a carpenter, or a blacksmith's son a blacksmith. Everyone is therefore free to take up any occupation he likes. As a result, a person takes up only an occupation which he is fitted for. This reduces the probability of the wrong man doing the wrong job. Before becoming General of the United States Army, President Grant worked as a tanner. He later became a famous general and President of this country. President Garfield was earlier a schoolteacher. President Lincoln was a farmer's son, and performed all jobs from the very lowly job of a woodcutter to the highest job of President. It is not the case here that absolutely everybody aspires to become a teacher, clerk, lawyer, or Government servant. In our country, the sons of artisans like goldsmiths, carpenters, and blacksmiths, as well as the sons of Brahmins start demanding salaried positions as soon as they have obtained a little education; and feel that the work of making pots and pans, making shoes, lathing wood, etc., is meant only for inferior people. Here the case is exactly the opposite. Here, men and women who have earned high degrees from eminent colleges do not hesitate to do any work that needs to be done. It is a man's industry and labor which are respected here, and not a salaried position which necessitates servility, as is the case with us. The street sweeper and drain cleaner here receive more respect than do the degree-holding Raosahibs, Raobahadurs, Rajasahibs, Nawabsahibs, and similar personages in our country.[7] I have heard that in England also an ordinary tradesman or laborer is treated with great disrespect, and that the King or Queen declines to meet such persons.[8] In India, of course, the castes which engage in the crafts and in commerce are considered inferior. Can prosperity be expected where the people whose industry contributes to the wealth and progress of a country are treated with such disrespect?

Growth of Cities and Communication Routes[9]

All the towns which have a number of machines and factories are attracting more and more people. Even so, it is not as if all the people stay in the same place and cause overcrowding. If a person is not able to manage in one place, he is free to go to any one of a hundred other places. This is a large country with many industries. This vast country is still not settled to any great extent, so that there is no difficulty in settling in a new place. These are the reasons why people are not compelled to stay together in the same city and reduce it to poverty, or starve to death themselves. A man who is capable of doing some sort of work will not starve anywhere in the United States. A person who is lazy and neglects work, or harbors false pride and will do only a specific kind of work, might starve to death—in which case, no one feels sorry for him.

Flourishing commerce and an increase in employment has led to an astonishing extent of growth of the population, land prices, and the number of houses, stores, and factories in large cities. Let me give a couple of examples of the growth of cities. In 1880 there were fifty large cities in the United States, which were famous for commerce and other important things; fifteen of these cities had not even come into existence in 1830. Only plots of land had been demarcated for them, but ground had not even been broken. Now the cities are flourishing to such an extent that the smallest of them has no fewer than 40,000 inhabitants. The city of Chicago, which now has a population of more than 700,000, was a thing of the future in 1833. There was some plan about building a city on that site; that is all. In 1834, a number of people settled there. It is said that the amount of money which would have been required then to buy the entire area occupied by the city today, would now buy a front of six feet on one of its large streets. Such is the increase in land prices there. Such also is the power of increasing population and flourishing commerce. The extent of the city's prosperous commerce can be estimated from the figures given below. The three largest items of trade in Chicago are lumber, food grains, and animals. Its annual sales include 2,000,000,000 feet of lumber; 900,000,000 feet of shingles; 1,600,000,000 bushels of food grain; 5,000,000 pigs; 2,000,000 cattle; and 1,000,000 sheep. In addition, its iron and steel factories are very important and profitable. There are a few iron and steel factories in Chicago and within thirty miles of the city, which produce steel bars for railroad tracks. Five hundred thousand tons of steel bars are manufactured there every year. They would suffice to encircle the whole earth once with railroad tracks.

Next after Chicago comes San Francisco, which has also experienced a similarly astonishing growth. In 1844, only fifty people lived in the area which is now the city of San Francisco. Today it has a population of 250,000. In 1847, a plot of land large enough to build a mansion there cost a hundred dollars. Today a plot of land that size costs twelve to fifteen thousand dollars. The trade of this city now amounts to $100,000,000. Across the Hudson River from New York City lies Jersey City. In 1840 the latter had a population of 3,070, which had increased by 1880 to 120,722. Similarly there is the city of Brooklyn, which lies on the other side of New York City and which is also known as its suburb. Its population in 1830 was 12,000 and had risen by 1880 to 566,000. In 1830 the city of Cleveland in Ohio had a population of less than one thousand which increased to 160,000 in 1880. Milwaukee in Wisconsin had only a hut or two in 1834; by 1835 it had grown into a small village, and by 1880 into a city of 125,000 people. Goods worth millions of dollars are being traded there today. What is known as the State of Minnesota today was just an uninhabited forest in 1840. In 1848, the entire State contained 3,000 people; now its population is 1,000,000 to 1,200,000. The growth of the two cities in the State, St. Paul and Minneapolis, is very astonishing. In 1880 St. Paul had about 41,000 people and Minneapolis 47,000. In 1885, the population of St. Paul crossed 111,000, and that of Minneapolis 130,000. Every year Minneapolis exports 5,250,000 barrels of wheat flour all over the world. The manufactured products of Minneapolis are said to be worth more than $54,000,000 per year. In the year 1884, 246,985 railroad wagons full of goods entered the city, and even more wagons left the city. The trade of St. Paul is similarly flourishing. It is the same story with very recently established cities, such as Duluth, Indianapolis, Kansas City, and Allegheny City. Wherever you go in the United States, you will see such cities rising up and growing overnight, like enchanted celestial cities—although they do not disappear at daybreak, but remain permanent and grow even larger day by day.

This speedy growth is the result of the industriousness of these people. The people here do not have the time to dawdle over their work; they are very conscious of the value of time. The storekeepers in our country conduct their sales in a leisurely manner, sitting comfortably, leaning against a bolster. The grocer takes a quarter of an hour to assemble his scales after a customer enters his store. Then he acts like a philosopher who has just come out of his meditations, still sunk in profound thought, and looks about him, ignoring all mundane things; and serves the customer slowly, in a preoccupied manner. Then some more time is wasted in bargaining. Had the people of the United States had such a habit of wasting time and sitting at leisure leaning against bolsters, it is doubtful whether this nation could have left behind any trace on this earth at all!

Another thing worth remembering is that these people do not look to the Government for everything. Although the Government of this country is an elected one, and although it is required to do anything which the people insist upon, in accordance with the law, usually no one goes begging to the Government for public works. If new factories are to be set up, roads to be built, railroads to be laid, canals to be dug, ships to be built, or just a small store to be opened, a number of people get together to accomplish the task. In this country there is a separate association for each task—sewing, shoe making, cotton carding, pottery making, glass making, and for making pens, needles, pins, thread, etc. The idea of guilds, which has been mentioned in the sacred Hindu books like the Manusmriti and other Smritis[10] and in the ancient dictionaries in our country, and which have now been forgotten by practically everybody there, has made unprecedented progress and reached perfection in this country. There is no task, big or small, which does not have an association to manage it. Just as there are associations for each type of industry, so are there very large associations for traders in all goods. Thousands of such associations are in existence: for example, associations of farmers, cloth merchants, general merchants, shoe-makers, garment sellers, flour sellers, fish and vegetable vendors, liquor sellers; traders in cattle, horses, sheep, or pigs; porters, blacksmiths, carpenters, masons, stone breakers, tailors, goldsmiths, etc. (It needs to be remembered that tailors, goldsmiths, etc., are not castes in this country, but occupational labels.) The members of each association help one another, and share experiences; they also discuss the ways and means for improving their work and making it popular and profitable, and for preventing foreign competition; after which they act upon common consensus. This gives them strength. These people are capable of running everything from a club with two members, to an association with hundreds of thousands of members; and doing so smoothly and properly, without noise or bustle. Most things here, like post and telegraph, railroads, and ships, are run by privately established companies. They have been granted appropriate licenses by the Government. These companies are the result of the people's self-reliance, and they daily give the people new lessons in self-rule. The four principles, namely, industriousness, collective effort, self-reliance, and self-rule, are like a philosopher's stone; their touch turns everything into gold for the nation whose people possess them. Their touch is so marvelous, powerful, and effective, that it cannot but turn into gold anything that these people take up!

The railroads and waterways in this country (which have become as easily accessible and as comfortable as royal routes, thanks to the unceasing efforts of these people) are extremely useful for commerce. It is difficult to even imagine their extensiveness. This vast country is more than twice the size—approximately two and a half times the size—of our country. The census of 1880 shows that the area of this country is 3,547,390 square miles. The natural features of the country are one of the important factors which have been instrumental in creating unity in this nation. With the exception of the State of Alaska,[11] the remaining 2,970,000 square miles form a contiguous landmass. The four borders of this contiguous land are British America, or Canada, to the north; the Atlantic Ocean to the east; the Gulf of Mexico and the free State of Mexico to the south; and the Pacific Ocean to the west.

There are large mountains in the east and west of the country, while the area in the middle is mostly flat. Several rivers flow from the mountains on both sides and from the highlands in the north to the center, and flow mostly into the Gulf of Mexico in the south. As most of the rivers flow through the middle of the country, the land receives sweet water in abundance, and makes it very fertile. In addition, the rivers are the great trade routes, and contribute in a very large measure to the internal trade of the country. The rivers here are also very long. The longest river in the country is the Mississippi (or the combined Missouri and Mississippi River). It is 4,500 miles long, and has an average width of 3,000 feet. Large steamers ply this river up to a distance of 3,900 miles. It is said that this river, together with its tributaries and branches, provides 35,000 miles of waterways for ships. The word "Mississippi" means (in the language of our Red brethren in North America) "The Father of Waters." The name seems apt indeed, when one sees the enormous expanse of this great river. An American writer, by the name of Carnegie, claims that the size and volume of water in the Missouri-Mississippi is equal in bulk to all the rivers of Europe combined, exclusive of the Volga. This great river is three times the size of the River Ganges in our country. The combined length of the rivers to the east of the Rocky Mountains is more than 40,000 miles, and the area along the riverbanks is twice as much in length, that is, 80,000 miles. In addition, there are great rivers like the Columbia, Sacramento, San Joaquin, etc., to the west of the Rockies, which traverse thousands of miles before flowing into the sea. Until the year 1880, 4,500 miles of canals were dug in the United States at a cost of $265,000,000, in order to connect these rivers and facilitate trade. The ports which are regarded as the largest, such as Philadelphia, Baltimore, New Orleans, and Portland, are located on riverbanks far from the seacoast. They are visited by thousands of steamships every year. They have large docks and are great centers of trade. The lakes in this country, like the rivers, are also vast.[i] The five largest lakes in America (Superior, Huron, Michigan, Erie, and Ontario) can be said to be sweet-water seas. They have a vast amount of trade carried on by numerous steamships and hundreds of boats.

The largest cities on the banks of these lakes, such as Duluth, Toledo, Buffalo, and Chicago, have begun to equal great seaports, such as New York, Boston, and New Orleans. Steamships are an invention of the American people which has greatly benefited the entire world. The very first steamship which traversed the Atlantic Ocean, and connected the people of the New and the Old World, sailed from America. These steamships do not carry on trade between this country and others (because that trade has already been grabbed mostly by England); however, there is an astonishing amount of trade within the country. According to a very knowledgeable man, trade amounting to $800,000,000 is carried on by steamships and other boats every year on the Ohio River.

The countless railroads in this country are another important means of facilitating trade. Until 1850, the railroad tracks and trains[12] here were quite poor, and caused passengers a great deal of inconvenience. Now the inconveniences, difficulties, delays at railroad stations, and the dawdling of trains are all gone. In 1830 only twenty-three miles of railroad tracks had been laid in the entire country.[13] In 1887 (that is, within fifty-five years of the beginning of railroads here) the country had 142,735 miles of tracks on which trains are now running.[14] Of these, 54,280 miles of railroads have been constructed during the ten years from 1873 to 1883. The total length of all the railroads in Europe does not equal the length of the railroads in the United States.[ii] In 1887 the whole world, with the exception of the United States, had only 150,012 miles of railroads in existence. The speed with which railroads are being constructed in the United States indicates that within ten years or so, this country will have more railroads than the rest of the world. (In 1880, only 273 miles of railroad had been laid in the whole of India; the very next year, 11,500 miles of railroads were constructed in this country. This will clearly show how far India lags behind the United States.)[15]

These waterways and railroads are like arteries in the body of the nation. Through them incessantly courses the lifeblood of the nation in the form of commerce.[16] The extent to which these two facilities assist the trade of the country cannot even be estimated. Every year the steamers and boats carry 25,500,000 tons of goods on the great lakes and rivers; the coasting trade carries 34,000,000 tons of goods; and the domestic trade by land and in railroad cars amounts to 291,000,000 tons of goods. The vast domestic trade in the United States, by waterways and railroads, is six times greater than the trade of Great Britain with other countries! There is no share of foreigners in it at all.

There is another astonishing thing which has contributed a great deal to the domestic trade and prosperity of this nation; namely, the telegraph and its subsidiary, the telephone. A marvelous network of 760,000 miles of telegraph wires is spread all across this country! It forms the nervous system of this country, like the nervous system in the human body, and is a very effective and vital part of the nation. Ever since Benjamin Franklin discovered electricity, the native people have begun to harness electricity to innumerable tasks. Electricity serves as a messenger through the telegraph and the telephone; it runs trains, lights lamps, operates machines, cures diseases, and plates metal! Few are the tasks it does not do. Every large store, warehouse, bank, government office, and large meeting hall has the telegraph. It can publish news sent from anywhere in the world—even when there is no person to receive it! Thanks to the telegraph and the telephone, it is easy to receive many different kinds of information, such as changes in the weather; prices of foodgrains, and of cloth, metals and coins at different places; etc.

Another factor which contributes to the prosperity of the country's trade is that no excise duty is charged on any goods, irrespective of the distance they travel within this vast land. Goods can be dispatched at a cheap rate by railroad and boat. And because they are spared the trouble of unpacking and declaring them at numerous places and the expense of the excise duty, they are available to all conveniently and at reasonable rates, besides yielding rich profits to the seller. The goods which come into this country from foreign countries are charged a heavy customs duty. Many people in the country claim that trade will be greatly encouraged if the customs duty is abolished. The levy of a customs duty on imported goods was very beneficial as long as the manufacturing sector of this country was not well developed, and the industries were not in a flourishing state; because the customs duty raised the prices of foreign goods, while the goods made in the country were cheap and were consequently bought by most people. Now the trade, industries, and manufactures of the United States are highly prosperous, so that there is no sufficient reason to retain the customs duty on imported goods. Even so, most people here oppose the abolition of the customs duty. The people here take great precautions to prevent the domination of foreign countries in trade and in other matters, and to prevent their becoming slaves of others. No one hesitates to buy goods imported from abroad, if the same type of goods is produced on a large scale within the country and exported to other countries. Such an exchange of goods involves no loss, only profit. But these people do not allow domestic industries or trade to be harmed by importing from abroad on a large scale goods which are not adequately used or traded within the country. This is worth remembering by the people of our country who look to England for everything, who rely entirely on England, and who use English goods to the detriment of native industries and trade. The American said that drinking the tea and wearing the clothes imported from England harms the industries of his country; therefore he would never drink such tea or wear English clothes, but would content himself with whatever good or bad clothes were available in his own country. And he also acted accordingly. That is why this country has reached such prosperity today. And what have we achieved? We have given our gold and bought pots of pewter in return; we have shut down our handlooms and started wearing cheap English clothes. Like the Indians of North America, we have succumbed to the lure of shiny, colored glass beads; and we have sold our precious gem-studded land to foreigners in return for glass beads and glass bottles filled with wine. Now we are screaming because the wine has started to claim our lives, and the fragments of broken glass have made gaping wounds in our feet. This is why our country is in such a wretched state! This clearly shows that the United States and India are on opposite sides of the globe!

Thus far I have outlined the factors contributing to the commerce and industries of this country. Now let us turn to the chief topic of this chapter. The industries of this country may be broadly divided into three types—agriculture, manufactures, and mining.

Agriculture

This is the chief industry of the people of the United States. Like all other things in this country, agriculture is also carried on scientifically, and is being improved day by day. The reason is that the farmers in this country are not illiterate; most of them can read and write. They read journals and books concerning agriculture, and make use of the scientific processes and chemical experiments which contribute to its advancement. The motto "E pluribus unum," that is, "One out of many," applies as much to agriculture as to other things. In this country there is a national society of farmers known as the National Grange.[17] The fundamental principles of the philosophy which supports it are revealed by the pledge of the society, which includes consensus on major matters, freedom of thought in general matters, and friendship in all matters. It also requires members to be mindful of achieving the progress of their occupation and their associates, and to exert themselves to divide all work equally and to ensure a fair distribution of its rewards. This society has branches in practically every town in the country. It treats men and women as equals. Women are granted all the rights related to the organization which men have. A historian of this society says that "every husband and brother knows that where he can take wife or sister, there will be no impurity." It is for this reason that the National Grange has made respectable women its members.

Farmers living in villages and on farms are deprived of advantages such as going to plays, concerts, and lectures, and of other means of enhancing their knowledge during their leisure hours. All their time, from sunrise to sunset, is spent in agricultural tasks. It is essential for them to have some amusement, and also to increase their knowledge. The Grange is engaged in unceasing efforts in this regard. In accordance with the society's rules, lectures and addresses on diverse topics by well-known and learned speakers are arranged several times a year. It makes arrangements to teach a variety of subjects to the men and women who so desire, during their free time. The farming community has gained in industriousness, progress, happiness, and wealth as a result of the knowledge derived from the information published by the United States Department of Agriculture, and from other books, as well as from experience; and as a result of the benefits of unity, and the knowledge of different subjects made available by the National Grange.

Since independence, the citizens and administrators of this nation have paid careful attention to the advancement of its agriculture.[18] The nation's first President, George Washington, personally supervised the Department of Agriculture, despite his various other duties. Men like Jefferson, Webster, Adams, and Clay, who were philosophers, leaders, and politicians, were farmers themselves. It is natural that such excellent examples should make people think of farming as a prestigious occupation, and encourage them to undertake it; and that farmers should be generally respected everywhere. One-fourth of the total wealth of the United States has been invested in agriculture, and one-fourth of the annual national product comes from agriculture.

The custom of the son following exactly in his father's footsteps does not exist here among the farmers, or among other people. They find it impossible that the countless men born in a family should follow their remote ancestor, and do the things in regular succession in exactly the same way—whether it comes to holding an axe, digging a canal, cutting a channel, plowing land; or whether it comes to making a honeycomb, building a nest with twigs, or making an anthill. Their inventiveness and scientific knowledge have been put to use in every practical matter. Machines are used even in agriculture here. On large farms, the steam machine for plowing and sowing is managed by one or two persons, and does the work of hundreds. On almost all farms, large and small, the machine for harvesting crops and binding sheaves is run by one man, and does the work of fifty or sixty. There are hundreds of such machines which are being used for agriculture. In our country, no one knows even their names, and no one would understand how they work by merely reading their description in books. The cost of the advanced implements and machines used by the native farmers in 1880 was $450,000,000, or Rs. 1,350,000,000. There is a vast area of land in the United States which is suitable for agriculture, but there are not enough people to work on it; that is why farmers find it necessary to take the help of machines. This necessity has greatly encouraged invention among the American people, and thousands of new machines are being created. Also people engaged in agriculture and other occupations use these newly created machines with great eagerness.

The census of 1880 shows that the United States (excluding the large Territory of Alaska)[19] has 1,500,000 square miles of land which is suitable for cultivation. (Our India has a total area of 1,383,500 square miles; this means that the cultivable land in the United States is larger in area than our entire country.) All the land in this country is new, because it was not cultivated by anyone before the English and other Europeans settled here. It was overgrown by forest and grass everywhere. Whatever people know today about the history of this country shows that the land here had remained untouched by a plow since the beginning of creation, until the time of European settlement. Needless to say, it is therefore a very difficult and laborious task to cut down the forest, and to plow and bring under cultivation the land which has become hard due to the growth of forest since times immemorial. But praise be to the industry and diligence of these people! So far they have brought under cultivation at least 297,000 square miles of land. At the beginning of this century, about 65,000 square miles of land were under cultivation in the United States. During the subsequent sixty years, an additional 150,000 square miles of land were plowed and made cultivable. From 1860 to 1880, 82,000 square miles of land were brought under cultivation.

It has already been mentioned that the system of landholders and peasants is not common here. The inhabitants of the Southern States owned large estates on which African slaves worked. Now the Black people have become free, and most of them have settled down in the same place where they lived earlier. They rent small farms from the owners of large estates, and work them. In all probability, they will buy the farms which they now rent, as soon as they are able to pay the price. The laws related to the purchase and sale of land in this country are very simple. In the Western States also, some people own extensive farms. But many feel that such classes of estate holders and peasants should not exist in the country. At present most farmers work the small farms they own. There are a total of 4,000,000 farms in the United States, and about three-fourths of them are independently owned, and cultivated by the owners themselves. Of the 4,005,907 farms here, 322,350 have been rented out; 699,244 are held in shares; and 2,984,306 are independently owned. Each farm has an average size of 134 acres; however, one would find at least 30,000 farms which are larger than 1,000 acres. Cultivable land is also available at cheap rates here. At present, an acre of land costs about $20 in some States. The price of land is $7 to $34 per acre in several Northern States along the Atlantic coast. Day by day the land becomes more expensive as population and the number of settlers increase. Land prices have more than doubled between 1850 and 1880.

The land which is already under cultivation, or can be brought under cultivation, is usually flat; and machines are heavily used in agriculture. Water is available everywhere in abundance. Farmers do not hesitate to put in effort and use machinery in their work. They exert themselves in every way to make this fertile land more productive. All these favorable factors have resulted in a great wealth of grains in the United States, which will continue to be augmented in the future. In the year 1880, 118,000,000 acres of land produced about 2,700,000,000 bushels of grains, that is, an average of about 23 bushels per acre. They included 1,750,000,000 bushels of corn, 460,000,000 bushels of wheat, 407,000,000 bushels of oats, and many other grains.

Corn, cotton, and wheat are the chief crops of this country. Animals, like hogs, cattle, and horses, are usually fed corn. Hogs eat nothing but corn. A great deal of corn is also sold to people. In 1880, corn worth $10,000,000 was exported, after supplying the whole country's needs. Until 1860, the people of the country needed to import wheat. Now it produces one-fourth of all the wheat which is produced in the whole world. In 1860, this country produced 173,000,000 bushels of wheat; in 1870 it produced 287,000,000 bushels; in 1880 459,000,000 bushels; and in the year 1884, 500,000,000 bushels of wheat. This gives some indication of the speed with which the production of crops like wheat is increasing.

Twenty-seven years ago, the native people needed to import wheat; but in 1880 surplus wheat amounting to $190,000,000 in value was exported.

The people of this country began to plant cotton in 1776. It seemed doubtful at first whether cotton could be grown here, and whether it would be profitable. However, when the decision to grow cotton had once been made, it was implemented wholeheartedly. Soon after the country became independent, a man named Eli Whitney invented a machine to separate the seed from the cotton fiber. Cotton plantations began to flourish at that time. A heavy tariff was imposed on imported cloth in order to encourage the use of this new domestic crop within the country, and to encourage the sale of domestic goods; naturally the native looms multiplied, and cloth was produced everywhere in the country. Before 1880 the cotton of this country was utilized mostly within the country; however, during that year cotton worth about $30,000,000 was exported from the country. In the year 1880, 5,757,397 bales of cotton were produced in the country, of which cotton worth $220,000,000 was exported. Two-thirds of this cotton was sold in England. The cloth which England manufactures and sells at a cheap rate in our country is made mostly from American cotton. The cotton here yields very fine and excellent thread.

There is a grain called rye, of which bread is made. It is also grown on a large scale here. In the year 1880, 20,000,000 bushels of it were grown here. Similarly, 44,000,000 bushels of barley, and 407,000,000 bushels of a grain called oats were grown; also 203,000,000 bushels of potatoes were grown. A great deal of hay is grown in the Great Plains of the east and the west. In the year 1880, about 36,000,000 tons of hay were sold in the market. The tobacco plant is widely grown here; 638,000 acres of land are under this wretched crop, which is why tobacco is produced in abundance here. Half of it is consumed in the country, and half is exported. There is a wealth of different kinds of fruit in this country. The value of the fruit grown in 1880 exceeded $20,000,000. Reliable evidence shows that the price of native crops produced in that year exceeded $3,020,000,000, and the crops produced in 1884 amounted to $2,721,500,000.

It has been mentioned earlier that livestock, such as hogs and cattle, are treated like vegetables here, and "farmed" like other crops. In 1880, there were 56,750,000 hogs here; and 46,000,000 cattle, of which 18,500,000 were milk cows. (The cows here do not yield merely a quart or a pint of milk, as cows in our country do. They are well-fed; and efforts are made to ensure their proper growth and physical well-being. These cows yield a bucketful of milk.) This country had 45,000,000 sheep and 12,500,000 horses in 1880; by now they must have greatly increased. Naturally, all these animals are useful to the country. Large quantities of their meat is left over for export, after supplying the 56,000,000 meat-loving people in this country. The business of curing the meat of hogs, etc., for export started a few years ago. The value of the meat of hogs, cattle, sheep, etc., exported every year exceeds $117,500,000. In the year 1880, 240 millions of pounds of wool were produced in this country. The annual report of National Butter, Cheese, and Egg Association (a rather strange name, which cannot be helped) states that the annual value of dairy products, such as butter and cheese, in the United States is more than $100,000,000. In 1880, the farmers in the United States had an income (that is, profit, after deducting expenses) exceeding $550,000,000. Everything is great when it comes to the great!

Manufactures

Before 1776 the thirteen English colonies of North America were under subjection in all matters. As they were under the sovereign rule of the English Government, only such strict laws were enforced in the thirteen colonies as would benefit England and its people. George III was King of England just before the colonies became independent States; his reign was quite intolerable to these people. A customs duty was levied on all imported and exported goods in the country. These people had no freedom to trade independently with other countries; there was a rule that they should trade only with English merchants at English rates. They were to mine iron and other ores, and send them to England, but not manufacture metals themselves. Moreover, many Englishmen even insisted that the colonists should not have the right even to manufacture a horseshoe nail. High customs duties were levied on all goods produced here and exported to England. Duties on exports, duties on imports, taxes on sales—all these perpetual levies really reduced them to exasperation. The colonists did not have the right to cut a tree which had a diameter of two feet at the height of a foot above the ground. These people were quite shackled by these and many other similar restrictions which signaled subjection. Their trade and industries received no encouragement. Their backs were bent under the heavy burden of taxation. Finally the Stamp Act and the tax on tea strengthened their desire for independence; and they threw off the yoke of England, and broke the shackles of English laws. In 1785, the war of independence was over and peace was established in the country; and the government began to run smoothly. Laws which would encourage the country's trade came rapidly into existence, one after another. This was the beginning of their days of prosperity. A number of wars were fought in Europe from 1790 to 1820, which disrupted the commerce of that continent and encouraged the commerce of the United States. From this time until 1860, there was no hindrance to the trades and industries of this country. Subsequently, the war which afflicted this country for five years was very detrimental to commerce. From 1866 to the present, the trades and industries here have been conducted without interruption, and all their losses have been compensated for; moreover, this nation has now become wealthier than England, which calls itself the richest nation on earth. As soon as the Americans settled here, they concentrated on improving their manufacturing to such an extent that within a few years the English felt threatened by them, and felt compelled to make strict laws intended to prevent the rise of manufacturing here. Until 1830, manufacturing did not flourish here; time was spent only on establishing peace in the nation and in placing manufacture, as well as other trades and industries, on a firm footing. The extent to which manufactures have advanced in this country now has to be seen to be believed.

Industrial manufactures are flourishing here, day by day. A few years ago England was the most industrialized country on earth; now the United States claims that pre-eminence. The use of machines for everything has carried every type of manufacture to gigantic proportions. Making flour with the help of machines is the largest industry.[20] This country has 24,000 flour mills, which grind 5,000,000 bushels of flour daily. In 1880, the capital invested in this industry was $177,400,000; and the value of the flour produced that year was $500,000,000. This quantity of flour is sufficient not only for the American people, but for all the people of Europe. The flour produced by the Americans is sold in large quantities in Europe, Japan, China, India, and other countries. Next to the milling of flour is slaughtering, which also uses machines. The animal to be slaughtered is stood next to the machine; it is killed, skinned, emptied of its innards, stuffed with spices, and packed within a minute. Within five minutes, it reaches the person standing on the other side of the machine. Chicago has a very large mechanized slaughterhouse; there are similar slaughterhouses in other places. In the year 1880, 5,750,000 hogs and 500,000 cattle were slaughtered, stuffed with spices, and dispatched for sale. A capital of $50,000,000 has been invested in this business; and more than $10,500,000 goes to pay its employees each year. In one year, 1,700,000 cattle; 2,200,000 sheep; and 16,000,000 hogs were slaughtered, stuffed with spices, packed, and exported to markets all over the world to feed people.

In the manufacture of iron and steel the capability of the United States is next to that of England. One-fifth of all the iron and one-fourth of all the steel used in the world is manufactured in the United States. In 1883, the value of all the iron and steel goods manufactured in this country was $400,000,000. The rapid and uninterrupted advancement and growth of this industry indicates that by the year 1890 the United States will manufacture more iron and steel goods than England. In the year 1870, 64,000 tons of steel were manufactured here; ten years later, that is, in 1880, 1,373,513 tons of steel were manufactured. The United States has many iron mines; and, considering the extraordinary industriousness of these people, the ore will not remain unused in the mines, but will be made useful for humanity and increase the wealth of the country. There are large factories also for making goods and machines of brass, bell metal, and other metals. A large amount of capital has been invested in it, and the goods manufactured amounted to more than $214,000,000 in value in 1881.

The lumber trade, or cutting timber and selling it for building houses, etc., is very large. I do not know whether such an industry exists in any other country. But I conjecture that other countries do not possess forests to the extent that the United States does; or even if they do, the people of other countries have certainly not made any progress in the lumber trade. In the year 1880, 148,000 people earned their living from this industry. A capital of $200,000,000 was invested in it, and the lumber was valued at $233,268,720. There are very large forests in the States of Michigan, Wisconsin, Minnesota, Oregon, and Northern California, and in the Territory of Washington. There are some areas which produce nothing but forest trees. Industrious people cut enormous quantities of wood in all these forests, and acquire wealth by selling it within the country and outside. Durable, beautiful, and valuable wood of numerous kinds—oak, cherry, maple, mahogany, walnut, etc.—is produced here; it is cut, dressed, and sent to Europe. The golden land of the United States produces four hundred different kinds of useful wood!

Next in size is the cotton manufacture. The capital invested in it in the year 1880 was $208,000,000; and the value of the cotton goods produced in the country exceeded $192,000,000. Large quantities of cotton grown here are sold in England and other countries; that is why not much cloth is produced here. Even so, enough cloth is produced to supply the people of the country. Next in importance is the trade in wool. The capital invested in it amounts to $95,000,000, and the woolen goods manufactured in the country are estimated to have the same value. More than 86,000 people are employed in this industry. The manufacture of mixed (wool and cotton) textiles was valued at $66,250,000 in 1880. In the same year, a capital of $19,000,000 was invested in silk manufacture; the value of materials used was $18,500,000, and the value of products $34,500,000. Knitwear—such as stockings, gloves, etc., made of wool, silk, and cotton; and those made of wool and silk mixed—which were produced during that year were valued at $62,000,000. The people of the country started making woolen carpets barely twenty-five years ago; the industry has prospered during such a short time. In 1880, the carpets, etc., produced in this country had a value of $21,750,000. Shoemaking is also an important industry. The use of machinery has greatly assisted this industry also. Fifty years ago, a cobbler in this country took a lot of time and trouble to make shoes, just like a cobbler in our country. In those days, a cobbler would feel quite satisfied if he produced one shoe per day. Now, with the help of machines, one man can make three hundred shoes a day! In 1870, there were 3,000 large shoe factories in this country, in which about 9,200,000 people were employed.

A few years ago, all the watches required by the people of the United States came from Europe. Now so many watches are produced in the United States that they not only suffice for all the people here, but are sold in most countries of Europe and in India. Like all other industries here, the watchmaking factories are very large and very advanced. In about 1850, the best factories considered it an achievement to produce four to five watches per day. Now twelve or thirteen hundred watches are produced per day in similar factories. There are four or five large factories which produce as many watches every day. They never stop working. One of the factories sends six thousand watches every month to London alone. Within a few years, all the people on earth will begin to have such inexpensive, beautiful, and convenient clocks in their possession. Similarly, the sewing machines made by the American people will be in use everywhere. In 1880, about $11,863,188 worth of sewing machines were manufactured. Also, silverware, gold ornaments, and other items of engraved design are made very well here. The craftsmen of the United States are very skilled in etching and carving wood. It is not possible to adequately describe all these industries in this small essay.

It is difficult to even imagine how rapidly industrial production has progressed and is still making strides. In 1850, the value of all manufactured goods was $1,060,000,000. In 1880, goods worth $5,560,000,000 were manufactured in this country. During the same year, the goods manufactured in England were valued at $4,055,000,000. This shows that the United States manufactures $1,505,000,000 worth of goods more than England does.

Mining

The golden land of the United States has become a land of gold not merely because of its fertile surface. Just as Goddess Nature has made this independent nation rich in all external comforts and conveniences, so has she deposited inexhaustible stores of gems and precious metals in innumerable underground chambers, in the form of mines, beneath the surface of this nation.[21] Goddess Nature works her magic in these innumerable, vast underground chambers for the benefit of the American people, and transforms earth into gold. Within this nation's four boundaries of East, West, North, and South lie sheer green pastures, fertile and rich fields, forests adorned with rows of sky-high trees, cities filled with a happy and prosperous populace, as well as seemingly bare and barren plains. Beneath all these, in deep subterranean chambers, Goddess Nature has stored many things, such as gold, silver, lead, copper, mercury, nickel, salt, coal, oil, combustible mineral gas, excellent varieties of stone, sulfur, etc., for the fortunate people of the United States. Just as a calf, while drinking milk, nudges its mother's udders with its head once in a while and makes her release more milk; so do the American people scratch the back of their motherland once in a while. She is instantly pleased; she brings forth countless metals and gems from her inexhaustible treasure, and hands them over to her children. These American people have grown so fortunate thanks to their industriousness and inventiveness that any handful of earth they pick up turns into gold.

Chief among the minerals in this country is coal. The area under coal mines on this earth is said to be 400,000 square miles, of which 12,000 square miles of coal mines are found in the United Kingdom of Great Britain. It is said on good authority that the coal mines in the United States cover an area of 300,000 square miles. It is not easy to imagine that three-fourths of all the coal mines on earth are found in the United States; but it happens to be true. It may be said that the abundance of coal is instrumental, to a large degree, in achieving the prosperity of all kinds of trades and industries in this country. Although this country contains three-fourths of all the mines on earth, the amount of coal mined here does not equal that mined in England. One reason is that coal mining in this country started not very long ago; and another is that these people are too busy mining enormous amounts of gold, silver, copper, iron, oil, and other valuable minerals to feel the need to mine coal. Even so about 87,386,000 tons of coal were mined in this country last year.

It is said that the earth as a whole contains 10,355 tons of gold, about half of which come from the American continent. Every year since 1880, $31,250,000 worth of gold, that is, one-third of all the gold mined all over the world every year, has been mined in the United States. Like all other industries, gold mining has also expanded rapidly. From 1851 to 1860, the amount of gold mined every year was worth $5,000,000 on an average. Now the gold mined every year is worth more than $31,250,000. The same is the case with silver. Silver worth $46,250,000 is mined here every year. It is said that about half the copper on earth is produced by the two countries of Chile and the United States together. In the year 1880, 252,000 tons of copper were mined in the United States; and four years later the annual production was doubled. In the year 1884, 63,555 tons of copper were mined. There are numerous lead mines here. Around 1830, an average of 8,000 tons of lead were mined every year; now at least 140,000 tons of lead are mined annually. Before 1870, very little zinc was mined in this country. Now 35,000 tons of zinc are mined here every year.

Mineral oil, or rock oil, is plentiful here.[22] A few years ago, factories were built here to produce coal oil. But it was discovered that there are underground supplies of this mineral oil in several places in Pennsylvania, and that oil flows out along with river water. Large wells were then sunk everywhere, and oil pumped out. The oil of the United States is now supplied to the whole world. Natural gas was found while deep wells were being sunk for mineral oil. This gas is plentiful in this country. In some towns in Pennsylvania, the steam engines in all the factories and mills are run on this natural gas. Cooking, heating houses during the winter, lighting lamps, etc. are done with the help of gas. In addition, gas is very useful in chemical experiments. It is used for purifying glass, iron, and steel. There are hundreds of gas wells near Pittsburgh; it is said that each of these wells produces 70,000,000 cubic feet of gas every day.

In 1849, it was discovered that the State of California contains gold. At once the people of the Eastern States rushed to the Pacific Coast. Since then, everybody has begun to get up and go west to mine gold. Large cities came up overnight, like enchanted cities, in the uninhabited forest areas like Colorado, Nevada, and California. Cities appeared where there had been forests before, and fields full of grain appeared on plains which had been covered by grass. It is enough to get the news that a mine has been found somewhere, or that something useful exists or can be produced at some place. These people become as if possessed and start rushing off there; and they overcome mountains of difficulties in order to attain their goal. A proper description of the industry and commerce of these people would run into large volumes. The details of this country's net annual revenue (after deducting expenditure) are as follows:

Agriculture	$550,000,000
Mining	$56,250,000
Manufactures	$20,500,000
The Fisheries	$7,250,000
The Forest	$7,050,000
Other	$7,250,000

Thus the annual revenue from all industries is $648,300,000.

The British nation is very famous as the richest nation on earth. It is an old nation. It has accumulated in its treasury, through industries and by other means, wealth amounting to $43,600,000,000. The republic of the United States is about a hundred and twenty-five years old. It has accumulated in its treasury, solely through industries, wealth amounting to $48,950,000,000.[23] No one is likely to imagine that the United States is even wealthier than England; nevertheless, this is true.

Philanthropy[24]

The people who came to settle in this country were not wealthy to begin with; and those who are coming to settle now are not wealthy either. But the hardworking people acquired wealth through their industry after coming here. Now the descendants of those people will be born rich. Those who are born rich in our country have gained notoriety "by hook or by crook."[25] Many fear that in this country, too, those who are born rich will ruin their hearth and home. Nevertheless, there does not appear to be any reason to believe that this country will be reduced to misery, like our country, through the deeds of such "bright lights" of their families (who would set their families aflame). The United States is like a gigantic honeycomb. Only worker bees survive here; there is no place for lazy drones who live on the labor of others. The worker bees allow the lazy drone to survive only as long it serves their purpose. Once that is done, they sting the lazy parasitical being to death.[26] The people who were originally poor, and who have become opulent today on the strength of their industry and education, know very well the reason for their advancement. They do not support lazy and idle people. And they do not throw away their really hard-earned money on celebrating the weddings of pigeons, cats, etc.;[27] on inferior types of luxuries; on giving banquets for sahibs and arranging fireworks; on watching plays and dance performances. They put their money to good use.

There are many wealthy people here who possess enough money to buy large kingdoms. They establish societies to help the advancement and education of future generations, as befits their affluence.[28] Trevor[29] and Corcoran[30] donated $100,000 each for the establishment of colleges; Williston,[31] Walker,[32] Hitchcock,[33] and Winkley[34] donated $165,000 each; Colgate[35] and Crozer[36] $265,000 each; Cheney[37] and Bussey[38] $330,000 each; Stone[39] $400,000; Phoenix[40] $1,325,000; Vanderbilt[41] and Vassar[42] $665,000 each, Clark[43] $825,000; a man named Green[44] $1,000,000; a man named Rich[45] $1,325,000; Parker[46] $2,325,000; Stephen Girard[47] and Johns Hopkins[48] donated $3,325,000 each for establishing colleges. Leland Stanford,[49] president of the Southern Pacific Railway and Senator from California, spent $30,000,000 to establish a university in memory of his only son, who had died.

This great generosity of these extremely wealthy people has helped the very praiseworthy cause of education. This country has no reason to fear the brainless "born rich" as in our country, as long as the rich people of this country put their money to such good uses; and as long as the people regard education as highly important, and also direct school education towards practical usefulness!

Notes in the Original Text

i. The length and area of the largest lakes in the United States are as follows:

	Length	Area
Lake Cayuga	38 miles	104 sq m
Lake George	36	110
Salt Lake	75	240
Lake Ontario	190	6,300
Lake Erie	240	9,600
Lake Huron	250	21,000

Lake Michigan	340	22,000
Lake Superior	360	32,000

In addition, this country has numerous lakes which are sixteen miles or less in length. All the lakes, with the exception of Salt Lake, have sweet water, and they are said to contain one-third of all the sweet water on this earth.

ii. It is learned on good authority that the railroads in all of Europe in 1880 had a combined length of 114,262 miles.[50] This shows that the railroads in the United States were 28,473 miles longer than the railroads of the whole continent of Europe.

Translator's/Editor's Notes

Preface

1. Ramabai's lectures had a varied reception. Poona's *Kesari* ornately eulogized "her own feats of bravery" as "hardly less important that those of the American women she describes" (*Kesari,* 28 May 1889; my translation). Bombay's *Indu-Prakash* (10 and 17 June 1889) published an anonymous letter questioning the success of women's education in the USA, and Ramabai's response. *Dnyanodaya* reported the gist of her lectures and pointed out alleged errors (1 August, 8 August, and 22 August 1889).

2. For the U.S. census data and other factual information Ramabai has drawn upon Carnegie, who in turn acknowledged his reliance on *Scribner's Statistical Atlas* as his principal source (Carnegie 1886: vii–viii).

3. This is most probably a reference to Gopalrao Joshee, who traveled around the USA from mid-1884 to September 1886, giving lectures on the glories of Indian culture and exposing the seeming deficiencies of American culture. The embarrassment caused to Anandibai Joshee and her friends, who had extended hospitality and financial help to both her and her husband, has been documented by Dall (1888: 136–43).

1. Voyage from Liverpool to Philadelphia

1. Rachel Bodley (1831–1888) trained as a chemist and botanist, and taught natural sciences before being appointed to the first chair of chemistry at WMCP. An active participant in several scientific societies, she became dean of the college in 1874; and was awarded an honorary M.D. degree in 1879. Her questionnaire survey of WMCP graduates and their professional success, made in 1881, was hailed as the first study of professional women in the USA. Bodley also had a special interest in medical missionary work (*NAW* I: 186–87).

   Bodley had written to Ramabai in late 1885: "My thought in inviting you to come to America early in 1886 has been that if the tidings might be sent to India that you braved a wintry ocean to witness Anandibai receive her degree as a Doctor of Medicine, you in a certain sense gave your sanction to her act and enfolded her and her work in your own future leadership" (*Letters:* 165).

2. Despite opposition from CSMV and Miss Beale, Ramabai decided as a matter of duty to go to the USA, "first, because the kind people who have given every kind of help to my cousin to study medicine want to see me, and have invited me again and again . . . Secondly, if I do not go, I shall greatly injure the cause of my countrywomen, for those kind people will think it very rude of me and the interest which they take in my countrywomen will in some measure be lessened" (*Letters:* 163).

3. It is not clear whether the term "Hindu" here refers specifically to the Hindu community or means Indian in general, as it did (and still does) in the USA. In this

chapter Ramabai has used the words "Hindustan" and "Hindustani" for India and Indian.

4. The word used here is the Sanskrit *jati,* also used in Marathi, which embodies the concept of type or species and therefore has several connotations, including caste, class, community, tribe, race, and nationality. The meaning most appropriate to the context has been selected each time. In the present case Ramabai probably means "nationality" as well, which was covered by "race" in the nineteenth century English usage.

5. Throughout this chapter Ramabai interchangeably uses two Marathi words meaning "ship" or "sailing vessel," and employs the equivalent for "steamboat" only for a boat on the Delaware, at the end of the chapter. The now prevalent Marathi word for "steamship" or "steamer" (literally "fire-boat"), which was already in use then, appears in this text, except in chapter 9.

6. Such accounts appear in chapters 5 and 7.

7. The word used here is *karnadhar,* literally "helmsman."

8. The word used here is *ghataka,* a unit of twenty-four minutes.

9. This is a Sanskrit quotation.

10. The word used here is the Sanskrit *jivanmukta* (one who is liberated from future births), which has a clear Hindu connotation.

11. Ramabai's references to Anandibai in the present tense indicates that this portion of the text is dated prior to February 1887. The blood relationship between the two women was rather remote; Ramabai's father and Anandibai's maternal grandmother being cousins (*Indu-Prakash,* 5 August 1889). Anandibai and Ramabai had corresponded with each other in Bengal in 1882 (Dall 1888: vi–vii), but their first meeting occurred in Philadelphia on 6 March 1886.

12. The Education Commission (also known as the Hunter Commission on Education) was in fact appointed in 1882, and Ramabai testified before it in Poona on 5 September 1882. The complete testimony is reproduced in Kosambi (forthcoming).

13. During his Poona visit, Dr. Hunter was invited to a meeting of the Arya Mahila Samaj, which was attended by almost three hundred women and a few men (including M. G. Ranade). Ramabai read a Marathi address, "signed by nearly fifty ladies," elaborating upon some issues in her testimony; and the gist was translated into English by G. H. Deshmukh. Dr. Hunter responded with a speech endorsing Ramabai's suggestions about "the necessity for a female medical profession," which had also impressed other commission members; and promised to initiate informal action, although the commission's purview excluded technical education (*Times of India,* 12 September 1882).

   According to Bodley (1981 [1887]: xiii–xiv) Dr. Hunter had Ramabai's Marathi testimony translated into English and printed separately, which was indirectly responsible for the formation of the National Association for Supplying Female Medical Aid to the Women of India (also known as the Countess of Dufferin Movement, after its president).

14. This refers to the National Association for Supplying Female Medical Aid to the Women of India.

15. The word used here is the ancient Sanskrit *Bharatavarsha,* from which is derived the current name "Bharat" for India.

16. The word *pranapratishtha,* literally "bringing life into an idol when it is installed in a temple," seems to be used here advisedly to suggest the sacredness Ramabai attached to educational institutions.

17. The liberal thinking of Quakers, in terms of gender equality, is mentioned at the beginning of chapter 8, "The Condition of Women."

18. The County Medical Society strongly resisted admission of medical women. The *Philadelphia Inquirer* (5 October 1883) reported the start of the thirty-fourth session of WMCP ("Among the new students is Mrs. Anandabai Joshi [*sic*], the Hindoo woman, who proposes to take a four years' course at the institution") and added: "The County Medical Society held an animated meeting on Wednesday to vote on the petition for admission of three women, graduates of the Womens' [*sic*] Medical College. After an exciting debate a vote was taken, and it was found that the sentiment of the society was strongly against their admission, the highest candidate receiving but sixty-five votes."

2. The "Nethermost World," or Continent of America

1. The word used here is the Sanskrit *jati,* which also translates as "community"; see chapter 1, note 4.

2. The Puranas are ancient sacred books of the Hindus, which range from cosmology to heroic tales in their contents and contain descriptions of marvels. The Nethermost World (*patal*) below the earth is described variously as the Netherworld and as a veritable paradise filled with palaces and parks, where even the sun emits only light and not the usual scorching heat. Here Ramabai presents a progressive critique of the ancient Sanskrit literature, which lacked texts on history, geography, and similar branches of knowledge, and implicitly acknowledges the superiority of Western secular knowledge.

3. Shankaracharya was a great Hindu sage of the seventh and eighth centuries A.D. who revived Hinduism in all its Brahmanic tradition of rituals, a tradition that had been effectively challenged since the fifth century B.C. by Buddhism and Jainism, which emphasized ethical action as the determinant of spiritual welfare, rather than ritual observances and caste status.

4. This would translate as the "honorable" popes. The suffix *-ji* is an honorific often attached to names.

5. Ramabai adds a note here referring the reader to Mr. V. K. Oak's Marathi book *Hindusthan Katharasa* [Tales of India] "which has an excellent description of Vasco da Gama's voyage in the section entitled 'The Entry of the Portuguese into India.'" The book was published in Bombay in 1871 (Date 1944: 255).

6. This is an allusion to a significant event in Hindu mythology. The contest for supremacy between the gods and demons led to a tussle to acquire Nectar hidden in the depths of the Great Ocean; and the churning of the Ocean produced fourteen Gems, starting with Poison and ending with Nectar.

7. The rupee was the currency used in India at the time, as it is now. A rupee (then

divided into 64 *pice,* instead of 100 *paisas* as now) was worth one-third of a dollar. The *mohur* was an older coin of pre-British origin, usually made of gold.

8. The reference is obviously to the Inquisition in Spain and Portugal, and witch-hunting in medieval Europe.

9. Here Pandita Ramabai has used the Indian figure *lakh* or *lac* (one hundred thousand). Wherever possible, I have transcribed the figures in numerals for easy reading.

10. This is slightly inaccurate. Cabot in fact visited North America first in 1497.

11. Independence was formally gained in 1783, not in 1781 as Ramabai suggests.

3. System of Government

1. The two sayings are quoted in Sanskrit in the original Marathi text.

2. Ramabai uses the words "created free and equal."

3. According to Hindu mythology, Time, which is infinite, consists of repetitions of a cycle of four eons or *yugas.* First comes Kritayuga (spanning almost two million years), which is ideal in terms of morality and general happiness. Next follow Tretayuga, Dwaparyuga, and Kaliyuga (in which we now live, and which extends to almost half a million years), which are successively shorter and characterized by greater moral decline. After Kaliyuga has destroyed the world, the cycle starts again with another Kritayuga.

4. This is a reference to the Indian goddess Satwai (a folk form of the goddess Durga), who is believed to write an infant's destiny on its forehead on the sixth day after its birth. For the Chinese Exclusion Act of 1882, see chapter 5, note 25.

5. The following description is, in fact, taken from Carnegie (1886: 99–100).

6. A *panchayat* is the traditional Indian council of elders (usually five) which settles disputes. Each village had its own *panchayat;* in cities each caste had its own.

7. This appendix does not appear in the book.

8. This paragraph and the next two sections, "Counties" and "States," are based broadly on Carnegie (1886: 101–102).

9. The sections "Supreme Court," "Congress," and "Senate" are based on Carnegie (1886: 369–84).

10. Ramabai states explicitly that some senators resign, when in fact it is only a matter of their term being over.

11. Sahib was a descriptive label applied usually to a British official (and by extension any British person) in India.

12. This section is based on Carnegie (1886: 384–91).

13. This was only custom at this point. The Twenty-second Amendment to the Constitution making this provision was adopted on 26 February 1951.

14. If the president is to be impeached, he is tried by the Senate, with the Chief Justice of the Supreme Court presiding.

15. Inauguration Day was initially set for 4 March, but was changed to 20 January by a constitutional amendment in 1933.

16. This section is based on Carnegie (1886: 449–65).

17.	A picture of the Star-Spangled Banner was reproduced on the frontispiece of the original Marathi book.

18.	The reference to Delhi Gate is somewhat unclear. Ramabai probably means the main gate to the pre-British ruler's palace (Shaniwar Wada) in Poona, which is a symbol of his military might and ability to control vast areas of the Indian subcontinent. The palace was destroyed by fire in 1827, shortly after the British takeover (in a suspected case of British arson), but the massive stone ramparts and the gate still stand as emblems of Poona's past glory.

19.	The currently prevalent Marathi word for "citizen" is *nagarik,* which literally means a resident of a city (Sanskrit *nagara*) and does not carry the connotation Ramabai was so concerned about.

4. Social Conditions

1.	This paragraph is based on Carnegie (1886: 19–20).

2.	This was a protest often made by progressive public leaders. As a member of the Poona Municipality, Jotirao Phule had voted against the proposed municipal expenditure on the occasion of the governor-general's visit to the city (Keer and Malshe 1969: xvii).

3.	Chapter 9 has a brief description of the length of railroads in the USA.

4.	This description of fire stations is based on Carnegie (1886: 83).

5.	Ramabai does not use different words for "state" and "commonwealth."

6.	This and the following three paragraphs are based on Carnegie (1886: 105–106), where he cites Fiske (1885). Ramabai's personal library includes a copy of Fiske with her signature on the flyleaf, followed by "San Francisco Cal, U.S.A., Nov. 26th 1888."

7.	Presumably as a result of Ramabai's visit and talk there, Gilbertsville established a Ramabai Circle and pledged funds for her proposed residential school for high-caste widows in India (Ramabai Association 1890: 12).

8.	Edwin Arnold's long poem *The Light of Asia,* which describes the life of the Buddha, was first published in 1879. It has gone through numerous editions in Britain and the USA, as well as in other countries.

9.	The phrase literally means "to win favors from Saraswati [Goddess of Learning] and Lakshmi [Goddess of Wealth]."

10.	Traditionally, when Untouchability was practiced, a village would have a separate colony of Untouchables on its outskirts. This was supposed to be a polluted area because they were required to perform the unclean tasks of sweeping streets, tanning and curing hides, etc.

5. Domestic Conditions

1.	The Marathi word used here literally means "paper covering."

2.	Traditional Indian houses had wooden windowpanes.

3.	Ramabai's postal address from July 1886 to April 1888 indicates that her lodgings were located at 553 North 16th Street in Philadephia (*Letters:* 195–213).

4. Traditional Indian meals are served on metal plates, with metal bowls.

5. As a Brahmin, Ramabai maintained a strict vegetarian diet all her life (Dongre and Patterson 1963: 39). A disappointed Sister Geraldine, who had expected a change in Ramabai's diet upon her conversion, accused her of clinging to "caste prejudices" and displaying unwarranted "pride." Ramabai wrote to her in 1885: "I confess I am not free from all my caste prejudices, as you are pleased to call them. I like to be called a Hindoo, for I am one, and also keep all the customs of my forefathers as far as I can. How would you, an Englishwoman, like being called a proud and prejudiced [person] if she were to go and live among the Hindoos for a time but did not think it necessary to alter her customs when they were not hurtful or necessary to her neighbours?" (*Letters:* 109).

6. See chapter 4, note 10.

7. Omitted from the translation here is a short sentence which plays upon the Marathi word for fashions, *nakhare,* which the author construes as *na khare,* or "not authentic."

8. Kumta lies on the west coast of India, about four hundred miles south of Bombay, in the northern part of the state of Karnataka.

9. Europeans turn pink quickly in the hot Indian climate, and were often referred to as "red-faced."

10. As the Chinese custom of foot-binding had entered the Western social reform discourse, so the Western practice of tight-lacing figured in the Indian social reform discourse on the "Age of Consent" in the late 1880s and early 1890s. The reformers advanced the physiological protection of girl brides as an argument for late cohabitation within marriage; the anti-reformers claimed that early cohabitation was no more harmful than tight-lacing, which was not banned by law (Kosambi 1998a: 135–62). Ramabai's exposé of American women's double standards anticipates by a century Chandra Talpade Mohanty's discussion of Western women's self-construction as "the normative referent" in a binary East-West analytic. Mohanty speaks of Western feminists' tendency to assume themselves to be fully empowered, aware, in control over their bodies, and enjoying decision-making freedom; and of viewing Third World women as passive, powerless, and exploited (Mohanty 1994: 199– 200).

11. Satwai is another name for the goddess Durga, who is believed to write the destiny of all infants; see chapter 3, note 4.

12. The weight is given here in *seers*; one *seer* approximates one pound.

13. In the 1850s the feminist protest against the tight, uncomfortable, and unhealthy dress worn by "ladies" resulted in the adoption of a new costume: a loose tunic, knee-length skirt, and ankle-length Turkish pantaloons. It was popularized most effectively by Amelia Bloomer, who wore it and publicized it in her feminist journal *The Lily,* and became known as the "Bloomer costume." The costume had to be soon abandoned because the public ridicule amounted to persecution (Flexner 1975: 83–84; Evans 1989: 103–104). The general movement for dress reform, however, had taken firm root.

14. Frances Willard (1839–1898) was a feminist best known for her association with the temperance movement which started in 1873 (see chapter 8) and which successfully

closed about three thousand saloons in some six months in the Midwest and the East. She was chosen secretary of the women's temperance organization of Illinois, and of the National Woman's Christian Temperance Union, which was founded in 1874. She was to serve as its president also, and tried to use this position to promote women's suffrage, which was opposed by the conservative members of the union, leading to long-lasting friction. In the 1880s Willard traveled widely within the country, promoting the establishment of the WCTUs in many states and territories in the country (*NAW* III: 610–19).

15. The Audubon Societies formed for bird protection in the USA are named after John James Audubon (1785–1851), a very popular ornithologist and artist (*DAB* I: 423–27).

16. This is a famous quotation from the Bhagavad Gita (chapter 2, verse 22) relating to death and the immortality of the soul. The soul is said to leave the old body and enter a new one, just as a man discards his torn clothes and dons new ones.

17. The word used here is *jati*. See chapter 1, note 4.

18. A Marathi proverb is quoted here in the original text, to the effect that "Every where the *palas* [Butea frondosa] tree has a triple leaf."

19. William Lloyd Garrison (1805–1879) started his reformist career by protesting against "intemperance and its kindred vices," but is best known for his anti-slavery efforts. He was one of the earliest to demand the "immediate and complete emancipation" of slaves, and spent thirty years advocating the abolitionist cause. Garrison was instrumental in the founding of the New England Anti-Slavery Society in 1831 and the American Anti-Slavery Society in 1833, and served as president of the American Anti-Slavery Society for twenty-two terms (*DAB* IV: 168–72).

20. Elizabeth Coltman Heyrick (1769–1831) was a British Quaker who campaigned actively for the abolition of slavery in the British colonies (<*http://www.spartacus. schoolnet.co.uk/REheyrick.htm*>).

21. Lucretia Mott (1793–1880) was an activist on many fronts: a Quaker minister and proponent of tolerance in religion, an abolitionist, and a pioneer in the women's rights movement. She helped William Lloyd Garrison to form the Philadelphia Female Anti-Slavery Society in 1833 (because women members were then not allowed in the American Anti-Slavery Society), and helped to organize the Anti-Slavery Convention of American Women. Ultimately she was to surpass Garrison's vision, and after the Thirteenth Amendment abolished slavery, she worked for suffrage for blacks. Mott exhibited a great deal of personal courage when threatened with mob violence on more than one occasion.

    Lucretia Mott's best-known activism was on behalf of women. Along with Elizabeth Cady Stanton, she organized the women's convention at Seneca Falls, N.Y., in 1848, and passed the "Declaration of Sentiments" modeled on the U.S. Declaration of Independence. She attended the conventions regularly and was also elected president in 1852. She was the first president of the American Equal Rights Association, formed in 1866. After the women's rights movement split into two factions in 1869, Mott worked hard, though unsuccessfully, for unity (*NAW* II: 592–95).

22. Wendell Phillips (1811–1884) was identified with the anti-slavery movement, and spoke eloquently at the meetings of the Massachusetts Anti-Slavery Society and on

other platforms from 1837 on, and was closely associated with William Lloyd Garrison. In 1840 he attended the World Anti-Slavery Convention as a delegate from Massachusetts, and supported Garrison in insisting that women be given equal rights as delegates. After the Civil War, when Garrison suggested dissolving the American Anti-Slavery Society, Phillips proposed its continuation and was chosen president. He supported other causes, such as prohibition, the rights of American Indians, and women's suffrage (*DAB* VII-2: 546–47).

23. Helen Hunt Jackson (1830–1885), a highly respected author of poetry and novels, devoted her later years to crusading for American Indian rights, and wrote *A Century of Dishonor* in 1881 as an indictment of the U.S. government for its conduct of Indian affairs. On a commission from the Interior Department, she surveyed the conditions of the West Coast Indians; when the report had no impact, she turned to fiction and wrote *Ramona* in 1884, in the spirit of her friend Harriet Beecher Stowe's *Uncle Tom's Cabin* (*NAW* II: 259–61). In a letter Ramabai mentions having read *A Century of Dishonor* (*Letters:* 174).

24. Alice Fletcher (1838–1923), ethnologist, feminist, and American Indian reformer, spent several years working among the Omaha Indians, and successfully petitioned the government to apportion the common tribal lands among the members of the tribe as individual holdings (later passed as the Dawes Act of 1887); she was appointed by the president in 1883 to carry out the apportionment. In 1885 she wrote a 700-page report for the U.S. Senate, entitled *Indian Education and Civilization.* In 1887 she was named a special agent of the Interior Department to implement the Dawes Act among the Winnebago Indians of Nebraska and the Nez Perce Indians of Idaho. Fletcher wrote several monumental ethnological works on Indian tribes. In the early 1870s, she joined Sorosis, a pioneering women's club started in New York; served as secretary for both Sorosis and the Association for the Advancement of Women; and worked actively in the temperance and anti-tobacco movements (*NAW* I: 630–33).

25. By 1882 more than 300,000 Chinese had already immigrated into the USA to work mostly as cheap labor in West Coast cities, which frustrated the American workers' bid for higher wages. In order to avoid imminent civil disorder, the Chinese Exclusion Act was passed in 1882. It banned the entry of Chinese laborers, strictly regulated the entry of other people from China, and denied citizenship to any Chinese person.

26. The Hindu calendar divides the year into six seasons of two lunar (thirty-day) months each. The year thus has 360 days, and the deficit is made up by adding an extra month—that is, repeating one of the months by turn—when necessary. The adjustment sometimes also requires that a month be dropped.

27. There is no such description.

28. Assam (where Ramabai lived after her marriage), in eastern India, is now a separate state in the Indian Union.

29. This is a Sanskrit quotation.

30. A word meaning "restaurant" is used for hotels in this paragraph, except once when the word *sarai* (lodge for long-distance travelers, often associated with merchant caravans) is used. Traditionally there were no hotels in India; travelers stayed overnight at temples or temple halls meant for such a purpose, or at *sarais*.

31. The word used here literally means the palace of the god Indra.

32. The amount mentioned is Rs. 6,000,000. Henceforth all amounts mentioned only in rupees in the original text are given only in dollars in this translation. Amounts mentioned in both rupees and dollars in the original text are retained unchanged.

33. The author of an unsigned interview with Ramabai states that she met her "at a fashionable watering place in America. She was staying there with some of those kind friends who took up so warmly and effectually the cause of Hindu widows which she had at heart . . ." (*Women's Penny Paper,* 25 May 1889). The reference is probably to Saratoga.

34. Hindus regard Ganges water to be so holy that drinking it or bathing in it is supposed to cleanse one of all sins.

35. The Marathi word for "dysentery" (*modashi*) has a double meaning, and the sentence can also be read as "The very thought has deflated my conceit."

36. The Puranas describe the earth as composed of seven islands, one of which has the golden Mount Meru at its center. A veritable heaven on earth because of its pleasant woods and forests, it is fit for the habitation of the gods.

37. Richard Heber Newton (1840–1914), a Protestant Episcopal clergyman from Philadelphia, served at All Souls' Church in New York City from 1869 to 1902 before going to Stanford University as the resident preacher. He was renowned as the foremost liberal Episcopal clergyman of his time (*DAB* VII: 474–75).

38. Ramabai's project was to establish a residential school for widows in India.

39. Kalidasa was a great Sanskrit poet and dramatist. Because of a lack of authentic biographical details, he is placed variously in the first century B.C. or the fourth century A.D. His *Shakuntala* was translated into English in the eighteenth century and became internationally famous.

40. Snow was a fascinating novelty for all Indians except in regions like Kashmir in the extreme north of the country, and its Marathi descriptions are couched in surprisingly similar terms, and appended with some didactic moral. Anandibai Joshee wrote to her husband on 9 January 1884: "Snow does not make a noise like the rain when it falls; it comes silently, it falls gently like very light feathers. It is very white and looks like powdered sugar. But when rain falls on the original snow, it solidifies artificially and is called 'ice.' It looks exactly like glass. If it remains in the streets by oversight, people slip and fall heavily, and are hurt in many ways. There is a Government order that every house-owner in the city must keep the area in front of his door clear. Therefore one has to go out of the city to see the real beauty of Nature, which I did when I visited Aunt [Mrs. Carpenter of Roselle, N.J.] during the vacation. One day we all played with snowballs, and I went with Aunt for a ride in a wheel-less carriage called 'sleigh' " (Kanitkar 1912: 225; my translation). A little later she wrote again on 31 January 1884: "Snow teaches us an excellent lesson; it falls so silently, no thunder can be heard or no lightning seen when it falls. In sum, it causes no disturbance. Besides, it makes all the surroundings as clean and lovely as itself. It gives equal treatment to all" (Kanitkar 1912: 220; my translation).

41. The Ramabai Association had been established in Boston in December 1887.

42. The actual word used is a *crore,* that is, 10,000,000.

43. There is no such description in the book.

44. The many mythological stories connected with Diwali include the one which Ramabai narrates here—Lord Krishna's killing of the demon Narakasura, who had harassed the gods and kept thousands of women in captivity. Ramabai chooses to ignore the conflict of good and evil implicit in the event, and stresses the aspect of political legitimacy. The four-day festival of Diwali marks the advent of the winter solstice and is celebrated with lamps and firecrackers.

45. This is a quotation from the ancient Sanskrit poet Bhartrihari, who describes the traits of men he characterizes as morally superior, medium, and inferior. Worse than the inferior type of men are those whom he feels unable to describe: "We know not who they may be!"

46. *Balabodha Meva* (roughly, Moral Instruction for Children) was started by the American Mission in 1873 as a journal specializing in amusing stories and poems, and illustrated information about animals and birds (Date, Kale, and Barve 1969: 177).

47. Henry Bergh (1811–1888) pioneered the movement for the humane treatment of animals in the USA, through street sermons and lectures, mainly in New York City. He set up the American Society for the Prevention of Cruelty to Animals in 1866, on the model of the Royal Society for the Prevention of Cruelty to Animals in Britain (*DAB* I: 215–16).

48. George T. Angell (1823–1909), reformer and philanthropist, established the Massachusetts Society for the Prevention of Cruelty to Animals (MSPCA); started a periodical, *Our Dumb Animals,* in 1868; formed the American Band of Mercy in 1882, and helped to organize local Bands of Mercy in order to carry his message to children in public and Sunday schools; and established the American Humane Education Society in 1889 (*DAB* I: 303–4). As mentioned in the introduction, Mr. Angell used the text of Ramabai's letter for "The Pundita Ramabai Humane Pamphlet," which was sold by the MSPCA.

   Ramabai seems to have been deeply influenced by Mr. Angell. Years later she reported that in her Sharada Sadan she gave the girls "humane education. That is a monument to our dear friend Mr. Angell, God bless him! Through him I learned what a good influence this has over children. In India, though people worship animals, they are not humane; and they treat animals most cruelly" (Ramabai Association 1898: 33).

49. This seems to be an error; Ramabai obviously means summer.

50. For example, in the 1880s an advertisement for potency pills commonly appeared on the front page of *Indu-Prakash,* the liberal Anglo-Marathi weekly newspaper published in Bombay, with which a number of famous social reformers were associated.

6. Education and Learning

1. Cited in Carnegie (1886: 131).

2. I have inserted this heading for easy reading. Much of this section is based on Carnegie (1886: 136–50).

3. The amounts which are given in rupees in the original text are converted here into dollars, at the exchange rate of three rupees to the dollar, as mentioned by Ramabai herself in the book.

4. Samuel Chapman Armstrong (1839–1893) was born and raised in Hawaii, and completed his college education in the United States. He enlisted in the army during the Civil War, fought at Gettysburg, and had been promoted to the rank of brigadier-general by the end of the war. He was subsequently appointed as the agent of the Freedmen's Bureau at Hampton, Va., and became greatly interested in the industrial education of emancipated slaves. With the help of generous donations he established the Hampton Normal and Industrial Institute in 1868 and ran it along creative lines. The institute became an illustration of "education of the head, heart, and hand alike" as the essence of education for life (*DAB* I: 359–60).

5. This extract is given by Ramabai as a translated quotation from Armstrong. I have not been able to trace it and have therefore not presented my retranslation of it as a quotation.

6. Friedrich Froebel (1782–1852), German educator, devised his own educational system, which was aimed at helping the child's mind to grow naturally and spontaneously. He opened his first kindergarten school in 1836 and spent the rest of his life setting up more such schools and writing books on the subject (*Chambers*: 523).

7. Elizabeth Peabody (1804–1894) must have been about eighty-four years old when Ramabai met her. For many years she was a Transcendentalist who associated with Emerson, Thoreau, and Hawthorne. She was strongly influenced by her mother, who ran a school in Salem, Mass., based on the principle that every child should receive the training which was appropriate to his ability. She taught in, and started, a few schools; lectured widely on education; and wrote ten books and fifty articles on the subject. In 1860 she started in Boston the first kindergarten school in the USA, then traveled in Europe for a few years to study kindergartens, and on her return devoted herself to promoting the movement in the USA (*NAW* III: 31–34).

8. A special prize was awarded to the St. Louis Manual Training School at the School Exhibits, held at the National Education Association convention in July 1888, at which Ramabai was present and was given a reception by the WCTU (*San Francisco Chronicle,* 21 July 1888).

9. Felix Adler (1851–1933), born in Germany and raised in New York City, where his parents had emigrated, was trained as a rabbi, but left this post to become professor of Oriental languages and literature at Cornell University from 1874 to 1876. Later he founded the first free kindergarten in American in 1877, the Workingman's School in 1880 (which became the Ethical Culture School in 1895), the Plymouth School of Ethics in 1889, the Child Study Association in 1907, and the Fieldston School in 1928. He was professor of social and political ethics at Columbia University from 1902 to 33 (*DAB* XI-1: 13–14).

10. Francis Wayland Parker (1837–1902) was born in New Hampshire, began to teach at an early age, enlisted in the army during the Civil War, and, after the end of the war, went back to teaching school and experimented with innovative methods of teaching. He spent a few years in Germany, where he studied educational methods, including the kindergarten, which he introduced in schools in Quincy, Mass., where he served as superintendent of schools, and in Boston, where he was one of the supervisors of schools. In 1899 he set up the Chicago Institute, with the help of a generous endowment offered to him. After two years the institute was trans-

ferred to the University of Chicago as the School of Education; he became the school's first director (*DAB* VIII: 221).

11. This heading has also been added. The factual information in this section is derived from Carnegie (1886: 343–45, 353–54).

12. The Vernacular Press Act was imposed by the Viceroy Lord Lytton in 1878 to censor vernacular journalism; it was repealed by the next viceroy, Lord Ripon in 1882.

13. Grover Cleveland (1837–1908) served as governor of New York before taking office in 1885 as the first Democratic president after the Civil War. In the congressional session of 1887–88 he supported revision of tariff rates, which he saw as evidence of favoritism to certain protected industries. The tariff debate raged while the 1888 elections were held, and Cleveland lost because of the popular perception that tariff reduction was a British policy. However, a swing in popular opinion on the issue voted him in for a second term as president from 1893 to 1897 (*DAB* II: 205–12).

14. The Indian National Congress was the organization established in 1885 by Indian nationalist leaders and their British (nonofficial) sympathizers, in order to obtain political rights and eventual independence.

15. Mathura is an ancient city in the north of India, currently in the Hindi-speaking state of Uttar Pradesh; Awadh (British Oudh or Oude) is a nearby region in the same state. By "Madhyadeshi" Ramabai probably means the language spoken in central India (the British Central Provinces, currently the state of Madhya Pradesh). Punjabi, the language of the state of Punjab in northwestern India, is somewhat akin to Hindi, but can hardly be regarded as a dialect of Hindi.

Ramabai was probably the first and certainly one of the earliest public leaders to promote the use of Hindi as the national language for India.

16. The Konkan area is the strip along the west coast and the Deccan area the inland plateau of the Marathi-speaking region, which currently constitutes the state of Maharashtra in western India.

17. Gurjars are the inhabitants of the southern part of the state of Gujarat which borders on northern Maharashtra.

18. Kanarese, now Kannada, is the language spoken in the region then known as Carnatick, which was partly included in the Bombay Presidency. Today Karnataka is a separate state which lies immediately to the south of Maharashtra.

19. The "language of the Demons" obviously means any alien language.

20. This spans the length and breadth of undivided India from Kanyakumari, the former Cape Comorin, at the southern tip of India, to the Himalayas, which form the country's northern border, and from the Indus delta in the west (now in Pakistan) to Manipur in the extreme east.

21. The rest of this section is based on Carnegie (1886: 350–62).

22. See Carnegie (1886: 352, 355).

7. Religious Denominations and Charities

1. The separation of state and church is also an underlying theme in Carnegie's chapter "Religion" (1886: 152–164), from which some ideas and information in this chapter are derived.

2.	Under the Charter Act of 1833 the East India Company undertook to meet the expenses of the Church of England in India, out of its profits from the India trade. After the transfer of power in 1858 the British Crown assumed this responsibility, and the expenses were charged to the revenues of the Government of India (David 2001: 44).

3.	Burning of witches was not really an American practice; hanging was the usual penalty.

4.	A Puranika is a person who narrates sacred stories from the Puranas. Ramabai's natal family eked out a living in this fashion, and she was one of the very few women Puranikas of her time. After her return to India, Ramabai used the Purana format for her lectures to women audiences to popularize her ideas of social reform.

5.	The several Shastras and the four Vedas (composed over the period 2500 to 1000 B.C., and the oldest literature in the world) form part of the Hindu scriptures which could traditionally be studied only by Brahmin men. Women and the lower castes were not allowed to read them or to study Sanskrit, the language in which they are written.

6.	Missionary activity was forbidden in the English East India Company's territories in India until the Charter Act of 1813 ended the company's monopoly of India trade. The American Marathi Mission pioneered Christian evangelical and educational activity in Bombay. See the section "The Indo-American Backdrop" in the Introduction.

7.	A *bairagi* is a religious mendicant who has renounced the world; *ganja* is dried hemp flowers, or marijuana.

8.	*Kaikadis,* a caste whose traditional occupation was making twig baskets, also earned money through acrobatic performances in the streets.

9.	Raosahib is a title. See chapter 9, note 7.

10.	Hinduism believes in the transmigration of the soul and the resultant multiple rebirths. The ultimate spiritual goal is salvation, or the merging of the soul with the omnipresent Divine Spirit (Brahma), which also frees one from the cycle of death and rebirth.

11.	This paragraph is based on Carnegie (1886: 167–70).

12.	See Carnegie (1886: 170).

13.	Ramabai was impressed enough by these schools for the blind to open a section for blind women at her Mukti Mission at Kedgaon, and to give them special education through books in Braille; the section is still in existence.

14.	The harmful effects of oil dropped in infants' eyes was a favorite theme which Ramabai elaborated upon, along with other traditional Indian child-care practices, in *Morals for Women* (Kosambi 2000d: 92–93).

15.	The reference is to the Deaf and Dumb Asylum in New York.

16.	The social reformers and nationalists G. G. Agarkar and B. G. Tilak were editors of the Marathi weekly *Kesari* and the English weekly *The Mahratta,* respectively. In their papers they exposed the irregularities in the internal affairs of the Princely State of Kolhapur, which was under indirect British control. The Kolhapur Libel Case stemmed from their support of the young prince against his chief minister, who allegedly maltreated him with the connivance of the British Resident. During the court case which followed, Agarkar and Tilak discovered that the documentary evidence in their possession was forged and that their informants were unwilling to testify. The two editors were sentenced to prison in Bombay and served their terms in July–October 1882. Agarkar's account of prison life, *A Hundred and One Days in Dongri Prison,* was published in 1882 as a booklet, and was the first of its kind in Marathi (Natu and Deshpande 1986: xiii–ixx, 1–37).

17.   The rest of this paragraph is based on Carnegie (1886: 173–75).

18.   The term "zenana" was applied to the inner quarters of a house where women lived in seclusion in traditional homes. This kind of seclusion was strict in northern and eastern parts of India, and generally among the upper classes.

19.   Shaivites and Vaishnavites are the followers, respectively, of the gods Shiva (the Destroyer) and Vishnu (the Preserver). Together with Brahma (the Creator), they form the highest trinity in Hinduism. There are said to be thirty-three *crore* (330,000,000) gods in the Hindu pantheon. Shias and Sunnis are the chief denominations among Muslims (formerly called Mohammedans by many English speakers).

8. The Condition of Women

1.   The Ramayana and the Mahabharata are the great Hindu epics; the Bhagavata Purana is a collection of sacred stories which are used for recitals and as a basis for popular religious discourses. The other works mentioned here are lesser-known religious works, which Ramabai deliberately refers to as "literary."

2.   Haihayarjuna was said to have a thousand arms. Sita is the wife of Rama (an incarnation of God Vishnu), on whom the epic Ramayana centers. While Rama is forced to live in exile in a forest, Sita is abducted by the ten-headed demon king Ravana. After a gigantic battle, Rama kills Ravana. Ramabai indulges in conspicuous exaggeration here, and her surprising reference to Sita as having killed Ravana seems to be a strategy of presenting an acceptable, empowered Hindu female figure.

3.   Harriet Martineau (1802–1876) remained single and pursued a literary career when her father's death left the family in straitened circumstances. Her serialized "Illustrations of Political Economy" were enormously popular, as were the 1,642 articles she wrote on a wide range of subjects. In 1837 (not 1840, as Ramabai states) she published *Society in America,* in which her feminist ideas found cohesive expression (Spender 1982: 125–35).

4.   This is ostensibly a quote from Martineau's *Society in America,* but it does not appear in Martineau's book and was obviously intended as the gist of her argument.

5.   The World Anti-Slavery Convention held in London in 1840 ruled, in spite of strong objections, that only men delegates should be seated. The American women delegates, including Lucretia Mott and Elizabeth Cady Stanton, were compelled to sit in the galleries and were unable to participate in the proceedings (Flexner 1975: 71).

6.   See Willard (1888: 94). Willard's arguments about women's right to preach obviously influenced Ramabai.

7.   Hannah Lee Corbin, an advocate of women's rights, was the daughter of Thomas Lee of Virginia and sister of Richard Henry Lee—and not of Robert Lee as

Ramabai states. Robert E. Lee, son of their cousin "Light Horse Harry" Lee, later became the general of the Confederate Army during the Civil War (<*http://www.stratfordhall.org/*>). Hannah's letters to her brother Richard Henry are not extant, but his reply dated 17 March 1778 indicates that she solicited his support for voting rights and tax exemption for widows with property (<*www.uchicago.edu/Civilization/America/Suppl35/Corbin.html*>).

Abigail Adams (1744–1818) was the wife of President John Adams. Her letter to him, written on 31 March 1776 and now famous, reminded him to redress some of the existing gender inequalities while making laws. It advised him to "Remember the Ladies, and be more generous and favorable to them than your ancestors," and to "not put such unlimited power into the hands of Husbands." John Adams, though an affectionate husband, dismissed the advice (Spender 1982: 83–85).

8. The reference to 1832 is unclear. Slavery was abolished in all British possessions in 1834; Oberlin College was founded in 1833.

9. Oberlin College was founded in 1833 as a seminary and developed into a rudimentary college. It "offered women a curriculum even remotely comparable to that available to men on the college level," and was "the first such institution to open its doors to all comers, regardless of race, color—or sex" (Flexner 1975: 29).

10. This paragraph is based on *RICW* (1888: 51).

11. Mary Wollstonecraft Godwin (1759–1797) wrote *A Vindication of the Rights of Woman* in 1792 to plead for equal education and employment opportunities for women. She was harshly judged by her male contemporaries, and the label of "hyena in petticoats" given to her is remembered long after her writings are forgotten (Spender 1982: 100–14).

12. Hannah More (1745–1833) was a member of the Bluestocking Club (see note 50 below) and a professional writer whose literary output included poetry and drama. She did much to improve the condition of the poor (*Chambers:* 951; Spender 1982: 76).

13. Sidney Smith (1771–1845) was an English journalist and clergyman, and a brilliant speaker. He supported liberal and reformist ideas through his writings, mainly in the *Edinburgh Review* (*Chambers:* 1241).

14. This paragraph is based on *RICW* (1888: 51–52). Emma Willard (1787–1870) supplemented the conventional schooling she received by teaching herself a number of other subjects, including geometry. After teaching in several "female academies," she opened her own Middlebury Female Seminary, and, after an unsuccessful attempt to persuade the New York legislature to support a program of state-aided girls' schools, the Troy Female Seminary in 1821, which was "the first endowed institution for the education of girls." The pamphlet she produced for this campaign in 1819, "An Address to the Public; Particularly to the Members of the Legislature of New York, Proposing a Plan for Improving Female Education," was a landmark document in the history of women's education. Although conventional in her views about the average woman's role in life, Willard nevertheless made available to her students all the scientific subjects, as well as the accomplishments considered essential for girls (*NAW* III: 610–13; Flexner 1975: 26).

15. This and the next few paragraphs (excepting the description of the Arkansas River) are based on *RICW* (1888: 53–59).

16. Vassar College was opened in 1865, Smith and Wellesley in 1875, Harvard Annex (which in 1894 became Radcliffe College) in 1879, and Bryn Mawr in 1885 (Flexner 1975: 36). Antioch College became coeducational in 1852, the state University of Iowa accepted women in 1858, and Wisconsin admitted women to its normal-school training course in 1863. Cornell was founded in 1868, and a special branch for women, Sage College, was added in 1874; the first woman student entered the University of Michigan in 1870 (Flexner 1975: 124–25).

17. This paragraph is based on *RICW* (1888: 59–60).

18. Matthew Vassar (1792–1868) was born in England, emigrated as a child to America with his family, and made his fortune first in the family brewery, then in his own brewery and other enterprises. The founding of Vassar College for women, opened in 1865, was his attempt to prove the intellectual equality of women, and was well advertised throughout the country (*DAB* X: 230–31).

19. The following quotations are taken from *RICW* (1888: 74).

20. This quote is taken from *RICW* (1888: 165); the quote that follows is by President James B. Angell of Michigan University and is taken from *RICW* (1888: 73).

21. Mary Fairfax Somerville (1780–1872) lived in Scotland and England, taught herself mathematics in her twenties, and soon gained proficiency. In 1826 she presented a paper to the Royal Society on "The Magnetic Properties of the Violet Rays of the Solar Spectrum." In 1830 she wrote *Celestial Mechanism,* a popular version of the work of the French mathematician and astronomer Laplace; and in 1832 *The Mechanisms of the Heavens;* her book became a required textbook for students at Cambridge (where she herself and other women could not study). In 1834 she published *The Connection of the Physical Sciences,* and later *Physical Geography* and numerous papers and monographs; and in 1869 *Molecular and Microscopic Science.* She mixed with the greatest mathematicians of her time, and received several honors (Spender 1982: 168–72; *Chambers:* 1246).

    Elizabeth Barrett Browning (1806–81) was a famous and prolific English poet, who married the English poet Robert Browning. She made an explicit feminist protest in her best-known poem, *Aurora Leigh* (Spender 1982: 172; *Chambers:* 193).

22. This is a well-known Sanskrit phrase.

23. This refers to Harvard Annex, which later became Radcliffe College for women. See notes 16 and 24 of this chapter.

24. Alice Freeman Palmer (1855–1902) obtained a college education on a loan from her parents, promising not to marry before its full repayment; and also paid for the education of her siblings. She graduated in 1876 from the University of Michigan while holding part-time jobs; and was awarded an honorary Ph.D. degree in 1882. She became the second president of Wellesley College in 1882, at the age of twenty-seven, and the first president who nurtured the institution's early growth. In 1882 she was involved in the founding of the Association of Collegiate Alumnae (later the American Association of University Women), which promoted women's educational interests. In 1887 Alice Freeman married G. H. Palmer, professor of philosophy at Harvard, resigned her post, and moved to Cambridge, Mass. The marriage led to a public controversy between the anti-feminists, who saw this as proof of women's inability to shoulder positions of responsibility, and the feminists, who saw it as betrayal of the cause of women's independence. Alice Freeman Palmer

served various women's educational institutions in official and unofficial capacities, and was closely involved in the struggle to transform Harvard Annex into Radcliffe College (*NAW* III: 4–8).

25.   This is a quotation from the Bhagavad Gita (chapter 4, verse 40).

26.   This and the next three paragraphs are based on *RICW* (1888: 165–66).

27.   Maria Mitchell (1818–1889) inherited her love of mathematics and astronomy from her father, who also trained her from an early age. In 1847 she discovered a comet, which was named after her; she gained international fame, and was awarded a gold medal by the king of Denmark. In 1848 she was elected to the American Academy of Arts and Sciences, Boston; she was the first, and for almost a hundred years the only, woman elected to that body. In 1850 she was elected to the American Association for the Advancement of Science, and in 1869 to the American Philosophical Society (as the first woman to receive this honor); in 1873 she was made vice president of the American Social Science Association. In 1873 she became one of the founders of the Association for the Advancement of Women; she later served as its president for two years, and as chairman of its science committee for the remainder of her life. In 1865 Matthew Vassar inducted Mitchell into the faculty of the newly opened Vassar Female College and built a special observatory for her research and teaching; she taught there until 1888 (*NAW* II: 554–56).

     That Ramabai was personally acquainted with Mitchell is indicated by the following note on the flyleaf of Ramabai's copy of *RICW* (in what seems to be her own handwriting): "Mariah Mitchel [*sic*] discovered a planet and immortalized her name for which Russia gave her a medal. She was Professor of Astronomy in Vassar when I was there. She showed me the large telescope and observatory; she is a noble woman of beautiful character."

28.   For Caroline Herschel see note 47 below.

29.   Jane Bancroft Robinson (1847–1932) graduated from Emma Willard's Troy Female Seminary in 1871 and obtained her Ph.D. in 1884 from Syracuse University. Her doctoral thesis, *A Study of the Parliament of Paris and Other Parliaments of France,* was published in the same year. She served as dean of the Woman's College and professor of French language and literature at Northwestern University, Ill., where she founded the Western Association of Collegiate Alumnae in 1883, which heralded the later American Association of University Women. Jane Bancroft made an extensive study of deaconesses, or women serving in the Home Missionary Society of the Methodist Episcopal Church, on whose behalf she exerted herself for many years and to whom she left her home in California. In her early forties, Bancroft married G. O. Robinson, a Detroit lawyer. She bequeathed $10,000 to the California Institute of Technology in Pasadena (*NAW* III: 183–84).

30.   Louisa Reed Stowell, M.S., was Fellow of the Royal Microscopical Society, and President of the Western Association of Collegiate Alumnae. She was a delegate to the International Council of Women, and read a paper in the session on education (along with Ramabai herself) on 26 March 1888 (*RICW* 1888).

31.   Pauline Agassiz Shaw (1841–1917) was married to Quincy Adams Shaw, a wealthy and philanthropic Boston businessman. In Boston she revived the kindergarten movement started by Elizabeth Peabody and others in the 1860s; opened some kindergartens herself and supported others, some of which were taken over by the

Boston School Committee; and also started a number of industrial schools. Another of her well-known and highly successful innovations was the setting up of day nurseries for working mothers in the poor sections of Boston, to which she added evening classes in various subjects. She founded the Boston Equal Suffrage Association for Good Government in 1901, and provided financial support to the weekly suffrage newspaper, the *Woman's Journal* (*NAW* III: 278–80).

Mrs. Shaw served as a trustee of the Ramabai Association from 1889 to 1898, and continued to be an officeholder of the American Ramabai Association afterward. In her annual report of 1899 Ramabai expresses her gratitude to Mrs. Shaw "for sending several wash-boards, washing tubs, iron stoves, and other things to help start a laundry" (American Ramabai Association 1899: 27).

32. Elizabeth Rowell Thompson (1821–1899) contributed generously to the suffrage and temperance movements, out of the wealth left her by her husband at his death. In 1873 she developed an interest in scientific research and gave $1,000 to the American Association for the Advancement of Science. The Elizabeth Thompson Science Fund, which was independently set up out of her gift of $25,000, was among the first such endowments in the USA made for the advancement of scientific research (*NAW* III: 452–53).

33. The *Daily Inter-Ocean* of Chicago published an interview with Ramabai in December 1887 (Sengupta 1970: 79).

34. The organization was called the Woman's Christian Temperance Union; Ramabai consistently drops the word "Christian," possibly in view of her Hindu readership. The Woman's Christian Temperance Union (WCTU) was formed in 1874. Frances Willard became its president in 1879; she organized WCTU chapters in every state and increased its membership to over 200,000 (Deckard 1983: 264).

35. See *RICW* (1888: 171).

36. Yama, or Yamaraj, is the Hindu deity of death, and Yami is his twin sister.

37. Mary Putnam Jacobi (1842–1906) graduated from the New York College of Pharmacy in 1863, received her M.D. degree from WMCP in 1864, and spent five years studying medicine in France. Her abiding interest in raising the standards of medical education for women led her to establish the Association for the Advancement of the Medical Education of Women (later the Women's Medical Association of New York City), of which she was president for many years. She was a professor at the Woman's Medical College of the New York Infirmary for Women and Children, and worked for many years as a physician at the New York Infirmary, Mount Sinai Hospital, and St. Mark's Hospital. Her essay won Harvard's Boylston Prize in 1876, and opened to her membership in several prestigious medical societies. Jacobi was among the earliest physicians to focus on the environmental factors related to illness, and took active part in the women's suffrage movement (*NAW* II: 263–65).

38. This paragraph is based on *RICW* (1888: 95–97).

39. Elizabeth Blackwell (1821–1910), an eminent physician and the first woman to graduate in medicine, was born in England and emigrated to the USA as a child, with her family. After being rejected by several medical schools, she was admitted to Geneva College in the state of New York, where she had to face a great deal of opposition and ridicule until she graduated in 1849. She opened a small dispensary for women in New York City, which she developed in 1857 into the New York

Infirmary for Women and Children, staffed entirely by women. She was assisted by two able women doctors, Marie Zakrzewska and her own sister, Emily Blackwell. The infirmary provided medical training for women; it also served as a model for similar institutions. Elizabeth Blackwell was instrumental in forming the United States Sanitary Commission in 1861, and selected and trained nurses for the commission. In 1868 she established the Woman's Medical College at the New York Infirmary, with high professional standards; the college functioned until the Cornell University Medical School began to enroll women students in 1899. She spent the latter part of her life in England, where she had a successful practice in London (*NAW* I: 161–65; Flexner 1975: 119; Solomon 1987: 35).

40. The New England Hospital for Women and Children was founded at Boston in 1859 by Marie Zakrzewska, who had earlier worked with Elizabeth Blackwell (*NAW* I: 163).

41. This and the next two paragraphs describing women in law are based on *RICW* (1888: 174–79).

42. Arabella Mansfield (1846–1911) was admitted to the Iowa bar in 1869, together with her husband, and became the first woman lawyer in the USA, although she preferred to teach rather than practice law (*NAW* II: 492–93).

43. All four men were eminent lawyers, orators, and statesmen or political leaders. Daniel O'Connell (1775–1847) and John Philpot Curran (1750–1817) were Irish; Daniel Webster (1782–1852) and Rufus Choate (1799–1859) were American (*Chambers*: 997, 357, 1903, 286). The original sentence from which Ramabai has taken these names reads as follows: "There has not been time enough yet for a woman to develop into an Erskine or Burke, an O'Connell or Curran, a Webster or Choate" (*RICW*: 179). Characteristically Ramabai has omitted the names of the two famous British lawyers and statesmen: Thomas Erskine (1750–1823) and Edmund Burke (1729–97) (*Chambers*: 465, 207–208).

44. Mrs. Myra Bradwell (1831–1894) pioneered women's entry into the legal field in Illinois. During the Civil War she actively participated in the work of the Northwestern Sanitary Commission; she helped organize the Sanitary Fair in 1863. The publication of the highly successful weekly newspaper the *Chicago Legal News* was her own ambitious project, while she also, together with her lawyer husband, set up the Chicago Legal News Company, a printing and publishing firm. She was one of the first women lawyers in the USA. Her application to the Supreme Court of Illinois in 1870 for a license to practice law was denied; she finally won the right in 1873 after a protracted battle involving the United States Supreme Court. Bradwell helped to organize the American Woman Suffrage Association, and served as an official of that body and of the Illinois Woman Suffrage Association. With her husband's support, she successfully lobbied several bills through the Illinois legislature. These bills removed women's legal disabilities; for example, they gave married women the right to their own earnings, and gave a widow a share of her husband's estate (*NAW* I: 223–25; Flexner 1975: 122–23).

45. This and the next paragraphs are based on *RICW* (1888: 134–36).

46. There is no indication that Beethoven had a sister. Perhaps Ramabai confused him with Felix Mendelssohn (1809–47), German composer, pianist, and conductor (*Chambers*: 915). His eldest sister, Fanny (1805–47), also a gifted pianist and com-

poser, published some of her works under his name (*The New Encyclopaedia Britannica*, 8: 6).

47.   Caroline Herschel (1750–1848) assisted her astronomer brother Sir William Herschel and made independent observations. She discovered eight comets, several nebulae, and clusters of stars; and in 1798 she published a star catalogue. Her achievements were credited to her brother (Spender 1982: 83; *Chambers:* 665).

48.   This section is based largely on *RICW* (1888: 226–29, 242–44).

49.   This is a Sanskrit quotation; see chapter 5, note 45.

50.   The Bluestockings were a group of intellectual women in the late eighteenth and early nineteenth century England whose association belonged to the private rather than the public realm. They included writers like Hannah More and the novelist Fanny Burney. Given the contemporary ethos which denigrated women's intellectual and literary achievements, the word "Bluestockings" acquired the negative connotation of ridiculous misfits (Spender 1982: 75–83).

51.   For Lucretia Mott see chapter 5, note 21. Elizabeth Cady Stanton (1815–1902) became interested in the anti-slavery and temperance movements at an early age, and was married to the reformer H. B. Stanton. Immediately after the wedding in 1840, she sailed with him to London to attend the World Anti-Slavery Convention, from which women delegates were excluded. She formed a close friendship with another rejected delegate, Lucretia Mott, which was to result in the woman's rights convention held at Stanton's home town of Seneca Falls in 1848. The Declaration of Sentiments drafted for the convention by Stanton, on the model of the Declaration of Independence, started with the self-evident truth that "men and women are created equal," and listed women's legal and social grievances. The first public demand for suffrage by women was made at this well-attended convention. Stanton's association with Susan B. Anthony, another feminist of repute, was long-lasting and fruitful. Her address to the New York legislature, protesting against the legal disabilities of women, resulted in 1860 in married women being granted the right to their earnings and the guardianship of their children. She also campaigned for easier divorce, and for sensible and comfortable clothing for women. She wrote copiously for newspapers, and was an untiring and popular public speaker. In later years she was strongly critical of the gender inequality in religion, demanded equality in church matters, and published *The Woman's Bible* in two volumes in the 1890s, which created dissension within the women's movement (Flexner 1975: 71–77).

52.   This seems to be a misprint. Ramabai obviously means 1848.

53.   See chapter 2, note 6.

54.   Mary Ashton Rice Livermore (1820–1905) was a bitter opponent of slavery and helped General Grant's army with hospital supplies as well as fruit and vegetables during the Civil War. Her greatest wartime accomplishment was the planning and organizing, with Mrs. Hoge, of the women's Sanitary Fair in Chicago in October 1863, which raised more than $70,000 for the Sanitary Commission. Other major northern cities were inspired to hold similar fairs, and together raised over $1,000,000 for hospital and sanitary needs. Mary Livermore also served as president of the Illinois Woman Suffrage Association and later of the American Woman

Suffrage Association, editor of the *Woman's Journal* established by Lucy Stone and others, and first president of the Association for the Advancement of Women (*NAW* II: 410–13).

55. Florence Nightingale (1820–1910), English hospital reformer, organized a nursing unit to care for the wounded during the Crimean War and strove to improve the sanitary management of hospitals. Subsequently she founded an institution in London for the training of nurses, and wrote *Notes on Nursing* (1859), which went through many editions. Nightingale received the Order of Merit in 1907 (*Chambers:* 989).

56. This and the next paragraph are based on *RICW*, pp. 215–18. Sorosis was founded in 1868 by Mrs. Jennie C. Croly, a recognized journalist who was refused a ticket to the dinner hosted by the New York Press Club in honor of Charles Dickens' visit, because she (like other women journalists) did not belong to the Press Club (Flexner 1975: 182–83).

57. Here Ramabai seems to draw an implicit comparison with contemporary India, where the few women's organizations which existed were founded and managed by men—her own Arya Mahila Samaj being something of an exception.

58. The New England Woman's Club was founded in Boston in 1868, the same year as Sorosis (Flexner 1975: 183).

59. This paragraph is based on *RICW* (1888: 198–99).

60. The American Equal Rights Association which resulted from the Woman's Rights Convention split in 1869 into the National Woman Suffrage Association and the American Woman Suffrage Association; their merger began to be negotiated in 1887 and finally took place in 1890 (Flexner 1975: 155, 226).

61. See Flexner (1975: 155).

62. The Territory of Wyoming was the first to enfranchise women, in the late 1860s (Flexner: 163).

63. In Manchester, "unmarried women householders were given the right to vote in local elections" in 1869 (Deckard 1983: 212).

64. See Flexner (1975: 224).

65. Ramabai does not mention her own contribution to the convention, acknowledged by Frances Willard: "Pundita Ramabai, in her white robes, was a central figure, and her plaintive appeal for the high-caste Hindu widows, a memorable event in the convention" (Willard 1889: 416).

66. Ramabai was present at the International Council of Women organized by the National Woman Suffrage Association at Washington, D.C., from 25 March to 1 April 1888, as mentioned in the introduction. The other delegates included Elizabeth Cady Stanton, Clara Barton, Hannah Whitall Smith, Mary Livermore, Susan B. Anthony, Lucy Stone, and Frances Willard. Ramabai delivered an address on "The Women of India" in the session on education on 26 March (*RICW* 1888: 12–18, 63–67).

67. Ramabai has based this account on Mrs. Thompson's "Hillsboro Crusade Sketches" in Thompson, Willard, et al. (1906: 57–172), also reproduced (with slight variations) in Willard (1886: 50–79).

68. Its full name was the Woman's Temperance Crusade.

69. Thompson's account, on which Ramabai relied heavily in this section, has been liberally used in this translation.

70. This brief account has been literally translated by Ramabai in the text; I have quoted it here verbatim from Thompson, Willard, et al. (1906: 75–76) and Willard (1886: 58–59).

71. The leader was Mrs. Thompson herself.

72. Ramabai gives this quotation in English (with a gist in Marathi); it is reproduced verbatim here.

73. Mary Clement Leavitt (1830–1912) was a teacher, advocate of woman suffrage, and temperance activist who helped to organize the Boston WCTU. She worked as a temperance missionary within the USA. From 1884 to 1891 she visited Hawaii, New Zealand, Australia, East Asia, India, Africa, and Europe; during this seven-year journey she established eighty-six branches of the WCTU and twenty-four men's temperance societies in various countries (*NAW* II: 383–85).

74. See *RICW* (1888: 57–59).

75. This is not historically accurate. Spain had been controlled by Muslims since the early eighth century A.D.

9. Commerce and Industry

1. This subsection and the next are based on Carnegie (1886: 416–24).

2. This heading has been added. This subsection is based on Carnegie (1886: 428–35).

3. This section heading has been added.

4. See Carnegie (1886: 75).

5. This section heading has been added.

6. See Carnegie (1886: 231).

7. Among the titles bestowed by the British Government on eminent Indians were Raosahib, Raobahadur, Rajasahib (all three for Hindus), and Nawabsahib (for Muslims).

8. See Carnegie (1886: 237).

9. This heading has been added. The section is based largely on Carnegie (1886: 49, 52–68, 301–3, 309).

10. The Smritis are the ancient Hindu codes of religious law compiled by great sages, such as Manu, on the basis of tradition. The Manusmriti, or Code of Manu, is considered to be the most authoritative of these codes.

11. Alaska was only a possession of the United States at this time. It became a territory in 1912 and a state in 1959.

12. The actual Marathi words used here are, literally, "iron roads" for tracks and "fire-carriages" for trains; the latter word and a Sanskritized version of the former are still prevalent today. The two words seem to have been coined by Madgavkar in his account of Bombay (1961 [1863]: 29–30) and in his earlier book, published in 1858, whose title translates literally as *The Marvels of Iron Roads* (Malshe and Chunekar

1970: 72–92). A Chinese visitor to the USA refers to the railroad train (which he rode for the first time in 1868) as a "fire-wheeled vehicle" (Arkush and Lee 1989: 27).

13. See Carnegie (1886: 285).

14. The rest of the paragraph is based on Carnegie (1886: 96).

15. Although Ramabai makes light of India's railroad network, the innovation had greatly impressed the previous generation of Bombayites. In his presumably eyewitness account, Madgavkar (1961 [1863]: 230–31) captures the excitement caused by the inaugural one-hour run of the "fire-carriage" from central Bombay to a city on the mainland (twenty-one miles away) in April 1853. The day had been declared a government and business holiday, and thousands of locals and out-of-town visitors cheered as three steam engines pulled a string of "twenty large chariots" seating special invitees—Governor Falkland of Bombay, other British officials, and the city's Indian elite. Madgavkar also reproduces a song composed for the occasion, to commemorate the advent of a new historical era.

16. This description of waterways and railroads is based on Carnegie (1886: 274–75, 278–82).

17. This and the next paragraph are based on *RICW* (1888: 138–39).

18. The rest of this section is based on Carnegie (1886: 183–205).

19. See note 11 above.

20. The rest of this section is based on Carnegie (1886: 214–34).

21. The factual information in this section is derived from Carnegie (1886: 241–70).

22. Ramabai uses the word "rockel"—the then (and now) prevalent Marathi corruption of "rock oil"—which is now used alternatively with "kerosene."

23. See Carnegie (1886: 3).

24. This section heading has been added.

25. The actual Sanskrit saying quoted here translates as "by any and every means; by breaking the pot, by tearing the cloth, by braying like a donkey."

26. The idea is derived from Carnegie (1886: 109).

27. The conspicuous consumption and meaningless extravagance (especially on wedding celebrations—of children and even pets) of the princes and the idle rich in India have been documented with a suitable critique by Madgavkar (1961 [1863]: 350–53).

28. The amounts gifted by the philanthropists, as mentioned by Ramabai, do not tally with the amounts mentioned in *DAB*, which is used as a source here. There is no indication of the book to which Ramabai referred.

29. For John B. Trevor, see note 35 below.

30. William Wilson Corcoran (1798–1888), banker and philanthropist, was a resident of Washington, D.C. In addition to setting up the Corcoran Gallery of Art and the Louise Home to support "gentlewomen in reduced circumstances," he made substantial donations to the Columbian (now George Washington) University, the University of Virginia, Washington and Lee University, and other educational institutions (*DAB* II: 440).

31. Samuel Williston (1795–1874) owned several business enterprises and donated money to religious and charitable enterprises. He founded the Williston Seminary

in Easthampton, Mass., in 1841. His endowments to Amherst College during his lifetime amounted to $150,000 (*DAB* X: 309–310).

32. William Johnson Walker (1790–1865) was a successful physician who became a financier and made a large fortune in railroad and manufacturing stocks. His contribution to American education totaled about $1,250,000, and the beneficiaries were Amherst, Tufts, the Massachusetts Institute of Technology, and the Boston Society of Natural History (*DAB* X: 366).

33. There is a mention of Annie McClure Hitchcock having provided funds for a men's dormitory at the University of Chicago in honor of her husband Charles, a founder of the Chicago Bar Association (<*www.lib.uchicago.edu*>).

34. Henry Winkley (1803–1888) made a fortune in the crockery business, and divided it among several educational institutions, including Williams College ($50,000); Phillips Exeter Academy ($30,000); Bowdoin College ($70,000); the theological seminaries at Bangor, Maine ($30,000), Andover ($45,000), and Yale ($50,000); Dartmouth College ($80,000); and Amherst College ($30,000) (<*http://www.virtuolology.com/henrywinkley/*>).

35. James Boorman Colgate (1818–1904) had a highly successful stockbrokerage in partnership with John B. Trevor, which was renamed Colgate & Co. in 1873. He was one of the founders, and for many years the president, of the New York Gold Exchange. In 1873 he founded and endowed the Colgate Academy, which was merged in 1890 with Madison University (which he had earlier supported); the combined institution was named Colgate University in honor of his father. His total gifts to the two institutions amounted to more than a million dollars (*DAB* II: 298–99).

36. John Price Crozer (1793–1866) was a cotton manufacturer, and had served on the Christian Commission during the Civil War. The Crozer Theological Seminary at Chester, Pa., was built in his memory by his family, who added $275,000 to the fund of $50,000 left in his will (*DAB* II: 579–80).

37. The name mentioned by Ramabai transliterates as Sinnay. I have found no mention of a philanthropist of that name; the closest approximation is Cheney. Benjamin Pierce Cheney (1815–1895) made his fortune in the express transportation service of which he was a pioneer. He left $50,000 to Dartmouth College (*DAB* II-2: 50–51). He is also said to have contributed $10,000 in 1882 toward founding the Benjamin P. Cheney Academy, which has eventually grown into the Eastern Washington University (<*http://www.ewu.edu/new/alumni/IDStatement2002.pdf*>).

38. Benjamin Bussey (1757–1842) made a fortune in foreign trade and left it to Harvard University. His bequest was estimated at $350,000 (<*http://www.virtuolology.com/benjaminbussey/*>).

39. Amasa Stone (1818–1883) was a railroad builder and capitalist involved in the construction of the Cleveland, Columbus and Cincinnati Railroad; the Chicago and Milwaukee Railroad; and the Cleveland, Painesville and Ashtabula Railroad. He gave $500,000 for shifting Western Reserve College from Hudson to Cleveland, and making it into an urban university (*DAB* IX-2: 70–71).

40. Stephen Whitney Phoenix (1839–1881), a graduate of Columbia University, had inherited a large fortune. He left a collection of specialized books and a legacy of $15,000 to the New York Historical Society; and his general library of books, to be

known as "The Phoenix Collection," to Columbia with $500,000 for technical use (<*http://famousamericans.net/stephenwhitneyphoenix/*>).

41. Cornelius Vanderbilt (1843–1899) was a financier from a wealthy family, president of the New York and Harlem Railroad, and of the Canada Southern Railway; and chairman of the board of directors of some other railroads. His gifts to Yale (where all of his four sons studied) totaled $1,500,000 (*DAB* X: 173–74).

42. Matthew Vassar gave over $800,000 to Vassar College during his lifetime (*DAB* X: 231). See also chapter 8, note 18.

43. Jonas Gilman Clark (1815–1900) accumulated money by shipping furniture and other goods from Massachusetts to California, and in real estate. During the Civil War he was prominent in the work of the Sanitary Commission. After visiting American and foreign universities, he founded Clark University in Worcester, Mass., in 1887. His total gifts to the university were $1,000,000—the largest amount given by any individual for education in New England up to that time (*DAB* II: 135–36).

44. John Cleve Green (1800–1875) was a merchant engaged in foreign trade, and a financier in New York. During his lifetime he donated generously to the Home for the Ruptured and Crippled, and the Deaf and Dumb Asylum. He also made very liberal gifts to Princeton College ($500,000), the Princeton Theological Seminary, and the Lawrenceville School (*DAB* IV: 551–52).

45. Isaac Rich (1801–1872), merchant, died one of Boston's wealthiest men. During his lifetime he gave over $50,000 to the Wesleyan Academy in Massachusetts and $150,000 to Wesleyan University in Connecticut. He also left his whole estate ($1,500,000) to the new Boston University, which he had been instrumental in founding (*DAB* VIII: 548–49).

46. For Francis Wayland Parker see chapter 6, note 10.

47. Stephen Girard (1750–1831), merchant and financier, was born in France, went to sea at an early age, settled in Philadelphia in 1776 just as the Declaration of Independence was about to be signed, became an American citizen, and amassed wealth in foreign trade. Girard was a generous philanthropist: he left $300,000 to the Commonwealth of Pennsylvania; $500,000 to the city of Philadelphia; and $6,000,000 in trust to the city for educating poor white orphan boys. Out of this trust Girard College was established. He was the first private citizen of the USA to bequeath such a vast sum for the public good (*DAB* IV: 319–22).

48. Johns Hopkins (1795–1873) was a merchant who made his fortune mainly from the newly started Baltimore and Ohio Railroad. He left in his will $7,000,000, to be equally divided between the Johns Hopkins University and the Johns Hopkins Hospital (*DAB* V: 213–14).

49. Leland Stanford (1824–1893) was a railroad builder associated with the Central Pacific Railroad (as president and director), and intermittently with the Southern Pacific Railroad (also as president and director). He founded the Leland Stanford Junior University in Palo Alto, California, in memory of his only son who died at the age of fifteen; the university was opened in 1891. After Stanford's death, a gift of $2,500,000 was made from his estate to the university (*DAB* IX: 501–506).

50. See Carnegie (1886: 296).

Literature Cited

Adhav, S. M. 1979. *Pandita Ramabai*. Madras: The Christian Literature Society (Confessing the Faith in India Series, no.13).

The American Ramabai Association. 1899–1921. *Reports of Annual Meetings*. Boston.

Arkush, R. David, and Leo E. Lee, eds. 1993. *Land Without Ghosts: Chinese Impressions of America from the Mid-Nineteenth Century to the Present*. Berkeley, Los Angeles, and London: University of California Press.

Athavale, Parvatibai. 1928. *Majhi Kahani* [My Story]. Hingane: Anatha Balikashram.

———. 1930. *My Story: The Autobiography of a Hindu Window*. Translated by Justin E. Abbott. New York and London: G. P. Putnam's Sons.

Balfour, Margaret T., and Ruth Young. 1929. *The Work of Medical Women in India*. London: Oxford University Press.

Berard's History of the United States. 1878. Revised by C. E. Bush. Philadelphia: Cowperthwait & Co.

Bhabha, Homi K. 1997. *The Location of Culture*. London and New York: Routledge.

Bodley, Rachel. [1887] 1981. "Introduction." In Pandita Ramabai, *The High-Caste Hindu Woman*, pp. i–ix. Reprint, Bombay: Maharashtra State Board for Literature and Culture.

Burton, Antoinette. 1992. "The White Woman's Burden: British Feminists and 'The Indian Woman,' 1865–1915." In *Western Women and Imperialism: Complicity and Resistance*, edited by Nupur Chaudhuri and Margaret Strobel, pp.137–57. Bloomington and Indianapolis: Indiana University Press.

———. 1995. "Colonial Encounters in Late Victorian England: Pandita Ramabai at Cheltenham and Wantage, 1883–86." *Feminist Review* (Spring), pp. 29–49.

———. 1998. *At the Heart of the Empire: Indians and the Colonial Encounter in Late-Victorian Britain*. Berkeley: University of California Press.

Carnegie, Andrew. 1886. *Triumphant Democracy, or Fifty Years' March of the Republic*. New York: Charles Scribner's Sons.

Chambers Biographical Dictionary. Edited by J. O. Thorne and T. C. Collocott. Rev. ed. Edinburgh: Chambers, 1988.

Chappell, Jennie. n.d. *Pandita Ramabai: A Great Life in Indian Missions*. London: Pickering & Inglis.

Chatterjee, Partha. 1999. *The Nation and Its Fragments: Colonial and Postcolonial Histories*. Delhi: Oxford University Press.

Clarke, A. K. 1979. *A History of the Cheltenham Ladies' College, 1853–1979*. 3rd ed. Great Glenham, Saxmundham, Suffolk: John Catt.

Dall, Caroline Healy. 1888. *The Life of Dr. Anandabai [sic] Joshee: A Kinswoman of the Pundita Ramabai*. Boston: Roberts Brothers.

Date, S. G. 1944. *Marathi Grantha-Suchi* [Index to Marathi Books]. Vol. I: *1800–1937*. Pune: S. G. Date.

Date, S. G., D. V. Kale, and S. N. Barve, eds. 1969. *Marathi Niyatkalikanchi Suchi, 1800–1950* [Index to Marathi Periodicals]. Mumbai: Mumbai Marathi Grantha Sangrahalaya.

David, M. D. 2001. *Missions: Cross-Cultural Encounter and Change in Western India.* Delhi: Indian Society for Promoting Christian Knowledge.

Deckard, Barbara Sinclair. 1983. *The Women's Movement: Political, Socioeconomic, and Psychological Issues.* 3rd ed. New York: Harper & Row.

Dictionary of American Biography. Vol. I, edited by Allen Johnson, 1957; vol. II, edited by Allen Johnson and Dumas Malone, 1958; vol. IV, edited by Allen Johnson and Dumas Malone, 1932; vols. V–X, edited by Dumas Malone, 1933–36; vol. XI, suppl. 1, edited by Harris E. Starr, 1944. New York: Charles Scribner's Sons.

Dnyanodaya (Anglo-Marathi weekly of the American Marathi Mission). Bombay. Several issues.

Dongre, Rajas K., and Josephine F. Patterson. 1963. *Pandita Ramabai: A Life of Faith and Prayer.* Madras: The Christian Literature Society.

Dublin, Thomas, ed. 1993. *Immigrant Voices: New Lives in America, 1773–1986.* Urbana and Chicago: University of Illinois Press.

Evans, Sara M. 1989. *Born for Liberty: A History of Women in America.* New York: The Free Press.

Feldhaus, Anne. 1995. *Of Water and Womanhood: Religious Meanings of Rivers in Maharashtra.* New York: Oxford University Press.

Fisher, Michael H. 2000. *The First Indian Author in English: Dean Mahomed (1759–1851) in India, Ireland, and England.* Delhi: Oxford University Press.

Fiske, John. 1885. *American Political Ideas.* New York: Harper & Brothers, 1885.

Flexner, Eleanor. 1975. *Century of Struggle: The Woman's Rights Movement in the United States.* Rev. ed. Cambridge, Mass., and London: Harvard University Press.

Forbes, Geraldine H. 1986. "In Search of the 'Pure Heathen': Missionary Women in Nineteenth Century India." *Economic and Political Weekly* 21, no. 17 (26 April: Review of Women Studies), pp. WS 2–8.

———. 1999. *Women in Modern India.* The New Cambridge History of India. Cambridge: Cambridge University Press.

Forbes, Geraldine, and Tapan Raychaudhuri, eds. 2000. *The Memoirs of Dr. Haimabati Sen, from Child Widow to Lady Doctor.* New Delhi: Roli Books.

Fuller, Mrs. Marcus B. (Lucia Bierce Fuller). [1900] 1984. *The Wrongs of Indian Womanhood.* Reprint, New Delhi: Inter-India Publications.

The Gazetteer of Bombay City and Island. [1909] 1977. Vol. 1. Facsimile reproduction, Poona: Government Photozinco Press.

Ghose, Indira. 2000. *Women Travellers in Colonial India: The Power of the Female Gaze.* Delhi: Oxford University Press.

Glover, Susanne L. 1995. "Of Water and of the Spirit." Unpublished Ph.D. thesis, University of Sydney.

Grewal, Inderpal. 1996. *Home and Harem: Nation, Gender, Empire, and the Cultures of Travel.* Durham, N.C., and London: Duke University Press.

Hewat, Elizabeth G. K. 1953. *Christ and Western India.* 2nd ed. Bombay: Wilson College.

The Hong Kong Daily Press (daily). Hong Kong. Several issues.

The Index (weekly of the Free Religious Association). Boston, Mass. Several issues.

Indu-Prakash (Anglo-Marathi weekly). Bombay, India. Several issues.

The Japan Weekly Mail (weekly). Yokohama, Japan. Several issues.

Jayawardena, Kumari. 2000. "Going for the Jugular of Hindu Patriarchy." In *Unequal Sis-*

ters, edited by Vicki L. Ruiz and Ellen Carol DuBois. 3rd ed. New York and London: Routledge.

Jog, R. S., ed. 1999. *Marathi Vangmayacha Itihas* [History of Marathi Literature]. Vol. 4: 1800–1874. 2nd ed. Poona: Maharashtra Sahitya Parishad.

John, Mary. 1996. *Discrepant Dislocations: Feminism, Theory, and Postcolonial Histories.* Delhi: Oxford University Press.

Joshee, Gopal Vinayak. 1886. *A Hindoo's Impressions of America: A Lecture Delivered in Rochester, N.Y.* Lunenburg, [Mass.]: Firefly Print.

Joshi, N. V. [1868] 1971. *Pune Shaharache Varnan* [Poona: Ancient and Modern]. Edited by G. D. Khanolkar. Reprint, Bombay: Sahitya Sahakar Sangh.

Kanitkar, Kashibai. 1912. *Pa. Va. Sau. Dr. Anandibai Joshee Yanche Charitra va Patre* [The Life and Letters of the Late Dr. Mrs. Anandibai Joshee]. Mumbai: Manoranjak Granthaprasarak Mandali.

Keer, Dhananjay. 1974. *Mahatma Jotirao Phooley: Father of Indian Social Revolution.* 2nd ed. Bombay: Popular Prakashan.

Keer, Dhananjay, and S. G. Malshe, eds. 1969. *Mahatma Phule: Samagra Vangmaya* [Collected Works of Phule]. Mumbai: Maharashtra State Board for Literature and Culture.

Kelkar, N. C. 1923. *Lokamanya Tilak Yanche Charitra* [A Biography of Tilak]. Vol. 1. Pune: N. C. Kelkar.

Kesari (Marathi Weekly). Poona. Several issues.

Kosambi, Meera. 1988. "Women, Emancipation, and Equality: Pandita Ramabai's Contribution to Women's Cause." *Economic and Political Weekly* 23, no. 44 (29 October: Review of Women Studies), pp. WS 38–49.

———. 1992. "An Indian Response to Christianity, Church and Colonialism: The Case of Pandita Ramabai." *Economic and Political Weekly* 27, nos. 43 and 44 (24–31 October: Review of Women Studies), pp. WS 61–71.

———. 1996. "Anandibai Joshee: Retrieving a Fragmented Feminist Image." *Economic and Political Weekly* 31, no. 49 (7 December), pp. 3189–97.

———. 1998a. "Child Brides and Child Mothers: The Age of Consent Controversy in Maharashtra as a Conflict of Perspectives on Women." In *Images of Women in Maharashtrian Society,* edited by Anne Feldhaus, pp. 135–62. Albany: State University of New York Press.

———. 1998b. "The Home as Social Universe: An Analysis of Women's Personal Narratives in Nineteenth Century Maharashtra." In *House and Home in Maharashtra,* edited by Irina Glushkova and Anne Feldhaus, pp. 82–101. New Delhi: Oxford University Press.

———. 2000a. "Motherhood in the East-West Encounter: Pandita Ramabai's Negotiation of 'Daughterhood' and Motherhood." *Feminist Review* 65 (Summer), pp. 49–67.

———. 2000b. "A Window in the Prison-House: Women's Education and the Politics of Social Reform in Nineteenth Century Western India." *History of Education* 29, no. 5, pp. 429–42.

———. 2000c. "Gender and Nationalism in Colonial Western India." Paper presented at the International Workshop "Gender and the Transmission of Values and Cultural Heritage(s) in South and Southeast Asia," Amsterdam, May 2000, mimeographed (also forthcoming).

———, ed. 2000d. *Pandita Ramabai through Her Own Words: Selected Works.* New Delhi: Oxford University Press.

————, ed. Forthcoming. *Mappings: Pandita Ramabai's Journeys and Encounters through Selected Writings, 1882–1921.*

The Letters and Correspondence of Pandita Ramabai. 1977. Compiled by Sister Geraldine, edited by A. B. Shah. Bombay: Maharashtra State Board for Literature and Culture.

Lewis, Reina. 1996. "Introduction: Making Connections." In R. Lewis, *Gendering Orientalism: Race, Femininity, and Representation,* pp. 1–11. London and New York: Routledge.

Loomba, Ania. 1998. *Colonialism/Postcolonialism.* London and New York: Routledge.

MacMartin, Charles B. 1995. "Teaching Race: Education at the Woman's Medical College of Pennsylvania, 1851–1888." *Collections* (The Newsletter of the Archives and Special Collections on Women in Medicine), no. 29 (Summer), pp. 1–5.

Macnicol, Nicol. 1926. *Pandita Ramabai.* Builders of Modern India Series. Calcutta: Association Press.

Madgavkar, Govind Narayan. [1863] 1961. *Mumbaiche Varnan* [Bombay Past and Present]. Edited by N. R. Phatak. 2nd ed. Mumbai: Mumbai Marathi Grantha Sangrahalaya.

The Mahratta (English-language weekly). Poona. Several issues.

Malshe, S. G., and S. R. Chunekar. 1970. *Madgavkaranche Sankalita Vangmaya* [Collected Works of Madgavkar]. Vol. 3. Mumbai: Mumbai Marathi Grantha Sangrahalaya.

Mani, Lata. 1997. "Contentious Traditions: The Debate on *Sati* in Colonial India." In *Recasting Women: Essays in Colonial History,* edited by Kumkum Sangari and Sudesh Vaid, pp. 88–126. Delhi: Kali for Women.

Martineau, Harriet. [1837] 1887. *Society in America.* 3 vols. London: Saunders & Otley.

Mayo, Katherine. [1927] 1998. *Selections from Mother India.* Edited by Mrinalini Sinha. Delhi: Kali for Women.

Mill, John Stuart. 1885. *On Liberty* and *The Subjection of Women.* New York: Henry Holt and Company.

Mohanty, Chandra Talpade. 1994. "Under Western Eyes: Feminist Scholarship and Colonial Discourses." In *Colonial Discourses and Post-Colonial Theory: A Reader,* edited by Patrick Williams and Laura Chrisman, pp. 196–200. New York: Harvester Wheatsheaf.

Molesworth's Marathi-English Dictionary. 2nd ed. 5th reprint. Pune: Shubhada-Saraswat Prakashan, 1994.

Morantz-Sanchez, Regina Markell. 1985. *Sympathy and Science: Women Physicians in American Medicine.* New York and Oxford: Oxford University Press.

Mueller, F. Max. 1899. *Auld Lang Syne.* Second Series: *My Indian Friends.* London: Longmans, Green & Co.

Nanda, B. R. 1998. *Gokhale: The Indian Moderates and the British Raj.* Delhi: Oxford University Press.

Natu, M. G., and D. Y. Deshpande, eds. 1986. *Agarkar-Vangmaya* [Collected Works of Agarkar]. Vol. 3. Mumbai: Sahitya Sanskriti Mandal [Bombay: Maharashtra State Board for Literature and Culture].

The New Encyclopaedia Britannica, Micropaedia, Ready Reference. 1998. 12 vols. 15th ed. Chicago: Encyclopaedia Britannica, Inc.

The New York Times (daily). New York, N.Y. Several issues.

Nieman, Donald G. 1991. *Promises to Keep: African-Americans and the Constitutional Order, 1776 to the Present.* New York: Oxford University Press.

Notable American Women, 1607–1950. Edited by Edward T. James. 3 vols. Cambridge, Mass.: The Belknap Press of Harvard University Press, 1973.

O'Brien, Sharon. 1989. *American Indian Tribal Governments*. Norman and London: University of Oklahoma Press.

O'Hanlon, Rosalind. 1994. *A Comparison between Women and Men: Tarabai Shinde and the Critique of Gender Relations in Colonial India,* Madras: Oxford University Press.

Our Federation. Fortnightly journal of the Woman's Temperance Union of Australia. Several issues.

The Oxford Companion to United States History. 2001. Edited by Paul S. Boyer. Oxford: Oxford University Press.

Padmanji, Baba. [1857] 1994. *Yamuna-paryatan* [The Wanderings of Yamunabai]. 5th ed. Pune: Snehavardhan Prakashan.

The Philadelphia Evening Bulletin (daily). Philadelphia, Pa. Several issues.

The Philadelphia Inquirer (daily). Philadelphia, Pa. Several issues.

The Philadelphia Press (daily). Philadelphia, Pa. Several issues.

The Philadelphia Record (daily). Philadelphia, Pa. Several issues.

Prashad, Vijay, 2000. *The Karma of Brown Folk*. Minneapolis: University of Minnesota Press.

Pratt, Mary Louise. 1995. *Imperial Eyes: Travel Writings and Transculturation*. London and New York: Routledge.

The Pundita Ramabai Humanitarian Pamphlet. 1888. Boston: Massachusetts Society for the Prevention of Cruelty to Animals, February.

Raikes, Elizabeth. 1908. *Dorothea Beale of Cheltenham*. London: Archibald Constable & Co.

Ramabai, (Pandita). [1882] 1967. *Stri Dharma Niti* [Morals for Women]. 3rd ed. Kedgaon: Ramabai Mukti Mission.

———. [1883] 1988. *Englandcha Pravas* [Voyage to England]. Edited by D. G. Vaidya, pp 1–27. 2nd ed. Reprint, Bombay: Maharashtra State Board for Literature and Culture.

———. [1887] 1981. *The High-Caste Hindu Woman*. Reprint, Bombay: Maharashtra State Board for Literature and Culture.

———. [1889] 1996. *United Stateschi Lokasthiti ani Pravasavritta* [The Peoples of the United States]. Reprint, Bombay: Maharashtra State Board for Literature and Culture.

———. [1900] 1984. "Introduction." In Mrs. Marcus B. Fuller, *The Wrongs of Indian Womanhood,* New Delhi: Inter-India Publications.

———. [1907] 1992. *A Testimony of Our Inexhaustible Treasure*. 11th ed. Kedgaon: Pandita Ramabai Mukti Mission.

Ramabai Association. 1890–1898. *Reports of the Annual Meeting of the Ramabai Association,* Boston.

Ramusack, Barbara N. 1990. "From Symbol to Diversity: The Historical Literature on Women in India." *South Asia Research* 10, no. 2 (November), pp. 139–157.

———. 1992. "Cultural Missionaries, Maternal Imperialists, Feminist Allies: British Women Activists in India, 1865–1945." In *Western Women and Imperialism: Complicity and Resistance,* edited by Nupur Chaudhuri and Margaret Strobel, pp. 119–36. Bloomington and Indianapolis: Indiana University Press.

———. 1999. "Women in South Asia." In *Women in Asia: Restoring Women to History,* edited by Barbara N. Ramusack and Sharon Sievers, pp. 15–76. Bloomington and Indianapolis: Indiana University Press.

Report of the International Council of Women (March 25 to April 1, 1888). 1888. Washington, D.C.: National Woman Suffrage Association.

Said, Edward W. 1991. *Orientalism*. London: Penguin Books.

The San Francisco Chronicle (daily). San Francisco, California. Several issues.

Sangari, Kumkum, and Sudesh Vaid, eds. 1997. *Recasting Women: Essays in Colonial History.* New Delhi: Kali for Women.

Sarkar, Sumit. 1994 (1985). "The Women's Question in Nineteenth Century Bengal." In *Women and Culture,* edited by Kumkum Sangari and Sudesh Vaid, pp. 103–12. Reprint, Bombay: Research Centre for Women's Studies, SNDT Women's University.

Sarkar, Tanika. 1999. *Words to Win: The Making of "Amar Jiban"—A Modern Autobiography.* New Delhi: Kali for Women.

Satthianadhan, Krupabai. [1887–88] 1999. *Saguna: The First Autobiographical Novel in English by an Indian Woman.* Edited by Chandani Lokugé. Reprint, Delhi: Oxford University Press.

Sengupta, Padmini. 1970. *Pandita Ramabai Saraswati: Her Life and Work.* Bombay: Asia Publishing House.

Shah, A. B. 1977. "Introduction." In *The Letters and Correspondence of Pandita Ramabai,* compiled by Sister Geraldine, edited by A. B. Shah, pp. xi–xxxvi. Bombay: Maharashtra State Board for Literature and Culture.

Shinde, Tarabai. 1975. *Stripurusha Tulana* [A Comparison of Women and Men]. Edited by S. G. Malshe. 1882. Reprint, Mumbai: Mumbai Marathi Grantha Sangrahalaya.

Smith, Sidonie, and Julia Watson, eds. 1992. *De/Colonizing the Subject: The Politics of Gender in Women's Autobiography.* Minneapolis: University of Minnesota Press.

Solomon, Barbara Miller. 1987. *In the Company of Educated Women: A History of Women and Higher Education in America.* First Indian reprint, New Delhi: Asian Books.

Sorabji, Cornelia. [1934] 2001. *India Calling.* Edited by Chandani Lokugé. Reprint, Delhi: Oxford University Press.

Spender, Dale. 1982. *Women of Ideas (and What Men Have Done to Them): From Aphra Behn to Adrienne Rich.* London: Routledge & Kegan Paul.

Spivak, Gayatri Chakravorty. 1994. "Can the Subaltern Speak?" In *Colonial Discourse and Post-Colonial Theory: A Reader,* edited by Patrick Williams and Laura Chrisman, pp. 66–111. New York: Harvester Wheatsheaf.

Sturge, Matilda. 1889. "An Indian Lady." *Friends' Quarterly Examiner* 23, pp. 217–29.

Sukhtankar, J. S. 1976. *Dharmanand: Acharya Dharmanand Kosambi Yanche Atmacharitra ani Charitra* [Autobiography and Biography of Dharmanad Kosambi]. Mumbai: The Goa Hindu Association.

Tharu, Susie, and K. Lalita, eds. 1993. *Women Writing in India, 600 B.C. to the Present.* 2 vols. Delhi: Oxford University Press.

Thompson, Eliza, Frances E. Willard, et al. 1906. *Hillsboro Crusade Sketches and Family Records.* Cincinnati: Jennings and Graham.

The Times (daily). London, England. Several issues.

The Times of India (daily). Bombay. Several issues.

Tocqueville, Alexis de. [1835] 1966. *Democracy in America.* Edited by J. P. Mayer and Max Lerner. New York, Evanston, Ill., and London: Harper & Row.

Tyrrel, Ian. 1991. *Woman's World, Woman's Empire: The Woman's Christian Temperance Union in International Perspective, 1880–1980.* Chapel Hill and London: University of North Carolina Press.

Vaidya, Sarojini. 1991. *Shrimati Kashibai Kanitkar: Atmacharitra ani Charitra (1861–1948)* [Mrs. Kashibai Kanitkar: Autobiography and Biography]. 2nd ed. Mumbai: Popular Prakashan.

Viswanathan, Gauri. 1998. "Silencing Heresy." In G. Viswanathan, *Outside the Fold: Conversion, Modernity, and Belief,* pp. 118–152. Delhi: Oxford University Press.

Welter, Barbara. 1974. "The Feminization of American Religion: 1800–1860." In *Clio's Consciousness Raised: New Perspectives on the History of Women,* edited by Mary S. Hartman and Lois Banner, pp. 137–57. New York: Harper Colophon Books.

Willard, Frances E. 1886. *Woman and Temperance; or, The Work and Workers of the Woman's Christian Temperance Union.* 5th ed. Chicago: Woman's Christian Temperance Publication Association.

———. 1888. *Woman in the Pulpit.* Boston: D. Lothrop Company.

———. 1889. *Glimpses of Fifty Years: The Autobiography of an American Woman.* Chicago, Philadelphia, etc.: Woman's Temperance Publication Association.

Women's Penny Paper. London, England. Several issues.

Index

156–57, 160, 162, 202–204, 207–208, 210–12, 227. *See also* Drinking

Livermore, Mary A., 25, 192, 260–61*n*54

Liverpool, 35, 55

London, 22, 112, 180, 235

Louisville, Ky., 27, 200

Luther, Martin, 139

Lytton, Lord, 148, 252*n*12

Machines and mechanical advances, 9, 106, 218, 220–21, 229–31, 233–35

Madison, James, 88

Madras, 59–60, 149–50, 159, 220

Mahabharata, 167, 254*n*1

Maharashtra and Maharashtrians, 10–11, 13–17, 39–41, 122; response to American society, 14–17, 34, 53

Maine, 188, 210

Mani, Lata, 14

Manorama (Ramabai's daughter), *ii*, 18–19, 22, 26, 29–30, 45*n*15, 48, 55

Manning, Adelaide, 20

Mansfield, Arabella, 184, 259*n*42

Manufactures: in Britain, 227, 232–33, 235; in the United States, 218, 222, 227, 232–35, 237

Manusmriti, 224, 262*n*10

Marathi language and literature, 10, 12–14, 31, 33–34, 39, 43, 53, 149; and Ramabai's enrichment of vocabulary, 42; and Ramabai's prose style, 39–40, 42; and Ramabai's writings, 18, 30, 46*n*21

Martineau, Harriet, 34, 167, 171, 186, 254*n*3

Massachusetts, 10, 74, 98, 132–33, 139–40, 146, 155, 171–72, 179, 186, 189

Meat eating: in India, 136*n*iv; in the United States, 35, 107–108, 113, 131–32, 231. *See also* Animal slaughter; Cruelty to animals

Medhavi (Ramabai's husband), 18

Melting pot, 8

Mendelssohn, Fanny, 259–60*n*46

Mendelssohn, Felix, 259–60*n*46

Methodists, 157, 166*n*i, 170–71

Mexico, 64, 69, 224

Michigan, 234

Michigan University, 141, 143, 175–77, 179–80, 185

Migratory consciousness, 17, 38. *See also* Diaspora, diasporic consciousness

Mill, John Stuart, 36

Milwaukee, Wis., 223

Mines and mining: in Britain, 38, 236; in the United States, 36, 38, 233, 235–237

Minneapolis, Minn., 184, 223

Minnesota, 223, 234

Missionaries: American, 10, 15, 159; American missionary support of British rule in India, 10; American women as, 25, 31–32, 194–96, 206; British women as, 21; European, 10; and imperialism, 21; wives of, 15, 195

Missionary activity, 10–11, 15–16, 25; critique of Indian society, 15, 32; by Ramabai, 24, 30 (*see also* Evangelization, by Ramabai; Proselytization, by Ramabai)

Mississippi River, 187, 225

Missouri, 132

Missouri River, 210, 225

Mitchell, Maria, 179, 257*n*27

Mohammedans, 62–63, 166*n*i, 214*n*vii. *See also* Muslims

Mohanty, Chandra Talpade, 246*n*10

Monarchy, 35–36, 80, 86, 96, 110, 141, 154. *See also* Kingdom; Republic

Monroe, James, 88

Montreal, 129

"Morals for Women" (Ramabai), 18, 22, 39. *See also Stri Dharma Niti*

Morantz-Sanchez, Regina Markell, 24

More, Hannah, 172, 255*n*2

Mormons, 156, 208

Moses, 169, 188

Mott, Lucretia, 115, 170, 190, 247*n*21

Mount Holyoke College, 29

Mount Meru, 125, 249*n*36

Mueller, Max, 20

Mukti Mission, 29–30, 48, 49

Mukti Prayer Bell, 30

Multiculturalism, 37

Municipalities: in India, 96; in the United States, 90–91, 96–97, 199, 210, 220

Muslims, 11. *See also* Mohammedans

Nashville, Tenn., 27, 200–202

National Congress. *See* Indian National Congress

National Convention for Woman's Rights, 190, 198–99, 247*n*21, 260*n*51. *See also* Seneca Falls Convention

National Education Association, 27, 146

National Grange, 228

National Social Conference (India), 31

National Woman Suffrage Association, 9, 199, 261*n*60

Nationalism, in India, 7, 13–15, 19, 26, 31–33, 41; as a male project, 13, 33, 41. *See also* Ramabai, Pandita, nationalism of

Nebraska, 27, 98, 132, 210

Negroes, 12, 77, 83, 106, 114–15, 118, 147, 163, 168,

Rakhmabai, 13
Ramabai Association, 22–25, 27–29, 128, 249*n*41
Ramabai Circles, 23, 29, 126
Ramabai, Pandita, *ii, 47, 48;* admiration of, for the United States, 22, 53, 167; alienation and marginalization of, 30, 32, 41, 45*n*8; American response to, 4, 9, 22–24; anti-colonialism of, 5, 7, 22, 31, 33, 36–38; anti-imperialism of, 5–6; Brahmin origins, mindset, and mystique of, 3–4, 17, 24, 31–32, 37, 39–40; Brahmanic lifestyle of, 17; as a champion of Indian women, 4, 18; as a champion of Indian women's education, 3, 17–18, 22, 33; as a champion of and worker for education of Indian widows, 4, 20, 22, 29; as a Christian, 4, 6, 24, 37, 39–40; as a Christian critic of Christianity, 40; and Christian theology, 19, 21; as a Christian wedge into Hindu society, 21, 25; Christianizing agenda of, 31–32; as a colonial subject, 4–5, 20, 36 (*see also* Colonial subjects); conversion to Christianity by, *see* Conversion to Christianity, by Ramabai; critique of American society by, 4, 9, 34, 37, 39–40, 53–54; critique of British society by, 4–6, 35, 38; critique of Hindu doctrine and society by, 30, 37, 39–41; critique of Indian society by, 4, 6, 32, 37–40; critique of Indian women's oppression by, 15, 39; as culturally Hindu, 37, 39; egalitarianism of, 30, 37; English education of, 4, 19–20, 24, 39–40; as a Hindu critic of Hinduism, 40; Hinduness of, 4, 24; Indian identity of, 6; internationalism of, 7, 31, 40; multicultural persona of, 4; nationalism of, 6–7, 30–33, 37–38, 40–41, 54 (*see also* Nationalism, in India); as a public speaker, 3–4, 17; Sanskrit education of, 3–4, 20, 31, 39–40; Sanskritized worldview of, 37, 39; as a social leader, 14, 41; as a social reformer, 39; as a social thinker, 4; spiritual quest of, 19; travelogue writing by, 5, 33, 46*n*21; vegetarian diet of, 24, 39, 246*n*5; as a widow, 3, 18, 24, 32; writings of, 5, 7, 28, 30, 32, 39, 42, 43*n*5
Ramayana, 167, 254*n*1
Ramona (Hunt), 116, 248*n*23
Ramusack, Barbara, 21, 44*n*6
Ranade, M. G., 13
Ranade, Ramabai, 13, 45*n*7
Reconstruction, 8
Red Indians, 35–37, 40, 63–64, 66–73, 92, 115–18, 144, 147, 227. *See also* American Indians
Religious denominations in India, 166*n*i
Republic, 35–36, 76–79, 82, 86–87, 140–41, 148, 218, 237. *See also* Kingdom; Monarchy
Republican Party, 8, 91

Rocky Mountains, 225; as a symbol of insurmountable obstacles, 173–75
Roman Catholics, 56, 64, 67, 131, 139, 141, 154–55, 186
Roman law, 188
Romans, 64, 79, 109, 138, 186
Russia and Russians, 148, 169, 180; immigrants, 117, 131

Sacramento River, 225
Said, Edward, 5
St. Louis, Mo., 146–47, 184
St. Paul (Apostle), 169, 171
St. Paul, Minn., 129, 223
Salt Lake, 238–39*n*i
San Francisco, 23, 25, 27–28, 146, 184, 222
San Joaquin River, 225
Sangari, Kumkum, 44*n*6
Sanitary Commission, 191–93
Sanskrit: education, 16–17, 20, 40; language and literature, 31, 33, 37; as a monopoly of Brahmin men, 17
Saraswati, 17, 37, 127, 168, 177, 179; as a title awarded to Ramabai, 17
Saratoga, 27, 122–24, 249*n*33
Sarkar, Sumit, 14
Sarkar, Tanika, 44*n*6
Scandinavian immigrants, 117, 131, 149
Scotland, 99, 140, 175
Self, 5–7, 40
Self-government: absence of in India, 78–79; in the United States, 35, 37, 78, 103–104, 104*n*ii
Self-reliance: Ramabai's advocacy of, 30, 37, 103; in the United States, 101, 103, 219, 224
Self-rule, in the United States, 219, 224
Sen, Keshub Chunder, 59
Seneca Falls Convention, 9, 198–99, 247*n*21, 260*n*51. *See also* National Convention for Woman's Rights
Sengupta, Padmini, 43*n*4
Shakespeare, William, 127
Sharada Sadan, 13, 16, 25, 28–31, 54
Shastras, 158, 253*n*5
Shaw, Mrs. Quincy, 25, 45*n*16, 180, 257–58*n*31
Shudras, 11–12, 157. *See also* Untouchability
Sinha, Mrinalini, 44*n*6
Sister Geraldine, 21–23
Sister Nivedita, 33
Skating, 109, 129, 135, 136*n*iii
Slave trade, 92, 114, 157, 163
Slavery: abolition of, 8–9, 16, 115, 168, 171; of Africans, 12, 26, 41, 83, 91–92, 114–15, 147, 163, 168, 170–71, 190, 230; of American Indians, 66–

MEERA KOSAMBI is former Professor and Director, Research Centre for Women's Studies, SNDT Women's University, Mumbai. A sociologist trained in India, Sweden, and the United States, she has taught, conducted research, and lectured in several countries, and has published widely in the fields of urban studies and women's studies. She is editor of *Pandita Ramabai through Her Own Words: Selected Works* and *Intersections: Socio-Cultural Trends in Maharashtra,* and author of several books including *Bombay in Transition: The Growth and Social Ecology of a Colonial City, 1880–1980.*